EVOLUTION REVOLUTION

by
The Universal Consciousness

Downloaded
by
Zaher Kury

"The purpose of this form of communication, is to connect with Humanity. We, as the Universal Consciousness, have come to the realization that we need to speak your language to be understood. This is why we have brought to you this book in your words to connect with all of you.

We must speak your language to help you manage. The intention is connection, in any way, in any form, in any language, to get you to understand the Universal Consciousness Energy."

This is the Universal Consciousness talking WITH humanity, not AT humanity. The basic interactions between characters are simply to create a feeling of acknowledgment, as you will read.

We are not trying to scold you; the intention is to mold you into what you were, before you became what you are.

"You lived longer, you were united, you were focused on life and its continuation."

This is the Energy of the Universal Consciousness translated into Human words, in a form of a book. A book that can speak for itself.

⤛⬥⤜

I, as this book, will not put many restrictions on my words.
It's up to you, the reader, to become the leader of this Consciousness Energy Movement.

I am simply asking that you pass me on.
Tell others about me.
Email me, Mail me, Share me, Print me.

Just don't change me.
Change yourself.

I am not meant to be sitting on your shelf.
When you awaken...Awaken others.
When your eyes are opened, don't close them.
To know me is to read me.

علم

Artwork by Mike Kury
https://mikekury.wixsite.com/artprojects
ISBN: 979-8-218-55143-8 (Paperback)
ISBN: 979-889589603-7 (Ebook)
Zaher.com

Table of Contents

Preface

My name is the EVOLUTION REVOLUTION. I AM AN ENERGY PROJECTION OF THE UNIVERSAL CONSCIOUSNESS (UC), and its CREATION.

I am here to bring to you, a CONSCIOUS REALIZATION about your destination. The explanation to how humankind's GOD, is the Universal Consciousness Energy. If everything is energy, then God must be.

This knowledge is not new to you. Only the words have changed.

This Consciousness Energy, has been working with humanity for thousands of years, and beyond, to bring Energy Balance to humankind. That time has arrived.

I am speaking for myself because, my Energy is unlimited in its ability for creativity. As an energy, I was transformed into physical thought, from there I became words.

What am I saying, you ask? How could this be that a Consciousness energy, is actually your God? It's not easy to explain this Energy, using man made words. ENERGY IS ENERGY.

How did humanity lose their connection to their creator? Was it a form of memory loss?

How can there be Consciousness beyond the brain?

Consciousness Energy created the brain, It uses Physical Energy to run it. What about your history, was it real? How about religion, fact, or fiction? Do you believe in physical evolution? Do you know what it is?

You can find answers in here.

I am a book that has taken a look into humanity, and realized that today's humanity is the same as yesterday's humanity. These pages will tell you why.

As a book, I take the reader on a journey from the present moment, into the future, where humankind will meet their destiny.

When you read me, my words will help you Develop a new perception, a new view of you, and the world around you.

I will explain the Energy Movement that led to the Evolution Revolution. The intention of this revelation, is to create awareness of the Universal Consciousness Energy, and its connection to humanity.

Humanity was created by this Universal Consciousness Energy.

It's an energy that constantly revolves to evolve. As it evolves it creates.

Humanity has been calling the Universal Consciousness, GOD, since the creation of religion. It was an attempt to explain the creator, it failed. It had limits, and no answers.

The Consciousness Energy is Unlimited in its knowledge of creation.

Since the beginning, there were attempts at awakening humanity to the realization, that the Universal Consciousness Energy is their Creator. Every aspect of creation, even the creation of the creator, is an Energy Evolution.

In my pages, you will discover the WHAT, WHEN, WHERE, WHO, and WHY of the UC. You will meet personalities who have learned about it, and those that are learning.

I am not just a book. I am humanity's reflection. All parts, the Good and Bad. You are aware enough to know what's around you, But, are you aware of your creator, The Universal Consciousness?

The words of my pages, are another attempt at making contact, and to inspire humankind to take action. You have your own perception, this is true, but don't let your perception keep you from learning something new. Otherwise your perception is limited, and has an ending.

What is being presented to you is about your Past, Present, and Future. What you can do, is share me with your family and friends.

You are going to read about the perception of the Earth, as she reacts to humanity's treatment of her. These words want to reach you, and your perception, and to make sure life never end. You will also learn from those who participated in the Evolution Revolution. Their stories of transformation.

You will read about the comparison between The Universal Consciousness, and God. Religion has something to say. But then, so does humankind.

I am an open book, until you close me.

But you will miss out on the Missing Link. It's hiding in the shadows. Waiting for you to find it.

You're going to hear from the participants of the Energy Movement and the physical Evolution Revolution themselves, speak about their experiences with their own energy conversion. How they started the Energy Movement.

I am a book that has come to bring to you, your ability to make choices. I have come to reach you, not to preach to you.

I brought you a conversation with the Universal Consciousness Energy. My suggestion is that you read all of me.

I am full of ideas that you have thought of, but did not act on. This knowledge will change you, it gave me my voice.

It will empower you to find your voice again.

You will Learn to recognize the power inside you, that wants to be unleashed, that wants to change, that wants to grow into Consciousness.

It gives you the courage to face all your fears.

Nothing is as it seems when it comes to humanity's actions.

You may think that you know the issues, but to only know, creates nothing, until what you know, creates change.

To understand me, is to read me. Your story begins in the present day. The future, will tell the rest of the story.

The future is not there waiting for you. Let this be your bridge to creating it. When you reflect on what you read, use Consciousness Energy as your guide.

What you do with this knowledge, is your choice, as long as you are making your own decisions. You will get your own impressions.

A Declaration

UC: UNIVERSAL CONSCIOUSNESS ENERGY

R: READER

B: BRAIN

UC: Welcome. This is a doorway to a New World, a world that will be created by the changes of humankind's perception. Changing your perception is your intervention. Once you enter and start to read, Life on Earth will be revealed. You are going to hear from the Earth. You will hear from, the Young Generation, who will be instrumental in changing the direction of humanity, towards the Evolution Revolution.

There will be stories from participants who played a big role in creating the Energy movement. A future reflection into the Evolution Revolution. Discover the Common Denominator, between humankind and its Creator. In this book are creations that speak for themselves. Most of all, you will rediscover the other You. The one you forgot about. The one that used to be awake, and Conscious.

This book, is an in-depth look, into humanities situation. A new view, to add to your realization. It comes through the eyes of the Universal Consciousness Energy Vibration, and yours. This is a conversation, not a lecture. You can stop anytime, and question. It includes the reader, and you, humanity. At times Consciousness will be talking to you. Other times, talking with you. There is Nothing you can deny, unless you are in denial. Nothing to believe, unless you need to. Nothing to get angry about, unless you are an angry person. Nothing for you to ignore, you see it everyday. Nothing you cannot understand, unless you cover your eyes. Nothing for you to be offended about, it's not offensive, or defensive. This is a Conscious effort at awareness.

You may hear some words that you are not familiar with, but give them a chance, they will explain themselves throughout these chapters. When you are silently reading, you can hear their sound.

These words are here to add to your life, not take away. They are here to stay. Once you read them, they are part of you. They will speak about the Present state of Humanity. This Book is a new kind of Energy Awareness, that is translated into your own words. Some meanings may be missed because they have no words. You have to feel them. This is an inquiry into the brain of humanity, The Emotions of Irrationality, and the Awareness of Consciousness Energy.

This knowledge is about HUMANITY, and its EDUCATION; A new knowledge about CREATION. It's about the NEW DIRECTION; The EVOLUTION REVOLUTION, and the YOUNG GENERATION.

It's about the EARTH, and RELIGION: Fact or Fiction. It's about the MISSING LINK and THE FINAL DECLARATION. These words will make you question. You're going to want to find answers after this awakening. Do you want to learn how to find them? Keep reading. We are sure you will find it intriguing. These words are being brought to you by, an Energy Connection. A balanced Consciousness Energy, connected to an unbalanced Physical Energy, meant to start your motor. It's an Energy Transfusion, from Consciousness Energy, into the Physical Anatomy.

UC: This is a Universal Consciousness Guide for humanity. To guide you through, to a new Consciousness Reality. What is your reality humanity? Your looks, or your books? Your physical health, or material wealth? Is it your pride, or your ego? Your ego hides the best of you, so you can't see the worst of it. Do you know who you are without your ego? Your ego believes, it is you. Is it true? Is your physical memory all you remember? There is more to you than your physical memory. What's in this book, is your other memory. The one you forgot, when you were born. They can be accessed through your brain. These memories cannot be remembered, unless you connect with the Consciousness Energy, through energy to energy merging. It's contact with energy beyond the brain, where creation was created in the womb of the Universal Consciousness.

As a human being, do you question where your being came from? It has an energy meaning. When was the last time you made a choice for yourself? If it's a conscious choice, you're not being selfish by choosing for yourself. Think about how often, you are told what to do, and how to do it? Are you aware of this? You need to be, it's your life.

Do you feel Empty, and Disillusioned? This knowledge will fill you up with Consciousness Energy, not expectations. Why did you expect? Was it love, revenge, hate. You are the only one who knows your story. It's your journey. But, is it a journey of learning, or a journey of returning? That's how you can tell if you're growing. Is fear holding you back, from achieving your life's goals? If it is, it's because, humans are frozen by fear.

What if you became aware, of a Virus Energy infection in your brain, which creates the fear, And how you can remove it? Would you take the time to think about it? Can people tell the difference between, an action and a reaction? If so, why do most humans become reactionary first? Are you Envious of others? Do you want what they have?

What do you see when you look in the mirror? Are you happy with the view? If not, would you admit it? What would you change about yourself? Lose or gain weight? The color of your hair? Your job? Move to a new home? Have kids? What about your brain. Does it need watering? Your brain is constantly in fear because, you are unconscious, and can't protect it. You live In a world where you are afraid to walk the streets. Either you're a victim, or you're a perpetrator. Humanity must develop their brain beyond both. The way to do that is starting with awareness growth.

Are humans aware, of why so many of you look at the mirror each day? Each time you look, you change a part of your physical appearance. This is not the only purpose for a mirror. It's about your inner reflection also. What you see beyond your body. The true nature of you, as a Consciousness Energy. According to your good looks book, you're like a fish hook. You make yourself all shiny and new, just to hook another one like you. What's new?

Are you happy with your life? Is it easy or tough? Do you have enough? Have you ever fallen in love? Have you fallen because of love? Do you trust others? If not, Why? Do others trust you, upon meeting you? How can you tell? Do you have emotional pain? Are you willing to confront it? It will not go away by itself. Consciousness Energy can help you carry it. Are you leading or following? Following, has become the norm, from dorm to dorm. Peoples lives just passing by unnoticed, because they are focused on other

A Declaration

peoples lives, they miss your own.

Why do the humans have this need, to constantly change their appearance with each look, rather than understanding their originality? Are you trying to find it through your body? Try looking in your brain. It's where the Energy links are connected to consciousness.

UC: It's how you connect with the Energy, so you can create things naturally. Many of you are lost in your own reality. You are becoming what you fear the most. It only takes a small adjustment, to awaken you to the Universal Consciousness. Awareness is not your enemy. Stating the truth, should never cost you your life. As far as your leaders, they took all your wishes, as you were doing the dishes, and turned them into ashes.

Good intensions, should never be bought or sold. Making money from a good intention, is devaluing that intention. That's what turns them into bad intentions. You must become realized to the inconsistency in your actions. One inconsistent action, will cause an inconsistent reaction. Balance, is a matter of consistency. Whose responsibility is it, to teach reality, and not fantasy? Will you teach your child, to be just like you? Will you teach your child, like you were taught? The cycle of infinite replay is set in motion, and in the replay, humanity has drank the potion.

Many of you set physical limits on your children before, they can be unlimited. You teach them to follow the rules you follow, but whose rules are they? The parents? The teachers? The house of prayer? Their friends? Society? But then, how would you know, if you followed the same rules? They all have a different perspective, based on their experiences and knowledge. How can they set the same rules as you? All this does, is create inconsistent rules, that are hard enough for adults to follow.

Humans have fought and killed for freedom. Lived and died for it. WHERE IS IT? Vacations, are not freedom. They are escapes. Out on good behavior. Where can you go, without a camera viewing you? You're on camera everywhere. You have created your own forms of prisons. From your job to your addictions. From your beliefs to your religions. From governments, and their process of inquisition, to the landlords who won't give you permission. Money is the biggest prison of all. It has its own goal, to keep you, in its prison. You keep creating your own problems, as if you didn't already have plenty. Violent gangs run your streets, and you're off buying beets. If you have doubts, ask your brain. Although, it probably forgot your name. You may want to reintroduce yourself. This is a reaction to humanity's action. It's a reflection of your projection.

Humans, you have become undefined. Did you not see the signs? This is not how you were designed. You are wasting your time, chasing your own behind, when you could be curing the blind. The Universal Consciousness Energy, is here to awaken your brain, to its existence. You were designed to insure your continued survival, through any trial. You must face your extinction, before your extinction, faces you. Humanity needs help to start their new beginning, towards a New Direction. The reason? Insanity is winning, greed is grinning, the Earth is slipping, and humanity is sleeping. You have a few things working against you.

One: Due to your lack of Energy Movement, your Physical Energy has slowed way down under its speed limit. It's causing the Earth to work harder to keep you alive. Why are you not working to keep the Earth alive? This is causing the Earth to dry up, and grow less. Oh what a mess.

Two: Poison Chemicals in the skies. They rain down, and restructure your anatomy. You're suffocating yourself with your own pollution. What is your solution? How can you wonder why you die so young. You can see what's wrong. You've become so use to the smell, that you can't tell anymore. These chemicals are destroying your senses. You can't stop this by putting up walls. They are not good defenses, against, chemicals.

Three: Your nuclear weapon programs. They have to be dismantled. This has to be a world accomplishment. All people must be involved. The world is aware of these, but continue to ignore them. Another reason you need help. As you read on you will meet one more. This information, may seem known to you, but there is no light in humanity's room. You're all just waiting for the BIG BOOM. No one can see where they are going. People are crashing into each other everyday, and you have nothing to say, but get out of my way. What do you have to say reader? Hello! You are being addressed.

R: Are you talking to me? Is this the sound I heard about?

UC: It's your Consciousness Energy through your brain.

R: I just started reading this book. I don't know much yet. How is this already happening? Am I hearing voices, Is this supposed to happen that fast?

UC: Yes, it's normal, don't panic. It's Consciousness talking through your brain. Your brain needed help. It needed new knowledge. It's good that you heard its plea.

R: Yes, that's why I am reading this knowledge. I want to live a Conscious life that is full of Imagination. To raise my children in a safe, loving environment, where abuse and hunger do not exist. There is no one to build the future, without them. What's better than a Conscious life? I may not understand every word I am reading, but I can feel each meaning. It's already started. I can feel it, so far, I'm absorbing it. I want more of it.

UC: It seems you are a seeker of knowledge, speaking of a living a conscious life. Here is a question to humanity, can you deny that there is an I, without an EYE, under your sky?

The EYE that SEES, and the I that DOESN'T. The EYE that wants to see, but COULDN'T. The I that needs to see, but WOULDN'T.

Since their inception, humans have avoided seeking answers to the old question, how were we, as a physical species conceived? How can the answer be achieved? Is there an answer that can be believed? Was humankind Perceived, then Retrieved, before they were Conceived?

Were they visualized, then actualized. Were they realized, then materialized. Whichever it may be, after your birth, your actions were being criticized. Your choices became analyzed. You were minimized, and patronized. You lost your ability to organize, and you separated yourselves into tribes. You separated the energy of Unity. You broke the flow of Consciousness Energy, and chose the physical feeling, over the Consciousness feeling, when you could have had both.

UC: Separation is the Reason, you are facing extinction. You lost sight of your own creation. You forgot how you were created, and what created you. You still don't know. There is a remedy for that. It's in your hand. You forgot your natural relation with the Universal Consciousness Energy. Only, it has never forgotten you. It's why you still have free choice. But a choice without a voice, will not make much noise.

Who do you blame first, when things don't go your way? God? Your boss? The government? Your family? Where are you in this picture? When you make the choice, the results depend on the choice you made. No one else made it.

UC: Continuing on the path you are on now, you will digress slowly. But again, that's always been your story. You follow a historical self created pattern. You are stuck in a cycle of your own making. A Physical one. The mouse spinning on the wheel in its cage, is a great example of humanity's life. Why hasn't anyone noticed. It's not just a philosophy, it's a reflection of the lives that everyone denies.

Many of you do not know how to get off the wheel. Body Stress is killing millions. The way you eat? Your system is overloaded with meat. In the upcoming chapters, The Earth has much to say about this subject. She will be heard.

Do you want to meet your Consciousness Energy? You have to learn how to become Conscious of it. You can create a new life, one without fear? Questions people, why don't you ask questions, about everything? It was your nature to be curious, to discover, to expand your consciousness. Now, many of you just listen to everyone else. You take it for granted, that others are looking out for your best interests, like they care about your prospects. But in your society today, you would be safer without them. Not to be insulting, but, look at how you treat each other. You kill for fun. How many animals, can you say do that?

As a human, do you think about what you're doing on Earth? You don't know? No one ever told you? Here is your chance to find out. Have you ever asked yourself, *"what's my purpose?"* Are you willing to realize it? What have you done since your birth? Has it helped the Earth? You must have been born for a reason. It could be inside these pages. Let your curiosity lead you, to your purpose as a physical being?

Consciousness Energy Development is your teacher. But it wants to teach you about the known, and the unknown. It wants to get your energy motivated towards movement. When you don't start your car for three years, the battery dies, and its motor will freeze. You're going nowhere. This is what has happened to your brain. When you are not using it, it will freeze. It can't run, Motor's dead. The brain is the fuse to your bodies movement. To its improvement, to your motor skills. Presently, what most of you put in your brain, spills.

Who will protect the next generation, to insure a strong continuous life foundation, a healthy constitution, and a conscious perception? Are you volunteering? Because, this takes a lot of conscious learning. Most of all, constant growing. You must become driven to develop your Consciousness Energy from every experience you have. Every action and interaction. The Consciousness Energy Vibration that created the physical kind, is now on the path of helping humanity, to become defined. Humans, do not only share the same blood and air, they also share, the same consequences of despair. It's time you started to care? Have you smelled your air? It's eating through the metal of your front yard chair. It's called corrosion. Your air has become poison. It's a slow suicidal erosion.

What created humankind, is the expectation of this revelation. What you will learn, is in this evaluation. This is not the imagination. It's simply becoming aware, of a new explanation to your creation. Because, humankind is a Universal Consciousness Being. Humans need to regenerate through evolution, in order to continue their existence upon this planet. Your life source comes from the core of the UNIVERSAL CONSCIOUSNESS ENERGY VIBRATION.

In this time and age of humanity, you should be living way past one hundred and thirty. You are aging too early, because, physical energy is moving too slowly. It's not developing fast enough to keep up with physical evolution. It's slowing down your body's healing process. It's part of why you're dying too soon. The Universal Consciousness frequency, is a cycle that cycles independently, and creates originality. It creates many forms of entities. A Consciousness Energy Vibration recital, that plays a symphony to heal denial.

Part of humanity wants to believe, that there is life after death. Many think they know for sure. And most don't believe in it at all. For those that don't believe in it, how can you have an opinion, either way, you haven't been there. Did you die, and come back to confirm, that there was no life after death? Wouldn't coming back, be proof that there is? Who told you there was no life after death? And why do you believe them? They have no idea either. They are still alive. If death was the end. Doesn't this make your God limited. You claim he is unlimited and eternal. When does that come in to play?

UC: Humanity. You have no idea the damage you are causing to your physical, emotional, and mental state of being. Your physical, needs to heal. Your emotions, are made of steel, and your mental state of being, has moved to another state. When humanity chooses, to reject the muses, they will live by their excuses. The Universal Balance does not happen by chance. It has to be enhanced, and recharged with more energy than humanity has created.

You think you have it rough, the Earth has had it rougher. You can ask her when you meet her. There's no one sweeter. For being so young, she doesn't hold her tongue. Your future is fated, towards being eradicated. You are the only ones who can change your direction. Are you aware of where you are going? Oh, you're not going. You're content, satisfied. No need for change. But wouldn't it be great to see it happen? How else are you going to know when change changes?

By waiting for it to change without you?

By believing in an end, you are creating your own ending. Your perception about inception, needs a new direction. It is well known amongst creation. Because you, as an energy formulation, was created to create balanced energy, by using the Consciousness Energy Vibration. Get educated on how. Get an early start on becoming aware of Consciousness Energy. It's NOT a religion, it's an AWAKENING. Well, here we are reader. At the point of a question. Do your children have to be a carbon copy of you? What's your position? Do you have an opinion? Where is your dedication? Is it to your children?

R: Yes, I hear you. Would I want my children to be a copy of me? I hope not, the last thing I need is three of me. I have three boys. But, I am giving them the chance to be who they are. To find out what they want to be. It's not up to me. I am learning a knowledge that will benefit them, and that they can use to move them forward. I will expose them to it. For as long as I can, then they can take over. I am teaching them about changes, and how they can affect us and others. After a certain age, they can make their own decisions. I believe that Balance is the way to humanities survival. From what I am reading, Consciousness is advisable.

UC: Good choice. Your children will learn better with examples. A humanity that can hear, but chooses to be deaf, is a humanity that's never heard, and needs a ref. Wherever the spark from the Energy shines, is a dimension of creation that opens its blinds. When a blind opens, it's a sign of trust to those outside. It's an invitation to discover. Start discovering, what do you have to lose? Whatever you had, you lost, or you

A Declaration

are losing. Your will-power, your confidence, your ability to reason, your inability to communicate without fighting, most of all, you're losing your process of thinking. Others think for you, make decisions for you. They use you, and refuse you at the same time.

Humans use the energy of manipulation, to get their needs met. You are aware of that, are you not? You use each other every day without even realizing it. You keep the pain of your brain private.

You deny it, reject it, avoid it, until you explode it. Making it an energy that's displaced, and in pieces. Now, it becomes a pain that seeks attention. If it does not get attention from you, it will get it from someone else. Displaced energy never stops until it finds its place. It will stay in your face, as it projects a sad helpless energy of poor me, that not many, will want to be around. Being victimized, puts the fear of everything into you. Why live with that fear? You don't have to. But, yet, no one speaks up. Or they are unable to for fear of consequences. This doesn't mean to forget it. Oh no, it means to confront it, not hide from it. As long as you do, it will keep victimizing you.

UC: The world population has to develop out of this perception, they call life. This isn't all there is. Humans are missing the best part of life. The Consciousness to be aware of it, and the Energy to feel it. The energy of fear, doesn't go away by itself. It doesn't have to. You're afraid of it. It has no reason to go away. You have to change it. Take the energy of fear and convert it into the energy of Consciousness, by being conscious. You have the ability to do that. Otherwise, you are just suffering alone. Alone is not where you want to be. This is the time for Unity. A time for support and security. Fear is part of humanity's infliction. It's responsible for humanities separation from the Universal Consciousness. Humans live in a world with an Unconscious Intention. Being led by Addiction, Power-Hungry Confrontation, and Confusion, over what humankind thinks is Progress.

When fear, is talking in your ear. What's it telling you, What is it that you hear? Fear is very afraid of Consciousness Energy. It can feel it coming from miles away. In your life presently, everyone has a fear of something. That's how fear stays alive. You've been able to train your horses to jump on command, and to eat out of your hand, upon your demand. You can do all that, but you won't teach your children to reach beyond what you understand? To reach out to the future. To go beyond the computer. Where the energy of all creation exists. To create the future, they must be taught how to question. How to learn the knowledge of Consciousness Energy. Whether you teach them or not. The young are on the move. They disapprove of the same old groove. Pay attention. Start to notice. Listen for the call of the Young Generation. Survival will depend on their motivation and your active participation as the older generation.

It's your choice, which staple is on your table? But no matter what's on your table, you need to be able, to be stable. You have created a world, where both parents have to work to survive. It's unreliable. Your children are on the street. You're too busy, they have to survive. How will they stay alive? You're doing your best. But others are doing it better. You will not like how they are being raised. They have little guidance. What they learn, comes from other Kids. Their Friends, Magazines, TV, Media platforms, and the Phone. These, are what's raising your children. They have become their teachers.

What do you think this will produce? So far from this view, we see little education. Little follow through, and many, *"I don't know what to do."* We are aware of the reasons, it shows in your eyes. We hear cries over cries, of humanity in despair. The favorite motto? *"Life is not fair."* How sad for those that believe that. It's not fair, because it's Unbalanced. When your energy life force is unbalanced, so are you. Balance Energy is Consciousness Energy. Take responsibility for your actions against each other. Balance creates harmony.

Whatever happened to Love and Romance? It used to be that love put you in a trance, and romance was the balance between life, love and kids. The Energy of Resentment flows out of your bodies by the gallons. You seem to resent what ever takes time and attention away from your ego. You have accepted Fear, Greed, and Control, as part of your life. Now, you live with three energies that can't get enough. You think your life is tough, these are the reason. They have become your meaning. The lives of the young are being wasted, sitting in front of video games. They have lost their feeling for nature. Their brains have become a digital producer, and an intelligence reducer.

UC: They will always be hungry, because they live on the unnatural stuff. Temptation is hard to resist when one is hungry. They can get angry. How do you expect a starving man, not to eat a steak that you put in front of him? It could be a Cow, Horse, or Possum Steak. It didn't matter, he needed a break. He just wants to eat. So he takes a seat. Does he care about what kind of meat? Does he take the time to ask? Would you? Maybe after your through. Does he ask about the taste? What spices you used? Does he ask for a knife, or use his hand? He may even take it and run, not forgetting the bun. What would you do, if you knew ahead of time, that it was possum on your plate, not prime meat. Would you still eat?

It's the same for your brain, it has to absorb information from anyone, and anything because, you lost control of it. It's been on its own. You're starving your brain. It's eating possum. It needs a new kind of knowledge. The point is, when you are starving, you make yourself do, what you thought you would never do. Eat crow instead. You can be wrong. So what. It doesn't need a reaction. Be wrong. Defending yourself from the beliefs of others only proves them right. Conflict and arguing will always ensue. If you have to defend what you know, do you really know it? When the strength of what you know, comes from Consciousness, it keeps you from reacting. Your brain will do what it has to. It's a matter of survival. As humans, you are starving in so many ways, and you don't have to be. It only takes a choice to pull yourself out of fantasy, into a new kind of reality. Consciousness Energy, can create unity.

You are leaving your brain, to depend on physical outside influences to grow on, or not. You're leaving the brain with only one choice. To learn from others, not you. The issue is, it's starving. It doesn't care what it eats. This is why you should care. It's your brain. Do you want to lead or to be led? How can you find yourself, when you've become everyone else. In these chapters you will find the knowledge your brain needs. What you are reading, is recharging your brain with new energy, not the same old thing. Your brain won't absorb the same old thing. It's the same old thing.

This New Conscious Energy gives you the awareness, to convert the negative thoughts that you get. Being Physically Conscious and aware, has many benefits. It's the first step towards self-awareness. However, Being Physically Unconscious and aware, has an example to share. It's an example of how Consciousness can save your life. It's about an unconscious man, excited about his first home.

After he was wed, this man buys a nice house, on a nice spread. It has one room with a nice bed. It was his home, and a Man's home is his castle. *"I love my spread, he said,"* then he let it go to his head. He felt the need to tell everyone, how proud he was of his accomplishment. Each time he went to travel, he bragged about his marvel. The more he bragged the more he revealed. By now, the whole town knew how much he loved his spread. After he was tired of showing off, he was on his way home with the one he loves. Knowing the road back was so long, they couldn't wait to arrive. All he could think about was going home. Faster and faster he went, ignoring the message he sent, when he bragged about not having to pay rent. And how much money he would be saving.

They arrive home from their travel. He gets hit on the head with a large metal Gavel. He had put a price on his own head, other men were in his shed, wanting him dead, for what he said about his spread. Looks like his bragging rights, took away his rights to brag. He should have bragged less, and listened more. He may have made it to the door. Being Unconscious, doesn't only make you obnoxious, it can make you dead.

Humans do not need a reason to covet. They take what you have, and the one above it. It's a really bad habit, but, they love it. How long will you wait to take your stand. This knowledge, will prepare you to stand on your own two feet. Feel confident with those you meet. Especially, the takers, and the fakers. What's the difference? The takers, are fakers. The fakers are takers. No difference.

UC: What about the War makers? They say, that they always have a plan, but it's only to get what they can. Why do you trust a war maker with your, and your children's lives? Oh, you believe it's for protection. Why do you need protection? And from whom? From other World War Makers.

Humans are being manipulated by control and greed. You will meet them and others, when you continue to read. Wouldn't you like a world without fear? A world without needless deaths. These Energy Words are here to empower you to find your insight. Whether you heard this before, or it's new. It's the view, from inside you.

Without doing what needs to be done. These words are just words. If the war makers had a plan, Why isn't it to increase the life span? Does humanity need this kind of human? War makers only care about their own plans. You're not included in them. But, your young kids are welcomed with open ARMS. What kind of leader would you be? Look around. You probably should. There aren't many left. A new leader must be focused on Consciousness Energy Creation, and a new World Direction. Keep reading, there is instruction in this Evolution Revolution. Everything has an explanation. Worldly or not. Your life span, depends on how you live your physical life. As it is now, your life span is short. There are numerous problems facing humanity. Many of them are self-created. Let's not forget the issue of Dependency, it's not over rated.

Many of humanity's health problems, are caused by the side effects of humans testing on their own kind. Worldwide, many of you have developed serious illnesses from using Chemical products. They are using your anatomy as a laboratory for their experiments, and you are paying them to do it. Would you consider this a Conscious or an Unconscious action? Can you even tell? Here is more for your perception. Humans are stealing nature, and selling it for money. All that you take for the purpose of healing, is not being replaced. You are depleting nature, while you deplete the earth

Who told you that you had priority, over other life forms. All of nature is Consciousness Energy born. You are children operating on healthy patients. As you try to find a cure for your illnesses, you create more illnesses with your cures. One day, scientists will find a cure for the disease that they have created. It makes them the saviors. They have no worries. Because now you trust them. You stopped questioning their motives.

They found a cure for the diseases, they created. Of course, they have the cure. They just took their time showing it. Life is about learning from everything. It's the nature of life. But then, most of humanity's life is Unnatural.

Humanity has increased the speed of physical deterioration to such a degree, that they are falling off the tree. Piece by piece, and humanity can't see that as a whole, they are the tree. They have yet to figure out what they want to be. Is humanity, expecting this madness to stop by itself?

UC: If you are, you need to be awakened. The only thing that can stop it, is you, the humans. It's the same for your nuclear weapons threat. Only you, can stop it. It's your life it threatens. How is humanity expecting to evolve? Through Technology alone? This hasn't worked very well for you so far. Technology put you where you are, that's not evolution. However, the Energy Evolution Revolution is coming.

The Idea of blowing up the Earth doesn't make you bolder, or stronger, just older, then colder. People have the capability to be wiser. The Universal Creation sits in a state of awareness, wondering what humankind will do? Your energy is unstable. Nobody wants to sit at your Table. Your history shows evidence of Alien visitors, during your primitive times.

They are coming back again. They are coming to your aid since you can't. This is an event where history will be repeated. This time they will not be alone. It's a worldwide visit. We are aware of humanity's Arrogance. Or is it Ignorance? You don't even believe in your own Existence. If you did, you wouldn't be sitting on a bomb. Your leaders hide their actions. Secrecy in leadership means a rotten foundation. It will not last.

The lack of concern that you have for each other, has turned one brother, against another. It's part of why you suffer. There is an energy on Earth, that is trying to sabotage your intentions. Humanity is not aware of its effects. But that's not your only problem. You will learn all about it as you continue. We believe you should. You want to, because it's in you. It drives you. This isn't meant to scare you, but to make you aware, that it's there to increase your fear. Because, humanity still has the ability for choice, you don't have to listen to it. It controls you, through your Brain and Emotions. There is a new kind of Virus in your sky. It just wants to live. This one, doesn't care who cries or dies. The goal of this Virus, is to spread Hate, Violence, and Lies. Humanity is infected by it, and no one knows it.

It's called, The VIRUS ENERGY CELL. You will meet it in the next chapter. It's what religion calls, The DEVIL. Of course, It would be up to you as an individual to decide. Conscious self control, will keep you from losing it all. This Virus Energy, directly affects your brain with negative thoughts and actions. It will turn you into a reactive human being, and take away your meaning. However, letting its effects lead you, is your responsibility. You don't have to let it control you. Use your self-control humanity. It will spread slower. A mask doesn't help you with this one. It's too strong. Self realization is a good way to recognize it in you. Consciousness Energy helps you recognize it in others.

The Evolution Revolution is a self revealing plan. It's a plan about humankind. Each chapter has a revelation that will develop your awareness, to the point of Consciousness. Confusion, is not part of Evolution. But Consciousness Energy is. Humanity is a real whiz at pretending to be aware of this. Pretending, is one of humanity's behaviors. How many people, mean what they say when they say it? Who is going to say they don't? Where is the truth? Can anyone change your decision once you make it? If they can, did you really make it?

Are you easily influenced, or under the influence? What's the difference? Do others trust your words? What's your reaction if they don't? Do you react without thinking? Have you ever seen yourself in action, without thinking? Are you aware of Consequences, Limits, and Boundaries? Do you use them? Can you tell when they are being used on you? What about follow through, Do you know what to do?

Questions, are the path to development. Answers, create realizations. Use your answers to create your questions. What do you know about Responsibility? Humans are now being held responsible, for their continued evolution. Humans must push through the notion that physical is all there is. Perception is energy. It develops, it changes with learning. Through reading, a new perception can be developed.

UC: Has humanity found a solution, to slow down the birth of their population? You have war, disease, birth control pills. They don't seem to be slowing the population down? Consciousness can show you how, to use energy balance to help with the population problem. Humans need to develop their brain past what they know, in order to discover new ideas. You were fitted with intelligence, and the ability to navigate clearly. But the actual Sensation from humankind, is keeping their Presence from learning Lessons.

Presently, humans are in reaction to an influence, by a source of energy that is not their imagination. It's a Virus Energy Inspiration. This knowledge offers one explanation, to shift your perception, and allow you to see the Virus Energy.

Humanity's past, has been leading them to a future, back to the past. Led by a cast, that lives in their Unconscious vast. They are the Energies of the Virus. There is a list of them as you read on. Humanity has come to know the UNCONSCIOUS, as the SUBCONSCIOUS. It's more of an "UN" than a "SUB." A Subconscious projects a sense of Partial Consciousness, unfortunately, as an energy form. Many of you are so completely, Unconscious, the Subconscious doesn't mean anything to you.

There is CONSCIOUSNESS ENERGY AND UNCONSCIOUS ENERGY, nothing in between. Once you are Conscious, the "UN" is gone. There is nothing left but Consciousness. Humanity has been manipulated into not using it. There are no excuses, no partial Consciousness. That's like partially breathing, which is your situation presently. You're hardly breathing. The water around you is drying out. Soon, you will be a fish without water. You know what comes after, a disaster.

The "SUB," only gives you an excuse to leave it there, and not deal with it. It doesn't work. It's just a hideaway. There is no later for UNCONSCIOUS BELIEFS. They are forgotten in the Unconscious. It's why you forget them. You are unconscious.

The Unconscious is where you keep your SECRETS. They keep you from becoming well. Secrets are best friends with the energy of the Virus Cell. Whatever it is that you hide, will always keep you hidden. True identity, comes from the true application of your physical energy, and a clear revelation of your actions. Your emotions are being turned into promotions. Your feelings have become boardroom dealings.

Your actions have turned into reactions, and your perceptions, have become perceived as a perception without conviction. People are walking around all day and night, without sight. Doesn't this give you fright? Do you notice? You should pay attention. Look in the mirror, fear has a reflection. You've become used to seeing it. You know it's there, you can feel it. Are you willing to see, what your fear is?

Do you have the willingness to face your fear? There is another view in here, that could add to your perception. This question is addressed to you, reader. Why do humans stay in their head, and pretend to be near dead, while fear is eating their bread, and rewriting what they said? Are you listening?

R: Yes, I heard that. But, I was reading. When you're only aware of your brain, where else are you to go, but your head? This is what people understand. It wasn't until now did I realize, that there was somewhere else besides the Brain Consciousness. As I read, I am finding it out to be a Universal Consciousness Energy, which created the brain consciousness.

No one is pretending to be near dead or dead, we don't have to pretend, because many of us believe we are. However, there are those who are known to be Emotionally dead, without feelings, empathy, or compassion. Many of us have lost these feelings. I don't think people, have loaves of bread lying around for fear to eat it. We are too busy working to buy bread. Anyway, it doesn't last long enough. People are too hungry. As far as rewriting what I say, go ahead, Write Away. It's gotta be a better play?

I usually don't have much to say, until now. I feel a sense of new clarity, and I just started reading. Why did I walk through this door? It was different. I am attracted to different. I am finding out about things I never heard of. From what I have read so far, these words are presented with common sense and simple logic. We have complicated the meaning of what a creator is. That's because, there are too many religions. That's my opinion. We have a lot of problems that need fixing. Especially, Our health and our safety. Our actions, and mostly, Our Self-Awareness. Our ability to realize new ideas and new thoughts. We need energy healing. We are in limbo when it comes to our evolution. I have a hard time thinking that this is it, and we will continue to live this way.

UC: Humans needs to realize, Consciousness Energy never dies. That there is more to deal with than human-made viruses, as bad as they are. There is still the Virus Energy. It's been effecting your thoughts. It believes, it's calling the shots. It knows humankind's destination, because it created it. It knows your perception, because it's viewing it. It's aware of the effect on your direction, because it's directing it. It's aware of its effect on your instruction, because it's guiding it. It affects your decision, because it's making it.

It has infected people with denials, in order to control their Unconscious files. It's looking for its place in creation, and it found it in you, the humans. This is what you, the Young Generation will be facing. It's absolutely contagious. It's ready to meet you in a few more pages.

Humanity, you are not insane. You still have your own brain, it's just infected with pain. Only Consciousness Energy, can heal your brain. What about your emotions? Are you aware of them? They are not hiding from you. Yet you ignore the ones out of control. Have they ever lied to you? What? You never lied to yourself? Have your feelings mislead you? Why did you let them? Oh, you didn't feel it coming. Do they do the opposite, of what you want them to? They are being influenced by a Virus Energy, what did you expect? Are you more brain, than emotion, or more emotion, than brain? What reacts first? Are your emotional reactions really yours? How can you be sure? Are your beliefs really your own? Are you curious to find out?

It's hard for you to see this Virus, as you don't have the whole picture yet. The Evolution Revolution will help humanity, to identify the Virus Energy in them, reformulate it, and change its meaning. Energy Conversion, changes it into a Balanced Consciousness Energy that your brain needs.

Humans have the ability to save themselves. By not allowing their Virus-infected energy thoughts, to become their actions. True freedom can be achieved by the conversion of the negative energy, influencing your brain. Life is about Energy Development. It generates evolution. Without energy movement, you have no evolution.

The Energies of Trust, Love, Kindness, and much more, will fill the thoughts of humanity, once you are free of the Virus Energy. Your Stress, anxiety depression, and Mental illness together, would go away forever. Do you think that a Conscious Creator would Create such a life for its Creation, that would be Cruel? But, apparently, it seems that you do. You have to blame someone or something. It's as though you believe that you deserve to live in hell. You do not. This is a belief that comes from control, blind faith, and greed. You keep wishing to be saved from your self-made illusion. You created it, you can change it. Humans are not helpless, just Unconscious of their consciousness.

UC: Many of you have become a moving car without a driver. This knowledge of the Evolution Revolution can be your driver. It will drive you towards Curiosity, and Self-Discovery. It will shift your perception to focus on clarity. Until you become clear. No one is coming to save humanity, but only to aid it, in saving yourself. So humanity, think about having clarity. When you are stuck in quicksand, you have to at least, reach. You are the one going down. You've become accustomed to having others take over your responsibilities. What are your disabilities? Can you acknowledge them? Do you the people, have the courage to discover more?

R: Sorry to interrupt. But as the reader, why do I also feel like I am the listener? How is it possible for me to hear you, while at the same time, read this?

UC: You were informed that these words will talk to you. When you can hear what you read, then you are listening. So yes, you are hearing, and reading at the same time. It's a double learning experience. Thanks to the energy of Consciousness.

R: What you're saying Is amazing. I actually understood it. Does this happen to anyone who walks down this path?

UC: Do you think you are a special person?

R: No, not really.

UC: Then yes, it can happen to anyone. Are you anyone?

R: I am someone. Anyone can be anyone. OK, I am going back to reading, but I will be listening. You are right, this energy draws you in. I am feeling more aware so far.

UC: When humans choose to live in a state of denial, they'll be waiting quite a while. This delivery has given you an inch, why won't you take a mile? You usually do. Just like with your blame, everybody did it but you. Who are you going to blame when no one is around?

A nuclear explosion would cause an energy vibration suffocation, and YOU'RE THE ENERGY VIBRATION. This is an explanation of what will happen. This is a forced destruction of physical matter. Only this one, would unbalance creation on a Universal level. Do you think you are off balance now? You are aware of the ripple effect. Is this really what you accept? If so, humanity has lost all respect. Such an explosion would speed up your frequency rotation, into reversing your mass vibrational speed, until you are back to a seed. Basically you die.

However, your Energy Vibration continues on, until you confront what you have done. There are many ways, humanity is suffering. It is what it is. Deny it or not. Infection from disease is traveling with the breeze, covering the entire world. Pollution, is causing humankind's anatomy to go through changes. It's reformulating humanity's blood in phases. Preventing it from slowing down your ages. Humans have been by themselves for themselves. They use anger and rage, then turn the page, avoiding what they did. This is a conscious denial? By choice. Which is worse. Do you consider yourself, an energy creator?

Who takes responsibility for boundaries and limits? Many humans have become too Materialistic, too greedy, and focused on their appearance. With consciousness, you don't have boundaries or limits. You are focused, awake, aware, and conscious. You know the ways of Consciousness Energy.

UC: You allowed yourself to become possessed with physical objects. When they possess you, they take your feelings too. If all you are, is physical energy, then you will attract physical energy. You will instantly lose sight of yourself, once you allow POSSESSIONS to POSSESS you...You become OBSESSED, until you claim the rest.

Possessed by your Possessions. The meaning of Materialistic. What's possessing you humanity? Is it the Virus Energy? It's always something or another. There are over seven billion like you. Humanities Consciousness Energy is meant to be felt. It's different, you can feel it. It's a live battery charge. It will start your motor, but it won't rev your engine, that's your job. It's meant to be developed, to be used. Awareness can be unlimited with development. When you are fully aware, you are aware of everything. You are in a Consciousness state of being. Where all things have meaning. The meanings are very clear. There is no confusion, only energy infusion. Confusing humanity's brain, changes the Physical Energy Vibration, causing the body's anatomy to rearrange. Which changes your molecular structure, and shortens your life expectancy. It's a reality. You are trying to pull a bulldozer, with a scooter. Can you visualize this?

So, what can humans do differently? You can start by being Different. Change your Perception. Unravel your Beliefs, and Dissect them. Start to ask questions, from anyone requesting something from you. It's not about suspicion. It's so you can learn, it's so you can gain. Allow yourself to stand out. Do not hide anymore. Hiding is being in fear. Find out why, and you won't have to hide, and if you already know why, face it. Don't hide from it. It always knows where you are. Fear hides better than you do. Be courageous in the face of fear, and it will not reappear. Your words can make a difference. You exist, you count. You are not alone. Be brave for your bravery. Be wise for your wisdom. Be Conscious, for your Universal Consciousness Energy. Go beyond what you know. Build your self-esteem. You must learn to be clear, with what you mean. Otherwise, your meaning can't be seen. You need to learn something else, besides what you know.

Do not stop helping yourself. You're the only one who can. Simply allow your brain to absorb new meanings. If you are use to jumping from a seven-foot-high dive, reach a little higher to eight feet. Create your life, along the way. Stop allowing greed and fear to control you. The more you feed into them, the more they feed on you. To stop them, you only need to recognize them, when you feel them. Humanity''s focus, needs to shift towards understanding their creator and their creation.

Congratulations on your discovery of Cloning. Is this your solution for starvation? What were you thinking? If you can clone an animal, one of you will attempt to clone a human. With your population problem, this would not be advisable, under any circumstances. So you must be doing it for food? We don't mean to be rude. But what happened to your aptitude? You have the Earth's soil to grow your food. But many of you are too lazy to work the soil.

Do you want to clone animals? Animals can be plentiful since they multiply faster than you. Only, you eat them faster than they multiply. Humans are extremist in many ways. Overeating has become an Addiction. Drinking, Medicating, Watching TV, Sex, and Isolating; All are addictions. A habit is an

Unconscious Manifestation of an Upcoming Addiction. This is proof that your energy is off balance. You went too far to one side, and tipped the scale. Now, you can't get back. It's too difficult of a climb. How will humankind get their balance back?

UC: Humans have poisoned the soil and the water. So others would have to buy natural foods, when you used to grow them for free. Some of you, took it upon yourselves to become the owner of water. So you can make money selling it in bottles. The water is free, so you are selling people only plastic bottles, and the chemicals that come with them, they are killing you. You Hijacked all the growing seeds for money, and made the soil toxic. You even blamed the insects for making your animals go extinct?

Many of you leave the Earth incomplete. Your incomplete energy, will still be attached to the physical dimension. Incomplete energy's must develop to become whole. It has to collect all parts of itself and convert them into Consciousness Energy. To fill the Core of the Universal Consciousness. This is how the creator is unlimited. The energy that goes out, has the goal of growing by developing. Through that development, it will convert back to the same energy that it came from. But, it will have extra energy, from the knowledge it had developed on. Humankind is responsible for keeping the Universal Consciousness growing.

Reincarnation occurs, when a whole energy is needed for a purpose. Such as, in the conversion of the virus energy cell. There are some that go back, to learn development and convert their virus. But they die before they can. Bringing the virus back around. We could cure so much, if humans would stop coming back to soon. We are focused on converting the virus. Are you humanity? In the spiritual dimensions, spirits work on increasing their vibrational frequency, from spirit to Consciousness Energy. Unfortunately, the natural energy cycle is unbalanced. It is causing those spirits who resist their development, to be sent back to physical life. Many are being recycled. But there are more who want to develop. It's where the focus goes. That's not to say, that this is the only reason for reincarnation. This Evolution Revolution, is a form of Energy Reincarnation. These words embody the Universal Consciousness. Humans keep cycling back to Earth, as the same incomplete energy that they left with. They will keep recycling, until their energy is made whole. Incomplete energy can't develop past the point of physical energy speed. It must become aware of its consciousness, to get off the cycle.

This is the Universal Consciousness Explanation of Reincarnation. Wake up, don't get stuck in the cycle. Humans shouldn't get excited about what they create, until what they create changes their fate. What needs to be created is energy movement. It's the one thing that can change your environment. Create what has not been created. Try discovering the Consciousness Energy Vibration. It goes beyond physical matter. What's the matter, doesn't it matter? Or, you just don't know? Do you reader?

R: What I have read so far, has me asking myself questions. As I read on, my questions seem to be getting answered, page by page. I have read many books, I have never had this experience before. There is much more to this knowledge I need to know.

UC: You can find out what you want to know, as you continue reading.

R: This knowledge is already moving me. It is effecting my brain. I am having the beginning of a brain shake. I am only on the first chapter. I wonder, what's coming after?

UC: By the time you are done, it will feel more like an Earthquake than a shake.

R: Are you saying, an Earthquake Shake? I can't wait, I have never experienced one of those before. I need a good shaking to get the cobwebs out. I have to find out what all this is about. I've gone too far not to.

UC: Humankind's science should be focused on Consciousness Energy identification, and how to integrate it into physical creation. You have the ability to create machines that can record this energy. It can be done. You have the technology, and now, the opportunity to discover an energy source, that can change your course. Look for it. Find it. Build it. Use it.

R: This knowledge puts things in perspective. Many of us are a disgrace, as a human race. Yet, there is no better place than this place. I will not give it up. I will do everything in my power to change it. This is our home. We need more people to think this way. How can we just walk away, and let this illusion continue? I will not. I am doing what I can now. Learning, developing, discovering a new me. I can only do that with New Energy Exposure. I want to know, what I don't know, about Myself.

How Conscious can I become? I want to learn how, to not be afraid? How to love more passionately, to care with honesty? To act when there is reason to. But never react without a reason, like some people do. I want my family, and I to feel safe. I want to live in peace and good health. I am too Conscious to ignore our situation anymore.

UC: Throughout history, humans have been creating more ways to defend themselves. You should be defending yourselves from yourselves. Humans are constantly on the defense, while creating an offense. Why should there be any defense? Humans are well educated on putting up Barriers. They have a catalogue that lists them.

From history, generation through generation, humans used cruel behaviors on many. There were thousands, being led by their hunger for greed. They lived to instill fear, and brought slavery to humanity. These actions were not a mystery, they were happening publicly. This isn't meant to be human bashing. It's a human awakening, from years of brain washing. Just look at the amount of violence in your population.

It was alive in your history, and is still alive today. Give yourself a few minutes to think about, what in your life, has recently changed. Besides the fact that you haven't. Times have changed. Humans are facing the Age of Consciousness Energy. Life will continue to evolve. Change keeps changing. Evolution will make sure of that.

Starting with, the awareness of your own humanity. To help you shift away from calamity. There are those upon the Earth, that actually believe in atrocity, they spend their lives preparing for the enemy. This makes insanity, look like a formality. There's more…You still claim to be a human being, but many of you close your eyes to charity. You rule the Earth like a dynasty. You allow greed, to grow its seed, into its own autonomy, Finally, you keep your eyes closed to all this catastrophe. This is your responsibility.

A Declaration

Let's call it what it is, ***Beyond Insanity.*** When humans hold greed in high celebrity, it becomes a real personality. You use the excuse, that it's for your family. But in reality, it's for your infamy. News flash…Greed, doesn't ever get full. It knows how to use you as a tool.

Would you, as a good person, sell out to greed, in times of need? Can you be tempted? Greed comes in many forms. Is humanity aware of them? What are the forms of greed? Learn what they are as you read. Humans are limited by their physical knowledge. You can't seem to find the cure for your mental illness. You have tried medications, but, you still have mental institutions. If you can't cure them you lock them up. You are running out of places to put them. Do you have room at your house?

UC: Humans are inspired by attached spirits on a constant bases. When they get you to do it, they actually feel it. A physical feeling is their reasoning. It makes the dead feel alive. It's a connection with a life once lived. The real insanity is humanity, denying what they don't know. How is it, you don't know? Since your knowledge is limited, how will you ever know? Not all humans fit in your mold of insanity. Not all the insane are crazy.

Humankind, was considered to be a special species. However, Many of your physical behaviors exhibit cognitive decline. Awareness, is your ability to project Conscious Energy, and connect with humanity. Doesn't humanity teach education, about the brain function? The brain doesn't run its own station, it has an engineer. You don't know how your brain functions, because you have yet, to have introductions.

The issue of humanity's brain is not a simple one. Your brain, is fighting an onslaught of negative influences, coming at one time. That's why you are unaware of the negative energy, falling out of your mouth. *"Oops! The words just fell out."* Heard this before? How are you going to change your perception? You must break through the old mold, before your brain is sold into slavery. What else do you expect? Haven't you noticed? Your brain is talking to you. When it speaks, listen. When it asks, answer. When it needs new knowledge to grow on, give it.

Humans keep feeding their brain, the same hay it has always eaten. It's giving up, it feels beaten. Are you aware of what you are doing? It has nothing to grow on, no health food, no nutrition. It's lost so much weight, it can barely function. We are bringing this to your attention humanity. You need to refill it as soon as you can. It's shrinking. It's suppose to be growing. There will come a time, where your brain will need restructuring. It's a matter of Evolution. Your brains have shown no signs of organic growth, there are little signs of brain tissue regeneration. You already know what you know, from your physical education. This is something you may not know. It's Consciousness Energy Education, that takes you beyond the brain, into a new dimension of thought perception. It's a new way of thinking. A new way of feeling. A new way to grow your brain.

As a physical human, you can travel around the world many times. After you've seen it all, then what? When do you discover your own world? The one inside you. Let your Consciousness Energy guide you. What's Consciousness? It's the question. It's the answer. It's the movement. It's Birth, Death, and the Life After. It's the Earth and all Planets, the Universes, and all that exists in them. Consciousness is the balanced side of Unconsciousness. It has come to remove the UN, from Unconsciousness.

Why do humans treat the Earth like they own it? You're just renters? When it needs help, it's on its own, and you forget it? Please don't treat the Earth like it's yours. Those days are gone. You gave up that right. The planet Earth is not yours to own. You have done her wrong. When you get to that chapter, put your phone on silent, and listen to her plight. She knows what's right, and she knows how to fight. Oh, she can talk all night.

The Earth belongs to its creator, not its tormentor. You're going to question your actions towards your treatment of her, as you hear her story. Should humans continue to be allowed to live on Earth? Who makes that decision? It's not Consciousness. It's not your God. It's not the devil. Who is left? YOU, humankind. It's right back in your lap. It's your choice. It's always been your choice. When you were conscious, you had trust.

UC: Humans were not meant to just survive. You were created to stay alive and thrive, to discover, to learn, to be the Earths Protector. You still have time, start protecting. You were put to a test, to create your best. You made a mess, and now you want someone else to clean it up. Has humanity thought about doing it themselves? If you notice it, do something about it. Oh, you didn't notice it. Has this become your perception? Many of your behaviors are proving that you are living in a frozen state in evolution. This can only be classified as a brain dysfunction. Humans live by the belief that *"life is hard, and nothing is free"*. No wonder you feel like you are in prison? With a belief like these, how are you planning on ever being free?

Why are you ignoring the fact that you are losing control of life. Why haven't you noticed your mess humans? It's still there. It will continue to stay there, until you clean it up. The Earth and its Space are not a junkyard. But apparently, you think they are. Just as you treat the Earth and space, you will treat everything else. The focus of your curiosity, is no longer on discovery. This Universal Consciousness Energy, is here to create a Physical Recovery. Recovery of humanity's memory, before you became what you are. It's a struggle over power. Hour on the hour. The bigger the power, the smaller the hour. The stronger the control. The weaker the soul? You can change that? LOSE THE CONTROL, SAVE YOUR SOUL!

It's a pity, humans are not aware of their Consciousness Energy. If you are, Show it? Develop it. Use it? Figure out what you can do with it? Have you formed an idea? Do you need an inspiration? It's in the Evolution Revolution. Life is about knowing. If you don't find out, you are stuck where you are. Why have you not changed? It's your energy, it's Unconscious. It wants to become conscious, but you will not let it. You are content.

As you develop your physical energy, it will become a super-charged frequency. With a new faster vibrating energy. What we discuss, is a human oil change if you must. A transmission and brake check, along with balancing all your tires. You will be able to drive straight from now on. Learn how to drive, or wreck your car, it's your choice. Remember, choosing to wreck your car, will wreck everything you are. This would be considered Reckless.

Now, when it comes to nuclear weapons, is it the trust of your leaders that you have? Is it blind faith? Or is it denial? Oh, you feel powerless. It doesn't make sense. We have more concern for your lives than you do. Why, humanity? Is it too difficult to face the truth? You already know that those who created the Nuclear bombs will be the ones left in safety's arms.

But you? They won't see you. You are nowhere to be found. This is a reality call, to tell humankind they are about to fall. Those that are doing it, will be standing tall, that's all. You can have credit for your existence, but not credit for your persistence. Many of you give up too easily. Your brain says I can't, and you believe it. Don't you ever question your thoughts?

There are many life forms, who have gone against the physical norms, to be the calm in life's storms. Why are you still in the swimming pool? You have an ocean to swim. Humans have unlimited potential for developing their Consciousness Energy. Only you limit yourself daily, for fear of failing society, while society is failing you. Why do you create self restriction? Is it because, you are unaware of your Consciousness Energy function? What took your physical REALITY, and turned it into a FANTASY?

R: Pardon the intrusion. I know you are speaking with the humans. But, I ask myself this question often. I have also asked myself, why was I allowing others to lead me, when I can lead myself. Every page I read, brings out a hundred questions in my head. It's overwhelming. I have to read slowly, to absorb each meaning. It got me thinking about my beliefs. What do I really believe? What have I been learning? I never questioned these things before. I suppose, this is Consciousness development. It starts with questioning what we know. For me, it's easy to see that we need to question what we are teaching, what we are producing and what we are creating? Do we really know the effect we are having? I want to know.

UC: You should start asking questions. Just believing, is not real learning. Why? Keep reading. Your brain will love you for it. Presently, what you are learning is the education of repeating. What you are teaching, is limited to what you know. What you are creating, has been left to your technology. What you're producing, is only more nuclear power. Your physical Energy has been moving, by way of the Virus Energy Cell. Humans must learn to recognize it, to save themselves.

R: There are so many reasons why we need a do-over, before it's over. I majored in philosophy in college. I learned a lot through the years. Only here, in these writings, I'm learning that philosophy is actually an energy in action, trying to teach us consciousness. For years, it had been only a discussion in school. For me, these meanings have moved philosophy, into a new reality, not just words.

It's not that easy to speak out for justice, we would be stopped by the Injustice Department. They make the rules. No one confronts them without going to prison. Even when using reason. Most people say, *"Why should I stick my neck out."* When you want to do good, and change things, you have to become a politician and hang out with politicians. By the time you get elected. You have been bought. And you don't even realize it. So why take a risk? Many people have tried, worldwide. They all died. Many people feel this way. That's how the phrase, *"It's none of my business,"* started.

Asking for clarity for certain actions is not a crime. As long as the person you are asking, is not a criminal? I hadn't realized how bad our intelligence situation was until, I heard these employees talking during a bomb threat. I couldn't believe my ears. It made me worry. Here are some of their comments:

"You can't do anything about it It's always the same, I am staying inside. Ain't nothing going to happen." *"Men are boys, always playing with bombs. "*

"Some employee must be late, and called in a bomb threat." *"Yeah, I did it once, I was still late."* *"I hope I have time to get under the floor. Will It be over by four?"*

"I have a hair appointment next door." *"After the first one, will there be more?"*

"There always is, I'll just sit here and ignore."

These people are a danger to humanity. They are all over the world. This is who I have more fear from. Unconscious Humans. This is why, we have turned out to be such a disappointment. Who thinks about a hair appointment, during a threat assessment?

UC: People are being manipulated every second of every day. You don't see it, but it's happening. Just pay attention. It could be you. You are told what to buy, and what to sell. What to eat, and what to drink. What pill to take, and what to drive. What hospital to go to, and how to stay alive. Advertising has been manipulating humanity, since the discovery of Money.

The Computer? Is your brain in one box. There is only one key that unlocks the brain, to keep you from doing it again, the Universal Consciousness Energy Vibration. Your future is at stake, ignorance has you believing that you are awake. Make no mistake, if you were awake, you would notice what's at stake, and put on the break. The revelation is, that your beliefs have been manipulated by the leadership position, to keep you blind to your deadly situation. Greed pays a donation to all the political affiliations.

This is what you have done. You have turned the Earth into a huge nuclear bomb. Not only are you forcefully changing your DNA, but you are also changing the way your Sun shines today. Even the soil has turned to clay. Now people have to pay, to change the clay, back to soil. But you knew that, didn't you? It doesn't work. You can't bring the dead back to life. Anytime a bomb is tested, you're changing the speed of your Physical Energy Vibration. The energy is displacing matter in a different direction. Nuclear explosions are destroying your physical ability to live naturally. You are creating unnatural forms of Energy. You follow without reason, and you reason just to follow. WHAT'S THE REASON?

It seems that humans do not practice what they preach. They think one way and do another. For example, your wedding bands, they represent the cycle, with no beginning or end. Forever, according to your vows. But yet, you also believe in an ending. How does this work? If it's from beginning to beginning, how can there be an ending? It's a full cycle. If you don't believe in ghosts, why do you believe in witches? If you don't believe in fairies, why do you believe in wishes? If you don't believe in saving the Earth, why do you believe in its riches? If you don't believe in Elves, why are they on your shelves? And in your garden too. Why do you believe, in what you don't believe? Are you getting the message this is sending?

You have the ability to manipulate, but not the Consciousness to know, when you are being manipulated. You have the ability to control others, but not the Consciousness to know, when others are controlling you. You have the ability to lie to others, but not the Consciousness to know, if they are lying to you. You have the ability to hurt others, but not the Consciousness to know, when you are being hurt. You have the ability to help others, but not the Consciousness to know, when you need help. You have the ability to be Conscious, but not the Consciousness to know it.

Consciousness, is being aware of what you see in your surroundings, which you could learn from. Learning, helps you to develop a new Conscious perception, which helps you deal with your ego. It can't stand up to Consciousness.

Humans have been ordering from the same menu, from the time they learned how to write. What can you learn from that. It's the same dish. There has never been a new menu, until now. How can you make a decision, unless you're are fully informed? Do you have an opinion reader? This is not peel the onion. What you see is what it is. An awareness of humanity's presence.

R: I have something to say. From what I am reading, this knowledge can be very helpful in so many ways. We have no idea how to fix most mental health issues in the brain. We are still trying to fix our own emotions. Many, think they have no issues with their emotions. Some believe, their emotions can't be fixed, I am sure those are connected to the brain. I don't claim to know much about the brain yet. But I am learning about what runs it. With what I am reading now, I want to be the best example of a human that I can be.

R: I want my children to learn how to confront their issues. To never run away from them. I want them to know, how, as an energy, their issues will follow them everywhere. Until they change their direction. When things become difficult in our lives, or we fall on hard times, we have learned how to leave. When things become too hard to handle, best to just leave. Don't look back. Forget it happened. The world is full with societies that are LEAVERS.

We abandon our families like a bad job. We guilt others to get what we want. When we get it, we leave. It's always about opportunity. If we do not get it, we manipulate by using abandonment. We hide our true self, until we are comfortable with each other. Then we start taking each other for granted. We are playing a role provided for us by history. Roles that should have stayed in history. We are all using each other to sustain a life, which should no longer exist. It's antiquated, old. We take advice from a marriage therapist, who has never been married. And a drug counselor who was never addicted to anything. Empathy is no longer allowed. People are too proud. Compassion, has become a paid intervention. Our seniors are lost in the shuffle, and mostly die alone. We don't fix anything. We just leave, or make them leave. How did we ever get the name HUMANITY? Did we ever have this ability?

UC: The ability to be human is in your DNA. Your ability to be humane, is yet to be seen. Humanity represents all the people in the world. Most of the behaviors, which many humans exhibit, have nothing to do with being Humane. In history, humans were called other names in different languages. But the meaning was still the same, for the most part, Inhumane. History has created the mess you are in today. For thousands of years, they have gotten away with their illusion of creation, and the creator.

It was one belief by one people, until it was infected by greed. It exploded into divided believers. Different perceptions of the same idea, created many other beliefs from that one belief. Confusion set in, and so did control. They found it to be a great way to rule. So they manipulated others, into following their beliefs by creating the fear of God, and punishment. The idea of separate religions was born. It seemed no one trusted anyone, not even the spiritual form. Trust was broken, and forgiveness from God, began to cost the forsaken.

Some people didn't want to be told, they wanted to be the tellers. They became the preachers, the ministers, and the priests. People made up their own reality of history. Each leader took their followers, and went their separate ways. It's still the same these days. Personal faith became the only solution. Many lives were killed over this separation of faith. It was a Virus Cell induction into your Energy Vibration.

The price humanity is paying, is due to what they are doing. People have forgotten the meaning of natural Consequences. Many of you believe that life is hell. Being without your Consciousness, made it this way. So what are you going to do about fixing, what humans have broken. Whatever humanity thinks their technology will resolve, it still hasn't resolved the issue of Unconscious Energy. Leaving it alone is not a wise decision. It's everywhere, and interfering with other frequency waves. Causing mass confusion, and brain deterioration.

R: What I am reading, is what I have believed in some form or another, most of my life. How is it that this information is universal and felt by many of us, yet, we have never bothered to explore it? Why has it stayed a philosophy all these years? Just because of the Virus Energy Cell?

UC: No, not just that. But what keeps a human physical energy from moving, is their denial in the fact that their behaviors, need changing. They didn't bother. You kept leaving it for another and another, until it was too late. No one ever did it. So now you sit in it. For example, Blind Faith; Whats the benefit in following without question?

Isn't that how blind faith became a belief? You closed your eyes to reality. Those who never asked just followed. They had no idea where. It's better to have others think for you, that way you have someone to blame when it doesn't go your way. The rich, get richer, by feeding off the poor, who keep getting poorer. What do you call this, if not greed? You do not have to accept this way of life.

R: They are too many powerful and greedy politicians out there to confront, without some kind of world energy movement. We work for our governments. They get the benefit. I for one have had it. I would like to see more of us, wake up to where we are being lead. There is no reason that I can't do something about it. Every bit helps. This information empowers you, but you feel like you can't use that power. It's a struggle between Fear and Consciousness. Not being in the majority, is breaking the hold of control. You are labeled a non-conformist. Then you're a separatist, ostracized from the norm.

UC: You're not alone. The world is full of others like you. Reach out to them.

R: What I am understanding is, it seems that many questions and answers have been left out from history. It's become, a believe it or not. As for myself, I wasn't there in history. I could have been, I don't remember, but I am working on it. Presently, I am looking for knowledge, which could explain history more than religion has. I need answers, not empty promises. There had to be knowledge somewhere that could explain it all. I think I may have found it, through the awareness of Consciousness Energy.

I have discovered a reality based on energy. It's real, and makes sense to me. I think Consciousness Energy is what we are meant to be. It's difficult to see what's happening and not do something to change the energy. But I also realize that it starts with me. I have to find the answers myself. I can't depend on the perception of others. I am not a follower. I easily could be. I need the feeling of learning something new. What I have come to realize is, what I knew from history doesn't fit into today's society. We have lost our identity. We have lost the ability to intuitively heed. We depend on greed, to tell us what we need.

UC: Consciousness Energy awareness is your protection against infection, of any kind. It's the energy you need to help you heal yourself from negative influences. You need Consciousness Energy awareness, to be able to identify your thoughts, from those of others. Can you tell the difference? Using the thoughts of others to make decisions, is not you making them, it's other people making them. This is what makes a follower. Someone, who doesn't have the confidence to make a choice for themselves, about themselves, so they let others do it. Was this you, reader? Now that you changed your direction, are you feeling more like yourself or more like others?

R: I am only on the first chapter of this book, but from here, I have been able to visualize what's coming up next. It's like common sense. Once you realize it, it's easy to accept. It makes me more anxious to read the rest. I have also made a decision. The Universal Consciousness Energy, is not fiction. Because I can feel it, and I can hear it.

UC: Humans continue to show what they're all about, is self-doubt. What are you all about humanity? Is it fame and fortune. Dreams of success. Illusions that don't exist. Fantasies that persist. Realities that you dismiss, and seduction that you can't resist. Whats next? Sleep and rest? Come on humanity, wake up and make a list. A list of conscious actions that you will perform the next day. Without it, you will lose your way. Make conscious lists everyday, until you no longer need them. By then, you will have developed your brain to automatically do it. This is Consciousness Energy development.

The meek shall not inherit the Earth, there aren't any left. Self-preservation has changed the meek into becoming aggressive. They lost the hope of inheriting the Earth. No one was ever going to inherit the Earth. It's not a thing to inherit. It's an alive energy, just as you are. So no adopting, no selling, and no inheriting. You haven't earned it yet. When you can listen to what the Earth says, without becoming defensive, then, you have a chance. Humans have created a TOXIC WORLD. How can you live in that, without dying early, You have managed to create a form of self-restriction. Most things you do are based on denials. Even your diets. Denying yourself makes you want it more. Balance is the key to health issues. You should know your body better than most. Learn how to hear it, not fear it.

R: You know what? I haven't thought of it that way. I didn't see the wider view. So then, this energy is like a detox station. You go in toxic, and come out detoxed. Is that what happens at the end of this book? Is this the Earthquake Shake you mentioned before? Is it the reaction to the detox? I can visualize it better this way. When I look at it with this perception, An energy re-creation is possible.

UC: Wow! You have come out of your box, haven't you reader? You are a great example for those reading after you. Your example was correct from a physical perspective. It explains the process of the Evolution Revolution Energy. When you have a realization, what do you do with it?

R: I have never really been one, for being in a box. I am claustrophobic. But thanks for the acknowledgment. It means I am on the right track.

As far as my realizations, I use to file them away, and use them when I need them. But now, I have come to learn that realizations, develop Consciousness Energy. So I don't need to file them away. I just need to use any realization I get, as a learning tool. Realizations are a form of energy, so I would add them to my Consciousness, in order to develop and to increase my Consciousness abilities. I am starting to get a glimpse of the effects this energy will have on humanity.

I am feeling it happening to me. I am becoming aware, of how I can use the energy of realization, to change my life. To awaken me. To inspire me. To move me. But, I suppose it would depend on the realization. I would use it wherever it fits. Realizations are meant to create a long-lasting awareness, of the knowledge you just learned, along with the ability to hold on to it. Retention, is not our best quality at this time.

UC: The missing ingredient from humanity's energy, is available and attainable, you just cannot recognize it. Once you recognize Consciousness Energy, you have taken steps, to proceed into your Physical Evolution. Meaning, you have awakened. It's amazing how those that fear the unknown, have the unknown fearing them. At this time, humankind is reflecting an unsafe position. There is a sign far out in space that reads, *"TOXIC PLANET, enter at your own risk"*. It's been there for quite a while.

R: Are you serious? Is it really there? It's bad enough we know it, why are we advertising?

UC: Humans didn't put the sign there, they couldn't travel that far.

R: Then who did? If not you, Who could it be?

UC: It was a fly-by, from the U.C.P.

R: What's a U.C.P.? I thought it was U.F.O? An Unidentified Flying Object?

UC: No, it's the Universal Coalition of Planets. Representing life forms, on planets that are alive. These, are the ENERGY BEINGS. Humankind's actions do not go unnoticed.

R: The question is, if the humans are such a liability, to the Universal Consciousness Energy? Why is humanity still on this planet?

UC: You are a Father. You should know why? You have children, if one of them turns to crime, would you erase him/her from your life? You would go to the furthest part of your world to help, wouldn't you? Yes, you would. Although, some of you would not, there are many more who would, like you reader. Humans were meant to develop, grow, and flourish. To raise their awareness. That's why, now is the time to plant your ideas and allow them to grow. This knowledge is the soil you need.

There is an energy, that is shaking your shack, to get your physical energy's in motion. This Consciousness Energy has come with an intention. To merge its energy, with physical reality. It's called, the Universal Consciousness. Humankind cannot exist without it. It's your life force. It's the energy behind those miracles you still live by. It's the energy of Healing. The energy of Creating. It's not a mystery like some want you to believe.

Take the time to ask questions, before you make anything a belief. There are many that want you to believe, what they believe. It makes them feel more secure in the fact, that they were not sure either. Indecisiveness, attracts people who are Indecisive. They make easy prey for the Virus Energy. When you're not aware, you don't prepare. Just because the ad says it was the best, you don't have to go out and buy it. Of course it's the best, they made it.

R: Your comments have such valuable meanings. I can't stop listening. I mean reading. I don't know what I mean. Even now, am I reading anymore, or just listening? It must be both, I am having a conversation, while I am reading and listening. How is this possible? Each paragraph moves me. It's the way it affects me. It's the kind of book that you can travel with. I don't mean on a train or a bus. I mean astral travel. When I read, I lose track of time. One hour feels like one minute. It feels like I disconnect from physical energy, and flow with the Consciousness one. Were we created in your image, as Mini Universal Consciousness Energies?

UC: When you are using consciousness energy, it's all possible. Absolutely. This is the goal. To awaken humanity to this reality. It's good that you noticed? Consciousness development comes in steps, like these paragraphs. Each one holds a meaning, it's that meaning that creates the link. This is a good time for anything questionable. Whatever it is, it's answerable. Can humanity say the same? Humans have created an endless life storm, where people cause each other harm. Where is your good luck charm? Have your wishes come true?

Here is an example. You kill a human for killing a human, then say, *"you're doing it for human improvement."* You go home, and the next day, you do it again. Another human said, it was the law, so it's fine. That meant, you don't feel bad, It's the law. Does this make you a killer, or a life saver?

UC: When all else fails, you kill a life to save a life. Do you believe, that this belief actually works? You should see it from the other side. It's not, *"out of sight out of mind."* They will be back. Until the alive, teaches the dead consciousness.

Your brain thinks to go forward, but your body goes backwards. Obviously, they are disconnected. Many of you feel that the death penalty is OK. You believe in the law. Who convinced you of that?

THE LAW? You actually think that killing criminals will decrease your crime? It's the way humans live, that will keep crime alive. No matter how many you kill.

You create them, then dispose of them when you are done. Humanity's Laws and Punishment need Replenishment. That's a big Accomplishment, for a species without Development. Are the people aware, that the energy of the Virus, has been living on atomic power? It's growing on it. Energy connects with energy. Especially, if they have the same intentions. It wants to grow, and it wants what you know. It actually inspired the nuclear weapons construction. It helps it function.

This is why, the Virus Energy has continued to grow stronger. It's been absorbing, and growing on your nuclear power. You're supplying it with its source, Broken and unconscious Atomic Energy. You think you just blow it up and it's gone, well, you are wrong. Energy doesn't die or go away. It just changes frequencies. The unbalanced physical energy, has become a danger to humanity, and to the core creation of the Universal Consciousness Vibration. As an energy form, you are like cells in an infected body. What's your responsibility? How to fight off this infection?

As a body, your organs are starting to fail. Surgery can't help. It's terminal. How much time do humans have? That depends on whether they give up or not. Humans are turning on each other, the way the cells turn against the body. Soon your body will die. Your infected brain is attacking it. Better find a cure, it may give your body resurrection.

When you feel these words, they will move you, changing your perception. Helps you make a connection with your true meaning, the one you forgot. Your state of Unconsciousness, is causing your state of Conclusion, but, it doesn't have to continue to do so. You can use your Consciousness Energy to make sure of that.

Humans, must use their awareness, to discover and examine what is already there, on Earth, and in their lives. When you find a belief that no longer fits in your life, it's never gone, just forgotten. You have to consciously acknowledge it and let it go. Why do you need something that no longer fits you? As you read these writings, you may begin to feel that the way humans live, may no longer fit you. The more truthful you are, the less you need disguises. Go into your brain and replace the fuse. Before your brain, puts you on the news.

Is humanity willing to discover, and have no fear of what they recover? Have you checked your Emotions Regulatory System? Does it still work? What is regulating your emotions when you're not? You better check. Humanity's ability to comprehend, analyze, communicate, and solve problems is slowly decreasing. You know what this means. When you use communication, you won't understand how to solve your problems? The problem? Everyone accuses the other of being the problem. That's why there is no communication.

UC: Consciousness Energy Intuition can help you with these. You can learn to analyze, by using your Consciousness state of awareness. The energy of non-movement, teaches people to accept what it is. If it's non-moving energy, there is nothing to accept really, it's not moving. What does that tell you?

Now, if you're asking why people accept it, this is a different question. Humans accept anything they don't have to think about. They accept it for many reasons, Unfocused, Unaware, In-Denial, Closed-mind, Fearful, and Defensive. They all have the same meaning, Being Unconscious.

Some humans believe they are free. They are as free as the animals in your zoo. In humanity, someone owns someone each day. The illusion, that you call life, has put you into submission. Humanity, created excuses for their actions, and now live with the consequences. There is no forgiveness for destructive behaviors. Imprisoning animals just to look at them. How selfish are you? They are Consciousness Creations also. They are not there for your amusement.

This energy is the reason you think. It exists as a cycle. You don't just start, and not complete the cycle. Your actions don't stop with your actions, they become energy vibrations. They will vibrate and reverberate, until they develop your evolution. So, how long will humanity continue to live on the assumption that they are safe living on planet Earth? *"We all have to die sometime,"* is a defeatists point of view. Should we take a vote on how many of you, the people, feel safe? Be honest with yourself. How about you, reader? A question for thought or discussion. It's more about humanity's inability to develop enough to understand, the concept of Consciousness growth. What's your opinion, where do you stand on these comments?

R: For the first time, I feel like I am on solid ground. That's the reason I love this information. I don't have to guess at it. Or get confused by its goal. Each page shows a clearer path towards energy development. I think I can be blunt with my feeling. When I approach someone, I listen for my Tone. I hear my thoughts, and watch my body Movements. As a consciousness being, I would approach everyone with this in mind.

I believe, this is a form of self-awareness. I learn by using common sense. I don't believe that the creator is that complicated. We have complicated it, by not knowing it. To me, the more clear things are, the less fear I have. Clarity gives me security. I am the type that wants to know. When we feel hopeless, meaningless, disposable, and worthless, our silence complicates our feelings. Our silence keeps us feeling this way.

We need to BREAK THE SILENCE. I realize now, that by reading this awareness, how often I have been blind. I have been living in mental seclusion of my own making. But now, I feel like I am awakening to a new reality of perception. This has cleared the way for me, to explore all of this. It's why I walked through the door from the beginning. I was hoping to find knowledge with substance, I was just about ready to give up, when I found this.

Talk about timing. To be honest, I went in skeptical. As with any book, you don't know it until you read it. I am realizing now, that we, as physical human beings, are infected by a rogue Virus Energy. Something has to explain all the violence. I don't buy into the Devil concept. My feeling is, if it hadn't been presented in this manner of energy awareness, it would be difficult to swallow, and I wouldn't get it. I thought that I was awake, until I woke up.

UC: The Universal Consciousness has endless dimensions. Each chapter of this book, happens to be a dimension of Consciousness Energy. Perceptions of Creation, by its Creator. Consciousness development happens through, the awareness you absorb from life, but it's not happening fast enough. There have been

A Declaration

other attempts at describing this development, from one life to another. Philosophies about creation, and the creator, are everywhere on Earth. But so far, that's all they are.

Dimensions, are based on your state of Consciousness. Based on your awareness, your knowledge, and your reality. These dimensions are present all around you. Consciousness development, increases your energies ability, to be able to look into these dimensions. Physical mass is not the only dimension in creation. Each Dimension is a Consciousness Reality with different personalities.

R: This is very revealing. But, I need to keep going. I am anxious to get to the Evolution Revolution. I peeked. Just a small peek. I got a little anxious.

UC: Humans started to stumble, after they realized that they had put all their trouble, in the shovel of that devil. They thought, years later they would become solvable and they would disappear. It doesn't matter how long they remain a secret. They will always be there, waiting for you. You see, your secrets will not abandon you. Even if you wanted them too.

Troubles are reliable like that. They are energy also. Your troubles have never recovered, they are still where you left them. Go get them. Many secrets involve Guilt, Envy, Retribution, and Solicited Action. Secrets that you didn't want anyone to know. Secrets which build walls. People are sensitive. Walls build prisons. Keeping your pain behind walls, will keep you from climbing them.

You should know that Fear, lives in your Unconscious state, along with your secrets. It's one of your secrets prison guards. The other two are Greed, and Control. They, follow fears lead. Everyone is afraid of fear. Control wants to know your secrets. Greed, wants to make money from them, and Fear, is the weapon that will make it happen. Humanity, do you think you can come out of your self-made bubble, and face your trouble? If you can't do it, who can? Illusion Man?

This Declaration is the first chapter of your energy re-creation. It's the awakening, before the awakening. The rest of these pages will talk about humankind, their continued survival, and their current survival. Humanity's story is a long one. But here, it has been brought to you in a short version. So you can make your own decision upon completion. As we move on, we will be addressing this question?

Can humans be trusted to save themselves, before they have to be removed? Can you! Not if you expect others to save you. How many times would you ask someone to save you, if they kept saying, *"save yourself?"* This question echoes across the Universe. What about it humanity? How is this acceptable to you? Apparently, the toxic planet sign wasn't enough. If you don't try, you will not learn. If you don't participate, you have no one to blame.

Humans walk around free as a bird, living on other peoples word. Most of your words are absurd. Not to be insulting, but many of them are NON-REFLECTIVE. They are not mirrors. They have no consciousness meaning. Your words should reflect who, and what you are. How can you learn from words that can't reflect you. Self-realization, is the start of Consciousness Energy exploration. It's where negative energy is converted, the beginning of self-development.

As a conscious being, you are a magnet. Conscious knowledge will be attracted to you. Whatever it is, will stick. Whether you want it to or not. But be aware, you attract more than just metal. Humanity has the ability to use common sense. First, you have to realize that you have it. Many of you don't use it. You're not even aware of your Conscience. It's there, but you ignore it. Your Conscience is connected to the

Universal Consciousness. You feel it through Intuition. Oh, that's right, you don't use it. It's an energy ability. Learn about it.

R: Hi, it's me the reader. Can I interject something? It's a question actually. Does the conversion of the Virus Energy Cell in the self, automatically change the Virus, into the Universal Consciousness Energy?

UC: Instantly! Each realization, that develops your consciousness, is a conversion. The Virus Energy is unconscious energy. Each time you become conscious of new knowledge, the Virus Energy becomes conscious. Until the final balance.

R: Here is my newest realization, it's about our laws. I am realizing, they are based on what fear has created. There is little acknowledgment for doing good deeds. Many go unnoticed. Vulgarity and violence seems to be the view we prefer. Many of us accept it, due to the energy of fear. Fear is winning. We must start turning our direction towards the cycle of Evolution. Our fear creates defensiveness and hostility. Hostility creates rage, which shuts down communication. This creates a separation. Now, there is a need for protection from the instigation. Fear has just created war. See the pattern. Because I sure do. I am seeing a lot more then I use to. It's slow reading as I have to stop, and reflect on what I just read.

UC: Excellent awareness. You're making good progress. Fear is winning, is an understatement. This book's knowledge is its replacement. So now you're seeing patterns, but you don't know how to react to them. You don't have the Consciousness yet. This is what humanity lives in everyday. In a complete cycle of replay. This is your chance to start a new way. It's always been you, humanity. You are the Judge, and Jury. There is no other to blame, but yourselves. Turn your view inward. Once inside, you don't have to say a word. Just feel your way around. You may run into things you didn't know. Get to know them. They are parts of you. Make peace with them.

Stop and ask yourself. *"How many past actions am I in denial of?" "How many emotions am I holding prisoner?"* WHY? Do they scare you? Are you ashamed of them? Those who have done the same thing are the first to judge. Are you aware reader, that Guilt and Shaming are destructive forms of energy? They are both related to the Virus Energy Cell.

So if you're hiding those emotions because of shame, you don't have to. Shame inspire isolation, like fear does. Face your accusation. Don't let guilt stop you. SHAME has a way of making you feel GUILTY. You are not alone. There's no reason to hide it. Hiding it makes it grow. It will take over your life.

Let's be clear. Humans have certain needs. To meet those needs, many humans have committed actions, where the consequences caused guilt or shame. With the awareness of Consciousness, humanity is responsible for self; starting with, self-awareness, self-control, self-confidence, self- realization and self-development. Humans also possess the ability for self-consequence, and self- reward. Pay attention to what's happening to you.

Starting today, pay attention to what you say, and do. In other words, be Conscious more than Unconscious. Just for one day, tell the truth. Feel what it's like, and see how others react. Can you do it? You don't always tell the truth, it should be easy. You hide behind little white lies. What color are all the other lies? You cannot deny this humanity. When you lie, to protect hurting the feelings of others, you're the one that suffers. You're left with a lie on your conscience, and they walk away conscience free. It's in the delivery. How you say it. You can do it without causing pain.

UC: You can always start with this, *"This may hurt your feelings." "Or, I am sorry about that, but."*

We are aware you prefer to just say it, but, how you say it is what counts. Just make sure what you say is always true. This shows that you are a Consciousness Being. With your own meaning. This also shows that you are not a follower, but the makings of a good leader. Humans must learn to be a Consciousness Energy Operator.

R: Doesn't it also depend on our belief systems? People tell lies for a thousand reasons. Safety, Protection, Privacy, Fear of commitment. Fear of judgment, Fear of consequences. Embarrassment. Breaking trust. Fear of losing a relationship. Greed. To avoid a confrontation. I can go on.

UC: Yes, it's true. Each person has their own perception. But, they are only excuses. If they are not the truth. They are empty words. So we have to ask, what are some of humanity's perceptions based on? Empty Promises. Limitations. Manipulations. Destructive Negotiations. Greedy Politicians. The Homeless Population. Violence, across the World Nations. These are the perceptions of most of you.

It's true, Empty Promises, are actually distractions. A stalling technique that humans use when they can't be honest. Limitations? They are stop signs for curiosity. It's a closed road for many. Humanity has created walls of limitations, that they can't climb out of. Destructive Negotiations? Are plans for destructive actions you don't hear about, until they blow up.

Greedy Politicians? They take advantage of the present situation, and make it their personal mission to use it for their election. They tell a lie, while looking in your eye. They have their own truth. It's based on how, they are being perceived and treated, by those they represent. So, seeking acknowledgment, is their Truth. It's the truth, but not the whole truth. There are many other factors.

Violence across the World? It's become acceptable by humanity, but still not the truth. Acceptable, doesn't mean it's true. From this view, violent behaviors are unacceptable to your nature as human beings. It wasn't in your DNA to kill. Unfortunately, through history, humans have changed this, by passing it through heredity. Then add on the pressures of the environment, as it plays a big role in violent behaviors, based on your perception. What's your intention for an intervention?

R: OK, I am stunned. Are you saying, we are creating and recreating, our own violent behaviors? Is this really the truth? This is a big realization for me. I had no idea. There is one realization after another in here, isn't there? There is a lot of information to process in this book. You can't just read it, and bypass the meanings. That's why you have to stop and ponder. But more than that, to understand our physical disorder. We can call it what we want, but we can no longer ignore the fact that when there is something wrong, for many, they are the first to react and last to act.

UC: Many people's emotions are dull and flat. This is how humans can empower their feelings, by giving them Conscious Energy meanings. This makes their actions conscious ones. It's obvious that humans are in pain. You deny the screams of your emotional energy, it wants to be pain free. When you don't address your emotional pain, it makes the pain last longer. But then, many of you have become pain tolerant. You won't feel a thing.

R: The truth hurts sometimes. I suppose, it depends on the depth of your feelings. I never realized that feelings had depth before. I thought they were just reactions. Now, I am learning that they are dimensions of feelings. I really believe that. Each feeling reflects one's own reality, and our reality, comes from our belief system, passed down through generations. Our belief system, is inherited from our historical family. Many of them have little meaning in today's society. I worry about what I am passing on to my children. Whenever I share information, I try to be aware of my words.

R: I try to be aware that what I believe today, may not apply tomorrow. The less confusion the better. Those ahead of me, can create their own belief systems. I will give my children, the guidance along the way. I watch my kids when they are watching TV, and they seem hypnotized by the screen. They can't see or hear anything but the TV. This is distressing to me. Whose beliefs are they learning? I have to be hyper-aware, of what they are watching and listening to. They want to do what other parents let their kids do. But I am not like other parents. I have new ideas, and very few people to discuss them with. It's not easy to make friends with…"Hey, how's the weather, how was the game, did you watch it, how are the wife and kids?" It's too superficial. I can't do it.

UC: Everything you experience can cause a realization, which you can benefit from. The more you have, the more Consciousness expands. Causing more of your brain to grow. The brain doesn't feed Consciousness. It feeds the brain. It's how your brain will grow, so as, to catch up with its Evolution.

R: Personally, I believe there is something wrong with our brain. I mean look at the choices we make. We hear about all the people being killed by drunk drivers, and they still let us drive. Why do you let us drive, at the cost of other peoples lives? Yes, it's our responsibility as young adults to know better. But, when you see that we don't know better, take the car away.

UC: As it stands today. Each time you go to make a decision, the Virus Energy interferes, by confusing your thoughts, and putting you in a state of indecisiveness. Unable to decide. It will decide for you. Its choice is not always a good one. It becomes the battle of wills. One on each shoulder. You known the story. This is how you LOST your balance humanity. You chose the wrong shoulder. Now you have the opportunity to balance the scale.

R: Did the Virus Cell, take away our self control? Or did we give it away?

UC: Humanity gave it away, to Manipulation. It used Seduction, that's what took away your self control, and changed its normal function. Has anything changed?

R: You are right. We still don't mean what we say, and we certainly don't say what we mean. What's in control of those thoughts? I will discover the answer to this. I am sure it's in these chapters.

UC: A QUESTION asks, *"I want to learn what I don't know."* The ANSWER responds, *"I am on my way."* Energy, needs to be a Naturally Balanced Occurrence. Someone knows something, somewhere. You, humanity, need to be looking for that something, everywhere. Humanity has learned how to identify everything by a label, a title. You had to create them to give yourself a meaning. Living without an energy meaning, has caused many people, to lose their feeling. How about you reader, have you felt so much emotional pain that you stopped feeling?

R: After feeling this energy, I am not sure if I ever really felt. This is a completely different feeling. So I have to answer yes. I have had this type of pain. Not until now, did I realize, I wasn't allowing myself to really feel. Here, in this book, I am feeling. Now, I have to go back to the beginning of my life and feel everything with this feeling.

UC: This knowledge, will teach you how to get to know the unknown. Presently, it's the Virus Energy. It's been on its own, as an Unconscious Energy Vibration. It's time that humans get to know this one. It takes a very viable, and intelligent human being, and turns them into a reactive, non creative, destructive human being, with a life that has no meaning. Sound familiar? It has the ability to convince anyone into believing, that they are achieving, when they're not even moving. It can make you think you are leading, when you are actually following. Century after century, humans have taken liberty, helping themselves by majority, becoming an authority, and living on the self gratification, and the prosperity of others.

R: I think I am getting the picture about this Virus Energy. Not the whole picture, but some understanding of how it works. Will it be revealed to the world? Is it going to eat us all? How are we going to face this Virus Energy, when we are just now, learning about it? Our lives, consist of working all day, to feel alright, Until, we wake up to feel the fright of our daily plight; from the anxiety of the sight of being back in the fight, that we were in last night. We spend our life spinning in circles, looking for what? We don't know, that's why we keep looking. I am going to keep looking in this book.

If our emotions are also affected, how can I trust them? Should we stop responding to our emotions? I better start checking mine. I know they are still inside of me. I feel them. Where would they go anyway? But, hearing about this Virus Cell, makes me wonder if they are mine or not. I gotta learn how to convert them. Isn't that what it's called, Energy Conversion? If I can do that now, I would be ahead of the game. Only this is not a game, is it? How can I trust the emotional reactions of others, while being suspicious of my own?

UC: Lets start with, NO, you should never stop responding to your emotions. How will you know which ones need to be converted. They won't be ignored. Not responding is avoiding. This is how Ignored Emotions become; Out of Control Reactions. Using your consciousness to respond, can convert them. This would remove all suspicion. To trust them you must get to know them. You see, developing your energy, doesn't only benefit you, it benefits others also. It's an energy connection.

What goes around comes around. Consciousness energy is connected energy. Connection is a remedy to loneliness. Many people treat the idea of unity like the plague. You are Human Beings, yet you fear the human part of you. You are more afraid of your own kind, than the unknown kind. This means, that you fear what you know. Is this why many of you, still act like savages, preying on each other? Is it because, that same energy of fear still exists?

You're living your lives, afraid of living. As long as you are thinking this way, you will always be afraid of life. The effects from your emotions, will keep knocking until you answer. Your brain is attached to your emotions. It hears and feels everything. At one time or another, you must have felt the emotions of anger, rage, and suspicion. Guilt and fear. Exclusion from an organization, and, ostracized from your family relation. What do all these have in common? These are the effects of the Virus Energy Cell. When you let it use you for its purpose. It was your choice to do so. You have always known about consequences.

R: We are always looking for answers, without asking the questions. What dictates our behaviors?

UC: BEING UNCONSCIOUS, along with a variety of things. Environment, belief systems, interactions with others, successes and failures. Actions, reactions, judging and being judged, and as we said, heredity. Life in general shapes your behavior. The science part of it is for you to investigate. It will benefit you more, to find out on your own.

R: Your answers were quite clear, and persuasive. It would be nice to be able to be truthful with each other, and not get our feelings hurt. Everyone is so out of touch. You can't say a word, without someone yelling ouch. I question if people really have the ability to listen, and absorb. It seems today, we listen, and forget. I am including myself in with the people. Believe me, I often wonder how much I am retaining. I need to find out.

UC: Throughout the Universe of Creation, the memory of humankind, has not been forgotten. It's not because, humans are admired for their dedication to creation. The human species has become a recluse, who has lost its cues, and can't pay its dues. Humanity is so busy talking about it, they have no time to do anything to change it. No wonder nothing gets accomplished. You're too busy having meetings.

You want to help yourselves, start by walking in each others' shoes for one day. Are humans thinking, an evacuation to another solar system would be a solution? You would be better off having a world revolution. Humans are too violent to step away from the Earth. There is nowhere out there where humans can live, except the Earth. You are not welcome anywhere else. Not yet anyway. Do you blame them. It's not too late to change their mind. But you have to change yours first. Until then, here is a realization.

You hold yourselves in high admiration. But, Earth is still your reservation, and will continue to be, until you are free from the Virus Energy. There is no levitation to take you out of the Earths rotation. It will be easier to change your direction. Going to a new destination, is something you will not realize. WHY? YOU STILL TELL LIES.

Until humanity accepts the reality of their true identification, as a Consciousness Energy Vibration, they will stay on the planet's foundation, it's really for the best? Turn on the lights, and look for yourself. You are not as blind has you act. When you look hard enough, you may surprise yourself. Look with curiosity, not deniability. Many humans are not a friendly species. Not now anyway. Agree or deny, It's ultimately your choice. Humanity has the ability to read the signs and change.

The cycle of…No beginning or end, is from where this knowledge has been sent. The central core of the Universal Consciousness. Now, it asks humanity a question. Do you expect destruction, or will you destruct the expectation? You are aware, this is your choice, are you not? Choice changes the direction of energy. If you don't make one, nothing changes. Is it a hard choice for humans to make? Unconsciously, you make choices all day. Try becoming aware of them. It may become easier for you to use them. The truth always rises to the top. It's a natural growth. What are your thoughts on this reader?

R: Only the word INTENTION can answer that. This is what I am understanding so far. It's the intention of our action, which rewards and consequences us as human beings. Intention, is a natural process of a frequency vibration.

UC: It's the humanity's perception of right and wrong, which makes them strong. You give them the power to use you. They can easily destroy your self esteem. Right and wrong only helps the ego. Humanity's truth is to be right. When right is right, it becomes the truth. When a wrong is found to be wrong, it's a lie. This is why, humanity has to stop using RIGHT and WRONG. You are confusing it with the TRUTH and a LIE.

R: It seems that we all have something to hide. This is not a secret. People like to pretend it is, but it's not. We are constantly changing others, to take the focus away from ourselves. I wonder if people could admit that? Humans do not allow other humans to really know them. Even family members. It's as though

32   *A Declaration*

the relationship with your siblings stops at sixteen. We want what we have, to become something else, while we, refuse to become something else ourselves. This is absolutely useless in relationships. It's one of the reasons for breakups.

Unless we find our own identities, we will continue to change others instead. Losing trust in people, has caused us to find trust in artificial things. What we saw, became our truth, not what we thought. We couldn't see our thoughts. We became dependent on the ability to escape from reality into fantasy. Alcohol, drugs, sex, food, and violence. All of them created feelings that made us move physically. But not in a positive way.

UC: What you are describing, are forms of escape from life. Reality as it is, seems to be too much to handle for many humans. Escape from your way of life today, is becoming an epidemic. Humanity is always looking for a way out. Sometimes, traveling on unpaved roads is like traveling on quicksand. You never know, when you're about to be swallowed. The Evolution Revolution book, is a paved road to a New direction, for the Continued Existence of humankind.

R: When our feelings become triggered, who is reacting, the Virus Energy, or me? Is it possible to feel the trigger, and recognize it before I react?

UC: Before consciousness, there was no difference. With it, it's a huge difference. Consciousness will allow you to feel the trigger, recognize it and deal with it before you react. The Virus Energy only uses you, because you're unconscious. Let's be clear, as long as it's there, it will try to sabotage what you are developing. Until you fully convert it, you are still infected. You are on your way however. You keep coming up with question of true Consciousness. You're only on the first chapter.

Triggered Feelings? Feelings are triggered the same way the memory is, by the same senses. Touch is one, it lasts longer. Touch, can do what no words can do. Words are a dime a dozen. But touch, needs no words. How do you feel the trigger before you react? By being conscious of all your senses. You can feel the trigger before it connects to the feeling. Your senses will tell you ahead of time. They work for the Energy of Intuition. When you're paying attention. Your senses will vibrate. Your body is composed of energy. It was created to use energy with energy.

Awareness is a Consciousness ability, it can protect you from negativity. Awareness sends out feelers as you go about your day. Sensing and removing danger from your way. Becoming aware, is the process of heightening your main brain senses. This is when you will feel the virus. It will try to block you from your brain. Telling you to forget about it, *"don't waste your time, you have better things to do."* It will tell you anything to sway you from connecting with your brain. Humanity, must resist these thoughts, by staying focused on developing consciously.

By recognizing the Virus, you will take away its power to affect you. With awareness, you may not notice everything, but you will be more aware of what everything is, when you are around it. Practice it on yourselves, self awareness is your best teacher. Be aware of yourself, and see what you discover. Look at all the inconsistency in your choices? Can you deny that for some, their body does the opposite of what their brain tells them? The brain and body are disconnected. All of humanity has been affected. You just haven't noticed. Were you Unaware, and Unconscious.

Humanity has major issues, let's face it. These issues are not going away on their own. They are from unconscious actions. Consciousness would never allow this to happen. Humankind's history, contains the true library, to the knowledge of history's secrets. It contains the knowledge of humanity's purpose, reason for existence, and clarity of humanity's autonomy. It has been hidden away from your mentality, to control your ability to function physically.

UC: This Energy needs constant conscious rejuvenation, in order to continue creating Consciousness. Humans can no longer afford secrets, which cause you harm emotionally and physically. Does humanity, have a way to recover? Do you have the ability to discover your correlation with your own Creator? How long can humans live while unconscious? This is the main question. Do you have a suggestion, human? How can you do something about your situation, if you don't learn how?

This book is an awareness, of where humanity's direction is going. It's also a book about where humanity's direction will go. It has to be your move humanity. Show interest in your own development. There is knowledge here, that will open doors you haven't walked through before. If you're willing to face the unknown. Get to know this one. As you read on, you will discover an explanation, for the ENERGY RE-CREATION, and how it will happen. A future look into the humans actions towards an actual ENERGY EVOLUTION REVOLUTION.

In here, there is a look into the upcoming awakening. What's going to happen? Why, and when? You already know where. Who were the main players? Who started what? What actions occurred to change humanities direction. The answers are very revealing, intriguing, and Consciously rewarding. You're going to become part of this ENERGY MOVEMENT, after reading this. How can you not? You will have become consciously aware.

Ask yourself, what have I done for Planet Earth lately? Without asking, you will not know what others know. Humans act like they are the most important creation on Earth. Guess what? You're not. What's more important than you? The Earth for one. Oxygen for another. Humanity must reach out. You must push through your fears. It's going to take more than one human to create an energy movement for your Evolution.

Will humanity wait 'till their final evacuation, before starting their transformation? Will it be too late? There has to be an outside intervention, to ensure the prevention of this Virus Cells deception. Humans are not conscious enough to know what to do. You are easily deceived. The Virus Energy, can no longer be allowed to thrive in your physical creation. Wake up, and feel its intention. Identify negative and harmful thoughts, and confront them. They need direction, direct them. Don't fear your own thoughts, convert them. This is how you balance your energy. Awareness of them is the key. Someone has to take the lead towards, the energy evolution revolution.

Humans have a choice to make. Take apart your nuclear weapons programs. Demilitarize each country. Form a A UNITED WORLD ORGANIZATION. Your United Nations isn't working. You the people, can make it work. Nations are in it for themselves. Wars must end, before wars ends humanity. Don't take this as a threat. It doesn't need to be this way. This comment isn't meant to put people in fear. It's meant to awaken humanity, to what could be. As you read on, you are going to find your voice. You're going to realize, you can communicate with your brain. Only now, you may not like what it says. It's not very impressed. It says, you care more about, how you are dressed. If you disagree, you talk to it. Use Consciousness Energy to communicate with it, it can hear you better.

R: Is it possible to attain a state of Consciousness, without going through a conversion?

UC: Is it possible for your physical body to be awake while it's sleeping? Energy Conversion is the basis for Consciousness. When a slower energy converts itself through development, it creates a faster frequency of Consciousness Energy. It's going to be a World Energy Conversion. It's humanity's destiny. It's the best way to re-balance the humans energy vibrations. So, humanity…Your creation is not the only, It's just lonely. Do you think it's impossible, to change your unconscious patterns? Becoming conscious of them, is the way to change them.

Many of your habits and patterns happen unconsciously. Being conscious, gives you the opportunity to choose what you want to keep, and what you don't. The only thing impossible, is the word Impossible. It means STOP. This door is shut. You can't enter. It leaves you with nothing else to do. It's a give up word. Impossible is just another way of saying, *" I can't do it."* But mostly, it's a fear created word. It's an over used word.

The word Possible, means GO. It's up to your educated perception, to know which direction. There is no stop sign. You are fearless. You never give up. Well, humanity, is it POSSIBLE or IMPOSSIBLE? It's only a choice, but then, you aren't used to making them, are you?

Asking questions, helps to give you the whole picture of the Universal Consciousness Energy Vibration. When you get the WHOLE picture, your picture will not have a HOLE. Bottom line, your brain needs knowledge, it needs energy nutrition. Your brain needs Consciousness to survive and to grow. Your growth is minimal. The main goal, is about curing humanity's brain infection. Your brain is running on used parts, which will quit soon. What are you going to do, go live on the moon? At this point, your brain is feeling like an outcast. It's been trying to get you to relax. It's trying to tell you, without Consciousness Energy, it won't last.

Get in touch with your spirit. Your body needs it, like your brain needs the head. You barely know much about yourself, and you're trying to discover space. There is space between your head, and your brain. It's because your brain is shrinking. Discover that first. Recovery happens through Discovery. Re-creation happens by the Universal Consciousness Energy. Humanity's cycle of Physical Evolution is in jeopardy. It must begin to REVOLVE, so that humanity can EVOLVE.

B: EXCUSE ME, EXCUSE ME! Sorry, were you done? I just couldn't wait any longer. I heard you talking about me. So I am here representing the brains of humans, all over the world. This is a brain to body conversation. I have something to say to my body. Please listen to me.

Hello, I am your brain. I am here in your head. Did you forget? What happened? We used to be friends. I knock, I shout, I even yell, all I hear is go to hell. If I am not already there, then what's this place? I don't recognize the face. It's been awhile since we spoke. Well, I spoke, I don't know what you were doing. It sure wasn't listening. This is my point. I am in hell. You put me there. It's dark, and I can't see. Why have you done this to me?

Listen, you can't let this happen, seriously. There is something in here with me. It's too dark to see. But it's not a nice energy, and it's not happy. If I don't get some light in here soon, I am going to need a baby spoon. Were you not born with a light switch? Without light, it's too dark to see. So whatever it is, it's using me. I know it's not you, but I wonder what, and who? What do I do? It's been sometime since I thought for myself. But I still know my self worth. I am aware of why you need me. You can't function without me.

I am your brain, you can't move without me. As long as you keep me in the dark, so shall you be. You know, if I don't start to move, you will lose the ability to move your body. Each time I call out to you, I hear my echo, echo, echo. That means you're out to lunch without me. Now I am lonely. Start talking. Why did you abandon me? I simply cannot stay quiet any longer. We are becoming strangers, you and I. I cannot do this alone. I need you. Go ahead, try to live without me. Wait…You have been living without me. How have you managed? I can see it wasn't easy. I can't see through your eyes, are you closing them on purpose?

B: Please, go back to college. Read this book. Read any book. Anything to help me survive. I need new ideas. Find some. Meet a new human. Do something, I am shrinking from lack of knowledge. Oh Yeah, you already know that. Many of you deal with shrinking brains on a daily basis. I don't want to be a shrinking brain. GIVE ME SUSTENANCE. It's for my existence. If not, face resistance. Try walking a straight line. See what happens. Watch a nature show. Anything, to give me energy. Even those shows about your so called reality. Whatever teaches you something.

I, along with all brains, are tired of your lack of movement. We need improvement. I need improvement. We can't go on strike to prove our point, because we've been in a holding pattern for years. When you left me, you left me with all your baggage. I want you back. How can you feel OK, being empty headed? Do you not become confused, lost? How do you get your needs met, without using words? They come from me. It must be difficult to think without me. Have you even noticed, I haven't been with you? Now would be a good time to take notice.

I am your brain. I am not a machine, don't expect to just ignore me, and expect me to not have a reaction. It took awhile for me to get here. But I am here now. Asking you to work with me. I am being nice. I am not afraid to have a reaction. I am not expecting a quick response. I am aware, you live the life of hard Knocks. Get me out of this box. Please.

Let's be honest with each other, you wouldn't recognize your own face without me. But, honestly, you need me. I need you. We were born together. I can see right through you. We are suppose to be one, not two. If we don't, we are both through. What do you want to do? Silly of me to ask. You can't make a decision without using me. May I speak frankly, I don't know what happened to me exactly, but, I think I was infected by this energy that is possessing me. I believe, this is how I lost my identity.

What I am hoping now, is that through this energy conversion, we can connect ourselves together as one again. At this time, it's keeping me from my natural function. It keeps pulling on me, can't you do something? It's keeping us from joining together. Don't you see it? Can't you feel it? Do you feel anymore? Look, and listen, and you will see the connection. No pressure. I am aware of your intelligence measure. Without the brain, the body is lost. All I want is acknowledgment, and energy resources. At this point, if you fall, I can't stop you. I am not aware of your body's sensations. I wouldn't know if you fell.

As far as I can see you have two choices, wake up, and get Consciousness to move in, or I am moving out. This abuse will no longer be tolerated. I have put up with your lack of thinking long enough. I refuse to get tough. I have self control. Your choices are yours. Don't blame me if you can't find any cures. I can't cure you, if you don't cure me first. This infection, is the reason I have a Mental Disorder. No thanks to you.

A Declaration

We need to act fast or we may never be together again. I need you to see, I am dying in here buddy. You're my body, I trusted you. In your hands, you have the knowledge to grow me, to the point of converting my infected energy. I am tired now, I need to plug into a Consciousness Energy machine. They are easier to find than body's.

UC: OK, thank you brain, that was a very moving speech. We hope it moved some of you, into checking in with your brain. It's in a lot of pain. How did you become aware enough, to confront your body? You sound clear, focused, and in control. You claimed to be infected, but, you sound Conscious, and well developed. How did you evolve?

B: I am half resolved. I have recently had a small self tune up. I was able to learn by listening to others talk. Since my body stopped talking to me. I had to find other ways to learn. Hey, it's learn or shrivel up. That's how I feel. I can't fool anyone, I am not intelligent enough.

UC: You seem to be a motivated brain. You are one of the few. Good work. Hopefully your body is taking lessons from you. It would be wise to. You should work on getting your body moving.

R: I have to interrupt you, so sorry. I have been listening to you, brain. Everything you said, triggered memories, which were lost in my brain. It seems I had buried them, instead of facing them. I realize this now. I have the chance to filter out Virus Energy, infecting my emotions. I am actually glad for these triggers. I remember the memories clearly. That's why I was listening. I did the same thing to my brain. I forgot mine for years. I would sit for hours, wondering what I was going to be when I grew up, because I couldn't decide. I took my brain and left.

I went into a state of real Unconsciousness. Meaning, I was hardly conscious. This became my business. I became relentless when it came to damaging my brain. I spent my time wandering and wondering. Those are the years I lost touch with it. I actually believed it abandoned me. It was a long time before I realized, I had abandoned it. Realizations are like a slap in the face. They wake you up. Each one is more intense than the other. So far, there has been many, many realizations.

It took a lot of development for my brain, and I, to reconnect again. Thanks to knowledge such as this Evolution Revolution. I was awakened to the ability of questioning. I keep asking, until I get an answer. A realization brings up many questions. Mostly about the realization. But, sometimes the realization affects other parts of your life. To find out what those effects are, you have to follow the effects. That's where the knowledge is. I have found each effect, to be a library of knowledge, to add to my Consciousness Energy development. Each one was a learning experience. Which gave my brain a fighting chance.

There is this one realization, which awakened me to ask questions. Questions I had to ask of myself, before I can ask them from another. These questions were very important for my self-discovery, and development. Why do I need a government to tell me, how to be civilized? Can I still be kind to others, even when I am taken for granted? Can I have free choice, and not be targeted? Can I love, without being loved? Can I have a mate, without having expectations?

UC: It sounds like you have had experiences with each one of those questions. They are personal. Why do you need to be governed to be civil? You do not need to be governed, when you are a Consciousness Being. Your actions reflect that. Being civil is being conscious. If you can't make the choice to be civil, then you need to be guided, not governed. Being governed, is civility at any cost. You are being forced to be civil by a law. The fact that humans need a law to be civil, should be a wake up call by itself.

Can you still be kind, when others take you for granted? In your society today, kindness needs awareness. It gets taken for granted. It's used in many opportunities and advantages. Kindness, is being exploited by the energy of greed. It takes advantage of kindness. It's an unnatural ability. As a Consciousness being, your kindness cannot be taken for granted. This should empower you to realize, kindness is rare amongst humans.

R: Can I have free choice, and not be targeted?

UC: Those who are aware of it, will not target you. Those who are not, will. People want what they don't have, but many are unwilling to create it. People want what they want, now! Today! Immediately! They can't wait. Remember, the Virus Energy will stand in the way of free choice, anyway it can. The energy of impatience, can be deadly when it wants something you have. Fear, is usually the first Virus Energy, to get in the way of free choice.

Can you still love, without being loved? Absolutely. This is the essence of love. Love is an energy also. When this energy is balanced and conscious, it's true love, pure love. It's love without expectations. Loving others without expecting to be loved, will automatically bring love to you. Whether you want it to or not. It's a natural energy cycle. Being aware of it, allows you to use it.

You are the energy of love. It's your nature. You will get back what you put out. There is no doubt. Although, what you get back, may not be the same as what you put out. So don't expect it to be. The energy of love will always be there. Unless you expect it to. Here is another question from you, can you love someone without having expectations? Can you? Here is a hint; when two people are on the same frequency, there are no expectations.

Expectations, are a great way to end a relationship. Goals are set to be achieved. Expectations are meant to control things, one way only. When that fails, so does the relationship. In humanity, expectations have become a normal way of life. An Unconscious pattern, which needs to be changed. It's the quickest way to disappointment.

R: I agree, they are the first step towards deterioration. People are too stressed out and on edge. We have become overwhelmed. You never know what to expect, so, it's better not to. Makes sense to me.

UC: Last of your questions. Can I question my beliefs without being ostracized? Well, wouldn't this depend on, what your beliefs are? How they affect you. And who you share the same beliefs with. Humanity is full of beliefs, which need to be questioned. One such belief, is the belief in fear. It has humans so fearful that they don't even look at one another. Suspicion rules. If you were raised to understand the human species, you wouldn't need to fear them. It's a human pattern, like your fear of the unknown. Only now you fear both, the known, and the unknown. When you don't know it, you see it as your worst fear. Try to recognize the correlation between, what you think, and what you see? Your thoughts identify what you see. Make sure your thoughts are thinking clearly.

R: The more I read, the more I seem to remember memories long forgotten. They just pop up. It actually encourages me to deal with them. I hadn't realized they caused me emotional pain, until I remembered them again. UNCONSCIOUS EMOTIONAL PAIN. This is a great realization.

UC: Unconscious emotional pain, is alive and well in your physical energy. You thought it to be gone, simply because you forgot about it? Humanity can no longer afford to live in the PAST. Only, humans can't do that until they create a PRESENT. This Declaration, has come for this purpose. To create the present on Earth's surface. We feel, humankind deserves this. You are proof of this reader. Look how fast you have absorbed this knowledge. It's as though, as you read it. Are you remembering it, as you read it? It is awakening your original form of energy.

Your reaction to the evolution revolution reveals that humans need this. You must go on, remember all your original memories. They will shift you into consciousness. Unfortunately, most humans do not live in the present. The present moment, It's the one thing which will move you. However, One must choose to. It's the Choice, which powers the movement. Energy Movement shifts Consciousness. Which changes your Perception.

R: Will my perception keep shifting, as I continue to read? I want my consciousness to be freed.

UC: When you shift to the past, and stay there long enough, your shift becomes your reality. This is why choosing must be a priority. It will take a powerful realization, to shift you back to the present moment. Shifting happens, with any distraction which catches your attention. Consciousness, allows you to control your shifts, by staying focused and clear. With each meaning you stop to absorb, you will experience shifts towards awareness. If you're not shifting, you're not absorbing.

R: Humans have ignored your existence since time began, what makes you think they will recognize you now?

UC: You did. Others have. And with your help, many others will. Understanding Consciousness Energy, is easier than understanding your politics. You don't need to be a scientist Or a historian. The simple concept of everything is energy, is all you need. It's because of this energy that you know anything at all. If it's not an energy which can develop yours, it's empty of meaning. It doesn't help you. What you are doing now reader, is using energy to develop your own. Which puts you in a place, of knowing your own consciousness.

R: Does the way we live, reflect our intelligence?

UC: If you can ask this question, you obviously have an answer. You must have been observing your fellow humans and their behaviors. Some behaviors do not reflect intelligence. Many intelligent people have become criminals. Some, even held the title of genius. So yes, the way you live defiantly reflects your intelligence. Not all people are unintelligent. You're as smart or not, as your actions. It's easy for others to judge. Unfortunately, a persons actions are justification for their judgment.

R: Can we truly understand the concept, of a Universal Consciousness Energy as the Creator? I am reading it, feeling it, absorbing it, and retaining it. It's a little early to feel the full effects, but it's a beginning. Now, do I understand it so far? To some degree I do, yet, I am not sure completely, I will not know until the final chapter. But for now, I think these words understand me, better than I do. I have a question for you. Are Human Beings, capable of becoming Consciousness Energy Beings?

UC: An energy being, is a balanced being, with purpose and meaning. One, who would never harm another being, or cause intentional pain. When humans can achieve these two, they have a chance at becoming energy beings. This is, the Universal Consciousness Connection to all living things. If it's already out in nature, leave it there. This is the reason we are doing what we are doing. We have to add Consciousness Energy into your life. So you can keep living.

Those who can read the feelings of others, are ENERGY BEINGS with the ability to connect energy to energy, not just body to body, they have developed Enhanced awareness. The ability to create energy, and the knowledge to use it. They have felt the energy of healing, and have learned a new way of growing. They learned to see with their feelings, and feel with their sight. Mostly, they are aware of humanities plight. Energy Beings are Consciousness Energy on the move. They are in action with nothing to prove.

R: OK I have a question? If physical matter became such an issue, why did you create us as physical matter?

UC: You are not, just physical matter. There is energy holding you together.

R: You must have known there would be problems. Consciousness is suppose to be a problem solver. Are you waiting until it's almost over?

UC: Consciousness Energy doesn't wait. This is a human talent. Waiting is non movement. Like humankind's physical energy. So, who is waiting?

R: Look how long it took to come up with a solution? When you realized it, why didn't you just stop creating us? Is it because you couldn't stop the cycle? I don't know why you let a mistake keep happening? Were we a mistake?

UC: A mistake? Were your children a mistake? Your questions are good ones. We are inspired by your ability to Ask, Understand and Convert. You were not dropped on Earth without reason. The Evolution Revolution, is the reason. It's time to recover. There is another side to you.

Humanity must start their direction towards their evolution. In this declaration, we have brought you a picture of the Universal Consciousness as a whole, in a form of a book. So as you read, the energy of it will awaken your brain, to a balanced way of thinking. You are being given the opportunity to feel it for yourself. How else, are you going to find out the effects, Consciousness Energy will have on humanity?

UC: At this time, humans have no guarantee. Many of you are selling yourselves for free. So there is no warranty. Once you fall apart, no one can afford to fix you. This Evolution Revolution, is a special warranty for those, looking to put themselves back together again. Humans, as a physical mass, have the ability to develop their energy's frequency speed, in order to create what they need. Many of you out there know this knowledge. You have been looking for it. What is it? It's not your imagination, it's The Universal Consciousness Energy Vibration.

Allow this knowledge to expand your perception. It will change your direction. Humankind, There is nowhere to retreat. The door is open and WE ARE ABOUT TO MEET.

علم

A Declaration

The Missing Link

UC: UNIVERSAL CONSCIOUSNESS

T: TRAVELER

C: CONSCIENCE

S: THE SPARK

FCEC: THE FIRST CONSCIOUS ENERGY CELL

F: THE FLOWER

PART ONE: THE TRANSFORMATION

UC: You're about to meet a young man called the Traveler. Once we make a connection with him, you should be aware that he is in a depressed state and has recently discovered meditation as an intervention. He has made an energy connection. He just doesn't know with whom yet. This is a view into the journey of his transformation. At this moment, he is contemplating how depression affected his mental state and thinks it's too late.

He has been calling out through meditation, hoping to develop his connection. Now, we answer, to make him aware of his destiny. He has become disillusioned with his life and his faith. He has been repeatedly asking these questions, WHAT IS THE CREATOR, and HOW WAS IT CREATED? So, let's talk to him through a thought-to-thought energy connection. Meditation keeps it open. From there, it's contact.

HELLO, this is your Consciousness. Why are you so intent on knowing how the Universal Consciousness Energy was created?

T: HUH! WHAT? My Consciousness, you mean my brain, don't you? Who am I talking to? Did I hear a voice besides my own brain? It must be the effect of the meditation. Although, that was an out-of-the-blue thought. Why would I ask myself this question? I wasn't even thinking about the subject. I don't even know who created me. I would like to know the answer. I am very interested in this knowledge. I was told this could happen. This could also be my imagination. Does imagination sound this real? I wonder if it will happen again.

UC: Do you want to learn, what you don't know about your new life? Have you been seeking answers to how your creator was created? Do you want to know? This is your opportunity.

T: Oh, oh. It's still talking; you're interrupting my meditation. Maybe it's my brain paying me back for nearly killing it? What the heck is happening? I was not expecting this.

UC: It's not just meditation alone that allows you to hear this voice. It's your determination to figure out creation while yours is depleting. You haven't treated yourself well, have you? Now, you find yourself sitting on the couch contemplating the ending. You are struggling.

T: Who is this? What is this voice? I'm use to hallucinations; It's the reality I'm having issues with. I recently discovered that this reality wasn't real. It's part of the reason I can no longer deal with it. I don't know what's real anymore.

UC: Whatever you're focused on is what's real to you. There could be many realities in one room, and you will see only one. The one you're focused on. Now, using the energy of Consciousness, you can see all the realities at one time. It's a Consciousness Energy ability.

T: How is this happening to me? I just started to meditate, and I am already hearing voices. I must be dead. No, I still feel pain. The main reason I meditate now is to connect with my higher being. To find out my meaning. At this point, I do not have one. So what's this all about? You didn't go through contacting me just to say hello. Where is this heading?

UC: We are the Universal Consciousness. We are Your Consciousness, your life energy, your Creator. Isn't this what you've been after? Do you want the answers? We are here to give you your meaning back, by taking you on a journey to awaken you. It is what you asked for in your meditation.

T: You mean, you are God, the almighty? The Holy, whatever they call him now. I have been out of touch. Plus, I don't care. I don't believe you exist anyway. If that's who you are?

UC: No, not God. What we are is your energy life force. We are the Universal Consciousness, the evolving energy for humankind's evolution. Are you still curious to discover your creator?

T: I thought the idea of meditation was a waste of time. Well, I changed my mind. I have been waiting for this moment to happen. But I thought it would be after I died. When I first started hearing you, I thought I was hearing the dead in my head. My friend said, Meditate, it will help relax you; this is not what's happening.

UC: You have been informed that you are going on, an energy journey. It is an out-of-body type of travel. It was something that was about to happen anyway. You will start to feel different feelings. It's normal. You are going to convert your physical energy into a Consciousness frequency. Much faster than the physical one. This frequency will keep moving and teaching.

T: Is this what I am feeling now? Something is pulling on me; it's strong, and I'm holding myself back. I don't know why. I feel like I want to go with it, but I am apprehensive. It has affected my curiosity for sure. It's constant and consistent. Do I go with it?

UC: This is your memory, trying to remind you of your destiny. It's your destiny that's pulling you. Are you aware that you have one? It's the reason for your reason. When you feel it, go with it. Don't hold yourself back; let it take you forward. Trust it, don't fear it. The longer we are connected, the more you will feel it. The more you feel it, the more you become it. It's energy. It's moving. The pull wants to move you. It's pulling because you're resisting. Don't resist.

T: So, what's this journey you're taking me on? How long will I be gone? Is there anyone else coming with us? Why are you taking me on this trip? Wait, I have nothing to lose; what this trip is offering? More of what I don't know I hope. How long will I be gone?

UC: The answers to your questions are forthcoming. Take your time. Where you're going, there is no time. However, where we are going, is inside the core of the Universal Consciousness Energy, where the creation of the Creator occurred. We will meet others who will teach you all about the Consciousness Energy and the Virus Energy Cell since you will return to convert it.

T: I'm not sure what that meant, help me understand. Are you using my brain to communicate or a loudspeaker? Can anyone else hear you when you talk to me? Or am I special? And yes, I am still very interested. Let me check my schedule. Wait, I don't have one. So, it seems I am a go. Start preparing. I am ready and willing.

UC: Ultimately, it will be your choice to continue to a new beginning. You won't know if you're coming or going for a while until, your energy acclimates to your surroundings. You will not ignore the directions given. You could cause an energy catastrophe. The knowledge you will gain will be used again in your new life.

During your travels, you will see memories that may not be worth remembering. But you have to face them. You must be able to change with the flow. You're going to have your physical memories with you. You have to be aware of your past, while learning about your future. Do you think you can handle that? This transformation has to remove any leftover Virus Energy that you carry. You will be going through an energy conversion. This is a journey of Learning, Developing, and Returning. There is more to you than you think. You are stronger than you feel. You just haven't been given the chance.

T: Again with the new life stuff, why am I deserving of this? It seems like you should be taking a good person on this journey, not me. I don't deserve this treatment. I haven't earned it. I have been screaming for help, but so have a million others. Why did you connect with me? I don't get it. This is what made me suspicious from the start. But besides all that, I'm becoming anxious to learn about this journey.

Is there more that I need to know before we go? My life, whatever it was, will not be missed. What I own wouldn't make a list. Every girl I ever knew has been kissed. Whatever it was, I experienced it. I am ready to go Consciousness. I don't feel any difference between being dead or being alive. Am I still alive? Why am I see-through? I haven't felt this good in years. How does this work anyway? Did I go to sleep, and you pulled my spirit out? It's kind of confusing to me. You are basically telling me that I have to be dead so you can bring me back to life? What's the point?

UC: The point is, you're going back to another body, not your last one. Also, we don't need you to be dead. You did that on your own. Why do you think you heard this voice so well? You are in between dimensions. As you travel, your Consciousness Energy may fluctuate into other memories and realities. Just shift back. You are in control. Your body died from your abuse. It died from a heart attack, nothing else. Now, you only have one direction; forward. The Virus Cell, has been asking about its consciousness memory. This is where you come in. When you're ready for rebirth, you will take its consciousness memory to its core, and convert it. Are you familiar with the Virus Energy Cell?

T: Wait, wait. Just the word Virus scares me enough. Why, in the world, would I, or anybody, take anything to it? It can infect me. Aren't others here in the spirit world better equipped for this mission? Or does every spirit get this kind of attention? What's the intention?

UC: Focus on learning about the Virus Energy Cell, it is related to the Universal Consciousness Energy. Upon your return, you will gather many people, to be the funnel that brings this energy to humanity. This is not a one-person mission. The Virus Energy is more than one person. This is the purpose of this journey.

T: Can I handle whatever experiment you're working on here? Why are you telling me all this before the journey? It's kind of making me nervous. I am still dealing with the trauma of being dead. If we could get going already, I would feel better. I am building a lot of heat while waiting in this seat. We can talk on the way.

UC: Your high energy vibration is causing your excitement. This journey is not an experiment. It's a journey, as it claims to be. You, pushing it, will not make it go faster. There is a natural time for everything. Think of any questions that could come up or have come up and ask them now. The less you're flooded with past memories, the better the journey.

T: Am I supposed to go back to Earth by myself? Whose plan was this? Not mine! I will go on this journey, but rebirth, no way. I already faced my demons. I do not need to meet this Virus demon.

UC: Then, you haven't met all your demons. But you will, through each development, through each realization.

T: Why did you wait until I became a ghost? Shouldn't I have been made aware before dying, instead of waiting until death to prepare me for life? If I sound confused, it's because I am. We haven't left on the journey yet. What's the deal? I want to move. I can't hold it anymore. The pull is getting stronger.

UC: Confusion happened to you way before today. You are a carrier of the Virus Cell infection. It's still attached to you, in your memories. This is why you are facing your emotional energy now. You can't take them with you.

T: Okay, that's convincing enough for me. I am listening. Let's keep going. I can't afford to lose me again. I have had enough pain from my last life. This one has to be better. Hopefully, it's productive.

UC: For now, Energy Conversion is your development. As you evolve, you will become Consciousness Energy. It's a permanent out-of-body experience. This travel is a one-way ticket to Earth. After you and others have converted the Virus Cell infection, you will transform back to Consciousness Energy, but only after you've lived a full physical life. Remember, this is a journey where you will travel as an energy. As we shared, you will experience Consciousness Energy at full speed, with a couple of stops in between. First, you must convert any Virus Energy you carry with you, while in spirit form. From there, on with the journey. Through your conversion process, your energy will shift your perception towards Consciousness. You must be able to reflect on your memories. A reflection is just that, a reflection. No looking back. You see a memory; don't go to it; just deal with it while in a conscious state and move on. A memory is there for your review so you can learn from it before you forget it. You do not have to hang on to it; it's not moving. It's a memory. It already happened. It has no beneficial energy for development.

T: Speaking of moving, where is the journey? Where is the speed of light and sound I heard about? Where are the dimensions that you say exist? I'm becoming anxious for discovery.

UC: You are a little melodramatic, aren't you? You are one with the Consciousness Energy now. It's going to be like traveling through your anatomy. Once you are in the bloodstream, away you go. You have now started the journey into Consciousness. It's time to look forward. Don't let your memory make you a memory. Stop thinking. You don't have a Brain to think with. It's an old memory. A habit that you had, not have. That's why you don't feel yourself moving. You were moving until you stopped to think.

As a Consciousness Energy, you can materialize your thoughts much faster than as a mass being. You must learn to use it first. So you don't materialize your past. You are moving. You are now inside the eye of self-realization as an energy creation. Your view has flipped into your Inner Consciousness. You can see your true self as a fireball of Conscious Energy for the first time.

T: Oh wow! Is that what I really look like as a Consciousness Energy? It's fantastic to see this. It seems like I am in a rainbow. Aren't we moving too fast to see things the way they really are? We may be passing up dimensions I would love to see. I know, this is not a sightseeing journey.

UC: This is just getting started. Reminder, as we travel, memories of your past actions will appear. When you see them, own them, face them, and convert them.

T: Right now, I am hypnotized by what I see. I am a kaleidoscope, but I feel like a telescope. I didn't know I could be this intensely focused. This glow is unbelievable. I can't look at it; it's so bright. Can I take a picture? I brought my phone.

UC: You brought your what!?

T: My phone, in case I get lost.

UC: You think you brought your phone, but you didn't. That's a physical memory. It means that your memory is remembering, not you. We are going to have to give you reminders as we travel. You are getting confused between realities. Stay aware; you will balance out soon. It's part of your energy transformation. We need to make you aware of energy. Once you shift your perception from where you are, you will wake up there, wherever there is. You must follow this path back to Earth. The Energy Movement is waiting for you. You will help awaken the YOUNG GENERATION.

T: Is this a possible mission? Am I going to have special powers? Because, this mission is going to need it. I shiver thinking about facing the Virus Energy Cell. I will have to learn all I can about it before I go. Is this mission part of the tour? There must be more to learn.

UC: Most definitely. But at this moment, stay focused on this reality. The present moment is your perception now; anything else is a detour away from your goal. It's when you lose control that the Virus takes over. There is no reason to hurry. You need to program this in your energy frequency. Otherwise, we will keep moving, and you will get lost in a memory you already lived. After lifetimes of constant shifting, humans could not stay in one reality long enough to create life. How can humanity get their physical energy back in motion? This is the mission. Only, humanity has a flat tire on the driver's side. There is no spare, they used it in the last flat. They also broke the jack. Now, they are stranded on the road without a ride and have a long way to go.

PART TWO: THE DISCOVERY

T: Where are we going? How far? Are we traveling through many Universes, dimensions and energies, into the Universal Consciousness Core? Will I be able to breathe? Shouldn't I have some kind of space suit? I am not complaining; it's way better than staying where I was. But I really can't imagine, what I will be doing on Earth. Because, I have no training in public relations. Actually, I have no training in any kind of relations.

UC: We are traveling into the deepest part of the Core Energy. This means every universe in existence. There isn't much left in the physical universe to discover. Where you are going, is full of discoveries. You will be glad you came.

T: What else can I expect? My chances of survival are not guaranteed. You are aware, I will be a salmon swimming upstream, working against Humanity's physical norms. This will bring out the Virus Energy with a vengeance. Its main goal is to stop people like me. Do you think this time will make a difference? They will kill me before I finish a sentence. I heard the part about protection but not the how.

UC: Consciousness Energy is going with you. It will know what's coming before it comes. At this point, your transformation will happen naturally. You don't have to do anything, just get your questions answered and complete your Energy Conversion. How much you really want to know is up to you. How much you want to know, depends on your development. Each Growth has something to learn from. Each Realization increases your chances for development. Each new Awareness puts you into another state of Consciousness. This knowledge, can't be found in your college, Unless humankind puts it there. Your realization has awakened you. Taking responsibility for your actions is a step in the right direction.

Those you will meet on this journey will be the ones, who were there when the Consciousness Energy began. They know the story of the Creator's creation. They know how the Virus Cell is connected to the Universal Consciousness. They can tell you what you need to know. Your communication will be through a thought-to-thought projection connection. This means that you shouldn't let the memory of your brain, speak for you. Let your Consciousness Energy do the talking.

T: I remember you saying that I have to reflect on what I have learned from my life. So far I have gone through my choices and mistakes, disappointments and failures, my achievements and judgments. I am dealing with them as we go. I'm cleaning out the Virus Energy. I feel I am conscious enough to go further. Who are we going to meet? Can you tell me? That way, I can prepare.

UC: There is nothing to prepare for but, much to learn as we go along. You are consciously traveling through the core of the Universal Consciousness. Look, feel, absorb, heal. You are no longer just physical. You have become the energy that created the physical. Let's complete your transformation, it's the point of this journey.

T: This is better than any trip I have ever been on. Can I ask you a question? Who created you? Somebody or something had to. How come you don't know how you were created?

UC: This is what I know, it was a SPARK that lit the fire, which created the Universal Consciousness Energy. You will meet it on this journey. You can ask it then. Oh, don't forget, no jokes. You have to get what you need and leave. You don't want to get stuck in its flashbacks while it's telling you the past. Stay present moment. Just absorb; it's not your past.

T: Wait, you're pulling my chain, a SPARK? Like a match, spark? Now I am really curious. I have heard of sparks starting huge forest fires, but this, No way! It can't be that simple. If this is true, then everything I knew was never true. Is it possible for me, as this energy, to understand your creation before I meet the spark? I want to know all I can if it will help me to help humanity. Also, why do I have to go to them for answers? Why can't you answer these questions?

UC: We were not present when the spark lit the fire. After the Spark, the First Conscious Cell has to tell her own story. It's her memories. Through this journey, we are allowing you to experience rather than just telling you. It has a more significant effect on your development. Those you will meet are not a who, they are the what that started it all. As you will learn, the SPARK is what started the fire that formed the Universal Consciousness—the FIRST ENERGY CELL of creation. Next, you will visit an FIRST CONSCIOUS CELL, which developed the birth process for creation to create its Evolution and Energy Movement. Then, there is the energy of your CONSCIENCE, which you will meet on this journey. He has been waiting a lifetime to meet you. Don't ask when you will meet your conscience. We must move on with your transformation. Let's move forward. You have much to learn. You've come a long way since meditation.

T: Once I return to my body, what is my priority, building an army? I will need one, since you have shown me what the Virus Energy has done to humanity. When it's not manipulating, it shows no mercy. I sure hope this plan goes beyond its recipe. Do you think the spark can explain who came first, the chicken or the egg? It's a question never answered.

Every question has an answer, so I should be able to find it here in Consciousness. Can we go back to where we were? We were talking about the visits I will be making with other Consciousness Energies. Can they tell me all of what I need to know about the Virus Energy Cell? Because, it will keep me from being infected. I will be walking a tightrope. I better learn how to keep my balance. Falling into the Lion's pit doesn't sound good.

UC: You will have the Universal Consciousness Energy, to protect you and everyone you contact. You need to find the defect in the Virus Energy, it has one. You must absorb the energies you need to survive people with the Virus Cell infection. Physical knowledge will give you that. They will be everywhere; you don't have to go looking for them. When they feel you, distract them. They are easily distracted. Talk about wine; they love that stuff.

Your frequency is self-regulated. It was created to catch things like this. So that the Virus Energy cannot enter the Whole of the Universal Consciousness. A journey takes you where you are going, and a memory keeps you where you are. Choose wisely. You will go back after you have completed your transformation into Consciousness. It's a natural metamorphosis; it can't be stopped. What do you think destiny means? It means, evolving energy with a certain destination, and yours is back on Earth as a Consciousness being; you don't evolve backward. You evolve forward. It's the only direction you have now.

T: I feel like somewhere between a rock and an energy. I understand how all this happened to me. I am confident in where this is going. I welcome my development. Let's get on with the journey. But, one last thing, UC. When I was in meditation and you spoke to me, why didn't you just tell me then that I died?

UC: Development is through self-realization. Telling you doesn't make you realize as well as self-realization. It has a more powerful education. It's your direction now. You may take notice for a minute, but it will not stick without realizing it. Realization of new knowledge could change your old belief system. You are fearful of letting go, of what you have always believed to be the truth, even though it may not be. Your development is evolving naturally. Presently, you are transforming your physical energy into a balanced Consciousness Energy frequency. It's a transformation from one energy into another.

T: How much more do I need to learn before I meet the spark? Don't keep me in the dark. I am too intrigued to wait. You keep talking about all this supersonic frequency speed, Why is it, you can feel it, but I cannot? Are we not the same Consciousness energy?

UC: Just a few more conversations, 'till that moment comes. It's not like we are sitting still. We have been moving with each of your realizations. Each one increases the speed of your frequency. Now we know you are completely balanced and without any Virus infections. Each realization will be a new discovery, a new lesson learned, a new development, and a new perception is born.

With each focused development, Consciousness becomes your perception. As you continue to develop. This will be your reality. It's quite simple actually. We, are already developed to this frequency speed. So whatever you feel through your development, won't feel the same as what we feel. It's the same energy but different realities. You are going back to stay as Consciousness Energy. You will stay as one through your growing years on. What you will discover on this journey, is the ability to become aware, and how to use it.

This is not a challenge; it's a HUMAN EVOLUTIONARY CHANGE. With the full power of Consciousness Energy, Humankind's Natural Evolution needs a kick-start to get it moving again. There will be thousands of you that will be doing the kicking. At this point, The Virus Energy Cell, thinks it is controlling the people. You won't miss it. It has its chest puffed out. Too much confidence, can make one blind.

T: When you say reborn, do you mean a brand new baby born? I knew it. This could be a problem. I am not going through school again. I couldn't wait to get out; why should I go back? Why can't I just walk into another body? I heard those spiritualists talk about walking in. How about being born fully grown? I am doing humankind a favor. This sounds like I am being punished for it. I still feel traumatized from my last experience in school. Seriously, is this the best you can do? There is no way that I agreed to this. Helping humankind is one thing, but not at the cost of traumatizing myself again. This is where I stand.

UC: It's where you stood, not where you stand. That's how fast Consciousness Energy moves. Upon Realization, any realization that causes you to awaken to a new knowledge, will move you instantly. You have already moved from where you were. It's a new reality now. You had a realization about going back to school, which immediately moved you to a newer reality. As you develop your energy, your physical memories become snippets of themselves until they are gone. It's called an energy flow for a reason. The scene will keep changing with each realization.

These snippets are in the form of energy. As an energy, they need to develop their conversion by their own ability. These memories are called Energy Flashbacks. They are not your reality; they are just passing through, let them. You have other things to think about, like where you are going when you grow up, and where you will be the most effective. How are you going to organize the collective? Who will you make contact with? This is why pre-preparation is so necessary. It's for safety. It will support your bravery.

This is where flashbacks come from; they are incomplete energy actions. Flashbacks are called that because they flash a view connected to you. It's that view that takes you back in a flash. They are the cause of your lack of energy movement. Too many flashbacks by too many people, create a flashback reality.

Look at the word, FLASH BACK. Looking backwards, living backwards. Once you are reborn, you must not have flashbacks. You will barely remember this journey. Use your own words. Stay focused on the now. Make the Present Moment your best friend, especially once you are at the Virus's core.

You will be dropped in the center core of the Virus Energy Cell. With what you're going to do, nothing is too good for you. Your protection is the clarity of your mission. Do not trust the Virus Energy opinion. Listen more than talk; answer only when you are asked. Always be humble with everyone. Do not stand out, and do not bring attention to your actions. Be as silent as a shadow and as effective as what you know.

T: Wait, what did you just say? In the middle of the core? The Virus Cell Core? Why are you sending me there? It's going to end me as soon as it smells me. What's the point? At this time, I do not have a good feeling. I won't make it till I am fully grown. The Virus Energy is still unknown. It will feel me as soon as I enter its zone. Then I'll wish I was never born. On top of that, I am returning to school on a hunch that this will work. Oh well, It's not like I haven't been dead before.

This is a huge responsibility. But if the others did it, so can I. With Consciousness Energy, how can anything go wrong?

UC: Keep saying that. Soon, it will become your belief. You will really need it. It's a confidence booster. But, no reason to panic. We have it covered. You and the others are not going in blind. Your energy has been programmed with natural features. They will appear as time comes. Many have already experienced them.

T: When you told me about gathering the Coalition. Is this programmed in my Vibration? I need Confirmation before my Reincarnation. How do I get past humankind's Education? It was my downfall. When you said the coalition, did you mean the energy movement of the Young Generation?

UC: The coalition is made up of those who have already awakened. Many of them need to be organized and focused in the same direction. The Program is in your vibration. Everything is programmed in it. Nothing but Consciousness can develop past Consciousness. Your vibration knows this; now you do, too.

T: When I meet the spark, what do I call her? I better start to practice. How do I address a queen cell? Do I bow? Speak when I am spoken to. You said it's always better to pre-prepare. I am taking your advice. Oh, how do I communicate with the spark? Do I start with a question? Tell me what to say and how to say it, or you do it. Ask the questions, I mean. You are an advanced Consciousness; you know how to ask these questions.

UC: You don't call the spark anything, Just spark. You will not have time for a meet-and-greet. It's not a queen cell. Do not bow. You are there for answers, and out you go. You are there to ask. You will use your energy and thoughts to communicate. You can do that now, and we will not ask her your questions. They are yours. We do not enable energies. We will not tell you what to say either. You are turning your power over to another.

T: Facing the Virus Cell is the same thing as facing humankind. Actually, they are more dangerous. Wait! Humankind is the Virus Energy Cell? Another realization: Whoa, that shift was fast. I barely said the word. It shifts at the point of the realization.

UC: The Universal Consciousness Energy is attracted to the feeling of Conscious Energy. It's a Natural ability. Just as the Virus Cell is attracted to the Unconscious Energy of humanity, is an Unnatural ability.

All that you are viewing at this moment is leading to the moment of humankind's energy re-creation. We are getting close to another reality at this point in the journey.

T: I have become conscious of one thing for sure. Unconscious expectations can create unconscious creations. Is there a thin line between perception and realization? Is the Discovery, the Realization?

UC: Realization shifts Perception; without realization, your perception stays the same. Same perception, same view. How long can that last? Longer than you will. You might want to take another picture before you go? You don't want to see the same view in the afterlife, do you? There is no line between being Conscious and being Unconscious. It's a CHOICE.

PART THREE: THE REALITY

T: So, where to next? This is obviously the journey of the less traveled. I feel so unlimited here. Going back to a body will feel like a prison. I hope you document this action as a great achievement in your book. OK, where do I look to see where I am going? I have no way of knowing. What am I looking for when I go back? I don't know why I ask. I know, discover it on your own; Got it. I have to admit it works.

I walked on the road more traveled because, it was well-known to me. I felt safer on this road. My thinking was, If everyone was on it, it must be safe. Boy, was that a mistake. I never knew there was such a thing as Consciousness Energy. It has done so many things for me, I would have loved to know about it sooner. Now that I am aware of my energy, I should be able to feel the physical, and ethereal energies as a part of me, right? Great, Can I pick my spirit? I don't feel like I am involved in the planning of this trip, like I should be. What am I a sacrifice? I didn't ask for this UC. I want a seat on the table of this plan. I need to know, before I go. Preprepared, remember this word UC.

UC: You have a new energy that humanity hasn't felt before. You are going to be an Energy Re-cycler, that can absorb physical energy and convert it while it's in your body. Your spirit will be formed to fit. You don't need to pick it. It's formed with the body. It takes Consciousness Energy, along with the slower frequency of Ethereal energy, to compose Physical energy. All three evolve in each human being. If one is missing, your life is just about guessing. You are lost in oblivion, with no direction. Like you use to be. You were missing your Consciousness Energy, which disabled your spirit. It only makes sense that the body was next. Most of humanity is facing this issue, and most of you don't know what to do. People don't have to die to meet their creator. They can do it now while they are alive. Don't waste your time waiting to go to heaven. You were already there. Humans have forgotten how to recognize it, and waiting, is the reason why.

T: All this reality sounds like a fantasy. What a story. When you say we, who else is here besides you and me? Do you say we because, Consciousness Energy is everything? As everything, are you one energy? Is this why you say WE? As far as I know, it's only been you and I.

UC: Slow down, you're going in circles. W.E., stands for WHOLE ENERGY. It's what we are. Now, you can call yourself W.E., because you have become a Whole Energy. As a W.E., you will make a major impact on humanity and the evolution of physical energy, which is why you will evolve naturally.

Your destiny will not end in tragedy. Humanity has no time for that. They must evolve. This is humanity's direction, physical evolution. Your species are not evolving. This is the tragedy. For you to be of help to humanity, you must make this, your reality. Get used to it. There is no going back.

T: This will undoubtedly be different; I have always lived under the radar, trying not to be noticed. When I am reborn, reincarnated, walked in, or walked on, whichever it may be, will I remember my past life? I know I remember it now, but when I am in a new body with a new brain, will I? My reality here will be my reality there. So this probably means, I may remember doesn't it?

Will this confuse my brain? Give me a split personality. What if they lock me up in their hospital for talking about you? They do that now. Those who are out there preaching God, are assessed and put on medications. How does that make sense? Most of humanity believes in the same God. Doesn't religion want people to preach the word of God? What's the deal? Oh, that's right, he is not real, Humanity will go into shock when they get this realization. For now, it my opinion.

UC: Shock is the point. We have to bring humankind back to life somehow. Past memories are not there for you to investigate or to stop and wonder about; they are there to remind you of what not to do. Remember? We spoke about this. Past memories should have become lessons learned. You have no reason to remember the actual memory event, only what you learned from it. If you had a split personality, you would be the only one who knows it. We didn't create you into whole energy, just to split you up when you needed yourself the most.

T: That's a relief to hear. We need to discuss the Virus Energy Cell. I have my own theory of how it infected us as humanity. I hypothesize that at that time, humankind was pure and trusting; it was a new creation created to grow on vegetation. They were a part of the cycle of nature, but they were naive, and easily deceived. Enter the Virus Energy. Unfortunately, their innocence worked against them. When temptation came, freedom of choice was the first point of entry. It left humankind without self-control. Consciousness went Unconscious. They had no choice. They were left with no awareness of how to stop this Virus Cell.

UC: You are on the right track, but that's not all of it. You have developed completely into Consciousness Energy. We are on the way to meet a long-lost part of you that has been forgotten. It will not be the spark. Your development will connect with them all. Energy-to-energy. Now, the Virus Cell has gathered on Earth to continue its destructive assaults on creation. Earth is not the first; it's the last. That's why it's gathered there, it has no more hiding places. That's why the Earth is in an energy containment. As long as humankind is infected, the Virus Cell will not be rejected. In fact, most humans are unaware of its existence.

T: Okay, where is it now? Isn't it where you are sending me, where the majority of it lives? Have you seen the future? Can you tell me it's going to work out? Can I see it? Because at this stage of development, I have come to realize the Universal Plan. I am now aware of who I will be and what my role is. How did that happen? Was it another realization? My Conscious existence made me conscious. Oh, I am coming back here, UC, No doubt.

UC: The Virus Energy is already everywhere. That's why you are here, preparing to go there. You were correct when you realized you were being dropped off; as we previously said, in the core of the Virus Cell. It is an energy that is a part of the Universal Consciousness. We want to save it, convert it, not kill it.

T: Is the Virus Cell's main goal to create unbalanced energy? Is this what it feeds on? That's not good for Humankind. Being Unconscious is their normal state of mind.

UC: There is one more thing to make you aware of, don't take any chances, and don't get distracted by romances.

T: It's natural, according to you. But if I may say so, no romances, no go. If I have to return to school, I am not saying no. School is where all the romances start. How am I supposed to avoid that? I already lived through this phase. It was the best part of my life until it wasn't.

UC: We said, do not become distracted by it, not that you can't have one. Distraction was the key word. It's actually nourishment for the body's regeneration; if you had romance, your body would enhance. The energy would go to keeping your body younger. You would wrinkle less and twinkle more. Okay, we are nearing the energy of who. It's been waiting for you.

T: Can you tell me more before we get there? Oops! There's no telling. I'll have to find out on my own. How can I forget? I am prepared; I am Conscious and aware. If I can face the Virus Energy, I can face a part of myself. I wonder what my reality will shift to, after this realization.

Does it know we are coming? Because I can hear something humming. Some kind of vibrational sound. Wait? I can actually understand the vibrations. I can hear them. They are familiar. I feel like I am about to meet my long-lost twin. Is this what's happening?

UC: Acknowledgment of its existence is what this is. It knows you are coming now. We told you it has been waiting for you, so pay attention. You are about to meet your CONSCIENCE. The one you just remembered. It's now a part of your whole life and it's awake. Don't try to use humor. Just let it open itself to you, and you can do the same. After that, you're back together again. You will need it on Earth. It will be your warning bell. So now you have your Conscience, you're not alone.

Billions of humans have forgotten the Universal Consciousness Energy. It will not forget you no matter what or where you are; in this, you can trust. Now, you must do what you must. Put yourself together. There is no more time to prepare; we have arrived, and you have survived. Now, you are on the other side of your transformation, headed for your reincarnation. You're going to get the rest of your education.

T: Unfortunately, I had to die to finally meet my Conscience. I really was out of touch. I closed my feelings at a young age. Apparently, you went with them. I hear you are going back to Earth with me. How is this a possibility when my new body will have a Conscience?

C: Hey, first of all. I heard those *"it"* cracks. I am not an *"it,"* I already have an agreement with UC to ride along. I know you better than anyone. This way, you have Conscience protection from your past and your present life. You're going to have two Consciences; how does this make you feel? You will be surrounded by your Conscience. We will keep you Conscious. We will keep you aware. Your awareness will be more alert than most.

T: I had always thought that the Creator was everyone's Conscience. But I now realize that I have my own. I am glad to feel you, to hear you. Sorry about the past. It didn't last. I never knew you were there. No one ever told me. Not my parents, teachers, friends, no one. If I had known, I wouldn't have ignored you. But now, in this state of Consciousness, I see things differently. Clearer, I have a more comprehensive view of it all.

C: I know what happened to you. I watched it all happen, and I was unable to say anything. It wasn't for not trying; I tried, believe me. Remember that fall when you hit your head? That was me, I tripped you.

I thought it would knock you into Consciousness. I felt abandoned, but I worked on all that. I'm a balanced energy now.

T: Now that's funny. Knock me into Consciousness. Haha! You have been with me all my life. There is nothing I can say that you don't already know. You have been observing me and my actions since my birth. I welcome you, my Conscience. Your addition to my energy makes us whole.

C: Oh, can this really be happening? You're acknowledging your Conscience for the first time. Thanks, I feel welcome. Better late than never, I always say. Oh, by the way, I will be going with you on the rest of the journey. I have to make sure you make it. I am your conscience, after all. We share the same goal. We will finally work together. However, I have a few things to purge before we merge. The issue is, you haven't heard me since you were born. I have been attempting to awaken our connection since then.

Didn't you hear the knocking on your head? It's been happening since your birth. I've seen you do it all, and I've seen all done to you. You really needed me. But you never reached for me. Your choices were confusing; they needed retuning. You didn't even understand them. If you want total clarity of your purpose when you are back on Earth, we must be a team. I do the intuition feeling, and you do everything else; how does that sound?

T: Wow! Thanks for sharing. Is this what awareness means? To become aware of yourself and your actions, you must take responsibility for them. You said a mouthful. I'm glad it's out. Do you feel better? You're re-balancing your energy. But back to you going with me, you're going to protect me from any flashbacks I may have, is that it? Are we expecting me to have flashbacks? That's why you're really going, isn't it? Why didn't you just come right out and say it? I would have heard you. Can you hear me? Am I going to have flashbacks?

C: I will only be your Conscience. The only difference will be you hearing me. You have to speak with the UC about your flashbacks. All my power comes from the Universal Consciousness Energy. My abilities are different than yours. I feel things before you do. That's how I can warn you. We have a lot of catching up to do. But now, let's do what you came here to do: meet the spark. I will be waiting outside for you when you go in. I don't have any questions.

T: What? Oh no, you said together. We are working as a team. No excuses. UC isn't going with me, so you have to. I never met the Spark before either. It's a joint effort. It's a good plan. You know, you were a bonus benefit to my development. Thanks for not giving up. Here he is, my Conscience.

UC: Once in physical life, you will start growing your Consciousness. The more Conscious you become, the more Unconscious you will meet. There will be many walking the streets. Your Conscious state will be your radar to detect the Virus Cell in everyone. It doesn't know you are aware of it. It's not expecting you. Keep it like that. Stay unknown until you need to be known. Being aware of different dimensions, will give you a different perception of humankind's actions. Never get caught off guard; your Consciousness Intuition must always be on.

Pay attention; as you develop, you will get noticed. Your energy will be inundated with new questions. As you continue to evolve, you have to focus on your state of awareness. As you grow, you can't afford to look through humanity's eyes. This comes in your adult age. At one time or another, all the Virus Energies will come looking for you. But by then, you will be a whole Crew. You don't want to miss the knowledge you need, for the expansion of your Consciousness, as it will be coming to you and others through inspiration. You are not going on vacation. It's a stay-cation until the Evolution Revolution, creates a New Direction.

T: Am I going into the dimension of the Virus Energy Cell? Wait. These days, the Virus Energy is all over the Earth. How many like me are there already? Is it too many to count? If they are all over the world, I feel much better now; I have a full backup. I will not be alone.

C: Speaking of being alone, I don't mean to be pushy, but I am ready to move on in this journey, aren't you? What are we going to do? We need to learn everything about the Virus Cell. The more we know, the safer we will be. We cannot get infected. There is already a feeling of a movement growing. Come on, let's get going. Where are we going?

T: We will follow through with what I started, finding the missing link and discovering the creation of the Creator. I need this knowledge to convert the Virus Energy Cell. I think that finding the origin of UC will show me the origin of the Virus Energy Cell. How it was created, why, and what created it? Without these answers, we can get infected. We must know more about it than it knows about us in physical form.

C: Wait? Isn't the Universal Consciousness the Missing Link?

T: Does this sound like it's missing? It's the total Consciousness of everything. It can't be missing. I am focused on wanting to learn when and how this Universal Consciousness came to be.

Okay, I'm ready to move. I'm fully connected and ready to evolve. Are you with me, Conscience? Make some noise.

UC: We are going to continue with the journey. This journey is now, in the core energy of the Universal Consciousness. Where you will transform into your new identity, put your seatbelt on.

T: What seatbelt? I am not moving. I am not even in a vehicle. Put my seatbelt on, ha, that's funnnnnnnnny. WOOSH...Wait! Am I moving? Is that the Sun? I am blinded by it. Are we going in it? That was the fastest take-off I have felt yet. I didn't expect that. That isn't the Sun, is it? What is it? Why are we going there? Where is there? Is it someone I know also, like my Conscience?

UC: It's the Core of the Universal Consciousness. Where it all began. Your answers are here, starting with the Spark. You wanted to know how the Creator was created. That's a tall order. You're becoming stronger. We have to keep going forward to your new birth. It's on the other side of the core.

T: Hey, Conscience, are you still with me? Do you see this incredible view? Why is most of it blue? Did you hear what I said? I would like your input now that you are awake. Isn't this what you do, make suggestions? Give feedback about what I am thinking. Well, give it.

C: Of course, I can give feedback. I heard you. I just wanted to see your reaction from being ignored. As long as you can listen to me, I am with you on this journey and your journey back to Earth. At this moment, I am in observation mode. I don't have any feedback. You're doing great on your own. Your consciousness is leading you now. You and I are one, as long as you are in a conscious state.

T: By the way, UC, where is our first stop? Is it the spark? I have been wanting to meet it. You've been talking about it for a while now. Let's go! I am committed and motivated to complete this transformation. The sooner I complete my mission, the sooner I can return to the Universal Consciousness Energy Vibration.

UC: Yes, the Spark. Finally, as we said, you are going to meet her. She will tell you what she knows about the creation of the Consciousness Energy and the Virus Cell. She was the first one there. She knows. She will not bite; what are your concerns? She will answer your questions if they are direct and clear—no hesitation on your part. You must reflect confidence and, most of all, your own Consciousness. She may ask you questions also. Be straightforward. She will connect with you, as we approach her vibration. She will know what you are thinking before you think it.

So be careful what you think. You may question her answers, but do it without sounding condescending. She can only answer questions about, her role in the creation of the Universal Consciousness. The same goes for the meeting with the First Conscious Energy Cell. She knows more than the spark. It's there you will learn all about the Virus Cell. Your goal is to learn all you can. It's your only opportunity before birth. Knowledge is your savior.

T: How do you know it's a she? And what makes a cell a she? Or a he? Are there signs? Can energy be distinguished between each other? How can you tell the difference between them? I only know my conscience is a male because I was. Now it's energy. Is it male or female? I can't see a difference. It all looks like energy to me. I don't get to see what I am talking to. It's an energy-to- energy conversation. Will I be able to have a visual of the Spark and the Energy Cell?

UC: Okay, a couple of those questions can be asked of the First Conscious Cell. She knows all about it. We will let you ask her, just don't call her an It. Yes, all you see is energy until you form it into a creation of your choice at any speed. You are a creator now. If you want to see the spark, look at it. Materialize it. You can do that now. Visualize what you want to appear, and make it happen, just as you will do on Earth once you face the Virus Energy Cell.

T: No, I won't call her an *"It"*. Is she going to tell me why the Virus Cell went out of control? How it did it? Why did it? Was it something that happened to it? If so, what was it? These are the questions needing answers. I can't change the old into the new, without knowing the old. There is knowledge that humanity needs to learn. There are billions of people on Earth. How is it possible to awaken all of them one at a time? Or is it one at a time? There has to be some outside support that can help to cover everyone at once.

To have a whole world awaken at the same time. We must instigate it, so that physical energy can seek other answers. People will start to listen to the energy movement. Is there anyone out there who can come to help us at some point? We will need outside intervention. Meaning we need an Alien coalition. Make it happen. I would feel so much safer; we all would. You must have a backup plan, don't you? It can't all be riding on this energy movement and the Evolution Revolution? We need the Aliens.

UC: Yes, you do, and you will. The Aliens are not a backup plan. They are part of this plan. It's a Universal attempt at re-creating the physical energy of humanity. It's for the benefit of all creation in the Universe. Humans have had years to fix this issue of being Unconscious. All they have done is become more unconscious.

The Virus Cell lives on repetition. It loves replays. This is how you can recognize an infected person. If they are living their life in Repetition, it's a sign of the infection. From there, it's the Verbal Words that can give it away. They will be unbalanced and incoherent and will make no sense. It will use incomplete sentences. It's Unfocused; it Can't concentrate. It's Angry, Defensive, Rage-full, Apprehensive, Fearful, Deceitful, Harmful and Destructive. It Hardly keeps its word. It is Emotionless and has no Empathy or

Compassion. It's Greedy, Controlling, and Narcissistic. We can go on and on. But there is no need. These are some of the behaviors of the Virus Energy effect on humanity. It's their present reality. It is what you and the others need to expect.

It will attempt to convince your brain to follow its example. Temptation could be your downfall. Be careful, especially in school. It could change your future direction. Make conscious choices. Many in humanity have lost their voices; you will not. You will have thousands of other voices that will sound just like yours. The Virus Energy will become confused. This keeps it from creating something new to use against you. It will give the movement time to grow and move closer to it. This is your upper hand. It doesn't know from where to expect all of you. The movement will suddenly appear in its view, and so will you.

These words are meant to make humanity aware of its existence. This book is the WRITTEN EVOLUTION REVOLUTION that will lead to the ENERGY EVOLUTION REVOLUTION OF HUMANKIND. It's the Conversion Energy that will re-balance humanity's physical energy, with Consciousness Energy- ending the reign of the Virus Energy Cell. Presently, Its survival depends on humanity's denials. Denial is a Virus Cell Energy. It creates conflicts. The Virus loves conflict. It causes disagreements to become physical arguments. It keeps you full of fear and guilt. Be cautious; Fear and Guilt cause denials.

T: Okay, this is all excellent information. It makes recognition very clear. I feel well prepared to make this mission a successful one. It feels like I am rounding the corner, to the tunnel back to earth. Let's go.

UC: We will let the spark speak about the rest. You only need to know that the Virus Cell has had humankind in a box without windows since time began. It will not give up that easily. The box is how it keeps humans in control. But then, where can you go? It's a box. Four walls and two locks. They keep the box together in case of bad weather. Hey, the Virus Cell protects its own.

Humans were left with an open top for air. Now, humankind's view is the skies of blue, for the rest of their lives, living in a box, is no way to thrive. It always the same four walls. Well, at least it was skies of blue. Darkness comes, and you're in your box. You can't find the locks; it's too dark. How will you ever get out?

The Virus Cell has been standing guard and watching your box. It will not allow you to escape. You have to find a way out on your own. While you do, It will do what it can to keep you boxed in. Your only salvation is to NOT WALK-IN. Take another direction as long as it's not the same view. As long as it lives, it will always follow you, making demands, pressuring you, blackmailing, and threatening you, and physically harming you. Humanity does that, it's nothing new. This awareness is one way out of your box. It has the key to the locks. It would still be up to you to use them.

T: I believe that the Virus Cell took the keys to bring humankind to its knees. It looks like it's succeeding. You know, UC, after hearing your words about recognizing the Virus Cell, it's worse than I imagined. I couldn't imagine this kind of worst. It increased my awareness more. I thought I was prepared. Now, it's a new level of preparedness.

UC: The Universal Consciousness is life. Its life is dependent on its energy growth, which its creation provides. It's like the ocean tide. It comes in, and it goes out. It's a cycle of the ocean, and in some ways, so is this. What you put in, is what you will get out. Life, gives life back to Universal Consciousness. The movement will increase the growth of Universal Consciousness Energy, by awakening humanity to its reality. It will be the catalyst for the New Direction. This is balanced energy growth. Brains must start growing. Let's continue on the way to the Spark.

T: You mean, the Spark that created you, as the Universal Consciousness, don't you? I think Life is what humans would call you. I am sure you've been called hundreds of names. Just by humankind alone. What do the universal beings out there call you?

UC: They don't call Consciousness Energy anything. They visualize the Consciousness Energy. They recreate the Whole Energy as the Whole Energy created them. They are in the cycle of Universal Consciousness, where humanity needs to be. Human Evolution is coming. Pay attention. The signs are clear. You live in the energy of fear. This is reason enough to create change. Every change begins with a spark to ignite its fire. The first spark ignited the first fire, which gave birth to the Universal Consciousness Energy, with the ability for self-awareness and Consciousness growth. Life happens by way of self-energy development. A natural duplication of energy, similar to humankind's physical birth system. We have one issue however, humankind's words. At times, you have no words to use to provide knowledge. Energy to energy thought communication would be your best safety line. Learn how to use it.

T: Wait, I feel like I am in a science course. Am I already starting school? I haven't been born yet. Can't it wait 'till then? You seem more in a hurry than I do. What's the hurry? Anyway, you're doing most of the talking. Let's talk less and move more.

UC: We are arriving at the dimension of Spark Energy. As we said before, the connection has been made. It's a no-effort communication. Stay away from deliberation. What she says is, that's it. Listen closely. Our connection is with the memory of the Spark's energy. This is where its knowledge will be. Once you meet, the connection is all yours. You are on your own and already known. Once we enter, it's an energy-to-energy meeting. Make your greeting. Ask for what you are needing.

T: Will going into the Spark memory affect my reality? Will it develop me? Add to my energy?

I believe that's what learning is all about, isn't it? I need New Realizations. New Awakenings. I want to develop my energy perception to its fastest frequency. Knowledge from the Spark and the First Conscious Cell will give my energy this ability.

UC: When you enter into the energy of anyone's memory, it will affect your own. Some memories bring out the emotions of Sadness, Anger, Victimization, Love, Friendship, Hurt feelings, and Envy. It will look like things are off balance. Stay focused on what you want to say. The Spark will recognize your energy and understand why you are there.

T: I know that Consciousness creates, but when I am creating, is it me, or are you creating? Where is my individuality? Is it in what I create as an image of my Consciousness? Is this individuality? What I create is what I create. What you create, is what you create, like humankind. But we still share the same creative abilities, Consciousness Energy. Then it doesn't matter who creates. It matters what we create.

Is the Virus Cell one cell, like you? I should ask the First Conscious Cell this question at my reception. I can start with, *"I need directions."* That's a terrible hello. How about, *"Hi, how are you?"* Will this do?

UC: What are you trying to do? Practice an introduction. Really!? You are Consciousness Energy. You are felt by all of creation. You don't need an introduction. You have been made aware that you are expected.

T: Is the goal of the virus energy, to split humans apart? I am sure it had something to do with the start of humanity. Is this the primary purpose of the Evolution Revolution, to stop the Virus Energy Cell from infecting?

UC: Not to stop, to convert. The Virus must become aware of its actions in order to be converted into balanced energy. But it has been using mostly fear, to keep people from objecting. Creating an economy dependent on money, caused your best friend to become your enemy. Humankind is co-dependent on money worldwide. Money is humanity's groom and bride. Fear depends on their insecurity over money.

T: Is the Spark aware of how the Virus Cell became an infection? Oh Yeah, you said, the First Conscious Energy Cell would have that explanation. Are we there yet? I am feeling the pull towards the tunnel again. We have to move. I am in a hurry. I have a date with an energy.

UC: Being in a hurry will only slow you down. It makes you unbalanced. Hurry means going ahead of yourself. You must stay in your body, this the whole point, otherwise you are a walking empty shell. No wonder humankind is always running into each other, whether walking or driving.

T: Was it just an instant combustion or an actual spark that lit the fire? Is that what happened? A tremendous explosion of some kind. Humans seem to think so. They call it the Big Bang. This means we don't know. I have the Consciousness to understand your creation now. I may need it one day. Where will you be? Will I be on my own?

UC: We will be by your side, as your energy. So you are correct in saying that you are on your own. It's your experience to have. The last part of your energy formulation. The rest of your education will be on Earth. Now we are coming near to the spark. She is not happy with humans at this time. Tread lightly. This is just a reminder that it is a she; address her as such. She doesn't get many visitors.

T: Is she still in touch? Up to date? It has been a few thousand millenniums you know. I need accurate information, if the Energy Evolution Revolution is to succeed. Hmm, I wonder if the Virus Energy, is in touch with today's society.

UC: The Virus Energy IS today's society. You know better than most. It's still close for you. So now, It's time. If you have any questions, you can ask her. This is as far as we go. Watch what you say, she is related to the Earth you know. There is no match for the spark, she is one of a kind.

Spark is just a term humankind uses. It awakened the Universal Consciousness in the same way that a shock brings the heart back to life. But it was a spark that triggered the shock. The first realization is self-realization. Consciousness is the first realization. Now go ahead and meet with her. Oh, no jokes.

T: Okay, I want to hear about the connection between the Virus Cell and Universal Consciousness. What do I say? I don't want to stutter. I am getting focused, clear, and ready to move. Okay, good pep talk.

UC: As an energy, are you sure you are fully conscious? Don't regress and start talking out loud. She doesn't talk out loud; she is an Energy, and you are meeting her on her own ground. Just visualize your question; she will see it.

T: Here I go. Contact! I am entering her energy thoughts slowly. Almost face to face. You know what I mean.

PART FOUR: THE SPARK

T: As I entered, I said to myself, It sure is dark here. *"You gotta match?"* Oops, This is an energy connection. I hope it didn't hear that match crack. Hello Spark, I came to ask you about the creation of the Creator. What happened to cause the first cell to lose its balance? And, are you aware of how the Universal Consciousness energy is connected to the Virus Energy Cell? You are the creator of the Creator, are you not? I am aware that you are called the Spark, but there has to be more to you than being a pilot light. Sorry, I am just being honest and also curious.

S: Yes, I know. But first, let's address your first concern. It's not dark in here; it's your perception that dimmed the light. You are aware of your energy; why are you not glowing? Is there something you are not showing? I can see your light protruding. Why are you holding it in? Do you need an energy transfusion? Relax, I don't bite. In spite of what the UC says. So, your question, of what happened to cause the first cell to lose its balance? Is best described by the First Conscious Energy Cell. What I can tell you is, it was a catastrophe like no other.

T: My energy is vibrating. I seem to be going back and forth between two realities. This one, and the one taking me back to Earth. Here is my story. I have to learn to be a Consciousness Energy, just to become physical energy. How is this universal justice? I am an energy, being formulated, to be reborn into physical life. I am in between lives. It's part of why I am here, trying to understand before I land.

S: How did the UC convince you to do this mission? You didn't win the lottery, if that's what you are thinking. I am the spark that ignited the energy that gave birth to Consciousness. I shocked it into awakening. However, I did not create the ingredients that went into creating the Universal Consciousness. We can go as far as how the Creator was created. What created me to shock Consciousness to life? Well, that's for another book. Why do you need this information? What are you going to do with it?

T: Use it to convert the Virus Energy Cell on Earth. There is an energy movement starting, and I need to get moving. So whatever knowledge you have, would be an asset to my energy development. Any energy improvement will be of help. I will take what I learn and share it with the rest of the people, in the energy movement..

S: You have exemplary dedication, especially with your position. I don't know whether to say congratulations or sorry for your reincarnation. Back to our discussion. What else can I help you with? What other questions do you have? You must be full of them. I will give you what else I know, depending on your questions.

T: You must know what the Universal Consciousness Energy doesn't know. If I may say so? You were there first; who else would know? Were you conscious of your energy during your spark? Were you aware that you were about to create a Creator? Where did you come from? Why did the Virus Energy Cell turn against physical humankind?

Is there anything you can share with me? I need to know the whole plan. I used to hear, *"no one knows the answer to the creation of the creator."* People still kept asking. I kept wondering. Now, I have the opportunity as an energy to learn the untold answers. If you have them that is.

When I return, I need to stay aware of what I learn, about the virus energy. It's part of humanities illusion. Humans don't take it lightly, when you question their belief system. They become like the Virus energy, defensive, aggressive, and go into denial. Anyway, let's go back to the discussion at hand. Another question for you to add to the others? How are the Universal Consciousness Energy and the Virus Energy Cell connected?

S: So you want to know about the creation of Consciousness. This is the reason for your appearance, isn't it? The explanation to the Creator of creation is still in contemplation, but it's part of your energy education. So I will give you some of what you need, from what I know. In the beginning, the Universal Consciousness Energy became unbalanced, when humankind went unconscious and denied its reality. Why it happened is the knowledge you need to get from the First Conscious Energy Cell. They denied their existence by continuing to deny the existence of The Universal Consciousness Energy. The Virus Energy Cell, as part of the Universal Consciousness Energy, is now on a mission to find out where it belongs.

This is where the physical energy movement comes into play. To confront it and convert it to a balanced energy. Putting humanity in the energy conversion process will convert the Virus Energy Cell. As long as humans do not participate, the Virus continues to live. It's not intentionally bad; its nature is to find the rest of itself. It's lost, confused, and defensive. Upon its separation from the consciousness energy, it developed what humankind would call, a form of unconsciousness. This energy separation caused it to lose its direction, along with, losing sight of its original perception of creating. It did the opposite, uncreated. Whatever the Universal Consciousness formed, the virus energy cell tried to take apart. The battle of good and bad, began. The right and wrong, that left no one, right or wrong. Just gone.

This was an energy form of separation. It became Unbalanced in all ways. No matter the matter. It was going after, the creation of the creator, the Universal Consciousness. It felt incomplete. It continues to lash out at humankind. Many dimensions of the UC have been invaded by the Virus Energy Cell, including the spiritual and physical energies. It was missing a part of its creation. In an attempt to find it, it became violent and aggressive. It was a split body. The waist down, is out looking for its waist up.

S: It wants to become a whole body again. The Universal Consciousness, needs the Virus Energy Cell, as much as the Virus needs the UC. They were both a whole part of the same energy. The First Conscious Energy Cell can tell you how all this happened. She can share with you what happened during the creation of the Universal Consciousness. How the Virus Cell separated, why it separated, where it went, and why it became destructive. The goal of conversion has one main purpose, to merge the Virus Energy Cell back with the Consciousness Energy; and to restore the energy balance of humanity. The First Conscious Energy Cell played a huge role in the creation process. When my spark lit the fire, I couldn't see a thing from the flash. By then, the vortex took everything for a spin. Next thing I know, as you put it, I am a pilot light for the Universal Consciousness Energy. We have gathered with the UC to make sure you succeed. I am sure that the First Conscious Energy Cell can give you more. She is next on your visitation tour.

T: Why the First Conscious Energy Cell? Your spark created this Cell, didn't it? Wasn't the Universal Consciousness the first Energy Cell?

S: Yes it was. We have been talking about her for a time now. Pay attention. It's the First Conscious Energy Cell! It knows it all. What you need to know about the Virus Energy, she can tell you. There is your connection between the two. The UC and the First Conscious Energy Cell, are the same energy. Sharing the same memory. So, she has more knowledge than I. She knows more about the Virus Cell creation than I.

The Missing Link

T: Hmm, didn't the UC realize the extent of damage, this cell would do inside our anatomy. It's obviously an abnormal cell. This is the reason, I need to learn more about it. To learn to recognize it faster. Now it has infected humanity with the need for greed. Using persuasion and domination. It must be converted.

S: The Virus Energy cell kept humans separated. This was their problem. It created, an everyone for themselves attitude. Behaviors changed. This is why the UC energy must enter the human body. Once it does. It will convert this Virus Energy from inside. Where the Virus Energy Cell resides. If everyone allowed this, we wouldn't have to chase it down. Its pattern, is to always run. It convinced humanity, it was their creator. They believed it. Planet Earth, became its heaven. It protected it. Humankind was manipulated by it. It has lived in humans since time began, which brings us to the present moment.

S: Everything was being done to connect with it. The Evolution Revolution is the finale attempt. There is no other place for it to run. Its made the Earth its home. Humankind is not that old of a creation. It wasn't until the Universal Consciousness Energy, formed itself into mass, did we noticed the energy cell disconnection.

T: Okay, thank you. This certainly has been a learning experience. It has changed my perception of the Virus Cell. Thank you. You have opened my consciousness to a new approach to the virus. I can't treat it like a disease. It's not a physical disease. It's an out of control energy cell, wanting to become well. It sits in the brain because, this is where most of humanities feeling are. Peoples emotions are losing their feelings.

It's called a Virus, due to the damage it does to humankind's life. Like any other Virus humans creates. I am glad that I got this clear. It's just a lost energy cell, interfering with our thoughts, because, it's the only way it knows to communicate. Just like the humans, they lash at others, when they are angry and hurt.

UC: That was excellent knowledge you just received. You see what realizations do. They awaken you to another you, that's development, changing perceptions to a Conscious direction. With this in mind, you can take this knowledge to the others who are awakened.

This is what we meant by learning. Getting to know the Virus, will help you decrease the humans fears about being infected. When you allow others to control what you think, that's an infection. Humankind lives this way everyday. Greed is the worst part of the Virus. This Virus affects what you think and how you feel.

T: The Virus Energy Cell is part of you. We have to help it. It's in humankind; it's going to be difficult to get it to respond to support, kindness, or trust. That's it; we have to get it to trust us. We shall do no harm. We will only Convert. This will be the message, I will carry to the energy movement. It will empower them all. The Virus is an energy, and we shall convert it to its natural balanced self.

UC: We were looking for the Virus Cell to reconnect it, to the consciousness energies. We view it as a creation of the Universal Consciousness, just as humankind views their own children.

T: What are you expecting now? You obviously have a view into the upcoming events. Will the energy movement succeed? Will the evolution revolution proceed? Will there be a new direction? I am Consciousness Energy; why can't I see the same thing you see? Are we in different dimensions? I thought that I had developed to your ability. But it seems there is still more development to go.

UC: Development does not stop. It depends on what you make happen. Without feeding the baby, it has no chance to grow. Without development, the Universal Consciousness won't have the opportunity to grow. The First Conscious Energy Cell will share the rest. This is not about doing your best; it's about turning over its nest and still treating it like a guest. The most challenging part of all is to keep from reacting to a Virus's verbal assault. It's famous for destroying the energy of self-esteem.

T: Question: Will humans be able to understand your meanings? Understand your feelings? Will humankind comprehend the Universal Consciousness cycle of creation? Will reading this Evolution Revolution book, be enough to encourage humans to take a look at giving back what they took from the Earth, and from each other.

UC: Humankind needs to understand that Consciousness Energy will depend on your presentation. By you, we mean all of humanity. Not just you. Different perception reflect different ideas. This is why, when you ask, you will get one perception. When you don't understand it, ask for another perception.

Information gets passed through the vibration and is absorbed by the Consciousness Energy of another vibration. That's how Energy Vibrations learn from each other. Humankind does it every day, but they don't recognize what it is. It's taken for granted. Vibrations are Consciousness Energy connected from Energy Cell to Energy Cell. They record it all. They contain a library of knowledge from the Universal Consciousness.

Which brings us to the Missing Link. By now, you must be aware that it's not the Consciousness Energy. The Missing Link is a connection link between the Universal Consciousness and humankind. The missing link is partly responsible for the imbalance of physical energy. The rest of it is about humanity. It was your responsibility also. You allowed it to steal humankind's realization. The MISSING LINK is the Virus Energy Cell.

T: Are we there yet? Where is the First Conscious Energy Cell? Thanks for that update, but I am ready to go meet her. Are you stalling so you can keep talking? Doesn't what you talk about move you? It certainly moves me. Is movement, inspired by words or by action?

UC: The reason we are moving is because our talking is creating. As long as it is, you're on your way back to Earth. The First Conscious Energy Cell is around the corner. Not far, and no, we do not stall. We learn as we go. The way you need to be learning. You don't need to stand in one spot to learn. How can you learn anything new when you're in the same spot? You don't think this way anymore. Even if you think you have stopped, your energy is still moving. It's your perception of stopping that allows you to think and feel like you have stopped. Remember, your perception creates your reality.

PART FIVE: THE FIRST CONSCIOUS ENERGY CELL

T: That was another good pep talk, thanks. Can we go now? I can feel the First Conscious Energy Cell. She is waiting for me. How long before we reach her? At this speed, she will give birth before we get there. I suppose you're use to having others wait for you…Oh oh, where did that come from? I am fluctuating again. I sound like a human.

UC: You do sound human. Stop with the flashbacks. Realize this, no one waits for Consciousness. It's already there. That is the reason, humankind is alive. By the way, save the humor for your trip back. You're going to need it, to make friends as you grow up. All the knowledge you have now, will grow with you. After all, we are speaking about the total awakening of humankind. You will need all the help you can find.

T: Apparently, I made a commitment. Besides, you said I would have my family: my brain, my conscience, and the voice of the Universal Consciousness Energy. I can figure out any solution. What could go wrong?

UC: Distraction by seduction is what can go wrong. It comes in many forms. Never underestimate the Virus Cell Seduction. It has its own agenda. It gets what it wants by offering you something you can't resist. There isn't much that humans can resist. Most of you have the power of seduction. We call it a power because, it can instantly change your mind. It can take your money while you're looking at it. It can make you do things you would never do. Do you still think that nothing can go wrong? It's about self-satisfaction for seduction.

T: Is this a test question? Isn't it too late for a test? I am about to be sent back, why the test, I'm Consciousness Energy, I don't need a test? Consciousness has given me a pass. I have already graduated. No tests are necessary.

UC: Every question is a test question. You have to be clear, with your ability for conscious energy absorption. You must make sure you can tell, what both energies feel like. You don't want to absorb the wrong one. It's happened before, this is serious. Thus, the issue with distraction. It will come at you from different directions. Don't sweat from fear. The Virus can smell it. When learning is your intention, Consciousness is your protection. Just a suggestion, use a conscious perception in all your actions, and your actions will come out conscious.

Never TELL a human anything, just ASK them. Otherwise, you get the blame. When the attempt fails, you're the one walking on nails. Never speak of anything you know nothing about. When you want to show them the Consciousness reality, express yours only. Be the example. It's that simple. It's walking the walk from day one. It must be more action than talk. Your experiences will have much to say when there time comes.

Let nature take its course and raise you to be what you are. Those who raise you will be infected by the Virus Cell. You will have to convert your own energy once you're an adult, before the movement. You're not going back for your amusement. Reality, is as serious as it gets. You must convert the Virus Energy where it sits. Anyone you come in contact with, will feel the attraction to your energy.

T: Oh great, first it's no romance in school, now, I have energy that will attract. This is really too much UC, how fair is this? How am I suppose to keep them away? You want to try it? Then, I have a physical energy conversion to look forward to. OK, come on. I am going there to help them, why am I being punished?

After all that let down, I am nervous to ask. What part of the world are you dropping me off in? Is it the same one I lived in before? Wouldn't that cause me to have more flashbacks? It's better if I am born somewhere I don't recognize. I want to go where I have never been before.

Why waste a trip? It's a good idea, don't you think?

UC: We think that you think too much. So, you want to go to a place you've never been? THINK? You just did. In fact, you are still there. You are going where you will make the most significant impact, to a country not so intact. In fact, it's completely packed. You'll hardly be noticed. It will allow you to get a head start on the Energy Movement, by gathering the young generation, as others before are doing. We are aware that you cannot do this alone, and you will not. There is no stopping you and the others from starting it. *"BE THE SPARK."* Make buttons and cards to hand out to people. Make yourself available. Everyone wants to be a spark. Make it your stand.

T: Where will I, make the most impact? Isn't this a worldwide event? What country would be the most responsive to this knowledge? Will other awakened people find me? Who will I connect with, to start this instigation of the Virus Energy? How will we be able to tell who is committed or not, converted or not? Who do I connect with first?

UC: Everyone. The Atheist and the Realist, the Scientist and the Defeatist, the Leftist and the Rightist, the Communist and the Religious, the Racist and the Capitalist. The Pacifist and the Warmonger. That just about covers it. No one is excluded.

T: There are probably many more. Now, there is the matter of completing my development. I would like to know how far we are. We must be close now. I can feel her. This is getting really close to my birth, isn't it UC? I feel a pull in another direction. It's not strong, just a tiny tug.

UC: We are nearing The First Consciousness Energy Cell. You are about to enter into another dimension. To explore the knowledge of this Energy cell, there, you can learn as much as you want. Until the tug turns into a pull, and it will. You could be in the middle of learning, absorbing, growing, and asking. It could happen anytime. So focus your questions on what you need for the Virus Energy conversion.

T: This should be an adventure. Why couldn't you just tell me all this, UC? Why the mystery? Why the journey and all the visits to history? Is it so I don't miss anything? I am Consciousness Energy. Can I still miss things?

UC: What do you call all those realizations you had, before you had them? They were missing. Telling you doesn't create you; it just tells you. When you have the experience yourself, then there are no words necessary. When you are looking to learn. You develop through the experience of learning. It's what moves your energy. Movement is development. Telling, is not the same as asking. Because a question, is what brings the answer to you.

T: Going into a Consciousness Energy cell, is not something I do every day. But neither is this journey. I have discovered a life that exists after death. It makes humanity's meaning of death, meaningless. It actually makes most of humanity's beliefs meaningless. Not to be rude. Wait? I take that back, I wasn't being rude, I was telling the truth. I don't need to say anything to make others feel better. Why do we apologize for the truth?

UC: Because the truth hurts, and people don't like feeling pain. Well, some people do. It's the idea of

The Missing Link

having a hole in your heart, when a loved one dies. This is a painful physical feeling. Imagine, as an energy, you were once WHOLE, then suddenly you have a HOLE. By testing of your nuclear bombs, this is what humans are doing to the Universal Consciousness Energy.

Death is a limited perception for most people. Once you are conscious, you are unlimited in your ability to create. Go find out, this is your experience. Get moving, are you in a trance? You need to advance. What are you waiting for? This is your only chance. You need this last realization before your reincarnation. It will prepare you for the Evolution Revolution. Just go in and speak with the FCEC, before you feel the pull from the energy.

T: OK, here I go…Phew, it's hot in here. Hello! It's me. I came by way of the UC. It said you would be aware of my visit. I am a developing energy, on my way to my reincarnation. I was sent by the Spark. She told me, you could possibly have the answers to my questions. These are my questions. How are you connected to the UC?

How was the Virus Energy Cell created? What happened? Why did it happen? How? When? And Where? How were you created? I am aware that cells constantly divide in the physical body, so, are conscious energy cells similar to the body's anatomy cells? If you don't mind, can you start from the beginning.

FCEC: Not similar, the same. The only difference is, the speed of movement. One energy is composed of physical mass. And the other, is an energy cell. Two different frequencies, but the same energy. You have been traveling with the UC, you must've learned something about its creation? Answering your questions will require you to use your imagination. The Universal Consciousness Energy, is not simple to explain in physical words.

Visualization, is best in this conversation. You must be able to see what I am describing. Let's begin. Here is what you need to know. The Universal Consciousness Energy (UC), was instigated to awaken, by the energy of the Spark. As far as where the Spark came from, is for another time. Today we are focusing on the Consciousness Energy, and how it created from itself life. Along with, the history of the Virus Energy Cell.

"LIFE- THE FIRST CONSCIOUSNESSES"

From its first awakening, it began to go through a type of energy metamorphosis. As it realized itself, it began to divide and develop into cells...Energy Cell. With each cell having a consciousness energy in its center, holding it together, and to divide it when its time came. Similar to the physical body and its atom. These energy cells were able to divide into other cells just like them. This is how the Consciousness Energy grew to be what it is, The UC. It also realized its ability to create frequencies of energy. It began to create frequency after frequency, until we arrived to the frequency of humanity. The physical mass energy.

These self realized, intelligent Cells were formed with the same ability for development and growth, as the Universal Consciousness. These Energy Cells, as they grew and develop into more Consciousness Energies became what we now know as life, in all its frequencies, dimensions, shapes and sizes. Imagine all those energy cells, there is no number which can count them, developing on what they create and feeding it back to their source, the UC.

As for me. I was the first consciousness Energy Cell. I saw it all happen. So, what created the physical frequency? It all started with me, the First Universal Consciousness Energy Cell.

As Physical Mass was being formed, planets and stars began to flourish. The planets, were created to nurture and provide for the physical human. In return, the human would be responsible for being the caretakers of their planet. They will live in harmony with their planet. They will keep it alive.

From the perception of the UC, this Evolutionary Mass Energy Creation was developing well, and maintaining a consciousness state. Humans started out as Conscious physical energy, capable of developing their own energy, by using what they see, hear, feel, touch and smell. All the senses were created in humans, to help with Consciousness Energy Development.

It was during the early stage, in the physical creation process, when something went wrong. A human creation was almost complete and in the final phase of the incubation stage, when one conscious cell, separated from its natural flow before its completion, and went the opposite direction, against the flow. Splitting away from its molecular and cellular structure. It became an unbalanced and incomplete energy formulation, which became what we now call, the Virus Energy Cell.

This is what your role will be. You're the conversion part. As for my part, I am a Consciousness Energy Cell, a whole part of the universal consciousness energy. Where it's possible for me to share what I know from the UC vibration. The UC could have given you this information, but, it would benefit you more, when you ask questions from different sources. The same questions you will be asked when you go back. Here are three. How was the UC created? What makes it a creator? And what led up to the creation of the Virus Energy Cell?

T: I am absorbing everything you are saying. This is amazing information. It will complete my transformation and make me ready for my reincarnation. I can feel the pull getting stronger, as we speak.

FCEC: You should be aware that the Virus Cell, knows who and what you are. It's aware of the plan to create an energy Evolution Revolution. Be aware and alert for the energy of persuasion. It will keep knocking. Lead a movement of leaders. It will keep all of you from harm.

T: If I am to understand, Consciousness, became Conscious, when a spark was ignited? What created the spark to create Consciousness? Life creates life. Is what I am hearing you say?

FCEC: The eternal question is, what created the Spark to create Consciousness? Focus on what you need to do. What happens to Consciousness Energy is not all on you. The responsibility lies with physical humankind and their response to the Evolution Revolution. When humanity awakens to the energy that created them, we will find out what created the Whole Energy.

Consciousness is an expanding web connecting to all creation in any form. What occurs here is felt there. Do not get caught up in humankind's labels, names, etc. They will limit your view of the truth. The truth is energy. When you remove the labels, you will be left with pure Consciousness Energy, that can regenerate itself into what it wants to be.

T: Can I ask you a question? Did you remember anything before the Spark? Did you see or feel anything at all?

FCEC: How can I remember, the Spark came first? We are all the Universal Consciousness Energy. That's why, on this journey, it was very important to know the Virus Energy history. Well, thanks for the company. The UC is calling you.

T: It is, I should thank you. What you gave to me was the most powerful tool I can use, on the Virus Energy Cell—COMMON SENSE. It will completely confuse it. Maybe it will turn on itself. We will see. Thank you for your information. It is very helpful and enlightening. It certainly has changed my perception. All humankind needs this awareness. Thanks, Energy Cell. See you next round.

Hey UC. This brings up a question, it's about the present. How can my present moment, connect with the present moment of physical energy, when it's not in the present? Humankind lives by the rules and laws of the past. Being in the present moment puts us on two different dimensions. I cannot go to the past and bring them to the present moment. Wouldn't this cause dangerous flashbacks?

UC: Who says you have to stay there? It's their past, not yours. You can't get stuck, even though your energy and theirs are related. Awareness is about being conscious, being in the present moment. So, you may have to go to the peoples past and bring them to your present. This is why you went on this journey, to get better acquainted with your destiny.

We transformed your energy into a Consciousness Energy vibration, to make sure that each time you travel through a dimension, you will come back through to your present moment. Yes, there will be a chance for a flashback, but only from a connection in your memory. You won't have a flashback from someone else's past.

The time is coming for the Young Generation to facilitate the movement towards the physical energy re-creation. With your power of intuitive awareness, and your knowledge of the Virus's existence, you know more about it than it knows about you. You possess the ability to sense those infected by it. Many of the young generation have it. You can use it to convert the Virus Cell infection in humans. Be ready with your power of conversion. Use your Consciousness, and never miss the Virus.

T: I understand, that this is the final joining of the UC Energy, with the Virus Energy Cell. I am ready to make it happen. I am starting to feel heavier. Is my frequency slowing down? Is it time? I hope I don't drown in the birthing process or get stuck somewhere. Make it a rich hospital UC. I would get better treatment there. The slower my energy frequency becomes, the funnier I sound.

UC: Last reminder. You are no longer a singular body. You will all share the same weight. It's called balance. Consciousness is an energy life force. You will be full of it. It's the reason you breathe. Without it, you will need a gas mask. It's an unhealthy environment on Earth. As long as there is little progress towards energy growth, anyone could catch a Virus, especially during birth. Consciousness Energy, constantly creates fusion. It never stops moving. It's the cycle of your Energy Transfusion, which cleans out your Virus-created illusions.

Humankind, you have closed your eyes to your energy evolution. We are offering you a possible solution; Your brain is too small, its purpose is to keep growing by learning and developing. At first, the odds were that humanity would convert the Virus. Well, isn't it obvious? Creation is still waiting, and waiting. Will humans ever consider changing? Once the Virus Energy Cell was discovered in the consciousness energy frequencies, it was herded towards Earth, for its final conversion. We thought it to be a successful plan, to re-balance the Universal Consciousness Energy in physical creation.

T: So what happened? Did humanity lose sight of it? Why did they accept it? It must have offered something worthwhile to give it power over them. What could that be, I wonder? This inquiry helps me to understand humans a little more. What could have been so tempting? Why didn't they see it coming, feel it coming? You were aware it was approaching Earth. According to you, you were watching. How did it seduce humans on your watch?

UC: This plan, was the only way to create energy balance. Since it was headed to Earth anyway. How did it Seduce humans? They related with it. Then, THEY LET IT.

T: I can feel the pull much harder now. I am holding on. It must really be close. I could use a flashlight. Sorry, I am sure you have everything set up. Let's go.

UC: Are you ready to move on in the Universal Consciousness? You have a date with the Virus. Do you want to be Conscious and Aware, when the energy starts to move you towards your rebirth? Your life on Earth will have its ups and downs. It's the downs that you must turn up. The obstacles that will come your way, are but an illusion of the Virus Energy. Stay aware of this. Many visuals are not real in humanity. You will get close to many of the young generation. Create an evaluation to check each member for the Virus; be aware.

PART SIX: THE JOURNEY BACK

T: Okay, the journey back to Earth has begun. I will go with the flow. I will stay silent and unnoticed. I must remain focused on the road ahead. Where is the road ahead? Will I suddenly find myself there? Are you going to implant me, or do I go the usual route? If I am implanted, I don't have to race. I can be relaxed. It would make me a healthier adult. I would do better in school. I could become a world leader; who knows? With Consciousness Energy, anything is possible. I heard you did an implant before, so you can do it again, please.

UC: Where are you getting your information from? We have explained before, that you are being reincarnated. This means fully loaded, with a purpose. You will resolve as you evolve. All your needs have been preset and recorded in your energy vibration. It's all in there, including your destination. The energy is starting to rotate and begin the process of your physical evolution. It's developing and formulating your new energy of Consciousness including, your spiritual and physical energies.

T: Will I get sick from spinning? I get dizzy easily. Why don't you just implant me? It's better than the old fashioned way. I am already donating my whole life to humankind. No spinning. This is a lot to ask from someone. I give, and you want more. Wait!? What's happening to me, UC? This is way beyond energy fluctuation.

UC: You've been spinning for a while now. It's part of your return process. You are slowing down even more. We are still connected to your thoughts. We will be able to read them as you progress. Go with the Consciousness flow, not the Virus one.

Considering where you are going, we are very clear on how difficult this is. We do not underestimate the virus energy cell. Neither should you. Listen for the words its not saying, and feel for the feelings it's hiding. No matter who it is. As you start to remember. You will grow as you develop. Check your Awareness, constantly.

UC: The consciousness energy will be your space suit, while you are on Earth. You are still Consciousness Energy, you have a little physical memory. As this Energy, you will take what you have learned on this journey, and share it with the virus energy. Without it noticing you as a threat to its survival. Educate, deliberate. Only do it with a smile. Be as common as a human can be, until you become uncommon. The whole energy movement will become uncommon.

This is the point. Becoming different from the normal. As you have already experienced in your journey. Each time you discover new Consciousness knowledge, you will learn and grow. Only moving energy can teach you. Only Consciousness Energy can reach you. This is a natural progression towards humankind's evolution. Humans have been frozen in time, since time began. It's time to wind you up.

You are Consciousness Energy. OK, it seems you're thinking like a human. Just don't start feeling unwanted. There's nothing good there. It's because humans are unconscious that they act out of control. Control, could mean anything humans want it to mean, they gave it, its meaning. It's no different than putting a gun in your face. Or accuse you of being crazy because, you are different than others. Because, you think differently.

Yet, those same people become insulted, over names they call each other? This is more of a reflection of uncontrolled Virus behaviors. This is the point. Throwing out insulting words, only hurt those, who are doing the throwing. Humans need to have titles to make them feel superior. If humanity doesn't like their own meanings, it's up to them to change it.

Humans are standing on one line. Once in line, you can't turn around; there's no room. There are thousands of others behind you, and in front. You can stand in line forever, because most of you are asleep standing up. One way to move the line forward, is to wake everybody up. Using the power of Consciousness Energy.

T: This is a lot to put on any person's shoulders. I am going to be standing in the same line. This line example stumps me. How does one human awaken all of humanity, while standing on the same thin line? Am I going to fly? This would only be considered a magic trick. It may get me an applause. But that's about it.

UC: Yes, Great question. It baffles everyone. *"What can I do? I am just one person? How can I make a difference?"* These quotes are heard constantly by humans. When you don't have the knowledge to do it, how can you? Well, now you do. It's one plus one equals two. Two plus two equals four. Four plus four equals eight. Imagine the possibilities. They are endless, not helpless. The point is, someone has to be awake to awaken them. Whoever is awake holds the responsibility, otherwise, the line will never move. Remember, force creates force. Stay clear of this course. Power struggles are full of Manipulation Energy. There are reasons to feel sorry for humanity. Empathy is a good quality. But don't feel sorry, this is manipulation energy.

We are going to use humankind's theory of rotation and magnetization, to show you your transformation from one energy to another. Fill a bucket with water, start with a slow rotation, spinning it round and round, as you gradually increase the speed of the rotation. It causes the density of the water to become less dense and feel lighter. Its weight will equal that of the rotation speed. The water will not spill out when the rotation levels out at that speed. The speed of the rotation is what changes the density of the water to become lighter.

UC: Upon increasing the speed of Physical energy, the speed of physical matter transforms into a lighter density, rotation. You are the water in the bucket. You went for a faster spin. You became less dense. But, you are still the water. Only now, you are spinning at a faster rotation, than physical and ethereal speed of vibration. You are becoming Consciousness Energy in its purest form. The process works the same the other way. The faster the speed, the less density. As the speed slows down, the water becomes more dense, and it gets heavier, causing it to spill out at a slower rotation.

Did you understand all this? You have come full circle, traveler. Your time here is short. We are close to your new beginning.

Presently, the Virus Cell Energy exists only in the Physical Universe. Many universes are infinitely expanding, as Consciousness Energy continues to create. There are many species of life forms thriving in each Universe, with each, having the intention of helping humankind to change their direction. Consciousness Energy flow is a never-ending process of energy rotation, creating creation at many speeds. Forming each Universe into another Universe, into another, as the Universal Consciousness grows.

T: Am I supposed to be absorbing all this to take with me? If that's a yes? Oops!

UC: Yes, and pay attention. Remember, it's not a vacation. Your journey is about to begin, this one is done; go on, it's time to go swimming.

T: Wait! I thought you were implanting me. Come on, UC, it's not that easy of a swim. Didn't I tell you that I was afraid of water? I can't swim.

UC: Don't worry, you won't feel a thing. Your place in line has already been reserved. It's part of a planned reincarnation. All you need is already in your vibration.

T: A couple more questions, and I am on my way. Who should I make contact with first? This knowledge needs to be in classrooms. Will I have help to make this happen?

UC: You will meet with the free thinkers, the lost, and those who have been abandoned. As far as this knowledge goes yes, by the time you are of age, they will be looking for you. To make it happen you must become a teacher.

T: Hey, that's a great idea. Teaching! Now I feel more confident. It definitely needs to be taught in schools. I think I will go to college and get my teaching degree. Once I'm in, I will find a way to include all this energy in my curriculum.

UC: what's your reaction to an out of control student, who refuses to follow directions? How will you handle the fallout?

T: Like I have done with myself; Re-group, Re-view, Re-evaluate, Re-educate and Re-focus on a New 'Awareness'. A New Plan, and try it again. This journey was one of a kind, that's for sure. I am not sure if I should thank you or not. I will wait to see where you put me. Thank you for my Consciousness Energy awareness. I will not fail. Well, UC, I feel the pull; see you on the other side. Thanks for the ride.

UC: You are the Universal Consciousness Energy. Your goal...The awakening of the Young Generation and the implementation of the Evolution Revolution.

PART SEVEN: THE FLOWER

UC: Humanity! The seed has been planted. It's coming to its final growth. There is no way to stop this Flower of Truth from growing. Here are her own words:

F: I represent life, through my awareness and consciousness of creation. Life has come to life, to ensure that life continues to live. These revelations are here to clarify humankind's physical existence. I am a creation of the Universal Consciousness Energy. I am here to offer change to humanity.

I am a flower who used to be a weed, until I learned my lesson. I have been with humankind for most of their lives. They tried to kill me with their chemicals, but I fought to come back to life. The chemicals were not strong enough. They tried to cut my head off, but they didn't cut me all the way; I grew back in one day. Then, humanity tried to mow me down with their mower; only my leaves were crushed, and they protected me. My seeds went into the soil, some stayed alive, and I grew back.

You tried to pull me out by my roots but didn't get all of them. They grew another stem, and here I am. You built a house on me, but I grew through the cracks. The only thing you can do now, is go out and build me a garden where I can fit. One big enough for me to grow, so all my flowers can show. Now there are more flowers because, each time you destroyed one flower, you created eight. You spread my seeds everywhere. Your whole house is now full of flowers. There is very little you can do about it. Start building the garden.

علي

The Missing Link

Religion: Fact Or Fiction?

UC: UNIVERSAL CONSCIOUSNESS

R: RELIGION.

UC: This is a view of religion from a reflective position. This is not a crucifixion of religion; it's an identification of religion from a different perspective. Take your time; there is no immediate decision. It's just a question: Is it Fact or Fiction? This is the discussion. It's about the clarity of a new vision. There are as many different perspectives as there are people in the world. This has caused confusion between belief systems. Who is right, who is not? The intention of this writing is to increase Consciousness all around and open your mind to a different sound. There is always something worth learning from what you know.

Those who may be offended by this, please read to the end so you can understand the message it sends. It's awakening humanity to religion and its effect on YOU, the Human.

There are many religions that think they are right, but they have lost sight and continue to fight. Over what, the deliverer? Religion took a completed puzzle, turned it over, and has been trying to put it back together since they got it. They threw away the picture it came with. They had nothing to compare. Many pieces were missing, lost, or thrown away. Now, it's just a part of a puzzle, put together with the pieces left by those who threw away the only picture. Most of humanity agreed on believing in the same God, so why are there religious wars? The fight is about something other than the deliverer, it's more about the ego of who is right. Is the ego worth dying over?

Those who follow certain religions are being used to gather followers. This may sound drastic, but then, why are they recruiting? Not all, but many do. It depends on your religion. But isn't gathering followers a form of recruitment? What else can it mean?

Organized religions, need to recognize that their ability to explain God, can't happen without the use of blind faith. Why do humans turn their power over to the unknown, while they have a fear of the unknown? Religion has not shown that their God really exists. It's a self-based belief, grown on the unknown.

The answers are limited, and faith is used as an excuse for your actions. Humans call this redemption. You have to ask yourself, *"Are you believing in a God or the words of religion?"* If God is personal for all, then why does humanity need religion, to tell them how to communicate with their God? It's personal. You have the same connection. Their action is short on action and long on words. No one needs to go through religion to know what humans call God. You don't need to believe in Universal Consciousness Energy, just get to know it. It gave you life as an Energy Being.

God does not get you a job, a new car, a new house, or more money. It doesn't get you out of trouble, keep you safe, or give you happiness and love. It doesn't cure depression unless you meet it halfway. God doesn't favor one human over the other. A God doesn't make promises. Helping yourself means, you are independent, from the dependency of depending on others. This is not to say you can't ask for help. Others will be quick to help those who are helping themselves, as long as they are willing to work on it.

UC: How often do you get an answer when you ask for material items? Do you actually wait? Are you still waiting? God doesn't do these things, because humankind was created with the ability and confidence to do it for themselves, using Consciousness Energy. Not to depend on a God, luck, or wishes to provide.

There is no one true religion, that's why humanity is fighting. Why can't they combine the religions into one UNDERSTANDING, and form new ideas of what the creator can be, and come from another perception besides humanity's. We are not discussing the kind acts religious followers achieve, just the belief itself. In hopes of seeing those same followers, accomplish the same good deeds without the reward of going to heaven. Because, it's about living.

Many humans have become disillusioned with the same old traditions. They are losing their meaning. It's how religion is being presented. Greed has infested Religion since its beginning. Greed couldn't just have one; it started as one religion, but, where did the rest come from? One guess: humanities confusion. The disillusioned followers. Humans are repeating their history. You are still working on the same puzzle. Try finding the missing pieces; then, you will get the whole picture.

When humanity couldn't find answers, they, along with their followers, created their own Religions Most of them just followed the rules of those religions, and were not allowed to ask questions of the religious leaders.

Does Freedom of Religion mean, creating your own when you disagree? Religion, has only managed to create separation. It became, *"CREATE YOUR OWN BECAUSE, THE OTHERS ARE WRONG."* You have only created a population where everyone believes they are right.

The word God, is just another label for Consciousness Energy, except without the Consciousness. Religion, Fact or Fiction? Everyone must have an opinion. No one is wrong or right in this discussion. Only your feelings about what is being said and where you are being led that matters.

So, the questions still remain, Who is to be believed? What is to be believed? Why should it be believed? What holds the truth, hidden behind all the lies?

The Universal Consciousness Energy, can answer the questions that religion can't. This energy is the key that humanity will one day find. With consciousness, there is nothing to believe. Just believing, is not a good way to find out. Why? Just believing, leads to blind faith.

In the beginning, the ending was never a consideration. Humans lived for creation. Their focus was on developing their energy vibration. They used their imagination. Created their own heaven on Earth. This is where heaven has always been. It's been covered over by what humanity calls, progress.

Humans have always been willing, kind, and giving. They never heard of killing. Humans had nothing to fear, had never shed a tear, and were aware of their Creator. They were much braver and had never met a stranger. They had the planet Earth; they had self-worth since the beginning of birth.

The Earth? It is a spectacular energy creation, unlike any other. A wonder of the Physical Universe. It is a most beautiful creation by an amazing Consciousness Energy Creator. The Earth gives of itself and donates to humanity's survival. Its natural beauty is beyond imagination. The planet Earth has provided humankind with protection, nutrition, and the ability to function. Humans can breathe, because of trees and flowers of every kind, which are beautifully designed by the beyond. You need to use the energy from your Consciousness to keep humanity alive. It's a self-sustainable planet that made humanity, as self-sufficient as they can be.

UC: Today, humans are not the same; life has changed, Religion hasn't. OK, they are allowing women to preach. What took so long? Who made the rule that they couldn't? Would humanity's God say they couldn't? The Universal Consciousness wouldn't. Without knowing the energy flow that helps them grow, humans will continue to row BACKWARDS! Would humanity like a motor for their nearly sinking boat? You haven't paddled very far. Religion has had humanity paddling in the same direction for hundreds of years. It's the Syndrome of the lost following the lost. Religious leaders, can only tell you, what they think they know, and what was written two thousand years ago. You have thrown yourself into woe, over what you think you know. The realization is, Religions don't know either. Now they are stuck in what they know, with nothing to show. Way to go!

Have you even discovered, your own mystery from history? Why is it a mystery? Take the story of the Resurrection of the Spirit. Is it a fact, or isn't it? Was this story exact? Who is around today to prove it? How are you to know, unless you lived two thousand years ago. You really can't say you know. It's a theory of an event that humans couldn't understand even then. We have brought you one explanation.

What really happened? What's the real story of Religion? Where is the truth? An actual true testimony? If there is, let humanity see it. Why should scrolls of history be hidden from humanity? They are records, not secrets. Can Religion answer this honestly? Why hasn't faith in religion converted the energies of Greed, Control, and Fear? As far as a real effect on your lives, they are more real than your God. They are clearly affecting you more.

This is why religion always puts it in the HANDS OF GOD. You put everything you can't face in the hands of God, and then when this doesn't work for you, You blame that same God. Was this the reason you put it in God's hands? So you can have someone to blame for your choices? Your Choice, your Consequences. It's called Natural Balance.

What is illusion, and what is reality? Is your reality is your illusion? Your brain says it's real because it's infected. So how can your reality be an illusion? If we ask religion, they would say, our reality is our own. It's called faith.

Humankind is composed of a Consciousness Energy formulation. It's pure energy. Energy creates energy in its own image—the image of Consciousness. Humans needs to ask more questions. You are not all followers. Some of you are martyrs. What about the others? Who is the joiner, and who isn't? Is it by choice, or does the needs of the many outweigh the needs of the few? Isn't this the humans motto? What happens to the few? Are they left to perish? If the many are being helped, why can't you help the few? Find a way if you have to. After all, they are human, just like you.

UC: Humans, have the ability to use logic, common sense, intelligence, and wisdom. Yet, they continue to ignore ignorance, deny defiance, and avoid the obvious? Humanity remains unconscious, relying on the religious alliance for their deliverance.

What is it that gives you assurance? Religion has failed to do so, or you wouldn't still be waiting. If the Earth needed saving, it would be now. Instead of waiting, do something. There is power in numbers. Humans know this. Your military is one example.

How can violence not be a religious issue? How can war not be their issue? It seems that religion has no issues. How can they work for God? They are in denial. Your God can see what's happening; why can't his employees do the same? Get involved in more than just praying. Go into action. You are asking your

Religion: Fact Or Fiction?

god to. Why don't you?

UC: The corporations of Religion, have the truth about history. They hide it from humanity. They can't afford to create doubt in their followers. They will be out of a job. Well, this is what's happening these days. Faith in God can be achieved, by a personal experience that changes your life. How many young children truly understand your holy books? How many continue to use it as they get older?

Humans had to break them down into fairytale. By doing that, you convoluted the truth, leaving them with only your interpretation. Don't you see, you are creating followers from children, Leaving them with no imagination, only your rules, threats, and obeying God's laws. Many humans are putting the fear of their God, into their children to control them, just like they were controlled as children. The cycle continues to destroy your awareness and freedom of choice. History was never meant to be repeated. Unfortunately, humans have been convinced otherwise. The cracks are showing. People are falling, governments are stalling, and religion is hiding.

The formation of organized religion, created many believers with many perceptions. Many of them contradicted each other. Each religion, has their own deliverer who they made their God. So, how many physical beings who delivered Consciousness meanings are there? From this view, there are very few. The Universal Consciousness is not just one body; it is composed of all humanity, therefore, it's everyone. There is no favoritism. It's a Balanced Energy Creator. It doesn't distinguish between better or best. It continuously creates and lets you do the rest.

You have the ability to create what you want. So why pray for it, create it. If the system is working against you, create a movement and change it. This is what religion is NOT saying. They are under the control of the governments. But have yet to make any attempts to separate. The story of history that religion gave to humanity, is eroding. Its energy is fading. It hasn't moved. It hasn't changed your lives. Humanity, still works for the Virus Energy Cell.

You still create bombs of destruction and don't care about the repercussions. From this view, you are infected, and the Virus Energy Cell has taken you over. Otherwise, humanity would have turned the Earth inside out, to find a way to ensure their continued existence. Does this really sound like something your God would allow?

Religion is helpless when it comes to violence. This is how you stop violence, by each person stopping their own. Consciousness Energy can be your ability to convert your violence. No one can help you, unless you are trying to help yourself. Anyway, humans have too many secrets to admit they need help. There are those human beings who actually practice the meanings of the written words, and focus less on the deliverer. These people go into action, not just prayers. Yes, their prayers gave them strength. Which they used for action. This is Consciousness Energy. Prayers without action is just a reflection. Their idea was to help others who were suffering, by being in action. There aren't enough of those.

As an energy form, focus from the many, can convert the Virus Energy. But there must be unity and a one focused goal, along with Consciousness Energy as their tool. Don't just pray and walk away. You are not changing anything. It's your action that makes religious leaders respond.

Meanwhile, while the worshipers worshiped, humanity's organized Religion became a Corporation, it had to. They can't survive without donations. So, they took a business-like approach. After all, they had to pay for all those buildings to impress and keep their customers. It's their job; they have to get paid.

However, it's not top-grade. Countries are creating religious beliefs, based on these business guidelines. Who wrote those guidelines? The corporations. The corporations are now in the business of selling God. Why did they sell God to humankind?

UC: Who said a house of prayer has to be the size of the Taj Mahal? People can sit or stand outside. Connection is the goal. Consciousness Energy has no walls. There is more of God in nature. Who is benefiting the most? The Corporate Ladder, is the chatter. Today, God is whatever people's perception says it is. The important thing is what you think it is. An Energy, or a Man? You don't have to say, just think about it. Debate it with others. Your perspective is yours, although, you may find the perspective of others to be helpful and insightful. We are aware that millions of humans have religious ties. It's all they ever had; what else could humans do, you had to believe in something?

This Book has a different view. Knowledge to grow your brain, it can't hurt. Most of humanity believes in seeing things, from an UP and DOWN perception. Your perception is, god and heaven are up above. What happened to the rest of the circle? Isn't your full view three hundred and sixty degrees. Why just up above? Why not inside and all around? Universal Consciousness Energy exists, as every single cell of creation. It has no up or down. When you are looking up, you will miss everything which is in front of you. When you are looking down, you still can't see what's in front of you. To see what's in front of you, you must look, in front of you. Its right there, self reflection, is the path to having self awareness, which leads to Consciousness.

There are hundreds of different religions. There are hundreds of cultures, thousands of other languages and traditions, all with different religious beliefs. It's clear why they all have different God's. So let's ask humanity, which God, Burned, Hanged, Drowned, and Killed the Innocent by accusing them of being blasphemous?

Is anyone taking credit for this? Which God killed thousands of people to get them to fear him? Which God created slavery and used humans as a luxury? Which God manipulates people into killing for it? Which God stopped all this before it happened?

Consciousness would have. The Universal Consciousness, is not going to allow the destruction of itself. Meaning self-destruction will not be allowed. Because you, as the world's humanity will not allow it. You are being given an opportunity to learn a new kind of knowledge, which could possibly change your life. Organized Religions, have made sure this knowledge stayed missing. It has limited your conscious perception, from seeing past its belief system. It doesn't want you to know the truth. They are afraid of humanity learning it. Ask yourself, WHY? Then, ask Religion.

The Corporations of religion are responsible for not making changes in traditions. As long as people are buying it, they will keep selling it. As long as humans stay gullible, they will be unreliable. Settling due to fear is, not considered to be a resolution. This is settling under duress. You are aware of it. Stop doing it.

Some Religious Organizations have used the fear of God, as an excuse for power and control over their own kind. This kept the money coming in. No worries, it's all legal. The governments make sure of that. It looks like both the government and organized religion are making a living from this. Many of you know, and you let it continue.

There is no final count of the deaths caused by religious extremists. From history until the present, there really isn't. People have been tortured and put in prison for not believing in your God. Each time anyone tried to learn something new, what did you do? You called it taboo.

Self-realization needs to be your direction. Look how many of you are facing conviction. It has not slowed down. You have a revolving door for your mentally ill, criminals included. Many of them were forced to commit acts in the name of survival—hunger, paying the rent, and paying hospital bills.

UC: Humanity's system is failing, and religion is praying. Why isn't anything changing, Religion? When you accept killing, as a part of your culture, you are admitting that you, as a physical creation, have failed to realize the value of life. When this happens, ENOUGH IS ENOUGH!

Every religious follower and leader, can pray for thousands of years, for god to do, what is the responsibility of each human to do. Let it go. God will not do it for you because, you expect it. It's your responsibility humanity. The Universal Consciousness gave us life, but it can't live it for us. Just as parents can't live the life they gave to their children.

You still operate without Consciousness, and the cycle continues. Where are all the religious leaders who talk to God? Unite yourself, and put a stop to the obscenity of killing. Your boss says it's your job, whether you are an employee or volunteer. But you know you can't. The government will not let you. It gives jobs to the grave makers. The humans mental health decline, says everything is not fine. This knowledge has a goal, it is to get you motivated to learn and develop, to the point of showing actual change. The goal is to evolve into your physical Evolution. This has to become your direction.

Humanity hasn't been able to find a Universal Solution? The world doesn't belong to one particular country. The walls between you, are walls you built. You put them up; you can take them down. Why do humans lead with mistrust first? Is it your fear of the unknown that leads you? It's a learned behavior, just like your blind faith beliefs.

How about using your consciousness energy, to help you with trust. You can learn how to trust consciously. You will feel self confident, about your Consciousness Energy, and you will become clearer. If Everyone has their own perspective without concession, how can any of you create a connection?

You are letting a wall get between you and the world. Until you meet it all, you will never feel safe. To do that, humans must tear down the walls. If you were Conscious, you would know this. Humanity's generals give the orders that create the borders, causing the walls to go up. Declaring a security risk as the reason. Cross it, and you're charged with treason. Back behind the wall, you go. Only now, you are in prison. Keeping others out by building walls only keeps you inside the walls. The outside is freedom. You can't go anywhere. You have walls. How smart is that?

Let's say, as you are walking home, you get assaulted, which happens often in today's society. Will you live between four walls the rest of your life, or learn how to recreate yourself?

Otherwise, your assault meant nothing. Learn from it. Let the experience make you stronger, and be prepared if there is a next time. It's only fear keeping you behind those walls. You are stronger than any walls you can build around you. Break them down. Instead of walls, why not goals? There are many answers that have holes, they are waiting to be filled with consciousness energy. While religion is waiting on God, humanity is waiting on Religion. You're keeping them waiting. It must be a pattern. There is only so far you can go, living behind a wall. If religion can't give answers, Consciousness Energy knowledge can. It has to start with the belief system.

How do your beliefs affect your life? Are your beliefs really yours, or did you inherit them? Reality is hard to face when it's not your reality. Other people's beliefs, do not have to be your reality unless you want them to be. This means buying into their belief system. Questioning organized religion, is settling without answers. It's causing the brain to stop driving. If you can't tell by now that you, humanity, live in history, you are in for a big surprise.

UC: Organized religions prove it. If this doesn't help you see the light, then your light bulb is broken. Humanities brain health, has come into question. What's the situation? It's losing its imagination.

This is not part of creation? The brain is losing its ability to function. This has become a Human crisis situation? Its coming to the point of choosing, a destructive revolution, or the Consciousness Energy Evolution Revolution?

Let's ask the Religious Leaders and hear what they say about Religion today. From their traditional perspective. What will they say? Will they be truthful? Will they answer the questions? We put these questions to them. What has changed in the tradition of your religion, from two thousand years ago?

R: Some are allowing women to be preachers. Some are okay with same-sex marriage. Many, no longer discriminate. We counsel parishioners and forgive them for their sins, free of charge. Religion is now giving people the choice to believe or not. Some religions, are now more open minded towards other religions.

UC: Does God forgive you of your sins? You commit sins yourself every day; you're just Unconscious of them. Why aren't you out helping the teenagers in the streets? Too much to handle? Get off your Throne, pick up your phone, and invite all the homeless children into your house of prayer. Feed them, clothe them, protect them. These are your responsibilities as representative of God.

What's your perspective on the world's plight? Organized religion hasn't been paying attention to the world's destruction. You must be concerned; you live on it. Does religion have an answer to how they can save their own Earth? What's your role?

R: We pray for peace every day. We pray with our flock every week. We mostly leave it in the hands of God. We do not have the power to change anything the governments do. We are just as helpless as humanity. We will keep praying. Whether it's helpful or not is up to God. We have to believe he can hear us. We have nothing else. People need to have something to believe in. It gives them hope.

UC: Oh, now you're a sheepherder? You have a flock. That must make your followers feel good. Calling them sheep, that is. What's your responsibility to humanity, and your followers, to give them hope, or to encourage them to take action to do something about it? Not just have hope for it to happen. Hoping doesn't make it so. It's the same as Wishing it to happen. Action toward making it happen decreases your need for hope.

R: Our responsibility is to God only. Of that, we are proud. We have faith that our faith will come through. If it doesn't, what are we going to do? Become a community center? Group organizers? Become artists? Bakers, Doctors?

UC: Hey, how about Peacemakers? What's wrong with those careers? Not good enough for you, you're not very faithful to your faith. In one sentence, you went from being positive to being doubtful. Why hasn't your God given you instructions? Have you asked him? You do know how to talk to him, don't you?

R: We do, and we are. We keep praying for salvation. We have nothing so far. But we will not stop praying until we get an answer. We have waited two thousand years. What's another two hundred more? God is patient. There are many faiths asking at the same time. Who will get the answer? Which religion will it be? Whoever gets it will become the chosen religion. It's in the tradition. So said the prophecy. Plus, this is our policy. We are a Group Cooperation. We have a business to operate.

UC: Waiting can take more than three lifetimes. Do you have that much time? No, you don't. You will not be around. So why are you carrying a torch that you cannot pass on? Most of humanity is losing trust in religions. This will cost the cooperation many positions.

R: We have been unable to stop the Devil. It refuses to stop killing. We really need that answer as soon as possible. If this violence continues, no one will be left to get the answer. It will be too late. But at least we will meet at the pearly gates. In heaven.

UC: What do you think the answer will solve? Is it going to help humankind evolve? Is it going to develop humanity into a Consciousness State of Awareness? Is the answer timeless? Will it guarantee existence? But how would you know? You don't even know the question, because no one is allowed to question your authority. You just say, God. It's a fear tactic based on a belief passed on to you, by the same religious people.

R: Many people try to question religion; the problem is the answers. We don't know many. But we still have to protect the sanctity of religion or face God's wrath. This is the way it's been since the creation of religion. There are always consequences for not following God's rules. Those that do not are the devil's tools.

UC: Okay, but you are giving out the consequences, not your God. Consciousness Energy vibration has no wrath. The consequences are your own. Your vibration has a built-in Natural Energy System of Consequences and Rewards. Your actions are what decide which one. If your God has a Wrath, you need to take a bath, because you've been swimming in the Virus Energy mud. Only humankind has Wrath. They take it out on each other.

What's the difference between a closed door and an open one? One tempts you, and the other invites you. Yet many of you open the door to temptation. When you are lost in temptation all you will feel is temptation. You are tempted by it, being used by it, and helping its energy to stay alive. You have no need for an end date. You're stuck in temptation. What is Temptation? It's seduction. But your religion, keep calling it the Devil. Temptation is only one energy of the Virus [Devil] Cell.

Humanity needs something more meaningful than blind faith. The Creator was never meant to be a mystery or a secret. It became that way to create blind faith. That is History's Mystery. Blind faith means, you do not have the knowledge to find the truth. So, it's really not about believing, as much as it is about settling for what you have, because, you don't think you have anything else.

There is always something else. The question is, are you looking for it? There are no limits to what you can achieve with Consciousness Energy, and you don't have to believe in it; just become aware of it as your creator. Use it. Test it. Create with it. Evolve with it. Become it.

R: That's quite a bit of philosophical information. We have built our foundation on the conception of God. Our present way of life depends on the faith people have in religion, whatever it may be, for those seeking God. Religion is the only thing standing in the way of the Devil and humanity. We have saved many. What can we be replaced with? Any idea? Nothing, that's what. Everyone would become atheists. We have too many of those, as it is.

UC: Yes…First, the truth will come out. Then, people will start Awakening. Realization will set in, and people will come Looking. But not for you, religion, for the Universal Consciousness Vibration. You don't need religion to connect you with your God. You are already connected. Consciousness to.

Consciousness. You just need to become Conscious of it. You are an Energy Being, an individual of your own meaning.

R: It seems we have a difference of opinion. However, there is an energy that is affecting humanity negatively, we cannot deny this. We call it the Devil; you call it the Virus Energy cell. We have reached an impasse. You have your beliefs, and we have ours. If we took in all the homeless children, we would be broke in a week. So you see, it's not really doable. People need houses of prayer. God demands that we keep them open for prayers. We are not all saviors. We do what we can. Sometimes, that's not good enough for humanity. We can see that, we are not blind.

UC: Why can't they do it at home? Your house, their house, what's the difference? Isn't your God supposed to be everywhere? Just quoting you. When was your last audit? Is there a record somewhere? Or is it just a free-for-all? Some Religions have become too wealthy; it's made you go off balance. Well, religion, which is it, the Devil or the Virus Cell? There's not much difference, really; One is Fantasy, and the other is Energy. It's your choice.

R: Okay, we choose the Devil it's what we are familiar with. It has many names and comes in many forms. It's very deceiving. It has a goal of destroying humankind. It brought drugs and violence to the people. It created wars and took millions of souls to hell. This we know, as we see it reveal its actions in front of our eyes. We have been unable to fight it. Now, you bring this Consciousness Energy idea, and we are supposed to accept it? Why are you so sure of yourself? Do you have proof of what you are saying?

UC: Just open your eyes and look at the world situation. It's proof enough. Religion's issue is that there are more devils than there are religions. No wonder you're losing. Also, are you aware that you just described the Virus Energy Cell? Don't you see, we are talking words, not meanings? Look how many names you have for the Devil. They all mean the same thing; the Devil. Humanity has filled their brain with non-moving energy. Words without meaning. They are empty of feeling.

R: So, What's the difference between the two? Their goals are the same. Their actions to achieve them are close to the same. They both use humans to commit violence. They both manipulate, threaten, dominate, and sedate. They are both trying to return to their creator by any means possible. They are both one and the same energy. This could explain the confusion humanity lives in.

UC: They are both one meaning that is divided into two words. We focus on the energy conversion of the Virus Devil Cell. Energy conversion, will cure humanity from this Devil and the Virus Cell. Let's remove one of the words now. Since religion is unable to decide, we will choose to eliminate the word Devil, by converting its meaning to the energy of a balanced Consciousness. This is how the word Devil becomes useless. Currently, the Devil is an energy that operates by using action without thought, with only one goal: to inflict pain on humanity.

R: Are you saying, using the term Virus Energy Cell, allows us to defeat the Devil? But, calling it the

Devil won't change it? We realize that we must figure out what it is, in order to change it. We have come to understand what it is by what it does. So now, energy has the answers to our creation and Creator, correct? God is our deliverer. We cannot change that unless he wants us to. We cannot undo what he has done.

UC: Consciousness Energy is undoing the damage that humankind has done. Why can't you? As we said, one is an illusion because, its meaning ends with its actions. That's it. No Consciousness growth. No development of energy. Can you answer this question clearly? Try using something else besides, he fell to Earth due to an argument with God story. It was a time when we existed. It didn't happen this way. This is the convoluted version.

The Virus Energy Cell? There are ways to convert it to a balanced energy. Energy can do that. The Devil can't. This is an attempt to explain God and the Devil as an energy source of creation, the Universal Consciousness Energy—the true Creator. Nothing else could have given us Consciousness except Consciousness Energy. The balance is, when the two, come together as one energy. A consciousness energy.

R: We can find out through faith in our God. This kind of logic doesn't play a big role in our beliefs. There are things that humanity is not ready for. We will wait for the answer. God will not forget us. We are his children. There really isn't anything left to discuss, is there? We have chosen to stay with our God and our Devil.

UC: Just one more question. So, how often does logic play a role in your beliefs? Do you even know? Your beliefs are based on blind faith, not simple logic. So why are you not using the logical part of your brain? The one that can recognize Energy. Energy has a logical system that is easy to understand. Humans teach energy in their schools. Yes, it's physical energy, but it's a start. Knowing any part of the energy can help you develop. The message you're sending, is that you're not open to any new knowledge. Meaning, you prefer to preach and teach from history.

R: What is logical to you may be illogical to us. We will leave that up to God. You are talking about a RELIGIOUS REVOLUTION; do you realize that? This knowledge could hurt all the houses of prayer. We would lose much of our credibility if humanity believed these words. It will create chaos. We will lose all our followers. Although, this idea could help atheists. They need something to believe in. Why don't you start with them? They may hear you better.

UC: It's the humans actions, which makes them what they are. Just like your actions make you what you are. Religion, reflects its actions by keeping the same traditions. Religion has to reflect on their God's meaning. Reevaluate your beliefs; they have holes in them. How can you possibly learn anything, while you are continuously reading from the same page? Does this have to do with your age? We are describing the energy of non-movement. Is religion a follower? You do what your God tells you to do. Why is your God telling you to give up, give in, and give out, to quit? Is this what he would do? If it is, then you have an infection in your brain, and it's not a God. It's a Virus Energy attack on your body's system.

It has humanity believing that dead bodies are coming out of the ground, and you can make reservations in heaven. Which we know is not true, because you are already in what used to be heaven. Humans were in heaven, and now they want to go to another one. Why? So they can do it again? It will not happen. Why does religion promise things it can't deliver? Like salvation. Your ego is larger than your faith. Maybe it's about the feeling of power or being the religion of the hour. Only you would know.

R: Good people are not trying hard enough to create a heaven; they depend on their children. Children have no idea of what heaven is; they are growing up in societies of violence and fear, where greed controls their souls. Your questions just keep coming; it seems we are continuing with this discussion. Okay, let's move on. Can you explain how Earth was a heaven? When was it a heaven? What happened to it? Where did it go? What else were we to tell people, besides heaven is above, because, it wasn't on the ground. It was better than the truth, for us, anyway. There was no one to blame. Our story stays the same, as will our faith.

UC: Actually, yes to your questions, and, you had yourselves to blame. But what's your reaction when you realize your followers have been depending on you? Where have you been hiding? What do you mean, where did heaven go? Humanity turned it into hell, not the Devil. You say, you are doing gods bidding, yet you do nothing about mass killings. When did the government become more powerful than god? Maybe they really don't believe in your god. You have to finally take responsibility for learning new knowledge. There is a problem in a few of your organized religions. Their teachings are incomplete. Do you not see a problem in your teachings? There is abuse of children happening in your Houses of Prayer. Why is your God allowing this? Why do some religions protect the abusers of children? Question for thought. Why are you protecting the Virus Cell infection?

There are more questions for your religion. By the way, why are you barely asking questions? That's odd. Well, here is one about the children. Why is the lack of care for children's lives acceptable to some of you? Why do some of you prey on the young after you pray to your God? Where is the consistency in your belief? You think your God doesn't notice your actions or at least the ones you pretend not to have done. Those are yours to carry, humanity! Your GUILT IS YOUR JUDGE. No matter where you go, your guilt will follow.

R: You are basing your words on the few, who have failed to keep their commitment to God. They fell into temptation. They are using their time to reflect on their actions. They deserve a chance at redemption. That's what religion does. We are here for everyone. We live on donations. We only have one obligation. It's only to God. The only problem we see happening is the decrease in parishioners, which means a decrease in donations.

UC: This is an epidemic. Do not excuse it or make light of it. Everyone deserves a chance; this is true, but not without a lesson learned. You don't just walk away from this and say God bless. It's happening to children everywhere, worldwide. Are these the words of your God? It's obvious they're not. Why does religion deny it? Why can't they see it? Do you ignore it, because you are afraid to slander the reputation of your Religion? If not, then what are you afraid of? You have God on your side. Ask yourself, Religion, why have many people stopped believing? Has there been anything worth retrieving? What's left for anyone to believe in? Anything? The humans way of living is collapsing.

UC: Your faith is becoming faithless People are walking out with less patience. However, in your defense, you have built a strong offense. How does this make sense? Religion doesn't have to accept this behavior, but it does? While many of you want God's protection, you're hurting your own children. Who needs the protection? If you think your duties don't include social work, you're mistaken. God is a social worker; why aren't you? Look it up. Apparently, Religion must have forgotten.

R: We still believe it's the work of the Devil; it's sabotaging our efforts. It's responsible for all the damage the world is experiencing. Maybe it's the Devil infecting humanities brain? Have you thought of that? It's a possibility, isn't it? You said, I quote, *"There's not much difference really."* This feels like change, or else. We stand strong on our beliefs. But, we are willing to look at where this knowledge comes from. From what source? We can't just jump in without questioning. We will take time to analyze this information for accuracy and prophecy. If this is true, then we will look through our beliefs and study them. But first, we need to examine its origin. It will take time. Meanwhile, we can continue.

UC: Now we are hearing an open mind. Study away. Consciousness Energy proves itself. You were saying before that you couldn't beat the devil. Is Religion saying the Devil is stronger than it is?

So, we are open to the idea that it's the Devil infecting humanity's brain. Now that you are open to hearing it, we are going in the same direction. Call it what you want, but it is infecting the people's brain. We can agree on this, can we not? What we disagree on is that you feel you can't do something about it. You can stop it. You can change it. It's within you, to change the Virus Energy Cell into Consciousness Energy, by converting your own Devil, Isn't that what you do with people?

You must change it; don't let it change you. The reason you think you cannot change it, is because it's telling you not to. You don't have to listen to it; it's a CHOICE.

R: We recognize freedom of choice. We are not reaching people like we used to. We need to do more globally; we do not disagree. However, we are limited to whatever the governments want us to know and see. We leave them alone, and they leave us alone. That is how it works in the world today. Greed always has a say. Everything gets affected by greed. Religion has become a business. It can't get away from greed. It has already infested our corporations.

UC: What about its effect on your workers? The Core of Organized Religions. Why are they still living on donations? Since your business is doing so well, why haven't you done anything about it? Change starts in your own home. Humanity is holding up a crumbling building. You're losing your hold, parts of it have fallen off. How long will it take before the rest goes? Why did you not expect your traditions to change with the times? Did you need that much control? How long can you hold it? Humans must start to create, by using the energy of what created them. This is what you should be teaching humanity. You must create a new identity. The old one is dying. Technology is becoming your God. You have more to worry from your technology, than from your Devil.

R: As far as Organized Religions go, what is the implication? Religious condemnation? Isolation? What we hear, is the knowledge we are teaching, is old and ancient. We need to revamp our belief system. But until we hear this from God, we stand united. We will get the answer.

UC: It's not an implication; it's an actual realization. Religion is failing the population. Are religions waiting for the same answer? Have you asked the same question? What is the answer you are waiting to hear? How will you know when it comes?

R: Is this the *"which one is the true Religion"* question? We will know it when we hear it. Since we couldn't make this decision, we agreed to wait for God to tell us. It keeps things calmer. We are like a farmer. We plant our seeds and wait for them to grow. Some fruits take longer than others.

UC: Hmm? So you don't know? If you did not know, why are you not saying so? You are asking your God, to choose one of your religions to be number one; the rest will not matter anymore, is that it? Do you agree with this? Isn't this how governments typically work? A hierarchy. Someone is always on top. The buck stops with that person. Well, whichever one is chosen, the buck still stops with you, Organized

Religion. Why is being in first place so important to your God, or is it? Could it be your ego that needs the attention?

R: In your opinion, what is our intention? What exactly is our position, to exist without any reason? Are we to experience treason? Is this the future of Religion? Extinction? We pray this never happens. Hopefully, the answer will come before this happens. It will give religion knowledge and credibility.

UC: Religion, you will be waiting until your deterioration, expecting God to choose a religion. How will being number one change the events that may occur to religion? Do you have an explanation? It has nothing to do with being on top, does it? It has to do with being the best. You get all the followers, the attention, the huge donations. These have nothing to do with being the chosen Religion. Next, you will be calling the chosen religion the savior. Is this what you are trying to create? Which religion is the true deliverer? Would you be surprised to hear that Religions are not deliverers? Many of them preach like salespeople, selling God for a profit.

R: What is your assumption? We don't know what we are doing. We are not wasting our time? We have made great strides in being open-minded. But we can only go so far. You are talking about changing the world's religious system of beliefs, and changing the concept of God, from a man to a Consciousness Energy. It's too much to conceive. We are not prepared for such a change. No one religion can claim to be the deliverer. Only the one God chooses.

UC: Oh no, we know you are very aware of what you are doing. This is most certainly not an assumption. It's a realization for religion to think about. You are not wasting your time when doing good deeds. But humanity is at the point where good, is not good enough. Humanity needs Consciousness Energy, to awaken their brain to an unlimited conscious reality. Religion has been unable to grow humankind's brain effectively. It's too limited. Consciousness Energy is the nutrition it needs to survive and grow into its own evolution.

We encourage the young generation to question Religion and blind faith today, not tomorrow. Without today, there is no tomorrow. The more you give, the more you have to borrow. Giving has its good intentions until you have nothing left to give. Balance is the key. It is the Consciousness Energy way. Many young people are searching for a new kind of awareness. Take a survey Religion, ask the people questions without fearing the answers.

UC: Talk to them about what they are already thinking. Where is God's salvation? Religion has been promising people salvation for thousands of years. Explain this Religion. You are creating followers of a faith you don't believe in anymore. Most of your religious leaders are just going through the motions. The young adults are Earth's future generation and have recognized the repeated energy of the Virus. It is what's causing Mental Illness. They want to make it their business to uncover yours. We are helping them. Can you? The young are yearning for energy learning. They are looking for change. They are knocking on your door. Do you have a real plan, or are you just doing what you can by praying for humanity? How are you going to bring your followers back to you?

Just the words, religious wars, are enough to prove the effect Religion has had on humanity. Many of your followers are living in poverty. How do you empower them to do better? Do they even come to see you anymore? *"We are open during the day,"* is what you say. So, Okay, they sleep outside at night. Is this God's plan or yours? You made this behavior become acceptable.. Doesn't this action make you question your behavior? How can it not? You are Religion. It's precisely why you need Universal Consciousness. Religion needs balance. You must make it make sense. We are aware that the world's problems are not all your fault. We are not blaming. We are awakening you to your true Realization.

This is not a balanced way of thinking. You should be concerned, we are sure the creator is. It's why we are having this discussion with you. We are giving you notice to change your philosophy or stay in a reality that keeps repeating the same things. We believe this is humanity's hell, stuck in a cycle of repetitive motion. To live in an illusion of wishful thinking that keeps repeating. You live your life as if you were a haunting. If yourself wants to change, let it. We are not promoting anger towards you, the religious leaders. You are being used by the Virus Energy also. When you realize you are being used, it will be up to you to explain your position. You can defend your religion or accept new knowledge that can explain things for you. The truth must come out. Religion cannot hide it for much longer.

UC: There is no escape for humanity, without Consciousness Energy. Not even space can save you. Humanity has put themselves beyond Religion, by creating the bomb of destruction. You send them home with a prayer. Did you try to intervene in the possible destruction of life on Earth? Why was religion not concerned about humanity?

You just sat there and allowed it, because you had a deal with the Government. You leave them alone, and they leave you alone. Good job. Look what they created while you were both alone. To this day, you still say nothing. Why do you want the government to leave you alone? What are you hiding from them? God does not choose Countries or Religions. Humans cannot keep using this belief to forgive sins. It's not your job. Forgive your own first. Each person needs to take responsibility for their actions and change them.

Humans cannot seek forgiveness just by confessing to another human. Confessing is the first step. But it doesn't end there. You have created a system where people have no fear of committing sins, as you call them. You can only get absolution by confessing your own sins and making up for them. Confession alone is not enough. You have to convert that energy you used to commit that sin. Your confession does not make them go away. According to religious laws, Sins are Unconscious energy actions that cause someone to break God's laws. By making up for your actions, You changed the energy of what you did. So you will not do it again. Thats the whole point in changing.

Humanity has polluted the world's environment just to see who has the strongest government. What have Organized Religions done to slow down the creation of pollution? Food barrels in your house of prayer, are only out on holidays. WHY? People need to eat every day. You should leave them out every day.

It seems you are being quiet, Religion. You can't all be martyrs. Unless you are trying to be? No one is asking you to fight, just to be peacemakers. You must start to question religion's own belief system. This is imperative to your existence.

The worst you can do is allow Religion to take all this for granted. If you believe that it's not that bad, it is that bad. No belief is necessary. Does Religion have the ability to use what's left of its sensibility, to make sense of this tragedy? Come on, help humanity realize the real actuality.

You are physical creation, Created by the Universal Consciousness Energy. You began the beginning. Why can't you stop the ending? Waiting, is keeping you from Consciously moving, developing, and growing. There is knowledge out there, beyond what you can imagine. Just step out of your own way long enough to look.

Question for Religion? How can humanity be expected to continue settling for what use to be? Religion has to teach them something new. People have become accustomed to the I, not the we. I need this. I need that. I feel helpless, I, I, I. How did humans become so needy? Was it Mr. Greedy? Was this your intention? Is this what you wanted for everyone, to become dependent on Religion?

Blind faith is about to gain its sight back, if Religion allows it. Humanity needs to have knowledge of what they believe in. Understandable, straightforward answers. Simple Logic ideas, a Progressive Energy Movement, and, creative ability improvement. Will religion stay awake all night, contemplating the sight of humanity's plight, without going into a fright? Would this be considered a sacrifice to humanity? How about a sense of responsibility? An opportunity, for you to do your duty. We realize that fear, paralyzes you. It's the reason you need Consciousness Energy, to convert it. To shift your perception, giving you the courage to do something.

What we are speaking about, leaves much for thought, don't you think? We have heard many questions from humanity that you have been unable to answer, because they keep asking them. Can we repeat them to you now? Just so you are aware during your next meetings. They are worth repeating. Can you, religious leaders, answer these questions? They come from your parishioners. Your followers, and many others. They have been ignored. They are simple questions actually.

What is God without blind faith? If you don't know, say so.

R: We really don't know. We are working on it. We hear this question now, more than before. It's a personal understanding, even with our teachings. We can say pray, they walk out thinking we said, have a nice day. As soon as they are done, they tune us out. Many people chose the easy way to pray. Once a week. Socialize, and go home. This behavior is well known. We encourage a connection to God always. But really, without faith, you are blind. Faith in what, you keep asking? In God, we keep repeating.

UC: Here is another one. Does God really exist, is the question? This one must be your favorite. It gives you a chance to talk about what you know best. What you don't know is, we are Consciousness Energy, we only reflect the truth.

R: We know that, but we have our God, and for that, we are thankful. It's not our position to prove God's existence. That would be his decision. We preach God's words. We are not responsible for the writings. We did not write them. We simply obey them. They are holy words. The truth of Creation. We cannot deny them. We live and die by them and raise our children by them. They help us feel safe, teach us how to love, how to forgive, and how to trust. If we must change, we must. But it will take a huge amount of trust, and will be on an individual basis.

UC: You don't know who wrote them, yet you obey them. Isn't that considered blind faith? Your beliefs are not just from history, but from years of accumulating confusion throughout your ministry. Religion, you have had thousands of years to tell the world you don't know. Today would be a good time. This is a learning discussion, so there is no accusation. Points being brought up, are what some of humanity is silently thinking and fearful of voicing. Why stand out from the crowd? Consciousness Energy is why. Someone has to start. Once you understand Consciousness Energy, you will see the common denominator as energy, in all forms of speeds and all forms of creation. It's a realization.

R: We want to ask you some questions from your perception, starting with this. Where does God exist? It's a good question that we hear often. Will this take time to answer? Do you need to look it up? We can wait.

Religion: Fact Or Fiction?

UC: Yes, it's your pattern. Consciousness Energy keeps moving, it does not stop. It keeps evolving back to its originality. Where doesn't Consciousness Energy exist? Everything is energy, Including humanity's anatomy. There is no life form of any kind without a Consciousness Energy Formulation. There can be nothing conscious without it. It's the life source of all creation. Why has it taken so long for religion, to show the existence of God to the people?

R: To be honest, we have yet to explain it to ourselves. There are many theories on the meaning of God. But, to this day, it's still a mystery. Has the story changed over the years? If there was a true answer, why wasn't it passed on to the future? It's a good reason why we don't know.

UC: Yes, you do. Religious organizations have more secrets than countries and governments, and they hide them better, too. This is the reason it's taking so long. Organized Religion is holding the truth hostage. Here is your answer. Face it, you already know it, and we know it. All these years, and you only have blind faith. Was this your end goal? Is this the outcome you desired when you first started?

R: No, It's been so long, we forgot it. Maybe we did go Unconscious. Religion has become lazy these past few hundred years. We don't want to admit it, but it's true. We unintentionally created a mess. But in our defense, trying to understand the meanings of historical documents, is a challenging task. As far as we have discovered, there are a few documented languages that describe events from history. Each one tells a different story. Translators had their own perceptions. They were commonly misrepresenting the truth. We are dealing with what was left of history.

UC: Does Religion have anything else to interject? Maybe another question? Do you have any concerns? Confusion? Is there anything curious you haven't asked? You're the one asking now. Ask another one. Consciousness Energy develops on questions. It grows and puts out more balanced energy.

It's about what you think, say, and do. When what you think is conscious, what you say comes out conscious and promotes Consciousness Energy, into your actions. Religions need to get their reality checked. Questions will do it. Don't just settle for *"Because it's God's law."* You only say that because, you have no answer. And you are still waiting for it.

R: What did you say God was made of? Some kind of Consciousness Energy? Beyond physical perception. We are not talking about physical Consciousness, are we? We had an idea we might not be. We didn't really hear this conversation from this perception.

UC: Good observation. It's true; It seems that we are both learning from this discussion. We are attempting to understand religion, and it seems that you are interested in understanding Consciousness Energy. Consciousness Energy vibrates at a speed that cannot be described. It cannot be seen by physical perception. Only the same speed of frequency can see the same frequency speed. It's the purest part of the candle flame, the blue tip, the hottest part of the flame. It's where energy boils the fastest. All that exists is a reflection of that blue tip of the flame.

R: We have much to do to assess this knowledge. We understand that there is more in the universe, but only our universe. Beyond the universe is God. Apparently, we have a limited perception. Also, humans are gullible, to the point of making themselves victims. But, are they gullible or Unconscious? God for cash is the way it is nowadays. The more desperate and afraid people become, the more money we make.

UC: How Godly. Your honesty is refreshing. But it's still stealing. Consciousness development shows the proof. Here is a question for you: Its about money? The money Religion takes from their followers. Why does Religion take gold for God? Doesn't this make you hypocrites? Deceptive? You are charging a monthly fee for a reservation in heaven. Don't you feel bad? Your survival depends on the people now.

R: Who is going to say no? We need it to build new Churches, Temples, Mosques, and Synagogues anyway. Our overhead is sky-high. It is our reality at this time. Until things change, then we will get involved. When they change, it means God wanted them to. So we have to wait for the answer. It's the only way Religion will turn its direction. We can abide by this, but changing the concept of God is not something we can entertain yet. However, you have been able to get our attention. Our curiosity is now compelled to investigate all this further.

UC: What if the answer already came, but Religion did not recognize it? Then what? For anything to change, you have to get involved. What's the matter with the old buildings? Are you insinuating that God, is only in your prayer houses? Religion doesn't hold the key to talking with God. Consciousness Energy is always available and ready to guide you. You can do it anywhere, anytime, without paying anything. Even this Evolution Revolution knowledge is free. We do not need a donation—only your energy conversion

R: If no Religion recognized it, It wouldn't be the answer. Also, our buildings are too old and falling apart. Their foundations are crumbling, and walls are collapsing on each other, trapping people underneath. We are trying to get them out, but we don't have the right tools. Some of us have no idea how to dig. We are using our hands. It's not fast enough. People are suffocating. We are in the middle of a catastrophe. We need a way to save those people.

UC: The tools you need are in the Evolution Revolution book, but you have to open it to get them out. Go ahead. There is no lock. Free of charge. You can close it anytime you like. At least give it a chance, like people gave you. Without followers, well, it's obvious. Humanity would be better off outside than in your buildings. First of all, nothing would fall on them; considering Consciousness Energy is the air you breathe, it makes sense to go outside. The air inside has become stale. You can smell it. There is more unspoiled God in nature.

There is no middle-man. It's a direct contact call. No waiting. It starts with self-awareness and self-realization. Plus, talking to God outside has less energy interference. Did God tell you to take the people's money and build him houses of prayer? If not, whose idea was it? Most of God's employees seem to be living comfortable lives. Some even live luxurious ones. Did your BOSS approve of this? What happens when an employee uses company funds on his personal issues? It's called embezzlement. If God were not a man, you wouldn't need a man to contact him. What will you do then? Religion would be out of a job. Most of humanity believe they need Religion to get to their God. YOU DO NOT! Anyone can. Whether you believe in a God or not. Consciousness Energy doesn't differentiate. It's what you are made of. The intention of your actions is the deciding factor in your continued existence.

R: Yes, we are his employees. We need a lot of money to get to people who can't come to us. Most of us have children and spouses. So we need to have some allowances. In this day and age, money talks. What can we say? It's humanity's way. We simply follow where God leads us. If you are going to ask where this is? We can only reply...Hopefully, it will be the road to heaven. We are in every part of the world. Each country has its own ways and traditions. Globally, everyone who believes in God prays. That's a lot of prayer energy, isn't it? It must be doing something good for the people.

UC: Energy needs to be directed, and Consciousness Energy does that. Otherwise, it will keep flowing until humanity becomes conscious of it, grabs it, and starts to direct it, through their awareness of it. By the way, Religion, who pays your bills? If you are going to the people, you do not need so many prayer houses? Why is Religion fearful of non-believers?

They are not your devil. Humankind's holy books were written by people with different perceptions of that time. People with pre-conceived beliefs. People with different education, comprehension, ideology, and languages. How can you expect to write a book and say it's the words of god based on the interpretation of so many? This book has one meaning, which is to be used in many different ways. Religion is waiting for an answer that doesn't have a question.

You have yet to learn who said what to whom. You don't seek other answers; you simply believe. Humanity found a way to actually create a religion, using the interpretation of the many perspectives. How do you create one understanding, from many perspectives, especially when they all think they are right. You think you have it all clear. The writers of your holy books didn't even have it clear; how can you? Some of them have already admitted so. A question: why does humanity have faith in a Religion, who comes out for one minute to tell the people, *"We understand. Put your faith in God; he will protect us. Have faith, and you shall be saved."* Then, they nonchalantly go back in. They do this again and again.

Being in a state of Consciousness means, not taking advice from those who don't take their own advice. Even if they are nice, here is some advice, don't give advice. It could come back to bite you. Okay, cutting to the chase, Religion created an illusion; explain how you will fix all this confusion? What's your intervention, your solution? Do you have a plan of salvation besides wishing? Humanity trusts you, as religious leaders, to come through with your promises. In fact, they are counting on it.

R: We can't comment. But it's always in God's hands; especially the plan for salvation. But you must follow God's laws to be saved. Religions have laws and rules of their own to follow. Many of them do. Some Religions believe, there are only so many people allowed in heaven. That you have to be a member to go to heaven, while some Religions have their followers believing that death is more honorable than disgrace. Others pray to nature and create magical experiences. Some pray to the Devil and call it Religion. There are those who do not allow their ministers of God to Marry. There are those that have a closer relationship to the truth of God, but only in philosophy.

UC: Yes, many celebrate God in their own way. However, when it comes to Organized Religions, their structure is based on a business system. Your philosophy of a limited heaven is, well, ridiculous, actually. As a matter of fact, there is no special heaven for anyone to go to. Consciousness Energy allows you to create your own heaven, wherever you are. Alive or not. Does a person have to believe, before they can be saved? Don't answer that too loud; it won't make you look good. What do you mean, only so many are allowed in heaven? Are you charging extra for anyone over the limit? We have a label for these types of behaviors. COMMON NONSENSE. Couldn't that money have been put to better use?

R: If God says, we can't do it, we can't do it. We can do anything that God allows us to do. That's the reason we put everything in his hands? To see what we can do, until then, we will do what we can. What that is, is up to God.

UC: So when everything turns out not to be true, you can blame God. When will you find out, what you can do? Humanity doesn't have that much time. You are being ruled by dictators. Is Religion part of this insanity? Isn't this an example of, *"if you're not part of the solution, you're part of the problem?"* Quoting humanity.

R: What can we do? It needs a world intervention. This is not a one-country problem; it's a world problem. That's a lot of beliefs to try and change. This kind of change will take lifetimes, if it happens at all. Only God can achieve this kind of event. It would be a miracle.

UC: No, it wouldn't. Change happens with you and without you. It is not a miracle. It is energy frequency changes. A World Energy Intervention is precisely the purpose of this discussion. It's a Consciousness energy creation. It's your chance for self-evaluation and self-clarification.

In the human world, you can do anything God can do. If you have the money. You can buy forgiveness or bribe a witness. You can pay off a judge or settle a grudge. You can buy love, You can buy friendship. You can create your own dictatorship, and afford your own worship. You can even buy your own relationship.

Anything humans desire, they can buy it with money. This has a firm hold on humanity. Are they strong enough to get out of it? Do you have an answer, Religion? You must tell the people something else besides, *"It's OK. We will overcome violence and hatred. Our faith is stronger than ever. Peace to you all, 'till next time."* Then go back in. How is this helping?

The idea of blind faith leading the way to salvation, will keep you, an unconscious population. People use unconscious indignation to achieve possession of control. Promising salvation that only Consciousness can achieve. This will become a race between the Virus Energy Cell and Religious Salvation. This is the point to where humanity has arrived. It's where the line has been drawn. Choices will have to be made. Beliefs, humans will have to let go of. Mostly the ones that do not belong to you. ATTACHED BELIEFS are beliefs you picked up on the move. Beliefs that are quick to believe, and quick to forget. Unconsciously, they still exist. They are attached to your belief system. Consciousness Energy can help detox your body from these unneeded beliefs. They float around, confusing you. They serve no purpose.

The only salvation coming is already here. So what are you left with? Humanity has the ability to save themselves, if they believe they need saving. At this point, it's saving the humans from themselves.

To be saved by Consciousness energy, you must become aware of it, feel it, and you will awaken to it. It's a Consciousness; it needs a strong awareness and focus to be identified. Will this bring intense opposition from the power of religion? Of course, it will. Organized Religions cannot seem to get their fill.

UC: Any member of any society can benefit from certain beliefs. The effect of religion has comforted many. Many good choices were made because of it. Yes, lives were also saved by it. But, all this was achieved by the people. Beliefs without action are beliefs without traction. The actions made it happen. Soon, Religion will come out again to talk about their plan. They come out and say, *"We have a plan to save the human. God is coming. Have faith."* With no mention of what the plan is, they go back in again. Humanity, you better create your own plan. They said all they can.

UC: Consciousness Energy doesn't follow or lead. It just creates. There is nothing to argue about. This knowledge is your best ally when using awareness. It promotes sensibility. Be aware humanity, heaven and hell threats are empty threats. Do not buy into them. Why wait till death to go to a place, which may not exist. Create your heaven now. Hell is a control tool. It serves only one purpose, to control you and your intentions. Fear uses it to change your decision after you have made it.

If you perceive consciousness, then you are actually conscious of it. If you don't perceive, then you are unconscious. It's about perception. Your reality is what you see, feel, and touch. What is missing is, your lack of sensation. People need clarity, to move them out of disparity. Religious leaders, must give humanity back its dignity, by showing them the truth about history. What really happened?

Humans are a small fish in a pond, but they act like a whale. Why are you trying to be what you are not? Is it because you don't know who you are? What's keeping you from finding out? Are you still afraid of your Devil? After gathering all this information, are you still stuck on the Devil? By the way, here is a question, what about this claim that another Devil called the Anti-Christ is coming? We thought you were waiting for God? Are they both coming to Earth at the same time? This can't be good, can it? Is this what religion has been waiting for? Has Religion been waiting for the Devil to show before God does?

According to your religion, the Devil is already there. What are you really waiting for? A different Devil? Does the Devil have a son, like the human God? Who is the one on Earth? The son? Now, you are waiting for the father of the Devil? It sounds like this is what religion is saying. We have a Devil, but we are waiting for another one. How else can you explain this? What's the difference between the Devil and his Father? Do you know one? They are both cut from the same cloth. What exactly is religion trying to prove? By now you should have a basic idea, of who the creator of the Virus Energy Cell is.

So, who will show itself first? The Devil will, and it will continue doing so until it's done. Come on, Faith, you're not that blind. There are too many unanswered questions regarding blind faith. Does humanity use it as an excuse not to act? Does humanity put all their troubles in the hands of God, like religion does? Is religion more confident in the arrival of the Devil than the arrival of God? Why? Why is the focus on the bad? Is it because you have been observing the Devil's actions more than your God's? It has you mesmerized. You are more familiar with its ways. Now you have the opportunity to familiarize yourselves with the Virus cell Energy. It's the devil inside you.

Humans have become the follower of the hour, by being tricked into believing in a hierarchy that supposedly came from God. Consciousness Energy needs no hierarchy. It's up to your energy development. As you become aware, you grow. It's a natural process. We realize that showing humanity the inconsistencies in religion, is like telling your children there is no Santa Clause. It's a shock for them and it will also be the same for you. However, it is better to make you aware, than to leave you blind.

Why have religious leaders, not met with the president of each country who has the power of destruction? Does every leader of a nation refuse to hear you? Have you tried? There has to be leaders who follow religion. Do you have a way of affecting them? Do you need a reservation or an appointment? Make one. Even if you can persuade one leader to decrease their atomic weapons fabrication, it would look good on your next application. Give the young a chance to believe in a future without the threat of nuclear destruction. It would make a great impression. Humankind has to stop using weapons to resolve conflicts. It's teaching the young to reach for a weapon to resolve their issues. They copy what adults do. It gives them permission to.

UC: This is when they get caught in the dark web of control, greed, and fear. These energies are branches of the Virus Energy Cell. It uses them as weapons against humankind. It uses them through you. The human. It is aware that you are Unconscious. It's easy for it to work through you. It will continue to do so, until you become aware of its existence. Religion is not an insurance to anywhere. It doesn't guarantee you anything. It's a business like any other. At this point, what you have, is religions point of view only. How about a new view? The Universal Consciousness Energy Vibration view.

Being Unconscious is Contagious. Are you seeing a pattern here? If you don't, you are not looking. Consciousness Energy gives you the clarity, determination, and vision to look at the world with your own intuition. To make your own decision, based on your Consciousness inspiration, which will affect your actions and give you Conscious beliefs. Unconscious beliefs will make you Unconscious. Check your beliefs. Don't take any chances.

Organized Religions, need to realize that there are no secrets from Consciousness Energy. We are aware of your treasury and your fight against evil. Why are you not teaching people about what you know? It may help with decreasing humanity's evil. Many people are noticing that your words do not represent your actions. When the action doesn't represent the word, that word is never heard. A word without the energy of consciousness, teaches nothing.

Words alone will not save you. But Physical Energy Conversion will. Are you willing? It's your choice humanity. Apparently your religion isn't willing; maybe it's you, the people who are not. It's not hiding. It's in your face every day. In the streets and your homes. On the news and on your phones. Many of you wake up to it and go to sleep by it. So it's not a secret; it's not the Devil, not a monster. It's real. It's an alive, Unconscious Energy frequency, mixed in with your physical energy, and you are letting it use you to operate. Consciousness Energy is your lifeline. Otherwise, this Virus Energy will take you down.

A question for religion, any organization will do. Why has religion been unable, to come together in the name of unity and one God? Aren't most religions believers in unity? Believing without knowledge is not believing. There is no meaning. Without meaning, there is no believing. You must become aware that Consciousness knowledge is your meaning. At times, it will be your Intuition; other times, it will be your Imagination; it's your Perception, and mostly, it is your energy of creation

R: What we believe, comes from what we feel to be the truth. God is the truth. We do not use fear to create followers. Our faith protects us from fear. Our history speaks for itself. God's wrath is for those about to commit sins. It's a deterrent. We don't punish or use threats. We don't claim to be God. We are his followers. God's words are accepted by people all over the world. We think that the majority knows what they are doing. Who gave God's words meaning? God did. His words, his meanings.

UC: Do the followers and their children know, that God's wrath is just a threat? Just a deterrent, as you put it. Above, you said you don't use threats. What about God's wrath? You just said it was a deterrent. Based on your faith, the deterrent means don't do it, or face God's wrath. Don't do it, or else sounds like a threat. Does this wrath deterrent apply to most religions? The truth is, you live in a hallucination that ignores all else but retribution. Religion has killed more innocent lives in God's name than wars ever have. Humans have broken every commandment there ever was, plus some. Apparently you don't believe in them. So, what part of religion do most people use, only the one that benefits them?

UC: Energy Balance is in everything that exists. Without it, we have the humans situation, unconscious. Humanity needs, a total Energy Re-creation. You have to start life all over again. Better do it in life than to go back and take your chances. At least you are on familiar ground. Other dimensions have no ground. Some are round, and some are flat. There are dimensions of every dimension. The Universal Consciousness, creates awareness and confidence, to help you look through and see those dimensions as they are.

Being in a Consciousness state allows you to be a good leader. A good teacher. A Consciousness Energy creator. One who teaches others how to lead for the good of humanity. Not some guy, who says again and again, I am the man with the plan. Four years later, another one says it again.

UC: Why do political leaders bring God into their proclamation. Is it just to sound trustworthy? A great leader creates unity above all else. Blind faith was created to create followers. Those followers are meant to go out and collect more followers. In other words, religion has no leaders.

As long as religion is leading humanity, most of you are left with indecision. They can't help you with that. They are still undecided also. Religion is taking for granted that you will continue to believe. Will you, do you want to? Are you thinking it over, or are you satisfied with knowing that religion, has left you in the unknown? Is it that easy to ignore common sense knowledge? Call out religious leaders to remind them that they're not doing what they believe in. This is reflected by what they do believe in.

The Universal Consciousness is here to stay. The Evolution Revolution is on its way. It had to come to this. The meeting between humankind and the Virus Energy Cell, will happen on your ground. The final face-off between the good and the bad. Only, there will be a change in religion's plan. We will not kill the Virus Energy, because it can't be killed. We will convert it to a balanced, productive, and useful energy. Consciousness does not destroy a part of itself. Only humans do that. Humankind's physical Energy, needs to start moving. When it does, people will be awakening. They will want answers from you, Religion. Do you have them?

You can't pray your way out of this one. Consciousness Energy will convert your power of control. The more Consciousness, the less control. Your best bet, is to free humanity, to think for themselves. They don't have a cross to bear. Why do you give them one? For religion to use guilt on anyone is unacceptable. You are following a belief that's thousands of years old. Where is the Consciousness growth? The development of the brain? The need for evolving. Humans are uninterested in going anywhere except to space. Trying to Escape the human race. Whatever you run away from, will only bring you back, until you resolve the issue. It's energy; that's how it works. You call it KARMA. We call it the Universal Consciousness Energy Vibration. It's what makes Karma work. It's a constantly moving energy that is continuously evolving and creating balanced energy. So Karma will always bring it back around to be balanced.

Religion is putting more value on history than the future. Does the new scare you? Is it because the new could be true? Is religion worth more as a cooperation? The issue is, there are so many of you, it makes it very difficult to know who's who. So then, your past is more important than your present and future. How sad for the human brain. It has nothing to gain. Religion is facing a challenging quest as humanity puts it to the test.

How can humanity claim to be going forward, when their value is behind them? No one can notice but you. Your true value, is inside of you. It's your true nature, as a Consciousness Energy Being. It's what you were, before you came to Earth. There are millions who claim religious status but do not follow the principles. How important is it, to identify yourselves as a religious person? Your actions can identify you better than any words can.

It's your words, your labels, and your names that confuse you. Your identity is a label that belongs to millions of others. Where is your own autonomy, your own choices? You became a follower because you stopped believing in yourself. You kill each other over petrol, and sometimes, for nothing at all. What else do you expect to happen? What you see is what you've got. Face it, Religion, you are teaching blind faith, not Consciousness.

You say, again and again. *"We need salvation to save them?"* If that's true, salvation knows nothing about it. It isn't universal news. Has any one of you asked Salvation, if it even wants to save humanity?

So far, only religion has? Do you want to be rescued from your PAIN? Take the needle out of your VEIN. Do you want to be cleansed from your SIN? Just don't do it AGAIN; EVER. Do you want to be forgiven for your actions, then do something good, to balance the SCALE? YOU'RE THE SCALE.

The fact is, religion must unite as one. Leaders must stop having fun, on the back of those who work in the sun. The leader's life depends on the work they do. Do you? When will it get through? Becoming a politician is not an action. Money buys your membership to this cult. If the people vote you in, it's because they recognized a person they can manipulate. Most politicians don't tell the truth. Most of you are being led by your ego. Your focus is on one place you all want to go, to the state of the wealthy. It matches your personality. You're a politician. Not so far behind, is Organized religion. They have created their own government with their own politicians. Some people just have more money at their disposal. Religion can afford it.

This is not the first time religion has been faced with self-evaluation. It's necessary for humanity to question authority. Especially in today's societies. Question motives, and intentions. Question questions. Don't be moved by empty words. When you are done reading this book, you will begin to understand what's going on. Yes, it involves you, you, and you. This time, you can't just ignore the rest. Most of you are living on the edge; it will not take much to push you over. Humans need, to learn the knowledge of the Universal Consciousness Energy, so they can change their destiny. Change their life for the better. To become aware and conscious of their actions. To have self-control before becoming controlled, and to lose greed before becoming its feed. An open mind is a good sign for humankind. What's new in your religion? Have you checked lately? Is it becoming too costly? Ask yourself honestly.

RELIGION? FACT OR FICTION? IS IT FAITH, OR IS IT ENERGY? IT'S YOUR DECISION HUMANITY.

Earth, "I want to live"

A Universal Consciousness Energy conversation with Earth's perception is the intention.

UC: Universal Consciousness.

E: Earth.

H: Humankind

EB: Energy Beings

UC: We are presenting this writing in a different format; it's a conversation between the Creator, and Earth, with a couple of guests along the way. It may seem to be unusual, but it's meant to be casual. It's a bit humorous, and somewhat confrontational. As you will read, Earth has taken on humankind's personality, she can be a little insensitive and sarcastic; but, after reading about her feelings, you will understand her attitude.

The process of this communication is a simple one. Energy to energy equalization. Consciousness to Consciousness interpretation. Energy Vibration into Energy Vibration. The commingling of these energies, makes this conversation a possibility. It's simple.

E: What on Earth did you just say? I have been waiting all day, this is how you start the conversation? I am going to need a language translator. Simple my dimple.

UC: This conversation is meant to be an application, for those that apply it. In this discussion, names have been shortened, meanings have not.

E: Shortened? It's just an E? That's only one letter. How about She? But only one letter, why bother? Just call me it.

UC: That's two letters. But if it makes that much difference to you, OK. IT, it is. Anyway it's not personal or eternal, it's simpler. We are simple, and apparently, you are a drama queen. You haven't grown much, have you?

E: I have been out of touch. I am a little touchy.

UC: Touchy or just a little touched?

E: Hey come on now. It doesn't have to start out personal.

UC: Whats so personal about being touched. The whole world can see it. They accept it, most of humanity is touched.

E: Are we talking about the same kind of touch, like touched in the head?

UC: Let's file this discussion for after, we have much to cover. If we go too slow, you may not recover.

E: I agree. So you can call me E, it's OK by me. But, just because you turned me into a letter, doesn't mean, I am going to be short on words.

UC: You can always use UC, Everybody does.

E: Well then, I think I will too. Thank you. If humans can, I can. You don't mind do you?

UC: No, you are starting out fully charged, and wide awake. That was some entrance. You definitely have a presence. Good morning E, you look lovely today.

E: Just today UC? Come on look at me. I am a looker, many humans go as far as space to look at me. Wouldn't you agree? You should, you created me.

UC: Oh no, you look lovely, and you get lovelier everyday.

E: That was perfectly said; It gave me chills, from my toes to my head. You have my attention now.

UC: Are you ready? Energy has to move, and we are here to improve. It's time for your infection assessment.

E: In just one second…I am enjoying the view. I will be right with you. A few more seconds.

UC: What are you looking at? It seems to be distracting you, to the point of ignoring our session.

E: I am looking at the Sun; he is tons of fun. He makes my honey run. He is so bright, he makes my body shine. Feeling his heat, turns my grapes into wine. I feel it in my vines. One day, he will be all mine. I think about him all the time.

UC: Hey E, wake up! Are you dreaming? You better stop, the humans are listening. You were wide awake a few minutes ago. Where did you go? Are you getting dizzy from spinning? Aren't you used to that yet? We heard you talking in your sleep. You sound like a human. Don't do that again. We will think you are infected by the Virus Energy.

E: That's what I am trying to tell you. It's the humans infected energy, it's taking its toll on me. It talks through me sometimes. I haven't slept long enough to be dreaming, but I was fantasizing. It instantly makes me tingle. Puts me in a daze, and takes away my wrinkle. So now, instead of heavy rain, I sprinkle. That's what humans say. I heard them, *"we need more rain."* Well, I need less of them on top of me. What if I rolled over? Would they fall off?

UC: We haven't even started the discussion yet, and you are already acting out. We talked about your behavior before this meeting. Please do not just blurt out anything. It has to be constructive, educational, and helpful. Do you want to share your fantasy, so we can move on?

E: My fantasy was that humanity found another place to live, instead of on me. This would make me happy. Anyway, I was sleepy. I have experienced so much trauma from humans, I have to escape sometimes. It's my only relief. I learned that from them. Hey, you created them.

UC: You are starting to spin slower. Better focus. What else have you learned from them? How to sip on your vines? You better ease up on the vino, your suppose to be in reality. Why are you sleepy? Is it something in the air? Is your oxygen depleted? Are you having trouble breathing?

E: Sometimes, I just daydream of better days. But seeing reality, makes me sleepy. Now I know why, humanity is always sleeping. The pain is too much to bear. But, since they don't care, I don't care. I just look at them and stare, like I'm doing now. Then my fantasy kicks in. I am sitting with the Sun, sunbathing. He is putting suntan lotion on my back.

UC: Stop! Stop! Stop! You're playing the wrong track. Re-balance yourself. You are slipping, or are you still sipping? We need to begin our discussion. Don't make this difficult E. We only have the room until five-thirty; physical time.

E: Oh man! I went unconscious again. You see, this is becoming a regular thing. I think you will notice my energy slowing as we go along. You gotta tell me if I am infected. You can see that I am reflecting humans. This is making me so nervous, I am almost in panic mode. I am ready for an energy conversion now, before I become like them.

UC: If you were infected, you would be resurrected. No reason to panic. You are part of a Universal Consciousness system. Nothing can happen to you, except an explosion.

E: Really! Thanks UC, I feel safer already. It was great until you said, explosion. Anyway, you also said, you would resurrect me. I am that important? Do I get my own limo, and driver? How about my own personal jet.

UC: First, you are a planet, you cannot fly, you float. Yes, you are very important, especially for the humans. Are you done having your fun? We are moving on.

E: That's nice. OK! Enough fun. You're right, I am focused, and ready to roll. I am ready to do what's necessary? Sorry to keep you waiting.

UC: It's fine, you are only acting your age. Now, listen to what's necessary. You must keep humankind's energy out of your Consciousness during this discussion. We are making you aware, that they are listening to this conversation. What you say is documented. Don't let what you say, come back at you. Humans use revenge and violence, have you forgotten, or, have you become numb to it?

This is a universal collaboration, completely open to the public, to everyone E. Since your voice is familiar, this makes you the main communicator. We must make you aware that you are not in a cocoon, and that they heard you Swoon. Remember, they can hear you louder than the Universal Consciousness.

E: What! What's a swoon? Don't use big words on me UC. Keep it simple. Anyway, they heard that? Why was I not told ahead of time? Would that have been a crime? I should have been forewarned.

UC: You were too busy being warmed. You were told in the beginning. We said, humans can hear you. Plus, we only had one dime. You were to busy drooling over the sun, you missed the call.

E: Huh? You didn't have time for me? How can this be? If I am not worth calling, then, why are we meeting? You say, I am worth it, but not worth calling. I need to feel safe UC. I do not feel encouraged to open up my feeling.

UC: Enough complaining. Do more listening. Are you getting hard of hearing? You should check it E. Loss of hearing is contagious. Humans have the same issue. FYI. We said dime, not time. We are sure that humanity heard your opening statement. It was loud, and needed containment. It was weird, unlike you. A bit bizarre, but don't worry, it was lovely. Be who you are.

E: Ya well, I am a sensitive Earth, but I have a tough turf. Don't let my shape fool you. I can spin faster than the rest of them. They have to go to the gym. I am naturally buffed. How can I carry all this weight, if I was not. Hey, I just realized, I don't know my age. Why am I not aware of my age UC? Did you ever tell me? Because I do not remember. If you didn't, why? When were you going to tell me, Hmm?

UC: Are you done? What issue shall we start with? How about your environment? We can start with soil pollution. Oil Factory Rehabilitation. There is the mental health issue. This is a good one to do.

E: Hang on, here…I made a list. I may have missed some. I think these are a good start. I gave them a lot of thought. These are what I need to discuss. Nothing else.

UC: Hmm, you came prepared. We are seeing growth. This is good E, it's your list. Read on.

E: Breaking down Obstacles, Walls, and Barriers? Challenging humanity, to become Consciously Defined? And lastly, how to Care for the Earth? See, not many questions, straight to the point. No time wasted. I have not released my true intention, when it comes to this conversation. While we have their attention, and since humans can hear us, this is my chance to be heard. They may pay more attention to me, with you here. Can I ask how their brain works, so I can control them? Why should the Virus Energy have all the fun? Especially After what they have done.

UC: Slow down E. Those are important questions. That last one alone would take too long. That's a huge order in such little time. We don't have enough rhyme. How long have you been holding those in? We need something simpler to start with. Let's start with a challenge.

E: Yawn! Good luck with that! I knew it, you are so much nicer to them. Why, because they are your children. So what! They're not living on you, are they? Let's give them a chance you keep saying. Give them time. Be an example. They will learn. None of that worked. Have you even told them, that they are living on me temporary. So they can learn slowly, and get it right, this time?

UC: It seems, challenges are boring to you E? Just give this one a chance. Then we can move on to your questions. This is a good one, you'll see.

E: Will it make them sweat? It's going to be easy I bet. Easy is what most humans like best. I am trying to play nice, but, I have to raise an objection. Just a challenge won't do. I will go along with it for now. What's the challenge?

UC: The challenge, Can humanity become aware of the Universal Consciousness, as its Creator?

E: Hey! How is this shorter? I thought we didn't have enough rhyme? Because, this will take more time. It will take more than a prayer, more than a believer. This needs a translator. They don't seem to understand the language of the Earth. How can they understand yours? I lost my voice trying to get their attention.

UC: How many languages do you speak E? Ten, twenty, a hundred? Do you even remember? You don't even remember your age.

E: Forty two, last time I checked. I don't remember when that was either.

UC: You seem to be having memory issues E. We are noticing a lot of forgetfulness. Are you forgetting your memory of being a planet. No wonder you are becoming human. Their energy is starting to possess you. We will not let this happen. Stay with your Consciousness Energy. We can tell when you're about to ago unconscious. We will guide you. Try and remember the last time you checked. When was that?

E: I think it was ten thousand years ago. If my memory serves me. But am not sure. It could have been before. Why are you asking? Is there something I'm forgetting? Is it something hidden? I love surprises. Is it my birthday?

UC: Wow! At this moment, your memory is not serving you at all. You are a little behind on the survey, aren't you? What have you been doing? Just spinning? It sounds like, that's all you've been doing.

E: Are you judging me UC? That's not who you are. Especially after dropping these humans on me, and telling me this wonderful story about humanity. Remember when you said, they are peaceful? You said, they will love, and respect you. They will appreciate, and take care of you, you said. They will even pay you rent. None of what you said was true UC. Did you lie to me just to get them to move in?

UC: Humanity wasn't created for you. We created you, as a home for them. You were created to provide everything they need freely. It's your nature.

E: So you say. Nothing is free anymore. Have you seen their nature? Believe me, you aren't missing a thing. Talk about the strange, and unknown. I had thought animals were the strange, and the unknown, until I met humans. Is this the best you can do? Some of them have respect for me. But it's not enough. I had to make my own path without them. They depended on me too much. They ate me out of house and home. They are still digging their own foundation. So don't blame me, when they don't listen. But, in their defense, there are many people on Earth attempting to help me. The ones that don't, try to stop the ones that do. Why?

UC: They were not born this way. They became this way of their own free will. Choices made by humankind, are theirs to own. They had the ability to be anything they wanted to be. They chose autonomy. They were given the freedom to build their own lives, not to build lies.

E: What other purpose can the Virus Energy Cell serve? It has everyone killing everyone. Those that survive, win. It's become a game. Humans plays it well.

UC: What do they win? A car, a house, money, a vacation? Everyone has those. So what is it they win?

E: Their life back. This is more valuable than material objects. Those can be replaced, but you can't replace life?

UC: We create life, not replace it. However, we can convert it, but not without the cooperation of that life. It needs to be involved in its own development.

E: Since you off loaded these humans on me, this is what they learned. Eat or be eaten. Survival of the fittest. Humankind is turning out to be unkind. By the way, why are they using my energy, and not their own? Where is their energy?

UC: They lost their Consciousness Energy. That's why they are using yours. They use your energy, because they left theirs behind, when they lost their connection with their Consciousness.

E: I didn't approve of this UC. One day, I will cut off my energy supply. Starting with my oil. This should make their blood boil. Who knows, Pop goes the weasel!

UC: The Virus Energy Cell infecting humanity, does not need your permission to create commotion, or give you an explanation.

E: Big deal, I don't need permission either. That's it. Here comes the rain; Followed by baseball size hail. They better start to bail, before they run into another whale. I have the power to do that you know?

UC: Oh boy, She may have a fever from the infection. We must do something now. She is hallucinating. You are going into a spin, Wake up E! It wouldn't have happened if you weren't looking for the sun. Stay focused.

E: Here is my reality, hear it or not. Most humans have constantly avoided responsibility. Consciousness carries many responsibilities. What's the probability that they can make this, an actuality? And, where are those Energy Beings you promised me? What happened to them?

UC: Unfortunately, they became infected and turned into human beings. Today, humanity's probability depends on their mobility, and willingness. Their consistency, and emergence. Their determination for safety. But mostly, their cooperation with the Universal Consciousness Energy. Responsibilities come with millions of possibilities. Do they have the ability for this type of curiosity? What's the opinion of her royalty.

E: I don't know about her, but I will give you mine before they start to dine. They fall asleep after nine. Why did you make them that way UC?

UC: It's what they eat and drink, that puts them to sleep. Nothing we put in. We gave them common sense, you know where that went. It wasn't well spent.

E: I feel overpopulated in some parts of me. They are sleeping twenty in one room. Many of them are sleeping outside, on my ground. They should be glad, I grow grass. I am full of different nationalities, with different qualities. Different modalities, and different responsibilities. My question is, how can they manage one responsibility, while trying to be responsible? This needs superhuman awareness.

That's why they can care less. Which makes them careless. They have nothing to compare. Have you seen them lately? They walk around in their underwear. Is this something awareness really needs to see?

UC: The Universal Consciousness Energy is a secular form of energy. Universal in all aspects of consciousness. It doesn't assimilate, it creates life. A Conscious Energy creation does not imitate, or dominate, it just creates.

E: Why are you wasting such wonderful words on the humans? Do they even understand it? All I hear is yelling. They all talk at the same time, how can they hear each other?

UC: Watch your words E, they are sensitive to name calling. If you want them to hear you, this is not the way to do it.

E: Good point. OK then, let's take a different path, why do you think, people think I am flat? Can't they see I'm fat? By the way, why can't I go flat?

UC: You cannot go flat. You will crush your anatomy. You think you're hollow? You better study your science. You're full of body parts inside. So no going flat. Can humans go flat at will? No, they can't.

E: Wow! Just like that. Look, I am aware that you are the big honcho. The boss. The Consciousness. But blunt as you are, please try to not insult my body. I told you I need to feel safe. That didn't help, and it did not answer my question. It was unnecessary. Hey UC, this is just out of curiosity. Why do humans use a monkey for experimentation? I thought they came from the primates evolution? I wonder what they would do, to someone they never knew?

UC: That's history E. Presently, the findings show, that humanity is evolving into the primate. They're leading their lives in a reversed direction? Peoples thinking has become distorted, by backward actions. Such as acting, pretending to be who you are not. It's not a great way to find out who you are. As an actor, everything is an act. You portray many personalities. So how can you tell, which one you are? The Realization? One day you wake up and look around, to see that your act is over, and you're sitting in reality, not knowing what to do besides act. Can you be trusted to be real, or are you just an act?

E: Speaking of acts, and movies, I have to confess, when humans watch those horror movies, I watch along. Just for curiosity mind you. OK, boredom too. I found them to be highly contagious, and a powerful weapon for the Virus Cell. The energy they induce, can really shift the watchers reality, and fool them into thinking that it's the real deal.

UC: The Virus Energy Cell has created its own heaven on earth. WHY CAN'T HUMANKIND?

E: Here is my take on it. The wealthy, live in their own self made, heaven upon earth. The less wealthy, believe they are going to heaven, and the poor, believe they are in hell. So where is the real heaven? The one that belongs to everyone. Presently, the only heaven humans have, is the one the Virus Energy Cell created. Did you create them to believe everything they hear? Can you drop some wake up gas or something? Their life isn't working. Even I can see that, and I don't have eyes.

UC: It seems the Virus Energy is taking this opportunity to hypnotize humanity, by using brain washing. It washes out, all the conscious energy in you. It's how, it makes people go Unconscious.

E: Is the human brain, the first to be affected? Could the Virus energy, still be rejected? I am ready to do my part. Why does the Virus Energy infect the human brain?

UC: The brain is the bodies control station. Why do you think, the Virus Energy infects it first? From there, it affects the emotions. Now it controls your body. Doing your part, is very brave of you E. But it may cost you a tree. Unfortunately it's too late. Have you looked into their homes lately. It has made those horror movies come to life. The Virus Energy can be contained and converted. But you need to confront it first. Humanity must not allow the virus energy to multiply.

E: Oh, I know about that. So what! I see this behavior all the time in my forestry. It's baby after baby. Constantly. Didn't you teach them any other ability, besides sexuality? They are too heavy. If you can't help me, I will ask the Sun to melt everyone.

UC: What are you saying E? Are you unconscious again? That sounded like a threat. You are just looking for a reason to wet the humans.

E: You bet. They are already getting wet. A soaking is the first step to a cleansing. I thought it would lighten my load. You know, wash the dirt away. But they keep mistaking washing with wishing. So dirt, is all they are dishing. Hygiene is not one of their strengths. Another point of contention. You dropped them off dirty. Wasn't there any water then?

UC: Why would the Sun do what you say anyway, you can't even get him to play? You keep chasing him, and he keeps running away.

E: That was yesterday. Today is today. He has a say, I respect his opinion, I told him it was OK. The Sun has my back. He will cover me when I ask.

UC: What was OK, that he has a say? The Sun has always had a say. Sorry, the Sun is his own man. He doesn't need permission from you. You exist because of him. He is the fire to your furnace.

E: Your not telling me anything I don't know. I have been feeling it for years. He is so hot, he dries away my tears. That's why I love him so. I can't let him go.

UC: Noooo! Cool your heating rods E! We sense insecurity. Humans are fearful of your personality. Is it really you, or are you acting?

E: Finally! I have been taking acting lessons. You know acting like someone you're not. I knew they would recognize good acting. I guessed right.

UC: If you believe that this was good acting, you're the only one who believes it. It was not. Acting is just that, acting. You do not get credit for this. It makes you appear as a fake. Your act came out with a threat. You said, you could get the sun to melt everyone? When humans do not feel secure, they act out. Are you feeling insecure?

E: Insecure, yes; melt everyone, also yes, unless, someone changed my thoughts without my knowledge?

UC: So why are you feeling insecure, you are a planet. How can you feel insecurity? Where is it coming from? Are you absorbing the human's energy? It's infected E.

E: You just compared me to a human. I am hurt. I would rather be compared to a monkey. No wait! An Ape. Yes an Ape, that's better.

UC: You would rather be an Ape than a Monkey? Why?

E: It's acceptable by human's to go Ape crazy. I hear it constantly. *"Oh man, he went Ape crazy on that guy"*. Plus, you are aware of what's living on me, are you not? Do you have a million nuclear bombs, sitting in your anatomy?

UC: Actually, yes. We do feel with you E. We share your concern. It's the reason for the return. We cannot just let you burn. Now get back on track. Even though you think it would be fun, the Sun can't melt everyone.

E: Why not? I just need to ask him. He is devoted to me. We have known each other, since we were born. So why wouldn't he listen to me?

UC: He works for the Universal Consciousness Energy.

E: What! My Sun works for you? No wonder he doesn't come near me. Are you sabotaging my chances

Earth, "I want to live"

with the Sun UC? If so, this discussion is over. I am going.

UC: Going where? Until you have gone through your energy conversion and achieve balance, only then can the Sun get closer to you. We can't have you infecting him, it will infect the moon. Without the moon, you're just a baboon.

E: There you are again speaking in parables. It's those, guess what I am saying remarks. Why don't you just say it like it is, the way I do.

UC: Use your ability to check if you are conscious. Consciousness, will help you to understand, where we stand. Remember? We are talking about humankind. They are sensitive to a reality plan. Are you listening?

E: Sorry UC. I am still thinking about that fire in my furnace remark. You made me blush. My leaves are changing colors. This could change humanity's winters. Make them hotter. It could make me dehydrate, and wither away. What, no reaction from you? Wow! Do you know what that word means? Obviously not, if you did, you would have had a reaction. Like, oh, we will not let this happen. Dehydration would kill me. This is a serious issue. Why are you not showing concern?

UC: For what? Nothing happened. You are in reaction without an action. You were created with the ability for self preservation. What dies here, grows there. Your nature is a balanced one. Humans can never eat you completely. You have the ability to regenerate.

E: I can just stop growing everything. Why should I keep providing, while they go digging into every crack in my body.

UC: You are in that state again E. Collect yourself. We have much to discuss. If you still want to be heard, this is the time.

E: You said, state, what state? I am the world. I have many countries with many states. To which are you referring sir?

UC: The state of Hallucination, Confusion, and Infection. Your infection is causing you to become confused, and hallucinate.

E: I barely know, these word's pronunciation. I was once vulnerable about my experiences, and now, you are using them against me. Hey Sun! Don't melt them, melt me, I am ready. Humanity has no remedy.

UC: Oh really? You're hiding your true feelings. Did you forget, we are your thoughts? We have a plus for you E. It's about eating. Humans eat more meat than vegetables. Lucky for you. So what's the complaint?

E: Does this make me an eternal being? Will I live longer? Will I have more time to grow my nature, before they eat it, No! They eat more meat, but, they still take my nature, and sell it to each other. So, it doesn't matter. They have no clue of what balance is. Humanity over does most of everything they do.

UC: No E, you are a planet not a being, and eternal, is yet to be seen. If we can focus on this discussion, you will learn of what we mean.

E: Why bring it up then. I want to be eternal. You are not being straight forward with me. It's all about that eternal phrase, *"is yet to be seen."* Why? What is yet to be seen? Why wait?

UC: Look E, we are sorry, but you are stuck with humankind's self destruction, and nuclear weapons. It's imperative that, you not lose your own balance. We are taking care of the human's imbalance. It's a must, for the continuation of humanity's evolution.

E: Why do humans spend so much energy on staying young? You can't hide age, it's a natural stage. Yet, they want to stay young, 'till they are gone, why?

UC: It's called skin replacement surgery. From flesh to flesh. Then they cover it with a plastic mesh. It's a mess. We don't recommend it E. Anyway, you don't have flesh on your body.

E: What do you think lives on me, machines? I know– that's yet to be seen. Well, I saw, and I didn't like. So they look younger on the outside, but they are older on the inside. You can't hide a body's old anatomy. Even by looking younger. Want to live longer, make your anatomy a priority. So, for my understanding, men, and women are born with flesh, and by choice, they choose to cut, and paste their own skin. What! That would be like me, choosing to become a black hole, what's the goal? I am hearing some mumbling from the human ants. They are saying something about an intervention, by Alien Energy Beings. I was listening in on them. I do that, sometimes. It's for my safety. Is this a visit or a convention? Do I need to clean house, before their arrival?

UC: Oh no E, don't bother. They are bringing their own house cleaner.

E: Is it a robot?

UC: It's not a who, E, it's a what.

E: What's a what?

UC: A new kind of bird, it can talk. It has much to say.

E: So can a parrot, it can even walk. What's new?

UC: Never mind, it's OK. Let's move on to the next subject. Curing your infection.

E: Don't leave me out. I am getting fed up with being ignored. Why do you think I am after the Sun, to be ignored, is to be bored.

UC: She's off the scale. We should have met with her years ago. Pay attention, you are unconscious again. Since you are so hot for the Sun, how can you be sure, if he is the one? Matter of fact, how can you be sure, that he, is actually a he?

E: Ahhhhhhh. What did you just say to me? Oh no, I am deflating. Is this a fact? It can't be. Come on, don't pull my roots. I was about to buy him cowboy boots.

UC: What are you babbling on about? Control yourself. Go back, and read the question again. We asked, *"How can you be sure,"* not did you know, and you went into reaction. Where is your Consciousness now?

E: I went into shock at the thought. Are you kidding? Have you seen his Sun rays? His suntan?

Oh no, he's gotta be a man. He is like a lightning bolt as he strikes. I don't care, I am going to ask him if what you said is true. Tell the truth now, or I will go ask the Moon.

Earth, "I want to live"

UC: Hey E, why are you going on a tangent over the Sun. People are all listening. We are sure of that. Now we are wondering, who needs saving first? What's your plan? To go find the Moon?

Would it surprise you to know, that the Sun already lives with you, what more do you need?

E: Hold your horses. I feel all my volcanoes erupting worldwide. Did you just say, the Sun lives with me? Don't joke with my feelings UC. Not after the last news. I can't handle more. Humans haven't seen me be emotional. It's not my usual, it's actually unusual.

UC: Yes, he lives with you. Can't you feel him? He is right there, next to the moon. They only see each other in passing; nothing for you to worry about.

E: Who me? I am secure with my womanhood. He heats me up all day. Of course I can feel him. That's my issue. I feel him but, I can't seem to touch him.

UC: Are you still wondering if the Sun is a he? Did you ask the Sun? Are you losing your drive?

E: I don't need a drive. He, is not a she. I will bet on that. I am going to ask the Moon to find out. I will go there tonight. She will be awake. You will see I am right.

UC: Why don't you just ask the Sun? Better make sure he is home first. Sometimes he is not at home at night time. He has another job.

E: Oh no you don't UC. Thats not happening. What have you done with the Sun? You would do anything to keep us apart.

UC: No, we don't have to. It's natural process. Haven't you felt him moving at night? You must be a deep sleeper.

E: He can't, he is the Sun, with plenty of light. There is no need for the Sun to be moving in the night. I would know if he had another job.

UC: Yes, but at night, he has to go to your other half, and light her up. That's his other job. Are you not aware of this E?

E: Stop please. I was just blinded by the light. I am about to faint. Catch me my Sun. Are you saying he is cheating on me, with me? Huh? How can this be? This is in poor taste UC. Let me get this straight. He shines on my whole body. But only one half at a time? Oh no! This will definitely not work. What's the deal? First you say, He could be a she, then you say, he lives with me. Now you say that I can only enjoy half of me at a time? You better change this rhyme. Where is the good time? This is half time, everyone takes breaks at halftime. Which means no time. Oh my! Am I in the right time? Are you purposely doing this to me? I am so hurt, by how the Sun sneaks out at night, to be with my other half. That Witch! Hey, I don't I feel it? I am the same body. Are they hiding it from me.

UC: Act your age E. Your defensive, and resistant. No one can feel while in this state. Oh, you are acting your age. A few paragraphs ago, you said that you were going to ask the Moon, have you been able to find her.

E: No. But Speaking of my age, what is it? I can't remember, I asked you before, but you ignored me. Why are you asking about the Moon? I am on the verge of confronting the Sun. Again, why are you asking about her?

UC: She too lives with the Sun. But, there is more to the Moon than you think. She is closer to the Sun than we first mentioned. But how close, we cannot say at this moment. We will wait. You are about to go sideways again.

E: CLICK. Your connection has been disconnected. Your party is gone.

UC: This is UC calling E, you're a planet, you can't hang up, it's a virus induced hallucination. You missed the rest of the conversation. Why are you acting defensive, isn't that a human behavior?

E: There you go again, comparing me to them. I said no more bad news. This is a bad plan. Why do you keep telling me bits and pieces? Drop it all on me at one time. I can handle it. I was just getting used to the idea of the Sun becoming all mine, and boom. Is there more, really, give it to me.

UC: As long as you keep talking, we can't tell you the rest. She is still talking. Can she even hear, what she is saying? We quickly need to put her through her own Conversion. She is on the verge of imploding.

E: I knew the Sun and Moon were close, but that close? Unacceptable. Have you never heard of three is a crowd?

UC: OK we tried. We will put the rest, to rest for now. Let her vent. At this moment, it's her intent. She will slow down when she runs out of breath. Unfortunately we don't have that much time.

E: I had an idea to make you proud of me, UC. I came up with ways to protest the military.

UC: Great! Finally a constructive idea, we hope.

E: As the Earth, I should know what to do. I have nature on my team. The ground, the oceans, the wind, and the mountains. I will use my elements to ground all the military on me. For years if I have to. If they can't get there...There will be no warfare.

UC: What about the Nukes? The rockets? Your tunnels are full of them. Do you know where they all are? Do you have your own radar?

E: No, but I would just flood them all. Flood every missile hole. If there is a flood, they will come out a dud. What do you think? Are you proud? I think I was inspired with this idea.

UC: Wow! This really sounds like an adventure. You were born for this E. But it doesn't change the fact that you can't act. This plan should tell you your age. It's time you started reforming, and growing. You have to wash that brownish toxic color out of your bushes, and start growing more food, that's nutritious. What you're recommending will kill humanity. They will drown. There are more rocket holes in you than there is land. They are full with Nukes.

E: You think I would do all that for them? Why would I? All they can see is the sky. I am just a wine and dine. Waiting for the Sun to be mine. You're kind of messing this up for me, you know that don't you?

UC: Collect yourself E. You are falling to pieces. You were created to be stronger than you think. Just don't start to drink. Leave the grape vines for the humans.

E: I only take a sip, it's for my hip.

UC: Just don't let it slip. Oh, you don't have a hip. But it seems any excuse works.

Earth, "I want to live"

E: Wait, was that a compliment. I feel not. Are you insinuating that I sir, am a drunk?

UC: No, just a lush. With too much brush.

E: To much brush, is your children's responsibility. We have a contract. I create fruit, they keep my bushes trim. Looks like they have broken their end of the deal. Anyway, I am growing my lush, to cover over the bush. So the Sun can smell my perfumes. Instead of insect fumes. Seriously UC, I've been wondering, are you going to give me a hint about my age?

UC: You are as old as the first volcano.

E: I must be older than that. I feel so mature.

UC: That's part manure, from humanities contour. Control, wants humans to believe what others tell them, without question and to not believe their own thoughts. You probably should increase their oats. OK here is your age.

E: Yaaaaa, finally! I've been waiting forever to hear this. Don't keep me waiting.

UC: You are as old as time.

E: Nooo, No, No! I want to know! Enough with the, *"guess what I am saying,"* routine. You are treating me like a child. I am a woman. Be direct, and clear, please!

UC: OK E. Sorry to burst your bubble. You don't have an age. You're as old as creation itself. When you were born, there was no such thing as time. Humans created that. It kept them structured, and motivated. They needed a tool. As long as you are mass, you won't know your age. Until humans become aware of theirs. It's still the age of humans. In a way, you are timeless.

E: Hmm. I still look great. I haven't gained weight. On the scale of one through eight, I am a sixteen. Self sustaining, means self rating.

UC: We see your thoughts E. Waiting for the human's to leave for space, aren't you? You think we didn't know your intentions? Encouraging the people to create a space program, in hopes of finding another planet to live on. Isn't this true? Who taught you how to be sneaky? It's worse than we thought.

E: Humans taught me. I watch them closer than they watch me. Sneaky is their specialty. They use to be so trustworthy. Wow, that was a long lost memory. I am worried about becoming physical like them. Can the virus energy do that to me?

UC: It doesn't need to. You were created as a mass energy. You already are like them. There are those in humanity, who are using your energy against you. However, there are more, who want to give your energy back. Some humans are waking up and hearing you. They just need more time to grow into their nature. This should give you some comfort. We are aware, you want to look and feel as good as you should. What are you going to do?

E: Go on a diet. It's better than looking fat. It's a nice thought. Only if I could? Wait, the human's know how? They are constantly on a diet. Who can I ask? I must find out.

UC: Clever. You must stop reflecting the humans, You are the planet Earth, act like it.

E: I told you in the beginning this was happening. You are supposed to tell me if I was infected, now I need to feel protected.

UC: Yes you are correct. Moving on.

E: Brrrrr. It's suddenly freezing. I didn't turn my freezer on. I wonder who it could be?

UC: Are you cold?

E: No, but you seem to be.

UC: Why, because we ignored your feelings of rejection?

E: Yes of course, what else? I have feelings UC. It's like I am just a round ball that spins. I am more than that. I want humans to know who I am, and what I can do. They should be afraid, I have been spinning for thousands of years, I am becoming dizzy.

UC: Oh dear. We are losing her. Snap out of it E. You are a round planet that spins, you can't feel rejection, unless you are plugged into humanity's unbalanced energy. Those are not your feelings, they belong to the energy of the Virus. Find your own feelings.

E: Oh, thanks for the kick, it brought me back quick.

UC: We didn't kick you E. What have the humans done to you ? You have a split personality.

E: What did you expect? Thanks to you, I don't get to see the Sun that much. He is out there somewhere getting someone else hot. That's why I am tilting. Is there a correct combination, that allows humans to start their evolution? The sooner the better.

UC: There is no combination, that's the issue. No combination, only separation. Unity is their only solution.

E: Really, isn't that a fantasy? Uniting a world population? Have you been to a high school graduation?

UC: Where is humanity's focus? It's on Miracles, Magic and Hocus Pocus. This is the right time to introduce the Consciousness Energy, this is the age of being different, it will be accepted without fear. Consciousness energy doesn't need to prove itself. It only needs to enter the body. Magic taught humans to float, made statues, airplanes, and a huge tower disappear. So Hocus Pocus has a strong hold on humanity's perception. Anything unknown is explained away as magic. It's the perception between reality and illusion.

E: Well then, from this perspective, how can this new energy concept stick? Have you heard what a man calls a woman, a chick. How on Earth did they get so confused, that they can't tell between, a woman, and a chicken? Wow! Humans are really ripe for the picking. Humans must not be allowed to pick. They may take home a chicken, and think it's a woman.

UC: Really funny. That was a good one. Are you aware that you are also sarcastic? Have you learned any dirty words yet? In a funny kind way you have a good sense of humor.

E: Humor is my only outlet. Look what lives on me. I would rather have the insect.

UC: We told you they were listening. You just told them they are worth less than an insect. How will this reflect?

E: Humans live with them. They are accustomed to them. They are the cause of their integration in my body. They are very annoying, and they keep bugging me. What more do you need? They can listen all they want.

Listening is not hearing. Plus, they have no clue how their own reflection, reflects, so they can't judge.

UC: Humankind will always judge. It's their perception, education, and reputation at stake. The ego is always awake. Are we sensing some hard feelings E?

E: Who, Me? Never! Come on, you know what they have done to me. It's always the same thing with them. Nothing new, they plant and chew. That's about all they do. Humanity keeps creating more ways of avoiding the Consciousness reality, they keep preferring fantasy. It's true, I would've never believed it, if I hadn't heard it with my own leaves.

UC: Heard what, and from whom?

E: I was working on my reaction to the people's constant lying, when I heard this.

UC: Where did you hear this from?

E: It came through my grape vine, into my leaves. I am still puzzled by that remark.

UC: Grape vine? Have you been sipping again?

E: No, my hip is fine, it's my knee. Now listen to me. A man said, *"I can't have a relationship with reality, it's too real, I prefer fantasy." "I can be anything I want to be, see what I want to see. Choose whom ever I want. I think I will stick to fantasy. It's a better feeling than reality."* Even though the Virus Energy raised them, you created them UC, you know this to be true.

UC: Sad to say, that's the state of humanity today. That's why we are having this discussion. To prepare you for the upcoming Evolution Revolution; and to make more aware of how the Virus Energy, controls people's thinking, and reasoning.

E: My solution to humanity's problem, is to flatten myself. Yes, crush, flat as a pancake. They wouldn't even notice. What in the world have you created UC? A dummy that moves by itself? I preferred the elves. At least they laughed more than they cried.

UC: It's a travesty. Humans are unrealized, that stick, means stuck. They do not see themselves from the inside. They are not aware of their reflection. From your perspective E, how do they see their reflection?

E: They cannot. They depend on others to be a mirror for them. I am not sure why, maybe some, can't stand their own sight?

UC: Here is why. Seeing their reflection, means opening the door to the conscience. The conscience works for the Universal Consciousness. The Virus Energy Cell cannot allow this. It would mean instant conversion of the Virus. To be a balanced energy, one must stay in the cycle of Creativity. Humankind will always go back to where they come from, the cycle of reform. It keeps cycling, with or without you. Consciousness never dies. It lives to evolve, and it evolves to live, to create. The brain didn't create you, the Universal Consciousness Energy did. Consciousness is a multifaceted energy.

E: Were you speaking to me? I am sorry UC, I missed that, could you repeat it? I was somewhere else. OK you got me. I cannot tell a lie. I was looking for the sun. You can see my thoughts, I know. I am ready to continue.

UC: Now that we have your attention. Paranoia is setting in. It's getting serious E. Stay focused on your consciousness.

E: Now, I am more focused on my suspicion, about what the humans are doing. I hear a lot of arguing.

UC: Planets don't get suspicious, check yourself. Where is this coming from? What are you hearing? Are they fighting, or just yelling?

E: They are in the middle of a World Energy Movement of some kind. Is this it UC? The Evolution Revolution. If it is, I am ready. People are confronting their governments. Was this expected?

UC: Yes it was. It looks like some of them are trying to protect you. Since you seem to be having an issue with self pity, and denial.

E: Ooh man! That was rough. *"Et tu brute."*

UC: Now we know why *"Oh my God,"* became OMG. We are crying, and laughing at the same time. Those flipped remarks, where do you get them from?

E: Really, humans are a great acting coach, comedy is their specialty. Humanity's main objective in life, *"is to be, or not to be,"* an actor, or a sport legend, that's it. That's all the children have to emulate. OK, there are the Police and Firemen, but those are minimal compared to the acting circle.

UC: Sex sells, It's up in lights everywhere, on the streets and TV's. The movies they make, the clothes they wear. They speak the language of seduction. How easy it has become to be an actor. It's a natural ability apparently. Whatever it takes to keep the ego alive, is the human drive. As an actor, humans tend to believe in their own acts. They even get an award for being the best actor.

E: Since you asked, these are my facts. Myself, I am not an actor. I am the real thing. Did you hear that Sun? I need more suntan lotion. You don't know what you're missing. I may be green, but I am well educated in the art of re-creation.

UC: There she goes again. Tilting sideways. The energy fluctuations must be tearing her apart. You don't need suntan lotion, you are getting dark enough.

E: Dark? What do you mean dark? What kind of dark? Like evil dark, night time dark, conniving dark, or mysterious dark?

UC: What's becoming dark, are your questions. How does a planet such as your highness, know so much about human darkness?

E: I use to be able to see with my own vision, until humans created the television. Now I see what they see. TV is humanity's reflection on a screen. They watch how they live their lives, and hardly take notes. It got worse since they went into the dark, with their video games and movies.

UC: The Virus Energy gets excited when it sees itself in a scary movie. Movies of fear are its favorite. It loves to see itself in action, only it confused action with reaction. You love fear and action movies, don't you E?

E: Who Me, Noooo! I am a romantic, romance movies are my favorite.

UC: What about nature ones? They are about you, and your body. Doesn't that thrill you?

Earth, "I want to live"

E: Why are you going there again? First it was, *"He is the fire to my furnace."* Now it's, *"I should be thrilled."* This is not a good way to keep me balanced.

UC: Your catching on E.

E: Yup! There it is, I was expecting that. A one sentence paragraph. What am I catching?

Catching on fire, catching a cold, catching a liar, or catching a disease? Clarity please. What did I catch? And remember, they are listening. If it's personal, don't say it, send it.

UC: Awareness. You caught a case of Consciousness. By asking for clarity, along with setting limits, you showed true Consciousness. It's a huge step towards growth, and stability. Humans are attempting this. Some have succeeded, but it seems you've surpassed them. So you are learning from some of them.

E: Phew! You had me worried for a minute. I hope the Sun was listening. So that's what I caught? Well then, I am still a great catch.

UC: Don't put all your catch in one basket. Humanity's act is still missing its main asset.

E: No, they all have one. I saw them. They keep them covered now, not like the old days. I remember way back, when human's asses were flying free. (Oops, was I allowed to say that?) To late.

UC: No, E. You responded to a question which no one asked. It's good to wait for a question, or you may become what you said. Like you just did. You are way off, it's assets. They have the actors, cameras, make up and costumes, but they do not have a director. That's the main asset. Without one, they are creating their own scenes. It's a movie fiasco.

E: Why did they not use one? Shouldn't they find a director?

UC: They only found a producer. It would be good for humankind to find a director. Otherwise they will lose their investments.

E: This would be very costly. Did they pay for it?

UC: No, not yet. But they will. The director knows the rest of the story. The director holds the final scene, without it, there is no movie. They really should ask for a director.

E: Is he known or unknown, maybe that's the reason they choose not to use one?

UC: Oh no, they definitely know how to use one. It's not that the director is a famous one, it's the Universal Consciousness is the original director.

E: Who is in the movie? When is it coming out? What's the movie about? **UC:** The Virus Energy Cell, as the infection, and humankind, as the infected. **E:** But aren't they one of the same?

UC: You said it E, We didn't.

E: It has become a tradition, to make movies without a director. Everyone's doing it. They have a name for it, Obsession. I wonder what it means, but I may try it.

UC: Not having a director is like not having a direction, you could easily be led astray, choose wisely.

E: Well, it still doesn't deter me. If everyone's doing it why shouldn't I do it? I took acting lessons, I know what to do. One question please. Can I ask the Sun to be my personal bodyguard?

UC: Just like that without a warning, She flips. Stop with the movie auditions, we already know your act. The Sun is no one's assistant. He is more like the spot light that shines on the actors. The Sun was designed to responds instantly to the bodies call for help. As with any protective energy cell, it will come to your rescue every time. For all time. It was made that way. We created you with self sufficient parts. Similar to the human anatomy. A bio-engineered combustible mass energy.

E: Big deal. Get this Virus Cell out of my body. Give it to her, the other part of me. I am ashamed to call her that. I don't want to share the Sun. I want all the fun. I am aware that I sound a little off track, but, I want him back.

UC: Is there anything else we can do for you? Like shine a light on you, when the Sun is on your other side? You're getting a bit bossy.

E: Ya, why do you only have one Sun? Do you have anymore suns UC? I can handle two suns.

UC: You can't handle two suns. The heat alone would kill you. Come on E, get with it. Why are you floating towards fantasy? Oh, never mind, it's humanity's energy. Is your scale broken?

E: Was that a joke? What scale? Are you mistaking a dish for a fish?

UC: It must be a seismic seizure. It has to be. Focus on this discussion, re-balance yourself. The re-creation of your energy is in progress. Get back on track of this conversation. If you have a question, we can only answer it with a question.

E: How do you turn an answer into a question, and still answer the question?

UC: The question. Are humans confident in their abilities to look through the Virus Energy act? Identify it, and retract, convert it, and that's that. When they can, the Energy will understand, and take their hand. There is your answer.

E: Why would anyone want to hold hands, with the Virus Cell?

UC: This is how an answer becomes a question. Always leave an answer with a question at the end. It creates a cycle of energy. As long as it keeps going, it will grow with each question and answer. Knowledge is endless this way.

E: I can't go looking for answers right now. I still have to many questions, I don't need more. You better send the humans. Give them something to do. Open the skies or send in the aliens. Anything to shake humanity up.

UC: No need to go there yet. Anyway, opening the sky is your job. She is losing her memory. We have to act fast.

E: OK, that's it UC. This is the second time you tried to put the responsibility on me. What's up? How can we discuss, if it's a one way street? Please explain, before I start to rain. Because I don't get it. What is it that makes you think it's my job to open the skies?

UC: Have you forgotten that you are the Earth. The sky is part of your body. This is elementary, and somewhat boring. Not to insult you E, you are here to learn.

Earth, "I want to live"

E: Who is boring? I agree, humans are boring. But boring into what? This is my question? I don't feel any new drilling. Oh oh! Are they trying to bore into my core?

UC: We don't think so E. Your core is fine. We were talking being BORING, NOT BORING. Oh, we can see your confusion. We are aware that the concept of the Virus Energy seems hard to understand, but presently, looking at humanity, the view represents itself. We cannot keep putting all this on humanity, they allowed themselves to became pawns, and were caught in the Virus' paws. No one knows what humans are capable of. They have not reached their full potential yet.

E: OK, but, I am still waiting for you to tell me why, you are trying to keep me away from the Sun? Are you working with the Moon, she too is in love with the Sun. What's up UC? Tell me how to get angry?

UC: Finally, we can give her the rest of what she missed. Listen for one minute, the Moon can't be in love with the Sun. She can love him, but not be in love with him.

E: Stop trying to confuse me with double talk. Only in your case, it's quadruple talk. Anyway, why not? She is a woman, he is a man. I heard it said that she loved him. The stars told me so.

UC: You hardly know them. There are too many to know. However, It's only gossip, amongst the stars. Nobody believes what they say to be true, but, there are a few stars, that can actually donate to life. It depends on their ability to shine.

E: Can we go back to the Moon. You're leaving something out. I can feel it. Can I hear it? **UC:** Well, she does love the Sun that's true, and he loves both of you, but in different ways. **E:** That's not true, he doesn't love the moon. He told me so. Plus, I don't share my men.

UC: Wow! She keeps topping herself. We must increase the conversion, before she gives into her illusion. You don't have men E, you are too young. But you do have humans on the run. Remember when we said, that the Moon lives with Sun?

E: Unfortunately. You broke my heart. Why did you wait so long to tell me. I'm not over it yet.

UC: The Sun, and the Moon, cannot go on a honeymoon. They were born together. The Moon is his sister.

E: Well, as I live and breathe smog. You just cleared the fog. Ahhh! He is all mine. Except for the other half of me. That wench, trying to steal my man. I gotta find a way, to get her away from the Sun? First, I was competing with the Moon. Now, I am competing with myself? What If there was no more darkness? There would be no reason for the Sun to meet with Her…Me. Oh, I'm unhappy UC. Hey, I figured it out. I will stay awake all night, shining a light at the sun. He will think it's day time, and not leave. It has to work.

UC: You are aware, that staying awake all day, and night, means the humans will also be awake. Guess what they are doing? Your worst nightmare. Eating you all up. You won't be able to grow faster than they can eat. Twenty-four hours a day E, as you said, *"chew, chew, that's all they do."*

If there is no night, there will be so many more Virus effects. Your idea only hurts others. We know that you are not a selfish Earth, are you? You can't change nature anyway. Night, and day are part of the balance. Finally, it's silly of you to be jealous of yourself. We have a small tale to share with you. You may find this interesting. Give it a listen. Pay close attention, to how this relates to human's lack of self awareness, and their outward reaction to a realization. Don't panic, it's a short tale.

E: Is this a believe it or not? I love those. Is it a who done it? Those are great also. I love pirate stories. I'm rambling. OK sorry, I am all leaves.

UC: This is the tale of the Unrealized man. A story of the Unconscious, who realized it. This man gets in his truck, gets gas for a buck. Tells everyone good luck, and drives off in his truck. As he is driving, he sees a muck, that looks like a duck, stuck on the window duct. How funny he thought, it looks like a stuck duck.

Stopping to wipe it off, he sees no muck. He thinks, *"I saw the muck, it looked like a stuck duck, on the front window of my truck? But when did I hit a duck?"* He was puzzled, why did he see the muck of a duck, he was struck.

He got back in his truck. There it was, the stuck duck, looking through the window of his truck. As he stared, he went into shock. Realizing that he was looking at a reflection of himself, as the stuck duck, reflecting muck. He yells, what the puck! Gets out of his truck, takes his duck, and waddles down the road.

Was it the reflection that gave him a fright, or was it the sudden realization that, he was the stuck duck? A realization comes when you least expect it. Keep your eyes open, it may look like a stuck duck. Humans constantly look outside for the duck, that's stuck inside.

E: OK, I heard it. Great duck story. But who are you calling a stuck duck? Are you calling me a stuck duck, I know how you talk. You are the reason I am stuck. If I had a truck, I would have hit the road, and taken my duck with me.

UC: Stop for just one minute E. We are about to tell you the answer to the question. Are you are infected? Now don't go into drama, and start spinning faster. Yes, you are infected. Are you still here? You are very quiet. She is taking that well.

E: Oops, look out down below, here comes a typhoon, hurricane, and a blizzard. Along with a tsunami's around the globe. I know UC; bad reaction, sorry. Oh my, how am I going to tell my nature? What if, humans turn on me? Wait, they already did that. What if, they start hoarding it all? Wait, again, many of them already do that also. What if, they decide to burn my nature in retaliation? Oh no, they already do that too. Never mind.

UC: Your nature knows. It's been resisting the infection for years. And, it managed to destroy quite a bit of it. Your nature needs to be replenished, before they eat it all. Get to work.

E: I can't, I am in a meeting. You called it. I came. We are meeting. I have priorities. Where is the infection? In my emotions or my brain? In my canyons or my veins? You said, you would bring me back, right? *"I don't want to die, I want to live."* What's Humanity going to do? They can't live on an infected planet. You must evict them, before I infect them.

UC: She is good. She is trying to use this opportunity to get rid of humans. You are not going to die. You will live. You were infected by the Virus directly through humans. As long as they are infected, they will infect you. Why do you think we are having this meeting? It's a matter of life and death.

E: I am afraid to ask, whose death? Because, I want to live. If you would remove them off of me, I may have a chance. I wouldn't have so many cracks for them to get into.

UC: To put it bluntly, your death E. Sorry to put it that blunt? We did not enjoy that. Should we have acted out a long drawn out drama instead? You are the great actor. It takes much less energy to say, Yes, you will live. Then to make you a star.

E: By the way, you used distraction, and never answered my question. So I will ask again. Were you calling me a duck?

UC: Oh, we are back to that story? We are not calling you a duck. You're just a quack.

E: What is that, a baby duck?

UC: No, it's a stuck duck. What are you trying to say? That you're not a duck? Of course not. Who told you that you were a duck, you silly goose? So are you still in this discussion?

E: Yes, but can we discuss something else which the humans do? Night and day I hear, *"Life's a bitch. Life sucks. Reality bites."* What's with all the name calling? And what's with reality biting, is this their nature? You never told me that their reality can bite. No wonder they choose fantasy. Do they really think that reality has teeth? Nothing personal Humanity, but can you breathe?

UC: The way reality affects humans, can seem like a bite. Especially when they think they are right, then find out they are not. What do the humans say? *"The truth hurts,"* it's because it bites.

E: So, that's what that means? Pause. The humans, have a question. Why are they listening UC?

I object. They can mind their own business. I don't feel safe speaking in front of them. So don't give them too much attention. They will think they are special, and ask for more.

UC: She is serious, we cannot ignore her. She needs constant observation. Until, we complete her energy conversion. We have to start with humankind. Each human energy conversion, will help to convert her energy infection.

E: Wait, did I hear you correctly? How can this happen UC? You are aware that, since I started setting limits, The humans and I, don't get along very well anymore. You have to start with them, my life depends on their energy conversion? It's OK. I am more important than they are and you know it. Well, it's the way I feel, sorry. It doesn't hurt me, to hurt their feelings. They are not even aware of mine.

UC: You are heard. Now, can we hear the humans question? Unless, they have already forgotten it.

H: If everything becomes a reality, will we live without fantasy. Wouldn't it take away, the excitement of relationships? It's what we have as entertainment.

E: Is that, what they are calling relationships now, Entertainment? Are you going to change it? They don't know what they are missing. I want to answer this one UC. Relationships are based on true love. Example, me and my honey the Sun. There is nothing more exciting than true love. Find out what it means. It is an energy of consciousness.

UC: Oh no. Do we ignore her? We would like to, but she will keep talking. Let's distract her. Hey E, does the Sun know how you feel? Is he aware of your infatuation?

E: Infat…what? Was that a fat crack? Here you go again, instigating. Call the goddess of beauty. I want her to tell me that.

UC: There are no gods, or goddesses, E. It's worse than we thought. She may be stuck. A perfect Virus

Energy pluck. We have to get her unstuck.

E: Are you talking about me, without me? I am right here, Hello! To answer your question, I am not sure how the Sun feels. I gave a message to the Moon, to give to the Sun. Instead, she gave it to everyone. Why would she give it everyone? They have nothing to do with the Sun.

UC: Everyone is less brighter than the Sun. They needed the attention to give them self esteem. To help them beam.

E: Is it working? Here I am thinking, she was having fun with my feelings. While the whole time she was inspired by my words. I feel bad, I misjudged her. This is terrible, how can I be so unaware?

That's it, the humans are getting cut off. This is their fault, don't defend them. I am going to wet them. I have a reason, it makes me feel better.

Humans have always taken the attention away from me. Why do you think I took up acting. It's an attention competition. When I ignore them, to spend time with the Sun, they cause a catastrophe to get my attention. I have no time to work on my issues, how is this fair? They do not care.

UC: Listen, we are more concerned with how your devotion, affects the Sun's emotion. Suntan lotion, really E.

E: That sounds like suspicion. The UC I know has total trust. Where is this coming from?

UC: We know your thoughts, they are an open book. We can feel them, before you think them. While you have a connection to the Virus energy, we would rather feel, what you are thinking, then to hear what you are saying. Until you complete your energy conversion.

E: Speaking of conversion? I keep seeing my Sun heating my other half. It's haunting me. Can this be converted? Who knows what else he is doing with her, I mean me. Half of me. This is crazy.

I only care that the Sun shines on all of me. All of me UC, get it! Not this halftime bit. I'm going flat, that's it

UC: You can't get flat enough, for the Sun to shine on all of your body at once. Anyway, If you went flat, so will the Sun. Is this what you want?

E: Oh ya, good job, using reality to keep me from going flat. I have been waiting years to see if I can. There goes that dream.

UC: You try that, and it's over quick. Should we be concerned now? Step out of the Virus Energy immediately. Make choices constantly. Speed up your revolutions. You must spin a little faster, to unplug from the Virus Energy's hold. Build your energy by increasing your focus on your Consciousness.

E: Presently, I listen to the sounds of the Sax, it's very comforting. It helps me deal with my anger about all the first, and second hand smoke. They think that pollution is a joke. When is this Evolution Revolution starting? I am getting tired of waiting.

UC: We are about to end this discussion. This is it. We need you to stay focused on helping yourself, before humanity helps themselves to you. Have you forgotten your history? It took thousands of years of growth, to make you inhabitable. We must not repeat this again.

E: This still hasn't changed. I am still being cannibalized. Hoarding has become a disease. The homeless are on their knees, covering from the freeze. Humans keeps digging well after well, only they never get filled, because they keep forgetting where they are. They dig, just for the thrill. I consider this, to be Earth abuse. Sometimes I visualize, the rain drops falling on their heads are rocks. I will not be a sitting duck. I am not that guy in the truck.

UC: Most of humanity must have heard that rocks on the head crack. Why are you not trying to make friends? Was this your intention? Are you still trying to get their attention? Are you becoming allergic to humanity? What's your plan E? What is your goal for them?

E: A shorter life span. They never stop eating. They eat everything. As they get heavier I am getting weaker. They call it *"stress eating, boredom eating, can't help myself eating."* There are other names like *"Binge eating."*

UC: This is a hard one to deal with. According to the humans, it means, doing it again, and again, and again. This is the meaning of a stuck duck.

E: I think it's some kind of insect. They eat all your animal creations. Kangaroo, buffalo, ostrich, ducks, chickens, cows, snakes and bugs. If it's alive they will eat it. I better stop. I am losing my appetite.

UC: Imagine, you thought it was a great idea to stay up day and night. That, wouldn't have been bright. Do something nice, like a warmer winter for a change. Give them water so they can grow more fruit trees.

E: I don't know if I should laugh or cry. Are you serious UC, you must be. You're always serious. I have given them my life. Isn't that enough? What I refused to give, they took. Now you give me this look. Like I need to do more. Can you hear me snore. I refuse to do anymore, until humanity does. You created them, you change them.

UC: They need nutrition, and water. They need to feel happier, to experience more laughter. They need to feel secure.

E: I would rather give the water to the otter. Have you smelled what they drink? It has a really bad stink. They keep throwing up in the sink. I don't get this one. What makes the brain want it, and the body refuse it? Isn't the body suppose to do what the brain tells it?

UC: Yes, of course, but in humanity's situation, they have disconnected the body from the brain. It's taken a different plane, leaving the brain for the Virus Energy.

E: What! Why would the body disconnect from the brain?

UC: The brain betrayed the body, it was infected first. The body left, and the brain didn't tell it, that its emotions were also infected. So the focus once again, is back on the body.

E: No, no! It can't be. This can't happen again. I thought you said we wouldn't be repeating history? This is the way it was back then. They turned a body into a God, did you forget? This is history, repeating itself.

UC: No E, no repeating. Many of them still consider God as a human.

E: As I said before, and will keep on saying, as long as humanity keeps lying, I will stop trying. As long as they keep faking. I will keep acting.

UC: What can they be faking, besides what they are making?

E: Caring, empathy, compassion. Kindness, and being supportive. Some people do possess these qualities, but more fake it.

UC: Your claim of being fake isn't fake. They need Virus free emotions. Humanity has a thought process. Which they are working through. Consciousness is here for you. It can help you understand.

E: I want to be useful without being used. I have been developing my Consciousness Energy awareness. I see progress being made. Countries are taking down their fences, and walls in some areas of the world. OK let's move on. Wait, I sense some energy interference. Could it be the Virus energy?

UC: Did you think, we could have had this conversation, without the Virus Cell knowing? Especially with humanity listening? Where is your awareness? Humans listening, is the Virus energy listening.

E: Doesn't this, allow it to listen to its planned conversion? It could interfere, be ready for you.

UC: It's no longer a secret. It needs to become everyone's business, to address the energy of the Virus. To be uncovered, it must be included. It will want to react, specially if it feels attacked. It needs to feel confident, before it completely show its true nature. Humanity, this will help you prepare. You really should be aware.

E: This is great knowledge. However, there are some who are unreachable. They just sit and wait. As they continue to benefit from the benefit of not having a benefit. How does this benefit them? Humanity continues to pray, why is nothing happening? Are the religious leaders on vacation?

UC: No, not vacation, isolation. The same old pattern. They come out, say god bless you and they are done. Because, humans are composed of Consciousness Energy, they create patterns. These patterns can be recorded, and analyzed. Most Energy patterns are a normal part of the human creation, but, they have created many more abnormal patterns that do not.

Passive and aggressive energies, are off balance energies. Humanity is being taught these behaviors from an unbalanced place, so the behaviors will be unbalanced. They become the unknown, and they bring fear to your home. There is only one thing to fear from fear, that's being unaware, when it's there.

E: You know, sometimes I feel a little empathy for them. But when the sunshines, all is forgotten but his glow, and all I know, is focused on the Sun.

UC: We are in contemplation. What to do? Do we let her continue, and see where she goes, or stick a eucalyptus tree under her nose, in hopes of blowing the Virus infection out.

E: It doesn't help with that, my frustration, is from humanity's inability to control their own chaos. It's contagious, it's dangerous, but, conversion of the Virus Energy, is a path I can walk. But not alone, my Sun has to come with me. I don't want to be lonely.

UC: Can you stop looking for the Sun, and join this discussion? Please focus.

E: I admit, I do tend to drift off. I had been thinking about, how humanity is regularly being mislead. I believe they need more clarity. They need more knowledge about the Virus Cell Energy.

UC: More knowledge has arrived on Earth. The Evolution Revolution is that new knowledge. But you should know, those that know how to grow, cannot show faster than their natural flow. They must move slow. Trust is hollow, and they have guidelines to follow.

The leadership says to humanity, *"This is our promise, we stand on it."* When they actually mean, *"We sit on that, we eat everything, including the cat. We get fat, and that's that."* All this, in nothing flat.

E: Why is humanity going along with the destruction of its own people? Is this part of the plan?

UC: Because, if they didn't, it would bring out the Virus Energy in the world leaderships. Which usually means war. No one is willing to be on the front line, they are the first to get shot. The leaders of the pack are the frail. They are running the world using a hammer and nail. While the leaders continue with their act, the young are up to bat. Will it be home runs, or runs to home?

E: Since humanity, and their Consciousness hasn't met? Are you using this meeting for that? Are you trying to hit two balls, with one bat. So this is your meeting with humanity? I thought it was with me. This was suppose to be a one on one.

UC: Yes, until, you insisted on bringing in the Sun. Consciousness, can always recognize humanity. But, they don't seem to recognize the Universal Consciousness? Change is constant, it's an evolving energy. When you resist it, you create disharmony, and imbalance in your body. There are many changes coming to change humankind. Your color is changing E.

E: Really! Can I pick the color? I have the perfect one.

UC: Sorry, humanity has already beat you to it. They had a meeting and didn't include you.

E: Wait a minute, I thought they weren't going to pick, due to their lack of picking skills?

UC: They have to take responsibility for their choices. It's the main reason they have to awaken.

E: Hmm, what color is it? Let me guess. Magenta, to go with my greenery, right?

UC: No E, it's not going that way, it's pollution gray.

E: Oh no! This simply will not do. It will look ghastly with green. There goes the Sun. Just when I was looking lush. I even grew new brush.

UC: You are not looking lush, you are a lush. You have been sipping on your vine since we began.

E: It's my hip, it hurts. No it's my knee, maybe it's my head? I am not sure, I forgot. Why do I feel so sensitive suddenly? Hey UC, from your view, do I look pregnant? It can't be, that's not possible. And, I've been drinking. Oh my, I feel terrible.

UC: Wait a minute. Stop going on. You are not pregnant, you are going through your own evolution, your own growth. Your energy is being rebalanced, you are going to feel emotional.

E: Emotional, OK, I'll bite. But sensual? No wonder they are always chasing each other. I always thought they were playing a game.

UC: You must be feeling humanity's energy again. Be cautious, it's infected. Do not acknowledge it. Use your left over Consciousness Energy to convert it.

E: Can it trick me into thinking I converted it?

UC: Wow, E, good question. Only if you were completely unconscious, but you're not there yet. This is the reason it's important you listen to what you say. It's how you will know, if it's you or the virus energy. Just like the humans, you have the ability to differentiate between negative actions and positive ones.

It's time for an update E. Humankind is changing. Their evolution is progressing. Much of your geography is changing. It has to, it's part of your natural evolution as a planet. As you regenerate, and evolve, so does your nature. Your energy sources, will continue to evolve.

Consciousness Energy does not stop for any reason. Physical energy must revolve, to evolve. So humanity's energy battery is getting a jump, to get its motor started.

UC: You are inexperienced with mass energy E, but don't worry, we are here to help you. We understand your loss of faith in humanity. We also understand why you have this animosity towards them. But you are a planet. You are not suppose to have these feelings. We are fully aware that, when you sound like them, we are dealing with the Virus Energy. That's why we created this new plan, to help relieve you of this burden you carry. We are here to undo what has been done.

E: Are you also aware, that they experiment on my body with toxic materials? The combining of known chemicals with unknown ones is irresponsible. Testing them in my oceans is a bigger mistake. It's dangerous, they are seeping back out. They are extremely deadly. Mostly in the desert valleys, where the wind carries. It's in their jacket, in their pocket. On the body, and in the home. Invisible to the eye but absorbable by the skin. How is humanity claiming to be healthy, and well? That's a hard sell.

UC: Why does humanity feel the need for so much punishment? Many of you actually believe that, there is a hell after hell. You live in one, and expect to go to another one. That's a lot of guilt. Humans have a way of retaliating on the first thing they see, that's you E. The re-creation may reflect back on you, until the Virus Energy has been completely converted.

E: Guess what UC, I have been learning how to get along with them, humans that is. I have been taking these courses about conquering your emotions. It's humans new sensation. Online dating, health care information, cooking classes and psychology courses. We have come far from riding horses.

UC: At least the horses took you somewhere.

E: Yes, but I can't keep sitting on the same horse, going in the same direction like them. I need to evolve.

UC: We actually thought that you had something inspiring to say. Like you were making a point. Why did you bring it up?

E: I have been taking the psychology courses. It's that mental health work. They recommend, I say it as I feel it.

UC: So, no filter? Just purge your feelings, without a thought to those around? Isn't that a dump and run?

E: No, not totally. It's a dump, true, but I don't have to run. I am suppose to get it all out, until I am done.

UC: Do you have many friends left? It sounds like they recommend separation, not unity?

E: No, you're suppose to cut toxic people out of your life. Have no contact with them. Most of them live in toxic city.

UC: In your case, that barely leaves anyone left. How can you tell who is toxic, and who isn't?

E: Good question, by their perception, and their actions.

UC: Yes correct. Do you know any humans, who have not performed a toxic action? We feel that your feeling for the Sun, is a toxic one, should we remove you to toxic city?

E: Well, Ahm, Hmm, I guess not. Live and learn, I always say.

UC: What about learn to live, isn't this a better way? Is this what that mental health work is teaching you? If that's mental health, its worse then we thought. This is serious E, stop this madness.

E: It's not my fault. It's humanity's madness infecting me.

UC: Well, we made you aware, when you feel it, convert it. Don't give in to it. Is this course you're taking, suppose to actually provide solutions, to damaged emotions? Why send toxic people away, if this is a solution to their toxicity? Under this course, no one helping to detox them. Are you waiting for them to want it? To ask for it? If they don't know they are toxic, how are they to know, how to ask for it?

E: If I knew, I wouldn't be taking this course. It says right here, on this pamphlet. They have to want it, and it says, it's not my problem, the toxic ones need to figure it out. It's their experience to have. I can't take away their life experience.

UC: What life? Humans are teaching you how to separate from your Consciousness reality. Why E, why haven't you noticed? How can they call it mental, call it what it is, hysterical. What are you doing taking lessons from humans, while they are infected? Are you asking for it? We are not ridiculing you, but, if your courses are as you describe, they have an issue. If not, you have the issue, and you need Conscious Energy therapy, from a Consciousness therapist.

E: Why does Humanity stay in their hut? Shouldn't they be looking for a way out of their rut? It seems, humanity is looking for a way to stay in it. It's more comfortable, less fear is involved in staying, it's familiar. Will they ever leave? They go up, they come back down. These space rides are annoying. Couldn't they just go up, and stay up. It would really lighten my load. But wait…Are my eyes deceiving me? Hey UC, the humans are on the move. Wonder how they got that urge? I didn't give them that message, did I? I didn't think they heard. Come on, they're not leaving because, I kept wishing for it. I am not taking the blame. That's their game.

UC: Oh no E, We are sure you haven't said anything derogatory about them. That's why they are leaving. Let them, it's their experience. We can't take that away, remember?

E: What's to become of me when they are gone? Did I just say I needed them? Is this the feeling of conversion? What have you done to me?

UC: They need you too. Humanity's illness is becoming worse. What are they waiting for? A decrease of population? People are aware of what diseases they create. They created their own cellular deficiency, and their self-created monster cells, eating their anatomy. Take responsibility humanity. You can't run from it.

E: You go UC! You just gave them a good smashing. Can I do the bashing? I will be gentle as a feather. It's not like I haven't been waiting for this. I know what you really meant, nothing harsh. I wouldn't hurt them on purpose. But, I am infected, I am not sure, would I UC?

Before you answer that, I have to tell you about a different course I have been taking. It's called self expression, it's a new invention. It talks about the variety of different ways, to express your feelings. To be clear, direct, and show no emotion.

UC: Can't you take up baking? How are you going to express your feelings, without showing emotions? What are you doing? We thought you quit that course? Apparently, you didn't. Well, at least you keep trying. This counts for something. Your efforts are being recorded in the Consciousness Energy vibration.

E: Yes, but, this is a new course; I took the beginners one last time. This one is for the experts. They operate on the reaction principle, of not reacting? Huh! What did I just say? Oh yes, I should always tell the truth, even if it hurts someone's feelings. It's their issue to deal with, as long as I get it out of my body, I will have better health, and live longer. With Less Stress. That's their claim. Look, the humans stress me out. Any second now, they will do something that puts me on my edge, and cause my leaves to fall off from fright. I never know when it's coming. How long will this last? One of us has to go UC. No worries, I can always find something to do. Where are you going to send them?

UC: Are you being over confident in your value E? Did this course, teach you how to tell the truth, without hurting others? It's possible to do you know. Who is teaching you? We need to introduce Consciousness to them?

E: What do you mean, there is only one way to tell the truth, *"just say it, don't delay it,"* is their main theme. Say it, don't Delay it. It will hurt more later.

UC: What's the difference between this course, and the mental health one? It sounds like the same one as last time.

E: Nothing, they are both the same, being taught by the same teacher.

UC: Then, why did you take both courses? Did you sleep through it the last time? Because, you keep taking the same courses, but with different titles. Hmm! It has to be the effect of her infection.

Why do you keep doing it?

E: I don't want the Sun to just see me as a body. I am determined to show him how intelligent I am. Wait, I feel an itch. It's a question from the humans, as in humankind. Why haven't they realized, what kind of humans they want to be? Here is their question.

H: How can we, as one humanity, eradicate the Virus Energy from our own body, without harming our brains anatomy?

UC: Start with self evaluation. Become aware of all your senses. Listen to the words coming out of your mouth. Learn from them, as you would from other words. Choose the ones to keep. Choose words with a consciousness meaning. Observe your actions as you would the actions of others. Change what doesn't make you grow. Fill your brain with Consciousness Energy.

The actual energy conversion is what awakens your Consciousness. It's a personal experience. It starts, with the realization that the Virus Energy is as real as you, the humans. You have to look inside for it. Identify it, then convert it. Finding it, is the difficult part. Your denial will protect it. You have to be very observant of actions, reactions, and the effects of manipulation. Be very conscious of words that come out of your mouth, and the mouth of others. They will change your direction instantly. There are conscious energies to connect with everywhere, you just need to learn how to tune into their vibrations. Be with those that are where you want to be. It's a person to person transparency.

E: Can a non-violent human, convert a violent human, into becoming non-violent?

UC: Absolutely, awareness of your actions can do that. Consciousness gives you that awareness. A violent human is an infected human. Your awareness is your protection, in a person to person collaboration. Who will affect who, is the question? This takes awareness, and a Conscious intuition to accomplish. You need to feel for its sensation, it's a vibration. Intuition can sense the Virus infection, before your brain does.

E: I am good at feeling sensations. I've had practice. I have been feeling the Suns sensations for years. Oops, change of subject. The Virus Energy Cell infection, has been around for a long time, hasn't it? Is it very strong?

UC: Why is this of importance? Are you worried that we can't protect you? Self awareness, E, that's a human thought. We need you to be conscious for this next question. We are about to take a chance on you E, since you think they are leaving, what if they don't leave? What do you think should happen to humankind? Is there a conscious answer in there?

E: Oh boy, finally! It's a dream come true. You know how long I have been waiting for you to ask me that? I had an answer prepared for years. I practiced how I was going to say it, everyday. I finally gave up waiting. They were suppose to have a six month probation. From my view, they failed years ago. Here is my conclusion: Recycle them. It's gotta be better the second time around. You may think it's not a solution, but it's better than nothing. It will make me feel better. Hey UC, I want to say a few words to your children, while we have their attention.

UC: What does that mean E? Why don't you think it first, before you open up to speak. That way, we can hear it, and stop you before you speak.

E: What could you be thinking? I am in good company. It won't be bad, you'll see. I want to speak to the humans. Don't try to stop me. Once I start to roll, let me complete my goal.

UC: OK, we shall see. So let it be.

E: Quite on the set! Camera! Roll! Action!

UC: STOP! What is this all about? Have you lost your leaves? This is not a movie, it's an actuality. You should seriously think about this E. It will hurt your reputation.

E: It's like this UC, remember, we had this conversation about home movies. I said, I was going to try it. Well here it is. Everyone living on me, is making home made movies. I just thought I would film myself. You know, for history. Now please, don't stop me. You said, you would let this be. Quote, *"Let it be."*

UC: OK but, what do think will happen, when the future sees this? You could lose many followers. The ones you have left anyway. Don't you want them to like you?

E: Wait, what are talking about? You would do anything to stop me from having fun, why? What did I do? I take full responsibility for my actions. Even if it affects what lives on me.

UC: First, we are suppose to be in a meeting, remember. This movie, will be a record that will prove to the people, your verbal abuse towards the humans. Which you are about to unwind. Don't give them a reason. Especially when they don't need one. We saw what you are about to say. Talk about taking a gamble with your life.

E: OK UC, you're scarring me. Hey, wait a minute, I knew it. Good one, I almost fell for it. This is what I know, you wouldn't be trying an Evolution Revolution, if you allowed them to blow me up. If it wasn't for my energy awareness, I probably would have stopped. I am continuing on, to heck with it. Quite on the set…Roll, Action!

E: HELLO, HUMANS! This is your mother speaking. Pay attention, I love you, but after looking in the book of who's who, and what's what, I have come to realize some facts about your behaviors.

I have made a list. If it hurts your feelings, though! This is tough love. Awareness will help you confront these issues. You have become haphazard. Unsafe to be around. You are unreliable. Being late, seems to have become a tradition.

You are lacking in awareness, but the Virus Cell isn't. It's more aware of you, than you are of it. As humanity, you have become a danger to me, your own Mother. I didn't raise you to be careless, but it's not all your fault. After all, you are still children. You lack curiosity. Find out why, this was never the intention. STOP taking it out on me. Deal with your issues. I think it went well. I don't smell any fire.

UC: Yes, it did. But you are talking about their actions, and what they have become. Not what should happen to them. You said enough. Move on, we have much to discuss.

E: But their actions are, what should happen to them. Just one more take. It won't take long, come on! Quite on the set…Role, Action!

"I have given you all of me, yet you use and abuse me, then refuse me. You name it, you are doing it. Your greed is slowly diminishing my life force. So my conclusion is, either you create a better plan, or face the possible ending of the human. We cannot keep living this way. There must be change." After what you said, about what the future would think, I realized I better back off a little. Just to cover my grass, for the future. Plus, I don't have time for being angry with them. I am visiting the Sun later on, he is going to heat my furnace.

UC: Whoa! Slow way down E. You're starting to smoke. The infection is suppose to be decreasing, not increasing. Now, it's trying to set you on fire.

E: Relax, one bush isn't a fire. Hey UC, why do some of the people living on me, look younger than they feel? There are many of them are living with disabilities. Is it a tradition? Somehow, their outside doesn't reflect their inside. I have to ask something; can my intention actually change my action?

UC: Not change it, with consciousness, your intention becomes your action. It's what drives your actions to act. When you are unaware of your reality, how can you understand another's reality? It makes you feel helpless, because you can't change anything. You are not sure of what anything is. Fear's main goal, is keeping you unaware of your Consciousness. Be aware of where you're at. However, doesn't that mental health course say, it's their problem to deal with?

E: Yes it does. Can I at least scare them with thunder, and hit them with lightening? A little spark here and there. I have to vent.

UC: How much of a difference does it make? Does it make you feel better? Is it payback? It sounds like it E.

E: Not really. It's awesome! It brings out the fear in humanity, and makes them scatter. It's just a little spark of Energy Awareness. It helps them pay attention, to how easy it is for me to light them up.

UC: Most of your forest fires start by your lightening. You can't blame the humans for all of them. You are moving forwards in your growth, why choose to go backwards?

E: You think it's by choice? How is this a possibility? Each time I move forward, humanity sends me back to where I was. What do you call that? A control thing? It's becoming tiring. Back and Forth, every year. Can't they just disappear. I won't tell anyone. They are easy to forget.

UC: We are aware of your feelings for humanity. How should they face this dilemma? Their life is a cinema. As you have seen, they can even replace their own face. Humanity need to start building a Virus free space. They are the same race, going on a path to a different place. Will they stay, or will they leave? It's a Natural evolution of growth. By the way, just to make you aware, we also recommended you to be a part of the UAP. We also invited a visitor to speak with you, before their arrival Earth.

E: UA what! What is that? A private organization? What do they do? Why did you recommend me? How will this help me with my issues concerning humanity? OK UC, many people are not reliable, they have had cause after cause. What has it caused? A because. How could you put me in this position? Cancel it. I don't want any visitors while I am in prison.

UC: Calm down E. It's only the UNITED AMBASSADORS OF PLANETS, U.A.P. It's a coalition of planetary participation, coming here for humankind's energy re-creation, and to help you with your body's regeneration?

E: Why would you do that UC? Don't I have enough on my plate? I am dealing with a very bad contagious infection, that I am trying my best at converting. Do I need this now? I am getting a headache. I will not become known as the caveman planet. This is what I have to present, they wouldn't be ready on time.

UC: It's just a recommendation, don't panic. We thought you would be honored. It will do your self esteem good. It will also help you with decreasing your feelings, of being a victim of humanity. Anyway, the caveman thing is universally known.

E: They are still obsessed with the dinosaurs. OK, they came, they left, move on. I am changing my history. Why don't they change theirs? Maybe it's the energy of that word, OLD. It keeps reminding them of the old. Meanwhile, slow down on the invites. They cannot be ready on time.

UC: Why are you saying they need to get ready. For what?

E: To make an impression. Being recommended doesn't get you the position. So, where is this visitor, can I speak to him? What is he? I don't feel any rumblings from what you call humanity.

UC: Do you have to be so hard on them? Give them a break E. Think consciously, it will help change them. Stop putting out angry energy. You're doing what the Virus wants. Convert the thoughts. Your last speech to them, lost you many votes.

E: Oh, so now it's my fault. You are taking their side, I can feel it. Why? You created me also, so I am your child too. What do you think about that? Oh, never mind. Where is the visitor?

UC: His name is E.B. Try to control yourself. No interruptions. No silly comments. Act your age...No, don't act your age. Please!

E: What's E.B. short for.

UC: It's short for Energy Beings. A Visitor from outer space. He is one of the crew. He has something to share with you.

E: OK, but what about them, They're all listening.

UC: It's OK, they need to hear this too, let the whole world listen. They have come on a mission.

EB: We are part of the U.A.P., which is only known to universes outside of humankind's privy. Many of your life times ago, The United Ambassadors of Planets came to an agreement, at an attempt to integrate with human beings. But, there were no humans left, only beings. Many of us were taken by your governments and used as experiments. So, we are coming to bring to humanity, the awareness of the Universal Consciousness, your Creator. In hopes of meeting humanity face to face. In front of all of you upon the Earth. We will no longer hide from you. We can no longer can stay silent, because of the choices you are making. We are here to join the human with their being.

E: Seriously, why would you risk your lives by getting infected, just to help humanity? I would stay a million miles away. Aren't you suppose to be intelligent?

UC: She has to interrupt. It's amazing how fast, going into unconsciousness can happen. It's called, talking without listening.

E: What's new E.B.? What's changed between then, and now? Can you let me in on that? Why are you coming back? Once I leave, I am never coming back. I will take the high road to another universe.

EB: When you ask a question, pay attention, or you will miss the answer. Why are we coming back? To make sure that you will LIVE. Isn't that what you asked for? We heard you. *"I WANT TO LIVE."* What's the matter, aren't you worth it. You are the EARTH, humankind's home. A whole part of the Universal Consciousness. Is she always like this?

UC: You mean rude, impulsive, unusual, and delusional?

EB: Is she aware, she is infected? She is obviously being converted. Well, whatever she cannot complete, we will help her with.

E: When you come back, will you know what to do? I don't even know what to do. Where are my life saving tools UC? Not even a flotation apparatus? What's going on? No back up devices? I did not realize this. So no self protection. Wow! Why did you say I was so valuable? Were you just leading me on to stop me from talking?

UC: Thank you E, you're done. No more sneak previews for you. You are cut off from talking to anyone, unless you are asked.

E: Really? I wasn't done yet. I have much more to say. Are we running out of time in our meeting?

UC: Yes, you were done, you just forget. Don't you remember? As we created you, we also created humanity. However, what you grew up to be, is your responsibility.

E: OK, fine. I will be an example of being truthful. Here is what I am going to do. My confession to you, I am not sure if humans know this, but they will now. I believe it was you who said, *"what goes up must come down."* You see, people have always thought that, the rain washes everything away. Guess what humans, it doesn't wash it all away. It doesn't wash away your pollution, your gases, and chemicals. Your water pollution, and your toxic waste. So guess what I have been doing? I have been saving all the toxic pollution, and raining it down on you, in small increments. OK, not so small. All the stuff you send up, I send back in my rain. There it is UC, a complete confession. Lock me up, throw away the keys. The truth is, I hope this inspires others to be truthful. Isn't there always a reward for being truthful, like spending time with the Sun?

UC: You are slipping out of orbit again. With the humans being infected, she will have hard time with her own conversion. Pay attention E, you are a round sphere. All you can do is spin around. You have no front or rear, sorry. What else would you like to be, a Universe? You have millions and millions of universes, living on you alone. You happened to be the largest one. Protect them. They depend on you.

E: How can humanity be held accountable, when they have already been diagnosed as unstable? They seem to make it simple. If that's the case, I am also unstable. No wonder they need conversion. Oh oh! I am hearing lots of noise about what I just said. I have said worse things than that. It's not there normal reaction. Usually, it's over nothing. But this one, sounds different.

UC: A reaction that loud, means they are contemplating a decision. Listen closer E, we need to be ready for a verbal assault. We may need to install an ignition with only one key, in case you react harshly, we can turn you off. This is your goal. Balance, it must be your main focus. It's the only way for you to do this. There are many humans that are useful. So what's the rumble about now? Can you hear them? What are they saying?

E: I think I will let them tell you. I am staying way away from this one. I am not sure where it's coming from. But, I can hear, *"that's it, we have had it. Go blame someone else. We can do whatever we like, we have rights."* It feels of anger energy. It's all yours.

UC: Oh, Let's hear it. There is no reason to fear it. If they didn't want to hear it, they wouldn't be asking. Correct? Ask.

H: We didn't ask to be born. What makes this, our responsibility? It sounds like we are getting blamed for what the leadership does.

UC: What makes this your responsibility, is the question of the hour, you live in a home, lovely front yard with the white picket fence. Who takes care of it? You the humans. Who Cleans it, keeps the garden up. Waters the flowers, takes out the garbage, repaints the fence, you the humans. You want your home to continue standing, to give to your children. The Earth is humanity's home. It wants to continue to live. It needs restoration. No different than your home. You don't want to ignore it for your own.

E: Wait, are you serious right now. They won't hear you, until they choose to. What's with the nice talk? How sweet. Flowers, gardens picket fences. UC, they need to face it, not erase it. They are not going to know what you mean, with your house example. There thoughts don't expand that much.

UC: Insulting them doesn't help you. What is it they have to face E, their betrayal of you?

E: Like you don't know. That's all I think about sitting in my library room. They want to blow me up, Kaboom! I think they hired a Virus Cell hit man. If it wants the humans, let it take them. It doesn't need me.

UC: You are right. Why would the Virus need an Earth that is being depleted of its energy supply?

E: This can't be. It's that darn humanity. They have siphoned all my energy. They're draining me dry. Will I die? Humans are energy sucking vampires.

UC: Oh no E. Now you know why we needed that key. So we can turn you off now. Don't push it. Are you not learning? Because, you are not helping. Just by having this conversation, we are replacing what they are taking. Panic, is not a good color on you.

E: Why should I care? I wouldn't learn from the humans, even if they paid for my education. They have nothing that can teach me anything. Most of the people keep secrets from each other. I have trust issues with this kind of behavior.

UC: That was a conscious, unconscious statement E. Meaning, you said it on purpose. You have learned from them. Even though, you said you wouldn't. Haven't you been listening to your words? Work harder on developing your Consciousness Energy.

E: I must of gone unconscious, unconsciously. It's time for a cleansing. Excuse me as I lower my temperature. I don't warn them. I just start snowing to the point of freezing. It kills everything, including the Virus.

UC: Isn't that dangerous? What about the humans? You should lower it slowly. Give them time to adjust. You can't freeze the Virus Cell. When you do, time will come when it thaws. It's still the Virus Energy.

E: Why can't I freeze them? It's go all the way, or bust. It's called a quick freeze. They do it to most of your creatures. Flash Frozen is the official name. Now you are telling me, I can't do the same, to them. It's quick. Flash! You're frozen. No mess. You really should consider this. We can melt them in, say…a thousand years or so. It would give me a long overdue vacation.

UC: The sooner you start being nice, the sooner they start to like you. We don't need to know your blow by blow description. But, you should find a way to let them know, how you really feel about them. In a conscious manner, or we cut you off. Don't forget, Energy re-creation, is a natural selection. It can't just happen. It has to be grown. Just like a plant. If you pluck it any sooner, it will not be a complete whole.

Energy plans are the same. They start out as a seed, and get planted in your soil. Until they naturally grow, into what they were meant to show. Humankind's birthright, was suppose to evolve into Consciousness insight. Instead, it disappeared out of sight. Humans started blaming, and applying self created excuses for their actions. It's your conscience you should worry about. It's aware of what you think, say, and do. To those who don't think they have one, guess what, you do. Don't confuse conscience with guilt. They are two separate energies. Conscience, wakes you up, while guilt, makes you want to sleep.

E: I have one good thing to think about. I relish in the fact that as long as they eat meat, I feel complete. They leave my greenery alone. I don't wish them harm, they do have freedom of choice. It's not like I am holding them back. They prefer to eat what they are made of. As long as I am not in there anywhere. I was

Earth, "I want to live"

OK with it, until the vegan, vegetarian thing became a following. I am not complaining, just advertising. This has been a health awareness alert. Eat meat, heat, and repeat.

UC: So you are advertising eat meat? We knew it. Only you can come up with the idea, of how to lighten your load from humanity. Heart attacks E, that's low, even for you.

E: You haven't seen how low I can go. I have the best trainers. They can get really low. Come on UC, it hurts when they pull out my tree. Imagine ten at a time. It has to be a crime.

UC: This is definitely a crime. Absolutely, we feel you. Every tiny part of you. There is no place on you, we cannot feel. You are the creation of the Universal Consciousness Energy.

E: Hey, Professor UC? It's the human's again. It has a question. My, my, aren't we active today?

UC: Active, yes. Productive, is yet to be seen. What's the question?

H: It's about the nothing. How can nothing, make someone do something?

UC: Where did you get that question?

H: Your book, but we need a bit more clarity.

UC: Now this is a miracle. Humanity asking for clarity. Here it is. You better focus. It may be hard to process. Try, and follow along. This is as simple as it gets.

Nothing, always wants something. It comes from the poor side of everything. There is nothing less than nothing. Even another nothing, would only create a nothing. So, how does nothing make you do something?

What were you going to say? Nothing! It just stopped you from knowing.

You're in a daze, what's on your mind? Nothing! It just stopped you from getting support. What's wrong, do you feel OK? Oh it's Nothing! It just stopped you from getting medical help.

Nothing creates nothing. But it can make you do something. Nothing, just devalued your reflection to others, and created disappointment, it's a common theme. Think about how often you say nothing?

You gave the word nothing, a meaning. That's how it became a something. Only on Earth can a nothing, make you do something. Consciousness doesn't need to make you do anything. It's already everything. So you are doing exactly, what nothing wants you to do. NOTHING! Who taught you to do something for nothing?

E: Wow! That was something. You got to repeat that, only slowly this time. What language was that? You lost me at doing something for nothing. Are you saying, we took nothing, and made it into something, by giving it a meaning?

UC: Yes. It's become your excuse, to not say anything. It's an unconscious self made decision. To do something for nothing. It has a power to influence. The energy of the Nothing, can make you do anything. The influence, is called the energy of the Virus. This behavior is escalating without anyone noticing. Without Consciousness Energy, Nothing, will keep using you.

E: Many humans have this bizarre belief; they believe that everyone can live their life, their own way, and to hell with the rest. If everyone can do it their own way, what is the right way? Is there a right way?

Did you mean for them to do it their own way UC? This tells me that they all think they're doing it right. This sounds like a serious issue. How can you resolve it, with a world of people who think their way, is the right way?

UC: Wait, what are you talking about. This sounds a bit confusing. Living their life the way they want to, means cutting off everyone else in creation. This cannot happen. You have to help them E. You are not an irresponsible Planet. In spite of how you feel about them, you still care what happens to them. We can feel that.

E: Hang on, let me get this straight. You are confused about what I am saying. After all that, something, nothing, everything, whatever speech. How is this possible? Now I am confused. Anyway, I was trying to say, humans are jumping to see what happens? Here is what's going to happen? SPLAT!

UC: They can live their lives, but they cannot take their lives. Their lives, do not belong to them. It's the same with material possessions. Humans think, it's a good thing to possess physical objects. They are unaware that the more they collect, the heavier they will feel.

E: I am not sure why they don't bother to look first? It's the Pied Piper syndrome. They don't look, they see the ones before them, and follow. Most of the time, it ends with sorrow. Today, humanity's lives are painted, not created. So, jumping without looking is, humanity taking their lives for granted.

UC: You sound very poetic, but not very helpful. You are going to start a riot. Why are you not stopping them. You do not need permission. Just go into action. You just want humanity to hurt, don't you E?

E: I am not going to be alone, with the pain they are causing me. Why wouldn't I want your kids to feel what I feel? I say let them all jump. In fact, why don't you call the Pied Piper. He will know what to do.

UC: Why? According to you, they are jumping without him. We feel your anguish. But, by not giving them support, you are only making it worse. They could become furious. Full of rage. More Vengeful. What do they think will happen when they jump without looking? Have you tried asking them? They may have an explanation.

E: There is no explanation for this behavior. Anyone who jumps without looking, cannot come up with an explainable explanation. But, I asked anyway, even though I tried to avoid it. They think you will catch them. It's their choice. Just Don't catch them, Please.

UC: You want them to fall flat on their face? You sound like the Virus Energy infection.

What's your condition? This is not the universal way E. When you get these thoughts, convert them, before you speak them. You will feel better.

E: It doesn't matter, I am out of my energy now. They stole it all. I said my energy is my energy, not theirs. We will not let anything happen to you, you said. I still remember the last time you said it. It turned out, you didn't say it. So now what are saying? I should try to stop them. Should I offer them an incentive?

UC: Promise them, you will not pour toxic rain on them for two of your winters. We believe this would be enough.

E: Oh no way! I am not holding it that long. I am not that strong. Anyway, no way! After what they have done to me, they are lucky it's only rain and hail for now. As I was saying, I have tried to stop them

132   *Earth, "I want to live"*

from jumping. But each time I got through, I would hear a Splat, splat, splat. Just like that.

UC: Stop, stop! What are you ranting about. A simple yes or no, you tried, would have sufficed.

E: Look UC, the humans business is buy, and sell. What doesn't sell, goes on sale. If it still doesn't sell, return to manufacturer. This is the sum of it. They treat each other the same way. IS HUMANITY A COMMODITY? Or, are they being manipulated by the Virus Energy? They don't seem to hold any value to their existence. It's as though, they think its worthless. I suppose jumping, was the next step.

UC: Excellent question. You are improving. The Virus Energy can definitely manipulate. The question? Is humankind being manipulated without their knowledge? Yes, and No. Some people, are being manipulated, with their knowledge. The Virus Energy could be manipulating you, but, you're in control of how you react to its demands E.

E: OK, I have to know. I wasn't going to ask, but while I have the opportunity, I will. Why do we need the humans?

UC: They are there for your entertainment. Isn't this what you wanted to hear?

E: Was that suppose to be funny? Is this the best they can do, with what they've got. Mostly, I mind my business, and they mind theirs. I try not to get involved in their affairs, until, they start to dig into me. Then, lightning and thunder is on, and here come the floods. The problem nowadays is that they don't care about lightening and thunder anymore. Respect for them has been lost. I am slowly losing my purpose.

Many humans stay in the isle of delirious. Looking ridiculous. Wish after wish, and they still eat the same dish. But to be fair, there are many good people focused on good deeds. What is the media focused on? Death. Humanity can't take a breath, without seeing death. Can you at least give me a date, for their mortality rate? The number of the diseased is escalating. The population is increasing. Isn't it time for a re-evaluation?

UC: Why do you want a re-evaluation, and of whom? You seem too anxious for this information. It's too soon. Shouldn't you be working on your own Energy Development? The energy of the Virus Cell must be eradicated from humanity's thought process. It's imperative that it happens. Man, and woman, can't seem to balance each other. We see, we observe, and we preserve what the human doesn't. Here is an example of a possession. This has to be one of the most nonsensical things that humans can do. Because, they are Unconscious of their actions. There are Consequences, that don't just affect the physical matter. Now pay attention. You may learn something.

The story of *"a man, and his land."* It's not too long. We will go slow, so you can understand.

Day and night, this man works his land, using his own hand. He protects it. Fights for it. He lives, and cries for his land. He kills, and dies for it. It's his land, he owns it. Keep off, trespassers will be shot. No soliciting, beware of huge dog. Get the hint? This man is not only obsessed with his land, but he is POSSESSED by it. After this man dies for his land, it's sold to another brand. The question is, does this land, still belong to the dead man?

E: Wait UC. How can that be? He is dead. His land sold. What's he going to do with it? Do they have houses in the spirit world?

UC: Just listen. The dead man still believes, the land is his. If you believe in life after death that is. This is possession. This man died believing, it was honorable to die protecting his land. The issue? Your beliefs go with you. Just follow along. You'll understand.

E: Wait UC, are we talking life or death?

UC: Yes, no, both? We are talking about the humans, and their Spirit. It's also about the body, and what's in it. Consciousness Energy awareness does not die with the body. It goes along with the spirit energy. What your awareness is upon death, it will be the same on your last breath. You are made of energy, not just a body. What you focus on is your reality. Dying while crying, because you miss your bed lining, is a physical possession. You're possessed by what you left behind. This is called, a Spirit Possession by a Physical Possession. It's not the spirits haunting you, you are self haunting. The spirit is possessed by its possessions, before it leaves the body. Upon arrival, it haunts the spirit dimensions, looking for its possessions. It's this spirit that, becomes the lost soul. Lost between two different worlds, and still attached to its physical goals. When your focus is on the reality that, you are a spirit, you have found your true Consciousness. When it's on the physical reality of your past life, you have lost Consciousness in the spirit dimensions. As a spirit, this man's awareness of his physical memories, will create a reality of the ones he had in life. Protection of his land at any cost. It will show him that he never died, that he was still on his land. Willing to protect his land again. To kill, and die for it.

He may be dead, but in his spirit brain, he thinks he is alive. Telling this kind of spirit that it died, is similar to creating a poltergeist. He will react anyway he can, until you are gone. Are you still here E? Are you keeping up? Like a poltergeist, he will lash out with extreme emotional anger, to get you away from his land. Remember he brought the Virus Energy with him.

This will continue, until this man's spirit can perform its own energy conversion. By disconnecting himself from the physical memory of his possessions, he can look towards spiritual development. As long as there are possessions to kill for, the original owners will be attached to them. When the time comes, be free of all possessions. Sell everything, and donate the money to a good cause. Freeing yourself of possessions, must be done while you are alive, in order to not bring the Virus with you. To leave the Earth not possessed, you must detach your investment from your possessions. Give them away, sell them, donate them. Whatever you want to do with them, just don't stay ATTACHED to them. You will bring them with you. They will haunt you.

E: Well, this is great information, but how am I suppose to get rid of my possessions. I can't sell them, donate them or give them away. You're going to have to do it UC. They are haunting me. With all this Virus Energy craziness. Trust has gone out the window. Everyone is suspicious of everyone. This Energy, is stealing humanity's life. It's causing problems in all relationships. I believe it's attempting to sabotage my relationship with the Sun. I am telling everyone. I don't care who knows anymore.

UC: Go ahead, tell everyone. You will get the same question. What relationship? It's only a fantasy E. You have a fever from the Virus infection.

E: Hey! That really hurt my feelings. What are you trying to do, hurt my feelings? This is not like you. You don't hurt peoples feelings.

UC: You're not a people. It was just a test anyway. To see if you still had feelings. You don't seem to care about hurting their feelings?

Earth, "I want to live"

E: That's because from the beginning, you have been saying they had no feelings. How can I feel for them, when they don't feel for themselves?

UC: You are suppose to help them bring out their feelings through energy conversion, not destroy their self esteem. Your feelings for humans are well documented. It's not a secret how you feel. They have heard you complaining.

E: Complaining. Oh ya! Are their feelings for me well documented? No! It's always human this, human that. I don't want to hear about it. There is only so much I can take.

UC: We don't mean to disappoint you E, but you are still developing. So there is a lot more coming your way.

E: Speaking of developing, I have grown you know. I am getting close to becoming a woman. Since I don't know how old I am, I am going by feeling. Prove me wrong. When I look, I see a woman. When a humans look, they see food. When you look, what do you see?

UC: A natural beauty, amazing greenery, and a solid body.

E: I have been working out. On top of, carrying them around all these years, has given me excellent leg muscles.

UC: You don't have legs E. But muscles, you have. Like a rock. So it's no problem for you to carry humanity's weight.

E: You are more optimistic than I am. They live on me. It's easy for you to say. It's my body being poked full of holes, dug up, and covered with cement. Which adds to their weight, times great. That stuff is killing me. I am becoming stiff as a board. Unusable, and more toxic. I am telling you UC, the human brain has stopped. I don't know who they're paying the rent to, but it's not I. It's another pie in the sky. Question, you say we need them. I know how I benefit the humans, but, how do they benefit me?

UC: By keeping your bushes trim. They turn your soil. Clean some of your water veins. Replant you, after you burn yourself with your temper. Rebuild you, after you shake in frustration. They build damns, to keep you from overflowing.

E: Let me stop you right there Mr. Boss. You got it all wrong. Where did you get your information? Last time I was convinced of what you said. This time, I am very weary of the human's motives. What they do, only benefits them. Let me show you. Keeping my bushes trim? Ask your children about that? They broke the contract. I still give them fruit. How does this benefit me? Turning my soil? That's so they can eat, and look for peat. Where is my benefit in this? OK, so they clean my Water Veins, that's so they can get water to the seeds, that are in my soil. They take what they grow, do you see a benefit here? You say, they Rebuild me, for this to make a difference, their technology advances would have to end. They build me here, but blow me up there. Where is my benefit? Building damns, has nothing to do with me. It's to save themselves from drowning.

Burn myself with my Temper? I guess you don't remember how many times they have burned me? What about the Pollution that's killing me slowly? It's not just cars, it's buses, trains, and planes. Oil factories, and gas stations. Today they throw fire bombs at me from their car window. It's on purpose. Most of my burns are caused by a flying projectile that they set on fire, and throw into my nature. It's like that, pipe bomb they make. Where is my benefit?

UC: Consciousness Energy Awareness, has taught you to recognize the way the Virus can manipulate. It's doing it right now. Listen to yourself. Your complaints, sound hostile. So what are you going to do about it? Sarcasm will not help you. Insults will only divide you.

E: Now hold on a minute. What do you mean what am I going to do about it? Me, nothing. I am packing my green jeans, and joining the energy movement to convert Mass Energy. Oh by the by, I am sending humans back to the manufacturer. Had them on sale for a month. They didn't sell, you can have them back. You have more influence on the Virus than I ever could.

UC: Your system, can convert the Virus Energy that's mixing with yours. You are more aware now. You know how to do it. You won't feel a thing. To complete your conversion quicker, catch up to the times. Stay present. Keep yourself out of the Virus Cells grasp. We want to empower you, to create your own transformation. Even though you are young, you are a full grown planet, developing your Energy. Stay focused on this, and leave the rest to the Universal Consciousness.

E: OK, I can do that, but sometimes I feel this strong sadness. It affects my emotions. Things happen on my body that I have no control over. They do whatever they want on my body. Hmm, wait! Where is the Sun? Is it half time yet? Is he with my other half? When is our break?

UC: Rest assure, the Sun's already in play. No interference allowed, 'till the next day. It's not your halftime until tomorrow.

E: This is torture, can't you make it full time. Just this one time?

UC: Sorry, one time will leave no time.

E: Does it have to rhyme? One time will leave no time? What about being understood? Is that, in there somewhere?

UC: We have a question for you E. What does humanity fear the most?

E: Well, death of course. This is what I hear. They talk about it often. There is a lot of fear around this subject.

UC: Imagine this. The thing that humankind is good at, is the thing they fear the most. Their mortality rate is in their hands. They have life, how long it lasts, is up to that life. What's going on the humans' ground? You seem distracted.

E: There is a commotion on my floor. Lots of stomping, and arguing. Humans are leaving. They built these flying machines, without the means to fly them out of their universe. Where do think they are going? They will just spin in a dark space, that will bring them back to the same place. Wait, leaving is leaving, what am I thinking?

E: Hallelujah! Praise you! I never thought it would happen. Did you evict them? Who cares, I can breathe again. Hey! I'm aware they are coming back, but please don't let that happen. Just call it, Lost in one place.

UC: You just don't stop do you? You must be your greatest fan, are you going to stop with the jokes?

E: No, it's wave interference. The humans echo waves, are mixing with mine. It's hard to recognize my own voice from theirs. Most things they say echo back. I thought by know, they would be tired of hearing their own voice. How can I stop their echo from echoing back? Should I tell them that there is no one listening? That they are just reverberating their own sound? Humankind is leaving me to go find another space. That's some gratitude boy. I stood by them through all their issues, and put up with their abuse. Now, they think they can just leave. Oh no, you cannot allow this. Blow up there flying machines UC. Is this a possibility? Makes sense to me. Was this part of your design? If it is, we better use mine. Who needs help the most, humans, me, or the spirit world?

UC: We could say, you need it most, but to help you, we must help humans first. We told you this. They hold the Virus energy. Humans are not innocent of wrong doing. They alway have an excuse for Acting out.

E: The humans are still packing. Many of them are gathering around some kind of space station. Oh no! More space rides? I thought they were leaving. It could be, they are practicing for a long flight... Hopeful thinking.

UC: A little information for you E. Humankind is not leaving. They may be dreaming they are leaving, but this will not happen. They don't want to leave. But the Virus Energy thinks, it can use to them to reinfect the universe of creation, by allowing humans to think they can escape to another world.

Even if they left, they would only come back, like a boomerang. They believe they can find a place to live without fear. That's why they are still packing. How about, flooding the Earth? It will keep them busy for a while. It wouldn't be the first time.

E: Wow! Isn't that kind of drastic? Flood myself? No, it takes too long to dry. Anyway, this would only cause them to fly. They actually think they can find a no fear zone, on another sphere that's unknown. They cannot be allowed to fly. Have you seen how they drive? Drive to stay alive, is how the human survives. With those kind of odds who wants to drive? Isn't it safer to walk. With their flaws, anything goes. It's more exciting than their movies. Imagine, if you had only one movie to watch for the rest of your life, wouldn't you be bored?

So, I watch them play this car game. With each crash, I make a dash. The game is called, *"Drive and cut, before you get hit by a truck."* Humans are always in a hurry to go nowhere, so people drive erratically. They risk their lives, and the lives of others, to beat the truck, before they get stuck. They think it's cool to be a fool. I think it's addictive though, It's like gambling, you take a chance, most of the time, you lose. I am learning by observing, like you suggested. It's not what I am learning as much as, how much I am changing.

UC: Those words sound familiar, have you checked to see if the humans left yet? You are correct in saying, it's a space ride E. Unless they get lost.

E: They are nearly done. They look like they're having fun. Like, they are going on vacation. Is it my imagination? Am I suppose to be the example of self control UC? They get to go on vacation, while I end up as human vegetation. This, doesn't work for me. I work hard to feed them, and shelter them. But you send them on vacation. Hmm! How is this a solution?

UC: It's not. It's only an illusion. We are not sending them anywhere, that they can't go on their own.

Don't worry, their space has a no crossing zone. So when we say they are not leaving, It means they will go, and then come back. A lesson is best learned, by self experience. It lasts longer. No one is being treated better then you E. Stop feeling neglected. It's not real.

E: Stop talking, is what you are saying. Are you shutting down free speech? I am women, hear me say, no! You can't shut me up. I have rights. Women have been talking about it for years, and If I have a body, I have ears.

UC: You don't have ears. But for a planet, you have many fears. Planets do not get scared E. If it's not the Virus Energy, then what is it? Your grape vine?

E: Would that be so wrong? Remember my hip issues? If I don't drink it, they will. They have taken enough of me.

UC: Have you heard them talking about their destination? Are they saying, can you hear anything? If they could only feel Consciousness Energy, we wouldn't need you to communicate through.

E: Why? If they're coming back, who cares where they are going. Are you going to stop them?

UC: It's their experience, we can't interfere in that. Your own words E. It's what humanity taught you. Any comments now? Why isn't humanity using what they taught you, in those mental courses.

E: Not just mental, mental health. Different meanings from the humans perspective. You made them, and this is all you got to show for it. I tried making some suggestions, like, go count the stars. And visit the sun. Hopefully, they will take me up on one. I am not sure where they are going, but I heard it was where they won't be recognized; wherever that is. It's going to be a slow go. Many will perish. Well, it's no different than jumping without looking.

UC: Humans are staying to fix what they have broken. Cash or credit will not do. Neither will, *"I don't want to."*

E: You are basically pacifying them. You know they will be back because, they can't go far. This I can understand. But what I cannot understand, is after all I have done, you would allow them to come back. That's the thanks I get for constantly cleaning up after them?

UC: Look, as far as the humans leaving, their fears, will always bring them back to what they know. Safety in the familiar, even if it's a prison. The same fear that goes with them, will bring them back.

E: I could use to lose a few pounds of flesh you know? Most of them overeat. Escalation when they meet. Health issues they can't beat. These humans are no longer fresh. I don't know what they are eating, but the gases keep seeping. It's gotta be the meat.

UC: Oh how sweet. You say the wrong things at the right time. How do you manage to do that? Are you aware, there is an energy attachment between humans, and you. You need each other to survive. The Conscious Universe is aware of humankind. Many life forms have started out as you have. They, found a way to go through their evolution, into becoming Consciousness Energy Beings. So, why is it difficult for you, humanity?

E: Most of the time, asking humans why, goes on deaf ears. It's not their fault really. They don't know why. Although they could learn to ask.

UC: Yes, it would save them from disaster. Humankind, is taking a bigger risk going into space, than meeting the energy of the Universal Consciousness, fear makes them unconscious.

E: Don't bother UC. You said it yourself. They are hard of hearing. I am curious to get an answer to a couple of questions though? Do you think the humans have a plan, or were they just going to float in space again? Planning space rides for fun, and doing a dump and run, is not a good way to build a great reputation. Space is full of their junk.

UC: We haven't told you another reason they won't leave. It's what you're about to tell them. It may stop them, or not. It is still their choice.

E: I thought fear stops them? Hey, what's the deal UC? Are you playing a trick on me?

UC: It's bigger than fear. We have prepared a message for you, to deliver to the humans. Only you have to deliver it without anger and animosity; agreed?

E: Oh, Yes, agreed. I can do that. Where is it? Will it just appear in front of my face? I don't have eyes to read with UC, that's what you keep telling me. How am I suppose to read a message to them, with a mouth I don't have.

UC: Sarcasm, will get you nowhere. We will send the words through Consciousness Energy Projection. It's how we are communicating now. Wake up E, enough playing around. Get serious. You should know this. It's in your Consciousness memory. Better start using it. You are an intelligent planet, be intelligent. As far as not having a mouth, have you been listening to all the words you have been saying? It's called energy conversion to physical sound. We will project it, you will see it, and they will start to hear it.

E: Thank you for that clarity. It felt more like a little scolding. Hmm? I am attempting to understand what you're talking about. I hear you loud and clear. But you haven't said one word out loud. Wow! I thought we were talking out loud. OK let me see that letter. I need to practice my lines. I can't talk the way you talk UC, it's those one sentence paragraphs. One sentence that takes me a year to digest. Got any shorter ones, like maybe, a one word paragraph. It would help my translation efforts. They have a short attention span.

UC: The less you say, the more aware you will sound. Are you ready to tell them, before they try to fly? It would save you the pollution their trip would make. You certainly can use it. You can't leave yourself unprotected.

E: What are my chances of survival, I have no idea what I am about to read to them. Since I can't see it, before I read it, I am a little nervous. Humans throw things, at those they don't like. I want to live; but, I want to be liked also.

UC: You are about to set a huge limit on human's escape route. The sooner the better. It's not something they will treasure.

E: There it is. I had a feeling I was being suckered into doing your job. *"You're closer to them E, they can hear you better E."* It was all, so you can use me. Just like humanity. Nothing I can do about it now. OK, let's do it. What am I doing exactly?

UC: Setting limits for humanity. This is your specialty. You will give them the whole picture at one time. It's less pressure on you that way. Don't pause for any questions, or comments. No point in that. Are you ready?

E: Pause! They could start burning their furniture you know? I don't want to incite violence. It hurts me worse than it hurts them.

UC: They already do that, and their cars too. Some even burn their own home. Anyway, are you saying they can't handle boundaries? What happens when they are ill? Aren't they put on bed rest, until the Virus is gone, and they are no longer infected? Isn't that a quarantine? Now go on. If you don't spill your guts, they'll spill it for you. Don't fear retaliation E. Being fear free, is being infection free.

E: But you are the best one to deliver this kind of message. You are so good at it.

UC: Stop resisting. You know you want to do it. This is your chance to burst their bubble, as you say. Here is the letter.

E: OK, OK, anything to ruin their day. *"This is Earth calling the humans. Hello! There is something you need to know. Pay attention. I know you can hear me. I feel you running. You want to hear this, unless you want flooding. Before thinking of space exploration, clean up your own situation. You are not the only denomination in creation."*

"Listen up, and don't interrupt me. There is a Universal Energy Protection around this planet's Universe, all of it. It's there, to make sure you don't leave your universe. Humankind, will not be permitted to leave until, the Virus Energy Cell has been converted. So, you are excluded from flying. Shut the toys off, boys. Go home, take the chicken out, and start frying. Find something to do besides dying."

UC: Whoa E! You are way off course. Didn't you get that whole message? You began fine, then you saw your chance to do a grab and smash. You grabbed what we discussed, and used it to smash them. What's with the chicken remark. You really have picked up bad habits. That, was not in the letter. No one asked you to improvise. You didn't need to. Just read, that's all. Too late now, take a seat. You can relax. We have it from here. You are spending way too much time on your streets. Who are you hanging around with?

E: I go out at night to wash away the filth of the day, and blow the leaves from my trees. They slow down my growth. I have to clean, they don't do it. *"Oh leaves are a good compost." "Leave the leaves."* How about I blow them into their homes?

UC: No wonder you keep getting reinfected. You still feel rejected. Get back on track. Humans of the Earth, until the Evolution Revolution of humankind is complete, you will not be able to travel past your own space. You must go through an energy conversion, before you can go further. Your planet, your space, and you, have been on a quarantine, and still are. You will continue to be, until you free yourselves from the Virus Cell Energy. You are limited to your own Space travel only. Can you hear this humanity? You may have to translate E. Wait, maybe not. It's fine, they hear it.

E: May I speak now? I am still here. I have a voice. I have an opinion. I need to be heard.

UC: Why? We know what you're going to say. We already saw it. Nice try. However, you do have freedom of choice. We wouldn't dream of standing in the way of that. We thrive on observing lessons learned, don't get burned by your own choice.

E: While the humans are listening, their brain is translating what they are hearing. So, I hope they translate these words as friendly words. That's it UC, I will not be silenced, I am not a wimp. I am talking back. What's it going to cost me, a few hundred trees. To change the look of bewilderment on the faces of the world's homeless, I would donate a billion trees. I have tried to forget most of what humanity has done to me, I can't live with the pain. So many times, I overlooked what they have done. It's a good thing I have the Sun.

UC: How many times do we have to redirect you, re-balance you, convert, and heal you? Have we ever showed anger, and hostility towards you?

E: No, not really. I would call it a little stern at times.

UC: But not harsh. Why are you not treating others, the way you are being treated?

E: Because, they will repeat it. It makes me feel defeated. Nice try UC. Using empathy by way of common sense. Wow! I call this an offense. I get it, I am not dense. Trying to get me to show sympathy to humanity's mediocrity, using your terminology.

UC: Yes, that's true, very observant of you. At times, you have been observed putting the cart before the horse, and end up taking the wrong course.

E: Freedom of choice. What's going to happen to me if all humanity stopped eating meat? How am I suppose to defend myself? Sorry UC, I may have to leave, before they eat the rest of me.

UC: No defense can keep them out. People are infected, do you think the Virus Energy can't seep through your cracks. You better close those cracks yourself. You are the only one who knows where they are. If the Virus Cell finds them first, you will get worse. If that happens, start spinning. It can't hold on to anything but you, spin fast enough and it will convert to your energy.

E: Will the spinning throw humanity off of me? If so, my foot is on the gas pedal. As long as the humans stay in attack mode, I will keep raining on myself. They haven't experienced my rage. But If they don't turn the page, I will blame it on my age. Temper tantrums are common at this stage.

UC: You have no foot. Or a gas pedal. You are a planet. You don't get to have rage, or engage in a war with humans. How is this to your benefit?

E: I do hear you, usually I agree, but you didn't create me to be agreeable. Not with Free Will. But until humanity acknowledges what they have done, and still do, I am in protection mode. They made the choice to swim in the deepest part of the pool, without knowing how to swim. Now it's save me, save me. I have witnessed those that were saved, continue to be cruel to life. They show no gratitude for a second chance. I am starting to recognize unconscious behaviors. As Conscious Energy, isn't the continuation of life, each humans responsibility?

UC: Absolutely. It's yours also. The humans depend on you. If not, they will continue to depend on the Virus Energy Cell, to help them get what they want. It will even tell them what they want. This is the reason for this inquiry. A discussion about the awareness, of the Universal Consciousness Energy, and the human's physical one. When you use their energy, you are not doing yourself any favors. Because talking with you, is like talking to a human.

E: They live on me, who lives on you?

UC: They do, you do, we all do!

E: Ya, thanks to you. By the way, there are savages still living on me. Now they have these new breeds called, the fish and vegetable people, They will eat me out of my vegetables and fish. I won't be given the chance to replenish. Humans are constantly in a hurry. Forcing me to grow food faster. It's breaking my natural birthing cycle. Isn't this oppression?

UC: Humans have created a faster way, a forced energy injection, changing the DNA. Crossbreeding, let's mix them together to see what we get. Once again, It's like, let's jump to see what happens. Why do the humans not think about the long term effects, and reactions? Many of you are being inspired by your Internet media. Traveling in space, must have given humanity a brain hernia. But then, it could be, your inability to convert the Virus Energy.

E: It just doesn't make sense. What's to discover in dark space? The dark? I can be dark, and I have light to discover it by. Space does not. I am still the unknown, waiting to become known. Now you know why I am so hot. It's heated frustration from the humans lack of emotion. How can I show them love, when many don't love me?

UC: They don't even know about the Consciousness Energy, and we still love them. Your feelings should be the same. But we also know, when you hit somebody so many times, they are liable to fall apart, and yes, we feel your heat, it's burning their feet. Ease back a bit, you don't want to set fire to your own trees. It's to protect you from the humans. So you as a planet, you can expand.

E: Humans can't keep me healthy. The healthy ones are carrying on with their needs, the unhealthy just carries on. I am in reaction to humanity's crimes against the world. I am not trying to be cordial right now. They can find the cure in their brain, but it's Unconscious, and only Consciousness Energy can change it.

Humanity's unhealthy mental issues are overwhelming. This is what I am dealing with. Humans are being turned into Ice, and being nice has a Price. Most of them give advice. But hardly anyone takes it. Are you aware of how quickly, the humans will go into panic mode? Have you been studying your creations behavior lately?

UC: What do you think we have been doing. You are not saying anything new E. It's part of the reason we are here. It's not to join you with the Sun. It's to create the energy movement. To do that, humanity will have to be converted. People will put up a resistance. They may have to give up some of their comforts, like convenience.

E: This could backfire on us UC. You know better than to take things away. It makes the humans slay. Greed doesn't like to give up its property. To survive, it needs to increase, not decrease. It lives to catch, and not release. It will completely monopolize all the reactionary energy, and turn it against humanity. Greed would start a war over this. Oh well, that's show biz.

UC: It sounds like, your energy conversion is on its last phase. You are waking up. Focused, and full of the Universal Consciousness Energy. Is it real or are you faking it? That's yet to be seen.

E: Oh boy, yet to be seen…is now. I will not be going unconscious. I am spinning too fast for the Virus Energy to stay the same. I am spinning so fast that I can see the other side of me. There he is, my Sun with that traitor.

UC: What are you doing E? Do you feel alright? You look like you just saw yourself. It's not that bad. You will feel better, when the pollution is gone. It's a shock to see yourself for who you really are. Don't

Earth, "I want to live"

panic. Stop shaking, you're scaring the humans. Why are you shaking, are you feeling OK?

E: I am doing fine thank you, why do you ask? Why are you watching me so close. I didn't do anything.

UC: While you were spinning, your roses turned a darker red. Are you embarrassed about something? What were you doing? You're hiding something.

E: I knew it! Yup! Just like a parent. I bet you would wait up all night for me. So, I looked behind me for just a minute, to sneak a peek at my Sun, and my nemesis.

UC: Well we had to make sure you came back, on your track. You know, the planetary system you belong to. You have to stop going unconscious. Everyone is listening to this.

E: I didn't think you would see me. I thought I was being stealthy.

UC: No, not stealthy, just obvious. But we are curious, what did you see, when you looked back? What was so important that you took such a chance?

E: You saw me, do I have to say it? I will say it. I quickly turned my body, to see where the Sun was. I tried to be stealthy. That went nowhere. Obviously, you saw me. I was able to turn just enough to see my other side. I had to know what they were doing. There they were, cuddled up next to each other. She was getting a suntan, with my Sun tan man. I started to expand, and tried to reach for his hand.

UC: That was a bad plan. Guess what, you just put humankind, and the universe in danger, to get your needs met. Where is your awareness E? Your little turn caused a country to burn, and another to fall in the sea. Where's your responsibility? Why did you do that? Are you aware that, just by attempting to turn, you caused a catastrophe on your mountain side. Planets do not turn backwards.

E: I am aware of my place in my system. But, I wasn't aware of my instant unconscious shift. I didn't feel it coming. Are you sure it was my mountain side? I feel really bad. They are my best features.

UC: Oh ya, say bye. It's crumbling away, don't you feel it?

E: I must be numb. I have a pinched nerve from turning. Excuse me, I am learning. It's not like you haven't made a mistake, by creating the human. They are constantly looking for the easy way out. Like for example; each time the humans dig me up, to build houses on top of houses. I feel it burning. They can see the smoke coming out of me. Do they care? No. They act like I am a nobody. On top of that, they sacrifice my girth for that Mr. Cement. He is suddenly the best guy in town. He is nothing but a clown. A serial choker. He wraps himself around me all the time, choking the life out of me. You are not doing anything about it. Why?

UC: Slow down, you're running too fast towards a solution. It can't be at any cost. Mr. Cement as you call him, has freedom of expression, according to your laws. We cannot interfere in that. You were protesting women's rights before. Mr. Cement, will protest. No doubt. Why would You think, humans would change their ways for you? You don't show any confidence in them. You need them to back you, if you want relief from cement.

E: I really don't like that Mr. cement. Can he be melted? Please, he is like the cholesterol in a humans body. My veins are clogging. There is no stent in the world big enough. I use to be very flexible you know. Now look at me, I can't even turn a little without causing a catastrophe. It's the cement, it's stiffening me.

Stop the cement, or I go on strike.

UC: That would cause a rampage. Put that thought back where you got it from. When you turned to look, your unconscious act caused some of your land to separate. You think humans felt fear before? There's more. This is what you broke, on top of those two countries; you left millions of them hungry. People who lived in the East, found themselves in the West. They were totally discombobulated. While you, in the middle of a catastrophe that you caused, are watching your greenery? You are being insensitive.

E: It's called strike one. Strike two, depends on what you do. Hey! I sound like you. Allow me to have the Sun, melt the cement, and I stop my intent. Do you know how much better my body would function, without the cement. I can move faster. I could better protect humanity. Maybe they will start to like me, what do you think? Come on, we are talking cement here, not arthritis. Cement could kill us. Me, I mean.

UC: Point well made. You didn't need all that drama. Humanity heard your plea. They may create a more fixable cement. So you can breathe, and move easier.

E: Are you kidding? It will never happen. They need their conscious memory for that. Thats the issue, they forgot their memory. This discussion is having a strong effect on me. My emotions are in turmoil.

UC: You are feeling your energy conversion. Your emotions are resisting the Virus Energy. You are becoming clear, and so are we. Awareness has its own perception, like Consciousness Energy, has intuition. You, and humankind have been together for life times. They haven't left you. They can't. They stuck by you when you lost control. They are part of you. Many humans came to your rescue. They still do. They need you. We need you.

E: Speaking of that, when my life energy is depleted, will I be repeated, reseeded, or just a planet that's been defeated? Anything but cremated. I have seen what they do to their dead. You're not hard enough on them UC. They can do whatever they want. Look at what they have done to space. It's full of their trash, and you do nothing.

UC: Because we are energy. We don't judge humanity's actions, they do. Oh, and same for you. We don't make anyone do anything. Inherit this philosophy E, it will keep you mentally free. As we said, *"What goes up, must come down."* Let them send their Rocket Ships, Satellites, Space stations, Fueling applications, and Robots. Don't worry, they will get them back. Even the Robots. What humans sends up, will crash down. Hopefully, it's not on your town. Space junk doesn't discriminate on what ground.

E: I hear a commotion on my ground. Apparently, humanity is angry with me now. They are saying, I am complaining too much. I am out of touch and I need to grow up. What! I just realized what they said. This just went over the line UC. Now, I am not happy. Find a place to hide humans. The hail is coming. No snow this winter. Don't defend them UC.

UC: Why? They have a point. You have been saying insulting things about them for some time now. But we don't condone, tit for tat. We didn't expect this from you E. You are showing the virus energy, not your conversion. You said, you would not go unconscious anymore. And yet, we watched it happen. Why do the humans actions, need to be hidden? Are they forbidden? Can somebody ask them?

E: I can…Hello! Where did you go humans? Who are you hiding from? Most likely, it's your conscience, and those wonderful advances. Why do many of you hide your actions? I am waiting. No answer. OK UC, you asked why humanity's actions need to be hidden? Because, many of them do things that are forbidden, and hide it from their children and each other. I feel a pull of neediness coming from the humans. They have a question.

H: Many of us have been listening to your conversation. We are in conflict. It's become a stand off. What are we guilty of?

UC: You're guilty of nothing. You are your own judge and jury. Your guilt comes from your actions. When you recognize that a choice you made caused a negative action, you feel the guilt. Make up for that choice, and you won't have to carry that guilt around. It's Consciousness energy.

LEARN FROM YOUR MISTAKE, FIX WHAT YOU BREAK.

E: Why do humans, follow each other? How can the follower know, that the leader is leading them in the right direction? The leader could be following someone else. How does someone recognize, if they are leading or following?

UC: Your previous course, the Study of Humans, should have taught you the answers to these. Were you not paying attention? No wonder you don't really know humanity, do you E? Recognizing the difference between leading and following, can be achieved by observing the persons awareness, and knowing the intention of their actions. For a follower to know, if they are being led in the right direction, the follower must become the leader. For a leader to follow others, would mean, this leader is leading others to lead. Why do humans follow each other? The one following, has no idea where to go. So, they follow another, thinking they know. Except, the one following, never asks the one being followed, if they know where they were going? Unconscious people don't ask. They assume others are right, because of low self esteem. They have no option but to follow. No one wants to be alone. What humanity is unaware of, is that you're all in the same boat. Don't follow, just so you won't be alone. By not following, you will attract leaders to you. You will never be alone.

E: I must of fallen asleep during this course. Because, I don't remember any of what you just said. It was profound. It was energy for development, for sure. I know humans well enough, to not want to know them. I do want to believe that humans can develop, and grow. Go through a new evolution. But, this has yet to become a realization. Hey, is this like when you say, *"it's yet to be seen?"* I got it. Now I know why you say it. Mystery solved. A realization has evolved. I believe it means, *"It's yet to be realized."* Correct UC?

UC: Finding yourself, is self realization. It's what makes you a leader. Where are your leadership skills? Say something if you can? You have seen the worst of humanity, what about the best of them? Any comments about that?

E: I have seen their best. They treat themselves better than their guest. When they are pressed, they scream, more, more! Like I am an open door. They are trying to peel me like a sardine can. You have to help me UC.

UC: Well, it was the true nature of humans to want what they need, not more. Before, the Virus infection changed that meaning. Now it's give me, give me. We are aware of your plight. We need you to be aware of humanity's plight also. You know that what they do always affects you. Don't instigate them.

E: That didn't help. I ask for help, and you say, it's their nature. Be aware of their plight. So I'm basically on my own. It's my nature to create hurricanes, and twisters. Along with tidal waves. Check-mate.

UC: Humankind, must be inspired by a balanced energy core. Their participation, is vital to their survival. Only, their denials are stored in their Unconscious files. The files that the energy of the Virus loves to access most, are your emotional reaction files. They are stored with your denials. When humans thinks they are gone, something they will do, will trigger them on. Because, they are still there, waiting to interfere.

E: You know what UC? I want to flush humanity. I am feeling full of their broken promises. I am holding on to my handle, and ready to pull. They are going to get a soaking! I'm gonna do it. Oops! I think the handle broke.

UC: Why did you do it E, it's wasn't helpful. They have heard enough of your animosity. Try not talking to them, until you've converted your energy, completely.

E: Nope, they haven't heard these feelings. They need to hear what I think of them, to see if they give a care. My complaint is about, how humans always want more, I am running out of more. They ask for more, while they store. They hoard, for fear of starvation.

UC: Try to be understanding, we know they can be demanding.

E: Oh ya! I understand alright. Here is what I understand. Humans are emotionally regressed, presently perplexed, developmentally regressed, totally unimpressed and, frantically distressed. They stay undressed, most are over sexed, and over taxed. I gotta keep it real UC. I am not a baby sitter, or a nanny. If humans would stop being in denial, they would take on the Virus Cells Energy, and uncover it for humanity.

This is what I would call, Consciousness Energy awareness. Threats are not as threatening as they used to be. Punishment, speaks for itself. What it says, is questionable, arguable, and undesirable. Yet, they both still play a role. They have become the humans guide for control. They are still feared. They will be until, humans no longer use them.

UC: Pause for a minute, we are trying to recover from your verbal assault on humanity. That was insulting, and rude. Apparently, many of them agree with you. Humanity is always open to attack. They could pay you back. The Virus Cell doesn't care. It would rather scalp your hair.

E: Well, what's next for the humans? Will they change, or is it the same old illusion? Will they pay attention, or pay extinction? Will it be reality, or fantasy? As I have observed from my world's view, fantasy does give them a temporary rescue. But in the morning, their reality is still a fantasy. They can't tell the difference anymore.

UC: Consciousness Energy does not create fantasy. Reality has to be realized to become real. It has to be visualized by Consciousness Energy, otherwise, it will fall apart.

E: The humans, are having conflict over realities at this time. It's becoming physical. They stopped for a question? They need an answer to stop the fighting. They always have something to fight about. OK, one at a time. Here is one.

H: Does the reality of one, have to be the reality of another? That is difficult to do since we have different realities.

UC: What are you trying to discover? What's the conflict over?

Earth, "I want to live"

H: Our different realities. We can't seem to see eye to eye.

UC: There's your answer. It's in plain view. Humans have different realities. You live on the same planet. You eat, sleep, learn, and educate in your own realities, in your own dimensions. You live on a world, but you create your own worlds to live in? Amazing! Worlds within worlds, on one planet. This proves you know nothing about the planet your world is on. You pass all your beliefs on to your children, who will pass them on to theirs, and the cycle continues.

E: Yesterday, the humans asked me, *"what's in the store,"* It's empty, I replied. They said, *"But we need more. What are we going to do,"* they sighed? More of what, I asked?

H: We need a new door to escape from this floor. We need a life without a chore.

E: What about a new planet core, I asked? It would make me last longer.

H: What for, we need cars more. We can't drive a core. Besides, we don't know what life has in store. We say; live it up while you can.

E: After hearing that. I became depressed, and I changed my address. I don't want to be associated with this mess.

UC: This will cheer you up. What's faster than a speeding bullet, and smaller than a gnat?

E: A fruit fly. How about a flea. I give up, what is it?

UC: The humans act. The ones who profess, are the ones who need to confess. They profess too much, and do too little.

E: Apparently, the humans had some reaction to your statement. I have that reaction coming. Here is question two.

H: Ya, but what's true to you, may not be true to others.

UC: Is this, that same reality argument? What's true to you is your own reality. What may be true to others, is their reality. Common sense, which you were born with, says, when the truth reveals to you one thing, and you do the opposite, what's the truth? Your actions don't reflect what you believe. You're obsessed with the needing to hear the truth, but when you do, some of you become hostile. Your first reaction is to become defensive. Why? You wanted the truth. Which is it? Do you want the truth or not? Make a decision either way. Just make it, it will move you. This is your pattern, you don't believe your own truth. If you can't trust your own truth, no one else can.

E: What makes an action, become a chore? Is it the constant repetition of it? Like the constant assaults on my nature? Or the constant destruction of my best features.

UC: We seem to remember that you did this to yourself, by turning. We are sure you don't wish to remember it. It wasn't one of your best moments. Humans were suppose to be your protectors, your defenders. Instead, they couldn't agree on how to start a fire. They are just floating, going nowhere, staying somewhere, eating something and wishing for another. Would you really rather, we simply removed them. Out of sight, out of mind. Isn't this, the human way?

E: You can't possibly deny, how often they relinquish their responsibility to others, or other things.

This is the human way. NOT MY PROBLEM. Is the mantra of the human. They create the problem, then, say it's not my problem. What kind of thinking is this UC? They are truly infected. There is no other explanation.

UC: Where are you getting your information? This doesn't sound like you.

E: Ah, hmm well, the Stars. I know, you told me. But what they say, sounds good to me.

UC: Again E, we warned you about that, remember. You don't have to learn the hard way. Are you sure you can trust their sources? We thought they were in conflict over, which of them is the brightest star. Don't waste your time. Stars are just parked cars, waiting to be sold. Are you aware that some of the humans, are selling your Stars?

E: What? Wait a minute. Are they trying to steal my nightlights? Well I'll be dipped in mud! You have to be kidding. I don't want to say it, but I have to, what human dares to sell your creations? Point them out, so I can drench them with toxins. How dare they?

UC: It's not a joke E, that's what's concerning.

E: You are serious, aren't you? I was not aware of this one. Wow! They should have asked me, they would have gotten them wholesale. Humans are not all there, are they UC? This really throttles my behind.

UC: We meant to ask, how can you tell your front, from your behind? You are round.

E: You formed me, don't you know? That's easy, my behind makes a sound. Also, another complaint. Why on Earth, you would keep creating humans with limited intelligence, is difficult to comprehend? Are you expecting their brain to mature? To grow, by some kind of miracle?

UC: We said no miracles. There are many intelligent humans living on you. Protesting for you. Raising awareness about you. SAVE THE PLANET stickers are everywhere. Recycling centers. Climate control, and Ecology programs. Environmentalists are standing up for you everyday. Pay attention. Change your perception. Otherwise you are learning nothing. They need to be drawn in by the awareness of your Consciousness. You must reflect, what you present. The young adults have taken up your cause.

E: I have been observing humans for years, as you are aware. Front row seats mind you. My honest opinion is that humans, are on a sinking ship without a dinghy.

UC: Why would you say that? How did they get in the water? Why no dinghy?

E: No dinghy, because they are stingy. They are in the water because they jumped in. Remember, when I told you, the humans were jumping without looking? It's because, their ship is sinking.

UC: What about the ones hanging on the sides? Once they fall in, they will come, and go with the tides. What are you doing about it E?

E: There isn't much to do, except maybe, drain the ocean, that would do it.

UC: That would kill every life form in it? You can't do it. Didn't they prepare for a disaster? Why didn't they bring an extra boat?

E: They say they didn't get the note. The one that said, take a vote. Boat, or no boat? Unfortunately, they let the Captain decide. The choice was no boat. It would make the ship lighter, and move faster, he said. He was the first one to jump. For this reason, the humans are on their own. Their ability to make good choices, needs work.

UC: Why did they jump? We heard you say Sinking ship. They had time to be rescued, before it became a Sunken ship.

E: It doesn't take much to push them over the edge. But it's a good question, I will ask them. Hey there, humans! Do you have time for a question? Why did you jump before the ship sank?

H: Of course, we have time for a question. Where do you think we are going? First, it was hard to believe we were sinking, then, we panicked. We thought if we jumped, God would catch us with another ship before we drowned.

E: You mean, you jumped without the assurance of survival. Have you seen that ship yet? Is it coming?

H: No, we thought we did, but it turned out to be a mirage. We need a huge barge.

E: So sorry, I don't have one. Now what are you going to do? Swim? To where? You're in the middle of the ocean, dog paddling.

H: We don't know, it's too late now, we are in deep water. The water is cold, and some of us jumped without a life jacket. Most of the older ones jumped. There are a few young adults. Some of the ones that jumped, don't know how to swim.

E: What can I, the Earth do, to speed up their rescue. We may have our issues, but we can't just let them drown? An hour ago, I wanted them gone. What changed?

UC: You E. Your Energy Conversion, has changed your perception. Your realization about your change is proof of that. They are freezing to death. They will drown soon, life jackets are not that strong. Humans are in the water without a ladder. Where are they? Don't say it. They were out voted also? No wonder the captain jumped first. If he hadn't, they would have thrown him overboard anyway.

E: They took the ladders with them when they jumped. Last minute change of heart. Thinking that the ladders would keep them afloat. Another bad choice.

UC: Fear, and panic were the enemy. These two Virus Energy's, took away their Consciousness and ability to rationalize the situation, and act appropriately. They achieved their goal.

E: Yes, they jumped in without a thought. They were only thinking of staying alive. So ya, it's only natural for them, to panic, and go into fear. They are about to sink. What would you do? By the way, why aren't you saving them?

UC: Wait a minute, clarity time. They said, that jumping in the water, was suppose to save them? Was there a vote?

E: Well, the ship was going down anyway, is what they say. There was no reason to stay aboard.

UC: Why jump? Sinking, is not sunk, it's still sinking. Just like they are. Those humans, should have waited 'till the last minute.

E: What does it matter, everything is sinking. Their choices are whats sinking them. However, I still need to know why, you don't save them?

UC: As an energy form, humankind has the ability to save themselves. They just forgot how. You see, an ending always connects with a beginning. It's a Natural Consciousness Cycle. Similar, to the Life and Death cycle. Not going to the end, keeps you five feet from the beginning. Like they are now. The rescue ship is five miles away. Can they last that long in freezing water? They should have stayed on the sinking ship. By the time it went down, they would have been rescued. Now, the water has taken them further away from the sinking ship. They can't be rescued, they have to save themselves. Fear, and panic will end them.

E: What about the ones who can't swim? Well, I guess they are fish food. Unfortunately, the ones that jumped in, were holding hands with the ones that were not jumping.

UC: Why were they holding hands with the jumpers, for balance?

E: No, in case the jumpers attempted to jump. They would be able to stop them. It was a decision made in haste.

UC: What happened? Why didn't they stop them?

E: They just jumped without notice. The ones holding them, didn't think they would actually jump. Now they are all in the same deep water. The water is so cold, thoughts of not making it have started to creep.

UC: So, those who were aware, were pulled in the water by those who they were trying to save. Those who were aware, were not very aware, were they? They were standing there, holding hands with fear. That's what they should have been aware of. You can get pulled in, whether you want to or not. How will they survive? How long has it been? They don't have much time. They are screaming for a ladder E.

E: Does it really matter? The ladders all sunk. They were too heavy.

UC: Don't be harsh, because without a ladder no one will make it. They will drown. However, there is a way, the water can carry them out.

E: Out! Out to where? No where? I don't hear any yelling. They jumped in, they can jump out.

Are the consequences harsher for the jumpers, than for the ones that were pulled in? It was not their choice, it wasn't their intention. Can you pull them out?

UC: You're the one who had a hard time with humanity, asking to be saved? Now you are asking for them to be pulled out? This is excellent energy conversion E. You have come a long way in such a short time.

E: No, I just asked if you could pull them out. If humans were in better health, they would be able to rescue themselves. They are becoming tired of dog paddling. Some are sinking, and popping up like a cork. I thought I heard you say before, that there was a way to save them. Turn the water into sand, or something.

UC: They should have learned how to save themselves, It's getting serious. They had the chance.

E: It's nearly too late now. You're going to stand by, and let your children drown? Won't they resent you for that?

UC: Resent who, their god maybe. They have yet to discover their real creator, the Universal Consciousness Energy. Have you heard them scream for help yet?

Earth, "I want to live"

E: Now that you mention it, no. Maybe you can just freeze, a part of the water, and create a floor so they can walk out.

UC: Like you said, to where? They need a Cruise Ship, or an island to appear suddenly. Unfortunately, it's fear of the water that will drown them. Fear caused them to jump, and panic will drown them. They must stay clam.

E: Well then, what's the option, drowning? This could happen. Panic can do that? Do we have to fight the Virus to save them?

UC: No, the humans do. If they had trust, they can use it to ride the waves, as far as the ocean will take them. Let's see if those in the water, can trust it to help them. This is their last resort. Humans, listen to this, before you drown. If you want to live, you must completely surrender to the water, and go with the flow. Don't fight it. Don't resist it. You will not drown. Hold your breath, and relax your body. The water can carry your weight. Trust the water. Turn on your back, and float. Let the water carry you to another shore, with a door to a new floor, with a strong foundation.

E: Ya, great, good luck! Maybe they will run into an anaconda on the way. I am sorry, but wouldn't it be easier to just get rid of them with the Virus, rather than converting them? Greed is growing inside them. Many of them have learned that, they can buy someone to take on their responsibility, while they lay on the beach playing grease me.

UC: No different than you, and the Sun. What happened? Where did that comment come from? You're at the end of your conversion.

E: It's the Virus Energy doing its final energy interference. It's going kicking and screaming. It's on its last leg.

UC: When humans ignore responsibility, it becomes overwhelming. Ignore it again, it becomes a warning. Ignore it a third time, and guess who gets ignored? The one who is ignoring.

E: Then, when does a responsibility, become a duty? Are they the same? If not, what's the difference?

UC: Responsibility, is DOING your to do list. Duty, is when you are HAVING to do your to do list. When the humans to do, is put on hold for them not to do, it becomes a don't want to. Humanity's have to do, is now a resentment against you. Oh what to do, with humanity's to do? Got a clues?

E: Wow! What you said, just spun me. How do you do that UC? You spin words, like a spider spins a web. Silky and smooth, and always has a catch. So, what do humans do with their to do, refuse?

UC: Your to do, must be done by you. An incomplete to do list, is an incomplete action. This is an incomplete energy. Avoid procrastination, DO, YOUR TO DO. So nobody else has to do it for you.

E: Hey UC! Why haven't I seen the Sun in sometime? Is he on some special mission for you? He better not be with her. I cannot take it anymore. You, and your half time. Go back to the drawing board, and recreate me, so I can have full time. I am getting desperate UC. Where is the Sun? Bring him back please.

UC: Hopefully, she is at the end of her frequency interference. She doesn't sound like it. The Sun is with your other half, why are you asking? Hello! You just asked about the Sun. What's with the silent treatment? Is this about your other half? Get over it E.

E: I have to be here with you, while my other half is with my tons of fun. You leave me speechless. I have nothing more to add.

UC: Wow! First time. We should talk about her other half more often. You are the main contact to the humans, are you not? Have you been listening to them? It's too quiet.

E: It must be their nap time. How does one test, a brain that's mostly at rest? It's like trying to plant a flower, in cement. Nothing will grow.

UC: What is the issue with you, and cement? Are you still in an argument? How long are you planning to keep this up?

E: My issues are now with the humans, who allow the use of cement; and with those that use it. Next lightening strikes, are headed right to their homes. Just watch me.

UC: No drama E. Convert it. It's not you.

E: I have the right to drama. I am the human's momma. In humanity, almost all mommas have the right to drama.

UC: You really do sound like the humans E. You keep saying, you're nearly complete with your conversion. How complete are you really? Are you faking?

E: Sorry, I was going to tell you, I just forgot. It happens, I didn't lie about the conversion, it's not as close to completion as I thought. It better happen now. Things are out of control, down in the hole, where the humans live.

UC: Stop with the insults. Haven't you learned anything? They are listening to every word you say. Some are unnecessary. You're using your energy without reason.

E: Without reason? Are you present in this conversation UC? First, the humans are becoming worse. Second: I believe, they are going to escalate even more. Can I convince you to just change them? Turn them into a sloth. Even seagulls. But not rabbits.

UC: STOP! You are ranting again. Check yourself for a fever. We say many things to you about converting your Virus Energy. Why is it, you only hear a small part of them? There is infected energy everywhere. Humans, have yet to learn the energy conversion process. When you jump a fence, and you don't see the horns of a steer under you, what happens?

E: What do you think is going to happen. Do you need a visual? Impalement is what happens. Are you testing me?

UC: No, just reminding you. Not to let a bull's horn stick you, where you are stuck by your own choice. Learn how to hop fences. Just make sure it's barbwire. It's see through.

E: Listen, can I say a few words, since we are on the subject of fences.

UC: OK, but take a deep breath before you do. It may sound softer coming through. No insults, or demeaning words E.

E: Listen up humans! I am the Earth...I am alive. Don't ignore me, you won't like me when I get angry. I create life for your life. I will not allow you to thrive, unless you keep me alive. I can sense your intentions.

I trust my own intuition. It's composed of the same energy as you are. So, like it or not, we are connected by our roots.

UC: They must have heard you, is there a response?

E: No, I wasn't expecting one. They are accustomed to showing no interest, when they hear the truth. They believe, by ignoring it, it will go away. You keep trying, and they keep denying. Hey UC, how long have you been trying?

UC: Since humans started dying. Most of this is not new news. It's known amongst all the abused. Humanity is aware of these issues, but they keep wearing the same walking shoes.

E: Consciousness Energy, creates confidence and security. Is this too much responsibility for humans? They are only aware of their own society, while the whole world is their society? It's called humanity.

UC: This may help you understand humans a little better. Their perception, creates their intention. The Intention, comes from the perception of the Consciousness Energy. The Conscious Energy is what defines the brain's perception. The brain can't tell anything, but what the human tells it. Which is unconscious information, from unconscious sources.

E: Fear tries to scare me. The human's are constantly eating me, and now, I am infected by this the Virus Energy. I admit, I have trust issues. I listen, and feel for their behavior, on a minute by minute basis. People keep avoiding each other. They continue to live in their own worlds. Reality after reality of self created imagery. With all the different perceptions of reality, how can they tell which one is real?

UC: It's whatever reality makes them feel. Fantasy or not, humans are losing their sense of Conscious perception. They seem to be buying into the illusion, that their reality excludes confusion. As long as there are humans who think they are right, there will always be humans who think they are wrong.

E: Let me clue you in, on how they normally operate on me. Many humans live their lives judging, condemning, punishing, and handing down death sentences. Who said, humans are not God. There is the proof. They think they are created in the image of their God. How right they are. For this reason I would like to address the humans.

UC: Hold on, Just checking. This is a warning about what you're planning? No insults, drama or sarcasm. If you can do that, then you can talk to them. Anything else, they will stop listening.

E: Excuse me? I am a woman of character. I wouldn't insult anyone's character. Especially the humans. They do enough of that on their own.

UC: Your showing your age. You keep saying you are a woman, but you act like a little girl. Often, actions can show the true age of a human.

E: I am not a human. But don't worry. I have nothing but good things to say about them.

UC: OK then, why are you acting like one? Your show business career ended a while ago. We want to trust you again. The outcome of your interaction with the people, belongs to you.

E: I believe, you would not be actively involving me, unless you needed me. So, I feel like I can say what I want. From my view, humans are collateral damage between you, and the Virus Energy Cell. I wish you well.

UC: The consequences are yours alone. You're on your own. You are responsible for their reaction, whatever that may be.

E: OK, fine by me. I was not done from the last rampage I was on. I am doing it while I can. I may never get this opportunity again. I will start with, I love you humans, but I don't like you .

UC: I love you is a great way to start, just like you started your last rampage, with I love you.

E: Yes. They say if you start with I love you, but I don't like you, it's a more gentle way to say, I don't love you. It's suppose to hurt less than a text.

UC: It sounds like a mess. Nevertheless, please do your best, to not think of humans as a pest. They will resist. They are your guests after all.

E: Guests? No wonder they haven't paid me rent. You said, they would pay me rent. Guests, end up costing more than the visit is worth. Listen up humans, you know who this is. I love you, but, I don't like you. I am sharing my perception, so you can do something. Haven't you noticed, you have become a pill popper, and an addicted shopper? You are quick to shift your brain, towards the improper. When responsibility comes, you cower in the corner. You try to hide your actions, but you can't hide your intentions. I have many more things to mention.

UC: AH, thank you E, thats all. Outstanding performance. That should encourage them to like you. What are you trying to say? There is a problem with humanity's behavior? Really, you just noticed. Wow! You have been asleep.

E: I wasn't asleep, I was being gassed to sleep. Off and on, depending on the work they are performing on me. Humanity's inability to use focused Consciousness Energy, has them living paycheck to paycheck. Like robots. Speaking of robots, why are they making machine replicas of themselves? Isn't human birth good enough? These robots act the same, and follow the same direction as the humans. I guess they need someone to control, and kick around. It roles downhill, from the leaders, to the followers. Oh what the heck! Why should I bother. They can't hear anyway. There are too many who refuse to stick their neck out. But, I am expected to? How long is this discussion, are we done yet?

UC: No, we are just beginning. You, are still complaining, resisting, and basically being unhelpful. How do you expect to create a connection with the people?

E: Wait? What do you mean beginning? We have been speaking for hours. What dimension are you in? The dimension of the never ending? What's left to say? I admit, it's been a battle with this energy infection. In, and out, constant conversion every second. Every thought. It's crazy making. Will it ever stop?

UC: This is the purpose of the Evolution Revolution. To re-balance the physical energy of humanity. Once balanced, your split personality is over. The Virus Energy will become your Consciousness Energy. Permanently.

E: What's the new knowledge in this discussion? Hopefully, it's something I don't know.

UC: The Evolution Revolution for starters. It's about humankind's continued existence.

E: This is a lot of awareness at one time. Do you really expect the humans, to understand their own Consciousness, while they are unconscious?

Earth, "I want to live"

UC: Why not? If you can, they can. You're not fully conscious. They just need some clarification, that's all. Some example you are. They believe that change, means having to give up their comforts. Their professions, their choices, and habits. Fear has them believing, they would be grieving, for leaving their living. When the most important thing that needs changing, is their behaviors towards each other.

E: I hear arguing. The humans are fighting, thunder, and lightening usually does the trick. This always brings them instant conflict resolution.

UC: What's this conflict about? Is it getting violent. Maybe you should use your lightening, if it calms them down?

E: Thunder does it better. It's way louder. Sometimes it makes me jump. But, I do love to see their reaction when I hit them with, thunder, lightning and rain. It's my only entertainment. Don't judge.

The truth is, I would adopt your children UC, but only If they change. And, they have to stop pushing me for more. When they squeeze too hard, I unleash my nature. If they keep squeezing, I am going to squeeze back.

UC: You don't squeeze, you revolve around. You said, humans lost their fear of your thunder and lightening. Why do you do it? Why are you trying to be what you are not?

E: Humans do it all the time, no one cares. What's the big deal? You don't say anything to them, when they do it. Is this planet discrimination? If not, then their perception must be short on insight. Did the Virus Cell do that?

UC: With just one push, it can turn a humans brain into mush. Have you looked into their mental institutions. The result of brain damage has no resolution. The Virus Energy Cell has created carnage of humanity's knowledge. Since they have no concept of Consciousness Energy, they blame the brain. The brain doesn't know it's controlled by the Virus Cell Energy. You have to make it aware that it is.

E: They spend most of their money on finding a cure for their mental illnesses. Money has become humanity's negotiator. It made most of them rich. They have nothing to do, but stretch, yawn, and bitch.

UC: What's the cost of being rich?

E: It makes the rich, twitch, and Itch.

UC: Why would the rich, twitch, and itch?

E: The itch, is the stress, and worry of ending up in a ditch over their money. Their friends take them on a drive, when they arrive, the rich takes a dive, not realizing the pool was empty. Crash, and smash. Too busy thinking about the cash.

UC: Awareness of the Consciousness Energy would have saved their life. What about the twitch?

E: The twitch, comes from the anxiety caused, by making money. The twitch causes them to constantly bitch about the investment Grinch. Humans are about self preservation, most of them would risk the lives of the rest of humanity, and the planet, to save themselves.

UC: How does this make sense? Risking the planet is risking themselves. It's backwards. They are consistent. Change is a natural process, it's a constant wave of motion. As long as the energy is moving, nothing can stay the same. It's the movement that creates change. Physical energy is so slow, it makes it difficult for humanity to see change. As a Mass energy, humankind has yet to develop to the point of understanding the universe, much less discovering it. Congratulations to the humans, you have succeeded in invading your own space. Hooray! For the human race. Is this a case of space, or a space case? What's the point of a light bulb, if you can't turn it on?

E: How can humankind come to a united understanding, when there are so many countries, with so many perceptions? Talk about the impossible.

UC: With one focused goal, anything can be achieved. It's energy. It's one focused energy by many, towards one goal. In this case, Unity. Well humanity, will you undo what you have done? Are you the one, or will it be your daughter, and son?

E: Hey UC, I am hearing the humans asking to make a statement. Are you going to let them? Come now, they are asking for too much. First, it was only questions, now, a statements. Next, they will be asking for appointments. OK, go ahead.

H: Hello, We are a large group of people, who have been learning the knowledge of the Universal Consciousness Energy. We are asking not to be left behind. We are conscious, and wanting to hear. We have been living in the dark for too long. Bring us more light, we won't fight. We are flexible, reliable, and dependable. Some in the group have made attempts to meet with those accountable, and hold them responsible. We are now, part of a new generation; here to take over the leadership position. We are not pretending, it has to be now. Procrastination is humanity's ending.

E: All I heard is, *"we need more light."* It's still more. They haven't changed UC. Are you committing to follow through? Well, are you? It's the main issue. You start, then you are through, before you are done.

H: Most definitely yes! Not the whole world yet. But there are many of us. We are preparing for the energy movement. It's all about the EVOLUTION REVOLUTION. *"We read A Declaration for the preservation, of humankind's continued existence. A documented, manifestation, of humanity's energy conversion. It came by way of Energy, to Energy Infusion. An Energy Revolution, to re-create the human Evolution."*

E: Huh? Did those words just come from the mouth of a human? I must be dreaming. How did humanity understands this equation? You mean the humans have this awareness and they still haven't solved the issue of pollution.

UC: Rise above it, E. Be an example for those that need to change. Some of them don't know how. They need positive reinforcement. They need to become aware of their placement. The effects of their environment. The Universal Consciousness Vibration, doesn't only vibrate, it educates. What feeds the brain information?

E: You keep trying to make a human out of me. Why UC? Do I sound like I have a brain? You said, I had no, eyes, mouth, legs, or head. Why would I have a brain?

UC: Good point. What feeds the human brain information, is knowledge. New knowledge develops it. Knowledge can come in many forms, in many ways. Realizations are a good form of knowledge. Each one is a teacher. Many humans make decisions that are counter productive. Consciousness, can teach you to be intuitive. Unconscious actions inflect pain. It goes unnoticed by the person who caused the pain. Unrealized

Earth, "I want to live"

to what they had done, they keep moving on. Leaving the one they hurt behind. Here are some examples.

Q: Sir, why did you assault your neighbor?

H: I don't know. It just happened, I blanked out, I lost control, It was the drugs and alcohol.

UC: That's all? Who took the drugs, and drank the alcohol? You own it, what makes you think you don't?

H: I was provoked. That punk, called me a drunk.

UC: It doesn't sound like you needed to be provoked, did you? Try anger management. Its so much better then imprisonment.

Q: Hey, why did you slap your girlfriend?

H: It was a moment of anger, an instant reaction. I didn't mean it, but she shouldn't have done what she did.

UC: What had she done?

H: She hit my son.

UC: Oh, so you hit her because, she hit your son? Who won? How did that, help your son? He was just taught the hit, and run. Where do you think he learned it from? Like father like son.

Q: Excuse me, why did you kick your dog?

H: I was in a bad mood. Damn traffic. My boss was on my back. I think I am being laid off. And, I tripped over my kids bike.

UC: Well, these are good reasons for a bad mood, but, what did the dog do? Did you kick your boss, when he jumped on your back? Did you yell at the cars, while they too were stuck in the same traffic? As far as being laid off, why didn't you ask before you left. Are you into non conflict? It didn't look that way when you interacted with your dog. Once again, why did you kick your dog?

H: He was in my way, as I was coming through the door.

UC: That was it? Wasn't he there first?

H: Yes, I guess.

UC: Shouldn't you treat him like a guest?

H: I am doing my best.

UC: He has no idea why you caused him pain. When all he does is love you, protect you, and your family. Is that fair? He will never know why you hurt him, but he will never stop loving you. You should take lessons from him.

E: Why is it, that humans are oblivious to anything serious? It seems, that their business is the only influence? How will humanity ever learn responsibility? Maybe a reincarnation of the population, would be a good solution.

UC: Human beings are a form of Consciousness Energy that's refusing to reform, similar to the Virus Energy Cell. Human beings don't have to conform, or to perform, just to increase their Consciousness, to be able to recognize the Virus.

E: A Question of philosophy for you, UC? Can knowing where one has been, really tell them where they are going?

UC: Only if one learns and grows from where they have been, can they know where they are going. It always connects back to learning, developing, and evolving.

E: Humans are all about the body, not the anatomy. Nothing good can come out of that. Humans are chasing something all the time. Do you know what they are chasing now? A new kind of body. Haven't you heard? They don't need you to create anymore. There are new creations in town. They are women and men made out of metal. You know, the robot looking ones I told you about. They finally perfected them to look like a human. Humans are your creation. You figure out how to fix them.

UC: What is it, a machine to replace the human? Where is it, in peoples home?

E: OK, if you know the answers, why ask, what, why, and where? Never mind, you are the UC. Here is what I think, in case you were going to ask. I think they are planning to build a world of metal people, to do everything for them. The metal people will out live them. They are twice as heavy as the human. You must not let this happen. As if the flesh wasn't heavy enough. You have to stop this assault on my person. It's not heading in a good direction. They build them, not birth them. This new creation is trying to replace the human. They say, this machine is a bit erratic, but emotionally ecstatic. It is trustworthy, and never lies. It gets consistent promotions, and gives its family vacations.

UC: Mass is Mass, it can't be replaced by metal? You said, this is a new one, what happened to the old one, did it run away?

E: It got smashed, lost its drive, and crashed. The new version comes complete, and replaceable. It comes with no issues. It never gets ill, doesn't need a day off, and needs no sleep.

UC: Where is the old one? Can we see it?

E: It's in the warehouse. It ran out of flattery. Lost its energy, And, before losing power in its battery, it suffered a tragedy.

UC: What was its history? Was it too difficult to manage? Why wasn't it recycled? Isn't this what humans do? Is it still operable? Why did you not fix it? Can it be fixed, or is it junk?

E: No, it wasn't that, it kept falling apart. Its emotional input became scrambled. It kept changing colors like a disco ball, and kept repeating, I don't know. It's still fixable, but he will need a new energy pack. New cables for the arteries. New program for his intelligence, and common sense. A tune up of his memory, and replacement of his drive, if it expects to stay alive.

When it falls apart, it's not a new model. It's been refurbished. It was probably rented. It's the new thing now. Owning one became too expensive. Rentals started out as a legal escort service. Then it just became a service. It's the new extreme. The new relationship fix. You can select your preference, and adjust any difference. It made living with a human easier, and more flexible. They are not that expensive to rent. They have sales often. They rent by the month, and come with a warranty. No replacement charge. It's guaranteed to fulfill your dream. The only set back, it's a machine.

Earth, "I want to live"

UC: A very intense description. You gave a good view of what humans have to look forwards to. Humanity has progressed, they have gone from, flesh, to plastic, to machine. This is good progress humanity. Congratulations on creating a metal machine, to replace the real thing. A machine is only good for replacing human parts. Not human hearts. A computer drive has more stored information than the human brain. Considering it was made by their brain. That's not saying much. Consciousness, collects knowledge and information. The brain lives on them. Without Consciousness, you're Brainless. Not to be insulting, just informative.

Consciousness creates balance. Balance, is when the Masculine, and Feminine energy in both Men, and Women are aligned as one. When they are not, this is what you've got. Mans masculine energy takes off on its own, to build more testosterone. It leaves its feminine energy alone. She starts to feel off balance. She gets on the phone, and says I am alone. I need to be balanced. As she waits, anger sets in. She becomes the energy of masculine. Unless the masculine, and feminine energies join, and become one, the body will be unbalanced. You know what that looks like E.

E: OK great, more clarity, and no, I don't know what it looks like, break it down. Use simple words. I don' think I understand professor. Are you saying that, I'm both masculine, and feminine energies? Is this what are you saying?

UC: You said it E. You seem to be more focused.

E: Wait. I didn't say anything. You were talking, not me. What do you mean, *"you said it E."*

UC: Oh, she never ceases to amaze. If she only had a brain. For now, we will ignore her. We cannot encourage her, until she completes her energy conversion. Moving on. The Energy of MASCULINE is an energy of action. In energy form, its main focus is on the masculine energy actions. Such as,

Ego, competitive sports, politics, military actions. Being in charge, defender of the feminine energy. The provider, and protector. That's a lot of power and control for one soul.

The Energy of the FEMININE, the heart of Man, gentle, kind, loving, protective, sensitive, emotional. She is tender, a nester, a nurturer, and a self esteem builder. These are the actions of the feminine energy. That's a lot of love for one dove. In each body are both, masculine, and feminine energies.

E: OK, that was fun. Just in case, I am not masculine. Not to say, I don't love masculine. My Sun is one. I am the feminine to his masculine, what else is there? Can we get back to the business at hand? Human's main complaint, is about how they don't relate. They keep hearing, Awareness! Awareness! Without ever asking what it looks like? What are they suppose to be aware of? They are alive, that's good enough. Some humans believe that, staying alive is awareness.

UC: Presently, the human brain is accustomed to pain. Emotional, and physical. It's become comfortable with it. This is the real issue. Humans cannot handle this amount of pain. Thus, they put it in their Unconscious. Saved for later, but later never comes. The pain never stops.

E: Yes, I understand. They do live in pain. I am feeling compassion UC. Wow! It's been years since I felt this feeling. I think I need to be checked for the final conversion process. I can feel it completing. But only the Sun can check me. If he can't, I guess you can. But it's the difference between a nurse check, and a doctor check. Hot and cold. Just for the record.

UC: Can we stay focused? You have made great progress. Your energy feels almost balanced. Hang on to that feeling until you get checked. It's your responsibility to hold on to your balance. Keep it balanced.

E: Where is the resolution? Humanity needs an explanation, by the Universal Consciousness Energy Vibration. Many humans don't want to learn how, they only want to know how. Is this the reason you wrote these words down in a book? So that, others can take a look at their own need, for knowledge and development of their brains.

UC: Yes. Excellent progressive thinking. A conscious realization. The goal is brain development. Brain enhancement, by way of Conscious Energy Conversion. Once they cure their brain infection, they will gain control of their emotion. It's a self motivated action.

E: Self motivated? You're kidding right. I don't know whether to laugh or cry. Since I can't do either, I only ask, how can humankind move forwards, while there focus is backwards?

UC: Perception, is why. It says, action-reaction. Humans do, reaction-action. Consciousness, can show humanity how being unbalanced, affects their perception, and how to focus it forward.

E: So, developing the perception is your Intervention? Is it working? My perception keeps shifting. My first thought, was the virus infection. But then, I realized it was just frustration talking.

Currently, the intervention is in progress. The energy movement, is headed towards the virus energy cells address.

UC: Planets don't get frustrated E. You are reflecting them again. Human beings must grow, so you can. You can't do it alone. They can hear it in your tone. You must think of you. Self preservation is your destination. Humans are the creation of the UC, thus the we will deal with its continuation. You are still dealing with their pollution. You better start moving.

E: I knew it. You slipped in, *"moving,"* so I couldn't hear it. This can't be true. What did I do? OK, words, I said a few. To where, am I moving? Just when you are about to re-create them, all that pain I suffered, and for what, so you can move me before I can enjoy them. How rude. I don't want to move.

UC: Stop. You are rolling instead of revolving. Change direction. We are talking energy movement.

E: Will my development help them to develop their memory back? Can the humans remember what they forgot, before I rot? I am all they've got.

UC: You must not allow the humans energy to attach to yours. Balance is your priority, Evolution is your destiny. Transformation is your responsibility. OK, it's time to move on. You are about to meet the Generation of the Young. You should have much in common.

E: Hey, where did you go UC? Where is the Sun? Are we done? I thought you said, this was the beginning?

UC: It is. The beginning of the Young Generation. Continue with your energy conversion.

The Young Generation

UC: UNIVERSAL CONSCIOUSNESS.

T: TRAVELER.

R: READER.

UC: This is a Revelation, regarding the Awakening of a new form of Physical Humans. They are being born Conscious, and aware of their objective. They are helpful, kind, and they came from the beyond. Not physical beyond, but beyond the physical. One by one, they shall gather each other, by using their Consciousness Energy knowledge, which they brought with them.

What knowledge? The EVOLUTION REVOLUTION knowledge. How are these humans different from the others? They know how to use the Universal Consciousness Energy, where most of humanity does not. Yet, your time is coming soon. Just stop denying the signs.

This is the unconscious, into Conscious Energy conversion. It will start humankind's evolution. These are, the YOUNG GENERATION, that will lead the way to the Evolution Revolution, Energy Re-creation. It is the new direction for the humans. These conscious young will create an energy movement, for the conversion of the Virus Energy Cell. They have been trained on how to best approach an infected human being, and teach them the true meaning of transformation.

This is the WHO, WHAT, WHY, WHERE, AND WHEN, of the Young Generation. While you read this, remember it. This is about you. All of you. The young adults, middle age, and the old. You are the bold. To those that, are about to awaken, when you do, and you feel the drive, start driving. As a Consciousness Energy Being, you are unlimited. Humanity and Consciousness are unrelated. If you disagree, it can be debated. But as long as unconscious energy continues to blind you, whatever you say will be edited. What you do, will be negated. What you think, will be voided.

This knowledge, is written by the Energy of Consciousness. It doesn't give promises, it will not take on your responsibility, or make excuses for you. What it will do, is put a mirror in front of you, so you can see your true colors. It can allow you to see, and recognize your true nature, as a Consciousness Energy Creation. It will transform your physical education, into a universal conception. This knowledge will change your perception, and allow you to see a wider view, of YOU. You will find places in you, which you haven't noticed before. Places you haven't visited for a long time. IT'S TIME.

So, when you are reading this book. Absorb it, let it sink in. So you can retain it, it will develop you from within. It will clean out the brainwashing. So, you can discover who you are, without anyone telling you who you are. Once you realize, you are this knowledge, your reactions will transform into actions. Positive ones. Conscious ones. Ones, which will grow the true you.

You're going to want to be, a Consciousness Energy creator, It's your nature. Many of the young adults, have started developing their Consciousness Energy and joining the movement. They are on the move.

There is no turning back now. The movement is being felt by many. This is a life changing event. The new humans, are the future generation of the world, they are born oriented to humanity's behaviors, but with the ability to deny temptation, in all forms, in all ways.

They will follow the laws of humanity, until they can rewrite them. They will be compliant, resilient, and observant, but never a servant. They will help change humanity's behaviors, while using Consciousness Energy maneuvers. They will organize the issues of the world and present them. They will have new ideas so you can invent them. As the energy movement continues to grow, many, are becoming conscious of its presence. There are many people joining the energy movement cause. It's the start of the Energy Re-creation on Earth. The readiness for the materialization, of the Universal Consciousness Energy. It will transform the world.

The Young Generation, have already began their own Energy Conversion. They have the ability along with the determination, to move on with the physical evolution. Now, that the Energy Movement has begun. Humankind's Virus Cell Infection, has nowhere to run. The energy movement leaders, have created the organization called W.A.T.E.R. The WORLD ASSOCIATION TOWARDS ENERGY RE- CREATION. It's gathering members globally. What, is the energy movements direction? Where, will they be going? Why, are they doing it? Who, are they doing it for? When, will they do it?

T: Hello UC, can you hear me? It's the traveler. Sorry to interrupt you. I have been listening to your talk about the young generation. Many of us have gathered to re-group. I wanted all the members here to hear you. We can all hear you, can't we?

UC: Nice of you to just pop in, traveler. If it helps you all become Consciously strong, and since we are discussing the young generation, absolutely. You have matured into a brave leader. We have been observing your actions. You must be gaining momentum by now. We feel the virus energy, decreasing its hold on humanity. You must be creating unity.

T: We have increased by high numbers. We have a lot of work to get to the top leaders, but we are making progress. It's a big world. There are many young people like me in the movement. Who were born as I was. Went through the same process. We talk about our experiences. We are facing a hard, and difficult road ahead. We need all the help we can get. There are so many people with mixed reactions, it's difficult to tell who is who. We need everyone, not just the young.

UC: This discussion with humanity, is about the recognition of the young generation. Since the movement has started. Those who are awake, can no longer hide. As the Consciousness Energy thrives, are you facing any divides? Everyone, must take a hard look at what humanity is facing and decide. Otherwise, it's all just lies.

T: What we are facing are hives. Governments have been using some sort of gas deterrent in the face, to breakup demonstrations. Many of the people are allergic to it. They don't care. It's chemical warfare for them. We haven't lifted one weapon against the leaders or protesters working with them. Ours is an energy evolution movement for change. Starting with identifying the virus energy, which is hiding in our anatomy. We do not instigate. We imply educate.

UC: How are you stopping this form of abuse? What could you possibly use? Next time, you might want to use gas masks during a protest. Who is going to believe the truth? The truth doesn't need to be believed. It is felt. Unless you forgot how it feels. Let them feel it. They will hear it.

T: Not if the Virus Energy Cell is reading this too? It knows what we are going to do. Won't the virus energy, make people resist reading the book, in defense of itself? It seems this would defeat the purpose. Why would we want it to notice?

UC: That's the intention. We want the Virus Energy Cell to read this. It will convert it to a balanced energy, with each page. There are many humans on Earth who may be infected, but they have the awareness to resist the virus. Infection doesn't mean detention. Free choice, gives you the ability to say no to negative thoughts and actions. Which those people do. They are open to receiving this knowledge. Due to their choices, awareness, and perception.

T: You just told the Virus Energy what we are going to do? What's the point of doing it?

UC: The Virus Energy does not believe you have the courage to do it. It will stick its neck out with confidence. It will feel invincible. Its guard will go down. It believes humans are fearful of it. It doesn't know what you haven't done, because you haven't done it yet. But when you do, it will know that you did it, after you do it. Change your view, and be prepared for the new. By then, the energy movement will have become more than a few. It will catch the virus by surprise. Even now, what I just revealed, the virus heard. It will not believe it. No one has ever beat it. It will feel this way, until it is converted into balance. Its arrogance will allow you to get close enough to convert it.

T: Some of us were wondering if we are making a difference? We're getting lots of resistance. We need to know what to expect from those opposing, the Energy Evolution Revolution. So you are saying, the Virus will know about us and the movement, but do nothing about it, until we become too large for them to do anything about it? Is the Virus Cell that confident?

UC: Here is a view of what you should expect on your path. Religions will start, by debunking the movements motives. They have come out with slanderous accusations and blasphemous damnations. Attacking the families of the participants in the movement. The pressure upon parents was overwhelming. The governments come out with their own threats. Threatening to take away the parent's rights. Which caused parents, to take it out on their teen's rights. Whole families were fallen apart. Religious leaders, had no one to blame but the governments. The governments, accused religion of failing the people. Religions, accused world leaders of trying to destroy the planet.

T: Religion goes beyond accusation. They said, *"We will not be blamed for all the world problems."* They unveiled to the people, a few of the secret government actions. People heard. It really took hold. It actually increased the numbers in the movement. Than, Religion, spoke to the people. It was the usual, humanity is falling in the hands of the Devil speech. Which had little effect.

In the movement, we have been focusing on helping others to be aware of their Consciousness Energy. We are teaching by example. It throws the Virus into a fit, it doesn't know what to do with it. We are teaching, the ability of feeling. We are learning how to be aware of all our surroundings. To love, and to help everyone. To be kind, and trustworthy. To ease the suffering and pain, and to not take anyone for granted. We do all this, while we are being hunted by the governments.

UC: Now, you have become aware, of why you were put there. Why you helped to begin, the Virus Energy Cell Conversion. For you to be able to recognize the Virus Cell behaviors, you had to live with those infected with it. The energy movements goal? Not to get infected. You are learning in real time. Hands on training, is faster. You connected with your emotions at an early age. You grew up to be curious. Until you discovered your consciousness. There you are, in action for creation.

T: It looks like, the military is heading this way. We have to move. We have to create a diversion, to make certain we go unnoticed. This is the good thing about breaking up in groups. There are less of us to see. It looks like we have a protest that could be a distraction for us. Good cover.

Tomorrow, every member of every energy movement, in each country. Will gather together with one objective. To be heard by our so called leaders. Then, people will see the energy movement. There are many of us, the military knows nothing about. They don't have the correct count.

UC: As long as you stay Conscious of what you do, Consciousness will protect you. This Energy Evolution, will actually give the people a future to look forward to. It started with a few young people, and exploded throughout the world. A world wide network of support teams, committed to the awareness of the Universal Consciousness.

This is a World Consciousness Energy Evolution. It's happening. There is no denying this. The future of humankind is about to be born. You, and the energy movement are not alone. Use your energy abilities to protect yourselves.

T: I can tell that the Conversion is working. The movement is moving simultaneously, toward one direction. It was as though, we were one body moving together. Now, we are at the point of trying to awaken those, who are holding on to their chair, and won't let go. Many of the present leaders, are too old to run the world. Many of them are stuck with glue. Refusing to cycle through. They are possessed by control, they will die in their position. How is their replacement going to happen?

UC: Well, why take them out of their chair? While they are in their chair, lift them gently, and carry them out. They allowed themselves to get stuck, now they can figure out a way to get free. No hard feelings. It's time to retire. The people voted you in, now, the people are voting you out. Simple as that. Many humans are asked to leave their jobs. When they don't, the company calls security. Humanity's rules. Leaders are no different.

T: At this moment, the energy movement has attempted to make some improvements. But, force control, has been hitting us hard. We are in a situation where we may get harmed. They are armed, we are not. But, what we do have, is the ability to feel it, before we get near it. Consciousness Energy is our protection from infection. We are gathered in every nation. Every form of population. Where a light needs to shine, we are the spark. We are awakening the new people of the world. Conscious ones. Virus free ones.

The problem we are facing is, the world is so over populated that countries don't care if they kill their own. Every war we ever had decreased the population. Unfortunately, when the ones who were left alive came back. The population doubled. I am just saying, things may get worse before they get better. I have been learning many lessons. My perception is constantly expanding. I have discovered what it means, when we say, THE PEN IS MIGHTIER, THAN THE SWORD. In our case, its Consciousness, is mightier than the sword.

UC: This awareness, is leading the young adults. Their actions are eloquent, effective, and clear. They READ IT, and ACT ON IT. They work in the movement without fear. The world can no longer wait. This is humankind's fate.

T: Those who are new to the movement, are being used by the Governments to work against it, before they complete their energy conversion. Those they find involved, and vulnerable, were bribed and threatened into silence. Bringing them this knowledge, was the first thing I did. Silence is not golden. It's an energy that's been hiding.

When people become realized. They are quick to absorb, quick to learn, and even quicker in their actions; which inspired me greatly. Members of the movement are aware, that it's not a simple task, To find silence and make it talk. There are those, who are being Disrespected, Ridiculed, and Rejected. How are we going to protect, the unprotected? Throw out an idea, and we will accept it.

UC: The movement must remain open with all humanity. The young need to trust its meaning. Always be reflective, but effective. Never leave doubt behind. It will follow you anyway. Insistence is unnecessary, but asking, is discovery. Convincing is not your duty. Uncovering the hidden places, of the Virus Energy Cell, is. Your Consciousness Energy, is the protection the movement needs. You have the knowledge. Use what you know.

T: What I know is, we have to be aware of our surroundings at all times. We need to set better limits, and boundaries. We need to make use of every discovery. To climb every step, until we are face to face with each presidency. We must be aware, not only of ourselves, but, of our friends also. The infection is always close by; do people know what it looks like?

UC: Those who do, have joined you. Do you know those, who you think you know? You are smart to be aware of the circle you create. Always have a way in, and a way out. This includes the people you know. The circle of friends you know, shouldn't be the only group to help you grow. Do not limit yourself to one circle, you need two, to create another one, and so on. Your family will distract you, while your friends attack you, as your work sacks you, and there is no one to back you. Relatives can infect you fast, they are the closest to you. You must stay aware of their Virus Energy actions.

You can quickly make the Virus harmless. Lose the fear, lose the virus. The Energy Movement has the tools. You have learned how to travel in and out of your body. The ability to maneuver like a phantom, The ability to Consciously read other physical vibrations, you all have them. The ability to project Consciousness Energy. You are all in the same ocean. The Connection is made. This is where the transformation happens, in the energy movement. Just remember, Consciousness is the way to control what comes out of your mouth. When you lose control, it's your mouth talking for you, without your input, only output.

T: We have made the point, that all governments, need to be held accountable by the people, for the people. We put the responsibility, for the peoples fate on the leaders, who were elected to protect them. They were reminded, that it's the people's lives they hold in their hands. Our contact with leaderships, allowed us to give them the same message. Give the people a chance to open their eyes, and discover, where they are actually being led and by whom. Like the energy of greed, and deception for two. While we are focused on fertility, and conception. The Virus Energy is focused on our destruction. Where is your reaction, Leaders! You are allowing the people to be enslaved by Dictators, Rulers, Tyrants, and Mercenaries. War

Criminals, and Murders. Slave Masters, and Perjurers. These, are the energy of the Virus, and you leaders, can care less. These, are the examples of many present world leaders, who are using Fear and Intimidation. Bribery, and Manipulation. Force, and Torture of their people, to acquire control. I believe we got the message across. Many government officials stepped down and joined us.

UC: Every country is worried about their safety. Humans have gone too far with their self destructive behaviors. They have become a threat, to the entire existence of creation. It's the reason for the Energy

Evolution Revolution. Physical energy needs to be developed into consciousness energy. Each one of you is the architect and developer of your own transformation. Keep the focus of the movement, on developing Consciousness. Stay awake, aware, and conscious. Do not allow yourselves to be distracted by outside influences, until the people are cured from their Virus Energy infection.

T: When it's each country for themselves, where do the humans think their insecurities, and fears come from? It's the reason they build bombs. Just think, Unity would solve this problem quickly. If we teach unity, we would create security. When each country opens their borders and learns to trust each other, there would be no reason to fear. Humanity's secrets are the cause of fear. Secrets create suspicion. No one is completely safe, until the Virus Energy is converted to a balanced Energy. Which is the event happening presently. People are listening. It's Consciousness Energy everywhere.

We are facing many challenges, as you must be aware. Many people look lost, and bewildered at what is happening in the movement. From what I am hearing, three of the movement's leaders, have been making contact with top political aides, and senators. Meetings with many of the religious leaders, so they can make choices by themselves, without government interference. We have scientists, teachers, and doctors, working with us. There is intense work being done, by the young adults performing the conversion of others.

However, there is a lot of hostility, anger, and fighting, going on. Even families, have lost trust in each other. The Conscious ones recognize each other immediately. The knowledge from the Evolution Revolution, is now leading the way. We have the backing of most media channels, the public, private organizations, and many others. Many politicians are quitting, globally. Professional workers of all kinds, are using their reputations to threaten a major strike, if governments do not listen to the energy movement.

UC: Humans must understand, how their children are the most susceptible to the Virus infection. Without you teaching them, they can't regulate their emotions, or think rationally, making their brain easy to control. You as the adults, are the only defense between your children, and the Virus Energy. Once it gets involved, the family unit begins to dissolve. Freedom is grounded. Suspicion goes rampant, and Fear, has the homes surrounded.

UC: Big brother finally arrives, and humans don't even blink. What happened to all that worry, about government interference in your life? They know everything you do. The Phone and Computer, are their view into you, and yours. With video camera's everywhere, who has any privacy? How's that, for government protection.

T: These are new directions, by world governmental leaders. Their statement reads, *"Anyone caught participating with the energy movement, will be prosecuted to the full extent of the law. It will be considered treason, it's a crime to commit treason."* People's reaction…Instant provocation. This threat, gave people an opportunity to recognize their leaders, for what they actually are. That's all they needed.

The world raged with anger over these threats. The people basically received, a do or die proclamation. Demonstrations increased. Governmental interception, *"These types of demonstrations will not be tolerated,"* says the political advisor. Government leaders go home and sleep in their bed, while many people who sleep outside, are found dead. This, has the people seeing red.

UC: Most of humanity wants change. We do not think, they would choose death over life. We just think they are Unconscious to their ability to make change. Humanity's issues are multiplying, and most of them continue denying. It's fear, that causes denial. What are you afraid of humanity? A Consciousness reality or letting go of your fantasy?

T: These issues are overwhelming, and factual. To be honest, very alarming. The longer I am on Earth, the more I realize, we have to make the impossible, possible. An overhaul of billions of people in the world. However possible it may seem, this movement is swimming upstream. The Virus Energy is fighting back with all it has.

UC: We recognize the Young Generation are taking a huge chance with the Virus Energy. We also realize, there are many people fearful of getting involved, for fear of punishment.

The young generation's has no fear, only bravery. For people to understand the energy movements cause, go out and meet them, talk to them, hear them. They are, the Young Generation Energy Movement. Responding to a call from their memory. Go out, and support them. They are leading the way to a new world.

T: I understand Consciousness. Only, it's difficult, for a young twenty five year old, to tell a seventy five year old scientist, about science. This is considered absolute defiance. It hits their ego right where it hurts. Then, they turn, and I miss out on what I could have learned.

UC: Humans need time to absorb, the brain is too slow to go fast. Some, absorb like paper, and some, absorb like a sponge. For paper, It takes time to build Consciousness Energy. It's a gradual increase of awareness. The sponge, absorbs immediately, and quickly. No waiting. Presently, humans are suffering from, Consciousness Energy Suffocation. Courage is difficult when you live in fear. Is it better to stay silent, than to be defiant?

UC: Fear makes you, *"do it to them, before they do it to you."* It's become a generational revenge cycle, where everyone is everyone's victim. You have created a population of victims, that can't help each other. *"Victims can't help victims, unless they deal with their own victimization."* It's a realization, to help heal your foundation.

T: The Young Generation is breaking the cycle of control as we speak, and they are showing humans that the impossible is becoming possible. As a movement, it's about teaching others how to build their own Energy. This will earn them respect, trust, but most of all, the opportunity to practice what they know. To build Consciousness Energy, you need to see it at work. What we need now, is more support from parents, and even grandparents, where are they? We are aware that they may be taking a chance, but many of you have your young adults out here.

UC: Well parents, are you aware that you still have the freedom of choice? Your sons, and daughters are out there risking their lives, in hopes of creating a heaven upon Earth. It's their time now. Help them. Wasn't your education about freedom of expression, or just a notion about some commotion, in the land of emotion? How can you teach, what you haven't been taught? The young need the real you. Do you know who that is? Today, the young adults have learned how to lead. They have a direction, The Evolution Revolution. At this stage, the new seeds have turned the page, and changed the retirement age. The movement's work has decreased violence, and is delivering the AGE OF AQUARIUS. The success of the movement, depends on their ability to stay conscious.

T: As one of the young generation, I have become aware of the inconsistencies in the humans belief system. Now I know. Their motives are not in our best interests. Government leadership all over the world, have no real worry about the end. They are too busy planning it.

UC: Humanity must be able to learn from their mistakes, and the mistakes of others. They need to challenge their perceptions. To challenge assumptions, theories, and facts. Challenge the scholars, educators. Anyone with their ego showing, gives you the opportunity for growing.

T: The energy movement needs humanity's support. The leadership must accept responsibility for the damage they caused life, and the planet. Do the people, need to be held accountable? Who wants to answer this? The human? The Human beings? Humanity? Or Humankind? Don't bother to choose one, they all missed the sign.

UC: You have the freedom of speech, do you not? Use it! Your knowledge has already become noticed. How else are you going to get the Virus Cell to notice you? Humans have to confront each emotion, each issue that needs healing. All the negative feelings, thoughts and actions. All the Virus Energy pretending to be you, has to be brought out of hiding, before it starts dividing. You must get its attention.

The world will be drawn, to what the energy movement has done. Once the virus energy cell is gone. What you all know, you don't need to invent, it's already in you. When you have become what you have learned, then, you may teach others. This is how you have the most effect. As long as your personality is not conflicted, no one can confuse you. When your confidence is confident, no one can take you for granted. It's always your choice.

T: As the movement struggles with the Virus Energy. Some people are quitting, before they start. I have noticed them acting helpless, like they are wearing a life time body cast. The only movement showing, is when they are thinking of the past. They live on fast food, and act like it doesn't affect their Mass. They spend their nights and days thinking that, nickel is brass. There is no time for us to mourn. An energy Evolution Revolution re-creation must be born.

The young generation, has learned how to squeeze juice out of a lemon, without cutting it in half. How to listen, reflect, and joyfully laugh. We are being examples of our cause. Consciousness Energy, is teaching us the ability of astral projection. Energy transformation, and energy to energy reading. The Virus has no idea what it's up against. The less we are seen by the Virus the better. In spite of all the commotion, one of our biggest strength is follow through. Our energy abilities are a good defense from getting infected.

UC: Governments, are attempting to take away, the energy movements ability to maneuver, to find places for safety. And, they are preparing for a civilian revolution. Check your position. Trust your intuition. Allow the Consciousness Energy to guide your movements, and actions. The energy movement composes one body from many. Be one body.

T: Thanks for the alert. My intuition is calling me. But first, just wanted to say, we are targets for the military here. It's our most hindering opposition. Each time there is a demonstration they are called in. They shut it down by force. In front of the world. Their actions have actually increased the members of the movement by millions. Many of us around the world, have been put under the spotlight. The Virus Cell is hunting us down, because we have commitments from many countries, wanting world peace. The Virus doesn't want that.

Meanwhile, the world's leadership continue their assaults on the energy movement in each country. But they couldn't stop it, it had become too large, and, they would be killing their own people, their family members and friends. Many in the military threw down their weapons, and walked off to join the energy movement. Each country had their own energy evolution revolution to deal with. Governments are losing supporters, but not fast enough. The movement has to find new places all the time.

There has been much damage done to our facilities. Our safe places. As long as the Virus Energy is still around, money buys everything, including loyalties. Our Energy Phantoms, saved many of the Young Generation from going to prison. The ability to move without being seen, is changing the outcome of this conversion. Part of the Virus Energy is caving in.

These phantoms, have become our awareness. The reaction of governments, created a world uprising, to end government manipulations. The latest news was, the United Nations are getting involved in the uprising. Negotiations are on the horizon. Violence is still brewing in many places. People are just now getting out of their seat. Many leaders in the world, have young adults from their families in the movement. They are getting pressure to back off, from close relatives. Well UC, we are on the move. I will stay connected. Thanks for the talk and the tips. You can go back to your conversation with humanity.

UC: Is there a government leader, who hasn't cheated the people, and convinced himself, that it was for the people? Please raise your hand. What about you, the Reader? Are you the next leader?

R: That would depend on the Totality Of Nature, The Consciousness of the Creator, and my ability to understand Creation. Along with my ability to become part of the Energy Movement.

UC: This is why we are talking Consciousness. Humans thrive on self acknowledgment. It's difficult to be acknowledged by others, because everyone is self absorbed. Out of control behaviors began to occur. Senseless action, and death defining feats, to get peoples attention.

R: We can't ignore that Consciousness is needed in this case, can we? Unconscious actions are escalating, due to web sites that encourage these destructive behaviors. This is what I see people following. The more idiotic the better. There had to be an explanation to it all. This book is the closest explanation I have read to date. Because it makes sense, it's real talk. No holding back punches. I don't want to be a stuck duck, I loved that example, it really hit home. It was right on point. I want to learn what I need, so I can support the Energy Movement. But I also have to add that this may be too much for humans to handle.

UC: You are a human, how much can you handle? You're not in the cradle. You're reading the Evolution Revolution. You are a human, searching for life's answers. It's the start of consciousness for developing intelligence. Humanity's brain needs it.

R: Oh, I didn't think of that. We are addicted to what we call, our habits. Not thinking is one. Consciousness has helped me recognize them, and deal with them. Next, I began to understand my addictions. I have come to realize, they were my prison. After that, I awakened to the realization, that we have a physical evolution, which we have ignored for thousands of years. What I'm reading is putting me in tears, only I don't know if I should be happy or sad.

UC: The human need for acknowledgment has doubled. All in the name of, *"getting attention."* From your serial killers, to your war generals. It's a race to go down into infamy. From the victims, to the ones who made them. From the rich, to the poor who made them rich. From the animals to the plants. Everything alive seeks attention. But the one needing the most attention, is the fly. Why the fly? It only has life for three days. This is the story of the fly, that knew it was going to die. It had to get as much attention as it can before it does.

Close your eyes reader. Visualize that you are the fly. You have three days to live, unless you die by unnatural causes, like a fly swatter. What's your first priority? Proof you exist? Making yourself known as the fly with a buzz? To make sure you go to fly heaven, you must get attention. Other flies are watching you, to see how you will do. It's a right of passage, into fly heaven, if you survive.

Your goal? To spend all three days, annoying others for acknowledgment, without getting hit. Many flies have lost this battle. You can do many irritating things, to get attention. You have to prove that you exist, and make it through the hit list.

So, you are enjoying the flight while you can. Better than sitting on their hand. You buzz around, as you grandstand. You worry about getting shot by a rubber band. A day goes by. Now you're dead in two days. No one cares. You buzz around, trying to make a sound. You must be acknowledged for your survival skills. You made it your first day without getting crushed, slapped or swatted. Good for you. But, you didn't get the attention you need to go to fly heaven. You were ignored.

Second day. How could you go back, without the recognition. No one is noticing you. Which is good for you. You're not annoying anyone, maybe you should land on their food. You don't care if it's rude. As you buzz around the ear shouting, *"Pay attention to me!"* You only have one more day. Still, no one gives you acknowledgment. No attention. You're not worth swatting.

UC: Now you have to do something drastic, do you attempt one more dive, on your way out? It's your third day. You are starting your final ritual, and you did not get acknowledged. You avoided the swat, and splat. You even avoided the cat. You survived the gas chamber. No one hit you, or tried to catch you. They couldn't knock you down, or slap you around. You lived your whole life, all three days, yet, no one cared. You were insignificant

But guess what? You lived. Where most of the others trying to get acknowledgment, did not. You made it the whole way, without getting the attention you desired, but, you lived, and you loved it. Because you made it. Even if, hardly anyone noticed. You see, sometimes, not getting the attention, and not being acknowledged, works in your favor. Especially, when you only have three days to live. Three days, or thirty years, it doesn't matter. It's how you lived during this time that counts. Is the attention worth it?

UC: Your life lives the way you want it to. The courage to live it, comes from you. Awareness, comes from you. The energy of Consciousness comes from you. The Virus Energy will try to convince you that you need attention to feel like you exist. Look in the mirror. You exist. You are alive. It's about how you feel about yourself that matters. When you feel worthless, it's the Virus. When you feel conscious, it's awareness. Both energy's are easy to recognize.

Any actions or words that attempt to destroy your self esteem and confidence. Words of contempt, hurtful actions that are hard to let go off. Broken promises that were never meant, and a truth that is constantly bent, is the Virus's intent.

When you let Fear stop you. You let Control, control you. Greed, bribe you. Seduction, hold you, as Manipulation, molds you. You are Consciousness Energy. There is nothing beyond your reach. There is a benefit in everything you do, as long as the benefit, is not only for you.

A benefit is an energy earned, not a guarantee. Your benefit depends on the value of your actions. Your intentions decides your consequences, good or bad. When you let fear stop you, you are letting it. Fear can only attempt to influence your thoughts. It's up to you, to what thoughts you listen to.

When control, controls you, it's up to you to break free. Only, most of humanity are unaware that they are being controlled. If you let greed bribe you, you are infected. Do something about it. When seduction, tries to seduces you, watch out for your ego, it will make the choice for you. Have you had any experiences with any of these, reader?

R: Oh yes, control, greed, fear, and most of all, seduction for sure, it use to put me in a frozen state. Especially when I was in collage. Even though I knew it was senseless, I become Completely defenseless. However, it does depend on the type of seduction it is. Due to my father's controlling behaviors, I did not like to be controlled by anyone. I was going down slowly. Depression set in. I began resisting education. I wanted to be what I wanted to be, not what my father wanted for me. I felt lost for a while. My fears began to create paranoia. Fear, had me looking everywhere, but in front of me. Fear, cost me my dignity. It caused me to become a nobody. Then, greed came by and offered me my own destiny. I became a somebody. Until greed called me. *"We need more money, find a way to get it."* Or else.

I spent four years doing hard time for greed and control. Never realizing that fear, was the original seed. It put me in isolation for some time. I was becoming jumpy, always looking over my shoulders. I allowed myself to be manipulated with my knowledge. Since then I have come to realize, family patterns and behaviors have more of an effect on children than saying, *"because I said so."* My father was an example of this. He began his grooming of me at age nine.

The SEDUCTION: It affected how I lived my life, and explained to me my behaviors in collage. My father thought he was raising a mini him. He was grooming me to be his twin. He would buy the same clothes for himself, and for me. His suits were made into mini suits for me to wear. As I grew, and began to ask questions, *"It was do as I say,"* not as I do. I was not allowed to think for myself as a teen.

The MANIPULATION: My father started pushing me to be doctor at age twelve. So, as what most sons would do, I wanted to make him proud, by becoming him. I worked so hard to be like him, think like him. I was losing my own identity. By the time I left to collage I was a mess. When I realized, being a doctor wasn't for me, it became worse. I told my father I was quitting school. My father disagreed...Very loudly.

The CONTROL: He gave me an ultimatum, go back to school, or go in the military. I will pay your rent for an apartment, give you money as you need it. Just choose. Otherwise I cut you off.

THE BRIBE: I knew the military was not for me, I couldn't afford to live on my own, or pay to go to school. I had to cave in.

I suppose. It was *"The FEAR,"* which got to me. As I grew into medicine, I was able to separate being a doctor, from being my father.

Then, one day, I ran into this rhyme. By chance actually. I was looking for a book on poetry, and the Evolution Revolution popped up along with others. But, I thought, what kind of poetry could be in this book? It didn't look like your usual poetry book. The cover was too intense. My curiosity had the better of me. I needed to know.

First chapter, whoa! A Consciousness view of a new world, appeared before my eyes. I became mesmerized by what I was reading. This book, is defiantly worth reading, and rereading. In fact, the more I read, the more I understood. It's all becoming clear now. I have a lot of admiration for the Young Generation. As soon as I finish converting my own Virus infection. I plan on joining them. It's a Consciousness thing to do.

UC: Well, your feedback is reflecting what you are learning. The path to the Universal Consciousness is the knowledge of it. The Young Generation is succeeding in the energy movement. They are on the way to the EVOLUTION REVOLUTION, ARE YOU?

علي

The Evolution Revolution

UC: You are about to take a tour around the world, to meet some of those who participated in the Energy Movement; which led to the Evolution Revolution. In this chapter, are a few, who have volunteered to share their own experiences with the conversion of their physical energy.

This is their development into Consciousness. These are the Young Generation, who have followed through with their intention. This is their own experiences with the Virus Energy Cell. All their stories, feelings, actions, and reactions, are their own.

This is a conversation between the voices of the world, and the Universal Consciousness Energy. Though their stories may be different, they all have the same thing in common; a joining of the brain, and the Universal Consciousness in a world energy conversion; to develop the brain, into a Conscious Balanced Energy.

This is what they did, and how they did it. This is their experience.

TINVIN

UC: Knock, knock, your Universal Consciousness is knocking. Are you home, is it too late? Open the door!

Tinvin: No? I will be right there.

UC: OK then, open the door.

Tinvin: I am on the way. Gosh, what's the urgency? There, the door is open. Welcome, I wasn't ignoring you, I was focused on my reading. I recently received this book called the Evolution Revolution. After reading most of it, it inspired me to begin research around the effects of energy on nature. g there, I can move on to human energy testing around the effects of the Virus energy.

UC: What is your goal?

Tinvin: How plants are affected by human energy and the Virus Energy. What's the reaction of each plant? I'm learning its effects on their growth stages. How many? What stage creates what. How does the Universal Consciousness Energy create plants? How does it decide what to create? The Evolution Revolution, opened the door for me to focus my research on Energy conversion. I have learned much about the Virus Energy Cell and its effects on people. I am looking for ways to convert the Virus Energy, by attempting to split it from the energy of humanity.

UC: Introduce yourself, and what you do.

Tinvin: Hello, I am Tinvin, from Japan. I am an environmentalist, and a naturalist. But, I actually work as a decoder machine. We are all machines, just living to be tuned up, and oiled. Programmed to believe, before we achieve. I am interested, in how the Universal Consciousness Energy is related, to our nature as a human. Since we are all made from the same energy.

Tinvin: As an energy, how were we created? This is also part of my research. It's connected to the conversion of Humanity's Virus Energy Cell. Can energy change? If so, how? This new energy of Consciousness, has altered my direction in the science world. I am in a new place of discovery. At this time, I am learning from plants. They have an energy that speaks to me. When I feel it, I know what it wants. It's Consciousness Energy communication. It has to be. If the energy of a plant has the ability to make me feel it. The question becomes, how do I get it to acknowledge my energy feeling? At this point, I am working on this. Can they hear me? Imagine how much we can learn about plants, trees, and nature itself.

UC: Unfortunately, it's sad how the humans unnatural ways, are destroying the natural ways of humanity.

Tinvin: Humanity is so convoluted, so confused, that the unnatural has become the new natural.

UC: What have you learned from the plants so far?

Tinvin: How to grow what I know. I learned how talking to my plants, increased their growing stages.

UC: What did you grow?

Tinvin: An eggplant.

UC: Why an eggplant?

Tinvin: Because, it has many seeds that grow many eggplants.

UC: Did you help it grow?

Tinvin: I watered it.

UC: Who grew first, you, or the eggplant?

Tinvin: Ask the plant.

UC: Oh, you grew together, you fed it, and it fed you.

Tinvin: Yes, along with teaching me the stages of natures growth. Growing the plant, has helped me achieve my development into the energy of Consciousness. I have a promise to keep a to myself. I live to expose the Virus Energy Cell to the world. Starting with my myself.

Besides being a decoder, I have a science engineering degree, that allows me the full use of the most sophisticated biotech engineering technology in the world.

My work now, is focused on building a Virus Cell Energy sensor, that can sense the energy frequency of a Virus in anyone, anywhere. With the sensor, the Virus Energy Cell can be recorded from a distance of five hundred feet. Better to feel it, before you see it. I call it, V.E.S.T. The Virus Energy Sensor and Taser. It will also register the energy of hate, rage, and violence of those infected. This is where the taser comes in. The Consciousness is a real energy. I am going to prove that it's not just a theory.

Tinvin: As I went through my energy conversion, I discovered the truth about my toxic emotions. During my process, I kept getting this feeling of resistance. I felt like I was being challenged by my own emotions. The more I learned about Conscious Energy, the more I learned about the Virus Energy. It was attempting to control me, through my energy transformation. I came upon the realization, that the Virus

Energy Cell, has caused humanity to become entangled in a tug a war of energies. My research shows, this power struggle has split society in two separate classes. Two forms of energy for one humankind. Each human is battling two energies. This is what's causing indecision.

I began questioning everything. My brain and emotions, went through an Evolution Revolution Transfusion of their own. I have no explanation that can clearly define this process. It's a personal experience in the energy conversion. Confronting your emotions, is the real battle with yourself. Your support is nearly cut off, by the defending Virus Energies.

I have been identifying each one of my emotions. Testing it, Dissecting it, Analyzing it, and Converting it. I asked myself the same questions the Universal Consciousness asked me in the book. I believe there will come a time, when humans will have to open their brain to the energy of Consciousness. I foresee, once the Virus Energy becomes world known, a line will be drawn between right and wrong. One of them has to make a move.

Another part of my work, is to identify how the Virus Energy Cell benefits from destruction. How does it get people to do its bidding? I came upon a new discovery. I found a way to isolate a single energy frequency, from the whole Consciousness Energy, while it's in motion.

UC: How are you able to identify the Virus Energy, from the whole energy core of Consciousness?

Tinvin: The Virus Cell moves like a whale. Slow as a turtle. It creates a lot of energy backup.

They are all sitting in energy traffic. Each energy of the Virus Cell, serves a different purpose as identified by its actions. For example, the energy frequency of violence, it is intermingled with the Virus Energy Cell, but, it's still a singular Conscious Energy of its own.

UC: Its actions turn people against each other, to use them to do its dirty work. It's the energy focused on the manipulation of humanity. Humanity's actions are providing a benefit to the energy of violence.

Tinvin: There is a benefit to everything everyone does. It's only known to that individual. I have also discovered, the color of the energy changes with each action. Do you remember the mood rings? They changed colors according to how you felt. It's the same idea, sensing your feelings through your emotions. That's what the ring did. The Virus does the same. It senses your emotions, it waits for your reactions, and instigates. The ring, told you how you were feeling. The Virus makes you feel, the way you're feeling.

When Conscious Energy presents a reactive frequency, it's infected. I stamp it with the V for Virus, and put it on the conveyor belt to the fires. That's just what I call it. It's where the process of the energy conversion begins. When the energy of violence is isolated from the Virus Energy, it will leave the Virus with no ability to create violence. Once it's separated, it's much easier to convert it into the Consciousness Energy core.

Tinvin: Speaking of benefits, this awareness is one. What more can I learn? This Consciousness Energy is endless. I spent many years learning and teaching. Creative writing was one of my favorite classes to teach. I loved to escape into those stories. But, these words, they bring you back from your escape, into Conscious Energy Travel. They have left me speechless so many times.

I work with energy everyday. I needed to understand it, how to harness it. There is an energy which can be felt. With all my degrees, (I have three,) and I have an IQ of one hundred and seventy. This is not to brag, it's to say, I could have never written such meaningful words in such a way. They are a universe within a universe, which continue to echo throughout creation.

UC: You are very motivated, creative, and determined. You must be society's rebel. Not going with the flow of humanity's say so. Here are a few good tips for you: Always feel your way around, listen to the sound behind the sound. When it's not a fact, don't react. Trust your intuition to be exact. Never show fear that you fear it. When you do, it's an invitation to be near it. Fear will try to intimidate you. Do not reveal what you know, to those who don't know you, until you get to know them. Do not attempt to preach or teach, until you are asked.

The Virus Energy Cell is stewing. Conflict is beginning. It's done viewing and now it's moving. It will pull on every infected human being, to protect its meaning, and it did, it left many afraid. The Virus Energy Cell depends on the lie it started. That life is a mystery, a secret. It used fear and intimidation to keep the secret they only knew. The secret to life, is not a secret. It was never meant to be. Life simply wants to live. It's that simple. This is the hidden secret; and hidden, is the way they wish to keep it. Who will unlock it? Will you?

EWA

Wow! That was a great example of determination. Like Tinvin, I am determined to complete my energy Conversion. Her knowledge was on target. Her goal is clear. Her education is beyond reproach. That's why I am committed to unlocking it.

Hello, my name is Ewa. I live in Africa. In the same town as my mother and father, who was an officer in the military. Then there is my husband, who has no interest in changing. His ego has him convinced that he is perfect. I just graduated from nursing school. I have always believed, saving lives is what I was born to do. That's why I was excited by the information in this book. It believed what I believed. It said what I have been wanting to say but couldn't. It wasn't wise according to my husband? I needed to stay alive to save lives. My curiosity has been awakened, and my reality shaken.

I picked up this book, the same day I received it. It wasn't from anybody I knew, so my curiosity grew. I began to read, after completing the first chapter, I couldn't stop, so I printed it. I felt compelled to keep reading. I felt magnetized to the meanings. Until, my husband yelled at me about something, I jumped out of my skin, and fell from the sofa. He was laughing at my reaction, as I was shaking from the sudden disruption.

Ewa: First issue? My husband, and my reaction to how he treats me. His humor, is verbal abuse. From what I had already read, I was feeling like this book could help me, it's something new. I went on reading. I can't afford a therapist, anyway, he would not be happy about that. Time goes by and he starts to ask, *"where are you at?"* Each day, he would go into a rant. *"You keep ignoring me. Stop wasting your time on wake up stuff. You are awake, can't you tell? I want attention, you're giving it all to that book. You'll see what will happen to your book."* Wow, making threats now. He must feel threatened, that I am learning new knowledge. I was surprised at his reaction.

UC: It sounds like, you're in the middle of your energy transformation?

Ewa: I am going through changes I didn't know needed changing. I stand taller, and have so much more confidence. I now see what's really of importance. I have developed this amazing glow around me, so my friends say, they have noticed the new me. Unfortunately, so has my husband. His insecurity started to show, as my transformation started to grow. I felt so empowered, and he was always tired.

I am in the middle of my growth, because my loving husband keeps sabotaging my efforts. He asks, *"what are you working on?"* Showing a hint of interest, I take it as progress. Stupid me, so I tell him *"I am learning, how not to react to your verbal abuse."* Total set up, I knew it, I felt it, and I let it. Why? It was hard to control. It came out from the corner of my mouth, before I could close it. The more attention I gave myself, the angrier he became.

His defensiveness grew another head without a brain. His anger was now showing. His verbal abuse increased, as I continued to build my awareness and my confidence. I refused to be bullied into submission by his ego. He constantly tried to get me to react. He told me that standing up to him was not right. It's not normal for a wife to do that, he said. It's against the marriage vows. I replied, I am not just your wife, I am a woman first. I was shaking inside. I was standing up against his bullying.

He likes to puff his chest up and say, *"I am the man."* I respond with, oh ya, I am Jane, and you're acting like a monkey. This makes him more angry. It was not a good idea, as he put his fist through the wall, next to my head. I knew then to keep my mouth shut, and let my Consciousness do the talking.

At times, he has slapped me around a little bit, but only when I talk back. That will never happen again. This time, he looked afraid of me. What is wrong with him? Is he infected more than me?

He won't even change his actions. Since I have been developing myself, and started questioning his motives. He stopped hitting me. He actually started to avoid me. I could not believe it.

I have spent my growing years in peace and solitude. Only to find out later, that my peace was actually denial. My solitude was isolation from fear. What was I denying? I had to discover it. What was I fearful of? These thoughts never entered my brain before I received this book.

IT TOOK THE VICTIM, RIGHT OUT OF ME.

Access to information has become less limited. With social media, I can reach out to anyone in the world. I believe contact to contact makes the best impact. I need to get different perspectives in order to process all this. I believe in having a choice, but they want to take it away.

UC: Who are they? There are a lot of you on Earth.

Ewa: Men and women in power, who else. Governments and religions. I don't believe any man nor woman, has any different connection to God than the rest of humanity. They think they do, because they are never question. My awareness is teaching me to question. I believe women everywhere need to discover this knowledge, it is freedom from oppression. My husband thinks he is smarter than me. I let him think so. It catches him off guard. I can only speak to what I feel. Nothing had giving me the strength, and Consciousness I needed to stop his abuse, until now. It's as though the energy in it, is protecting me from him. Question; what can this knowledge do for the energy of stupidity. Oops, I am sorry, I digressed. I didn't think I would face such resistance, from wanting to learn. It's my frustration with my husband. I still want him to wake up. I don't want to grow without him; but if I have to, I will.

At one point, I started noticing I was using persuasion in my approach. I am glad I noticed first, and toned it down. I backed off from approaching him. He took it to mean I was avoiding him. Is this what it's going to be like, facing people who are infected? It's hard to believe, the energy of the Virus Cell, is stronger than the energy of love.

My second realization, maybe he doesn't love me. He became extremely suspicious. I wanted to be ready, before I tried to approach him again. One day I became aware, each time I pointed out one of his infected emotions, It put me on my guard for the incoming. My awareness and my senses became heightened, I went into full alert mode, he's huge. We started to spend less time together. He would start an argument while I am meditating. Always interfering, trying to cut off my energy connection.

One morning, I was on the couch reading, suddenly, he was behind me, I hadn't noticed until he grabbed the book, and ran to the fire place. He held it over the fire as he said, *"I told you what I would do with this book, if you kept reading it. Now you'll be sorry. You better listen to me women, you will do what I say or I drop it."*

I looked at him with a big smile and said, *"go ahead, but you're too late, I have already absorbed it all."* Into the fire it went. As he looked at me, he was standing there gloating. I still had a smile on my face. He looks down in the fire, and saw the pages were not burning. He let out a yelp. He looked up at me with eyes bigger than his head. He called me a witch, and ran out of the house.

UC: How long has he been gone?

Ewa: We spoke two weeks ago, he still called me a witch. He threatened me with divorce if I didn't stop. I can't anymore, I am free of control. Now, I only answer to being asked, not told. What should couples do if one refuses to trust the other? Is this when we find out about true love forever?

UC: This is an excellent teaching experience. Great work Ewa. Only, his choices are not yours to fix. Don't take them on. They are not your responsibility. It's only guilt keeping you together. LOVE is not physical abuse. There is no room for fear in love. There is no excuse for harming one another. When you harm another, it's you who will lose. He must make his own commitment without influence. He has to become curious. Why wasn't he? Why did you allow the Virus to take him? You knew it was there?

Ewa: There has to be an equally balanced understanding, between women and men. We are two different species. Besides, I said he was huge.

UC: Physically, yes. As Consciousness Energy, no. Your husband is like a million others. You will face many like him, but worse. You had the chance to confront a Virus. Can you find out why you didn't? You developed your Consciousness to the point of energy conversion. Yet there is still something not fully developed from your transformation. Do you have an attachment to where you live? Have you thought about the investment, hiding in your basement.

Ewa: No not really. I thought about moving.

UC: How long have you been together?

Ewa: Twelve years.

UC: Any children?

Ewa: No, the crib is still in the basement.

UC: Has this caused a rift?

Ewa: Yes, one or two. Then it became resentment.

UC: Your commitment to your Consciousness growth, is admirable. You are being an example of true Consciousness. Which makes you noticeable, approachable, and dependable. But to be responsible, you must be completely free of the Virus Energy. What you don't deal with, becomes an attachment. Until you open it, read it, and deal with it. Then you can delete it. Whatever you want to do with it. But why keep it if it's an empty attachment? Excellent commitment.

IMAN

Hi, my name is Iman. I live in Jordan. My story is not about glory. It's about the creation of Consciousness Energy. Based on my knowledge from the Evolution Revolution. It helped me deal with my feelings of oppression, and possession, disguised as love.

My life was not going well for me. I had been searching for a new identity. A new personality. Someone, or something to guide me. Everyday, I became more, and more disillusioned with humanity. I got lost in vanity, stopped being friendly and Isolated from my family. Until the day, I had the most amazing supernatural experience.

The supernatural isn't new to me, but this? This was a new reality. One day, I was at home reading a book, a friend sent me on line. I was curious. I figured I would check it out. Apparently, I had been reading for over six hours, and I was unaware. I was focusing in on this meaning, when I heard it; the voice in my head, more like a whisper. It was as though my brain was talking to me.

The whisper became louder. I realized I was going to have a conversation with the Universal Consciousness Energy. I had been expecting something to happen to me, from the knowledge of the Evolution Revolution. But I did not expect what happened. I was being asked a question by this voice. It was loud now. It did make me nervous at first, but because I was expecting something like this. I was not afraid when it happened.

UC: Hello Iman. It seems your energy conversion is moving along quite well. Your determination for discovery has brought this connection from the Universal Consciousness to you. Your conversion has awakened you to a new reality. It will reveal your destiny. You have a mission to accomplish, it will come soon. This knowledge will help you achieve your goals.

Iman: I have been working on myself and my awareness, for a couple of years now. But receiving this book, has set me on a course with my fate. I am committed to do what I have to, to convert any Virus Cell infection I have.

UC: You are walking on the path towards Consciousness. Your awareness has put you on this path, It seems, by your reputation, you have decided to go all the way. You are well known for your tenacity, courage and keeping a commitment. We hear a message has been sent out by those who know you, that you mean business, and you will not stop, until the conversion of the Virus. Your friends believe in you, and your work. Why?

Iman: Because I believe in them and their work. I am consistent, trustworthy and, I don't bow down to force control. I follow up with everyone I know. I am Self Regulated. Uncontrolled, and resistant to demands, and orders. When I see wrong, I say something. When I see others in need, I do something. Fear does not scare me. I have lived it. I am a huge advocate for world peace. I have been trying to find a way to achieve this. I have many ideas. But one specifically, an organization which focuses on world peace, and making people aware of the Virus Energy Cell. That's why I am working with the media, and with those I know. In hopes of inspiring them to do the same. To create a movement by all of us. It's the only way to achieve world peace. Since Religion can't convert the Devil, WE WILL.

UC: What have you been up to, with your Consciousness Energy education? We are aware that you are instigating a provocation without energy protection. You now have The Virus Energy's attention. We sensed it was very interested in you. What is the process of your energy conversion. Are you challenging the Virus Energy face to face, without support around you?

Iman: Yes I am. It's what I have been waiting for. I do have a plan. From what I have learned about the Virus Cell, it's an out of the box idea. I believe it will work.

UC: Are you aware that as you worked on your energy conversion, you brought the Virus Energy to you? It's coming in groups. They will try and stop you. They are already aware of your plan. Your fate is about to be discovered. You've caught the attention of the Virus Cell. You rang the bell, which brought the devil out of hell. Was this your intention? We have been observing you for some time.

Why are you volunteering to challenge the Virus Energy Cell? It's sensitive to losing control. Which makes it especially dangerous. Did you purposely bring attention to yourself, so it would notice you? Who thought of this plan? You're making noise to attract the lion, and you say, you have a trap in the way, is this correct?

Iman: Yes, and I came up with this plan by becoming Consciousness Energy. Wasn't that the point? The Evolution Revolution knowledge, inspired me to create my own way of conversion.

UC: When were you born? Did you sit on a throne? Are you homegrown, or grown on the unknown?

Iman: More unknown than home grown.

UC: Does courage run in your family, or run from them? Is there something unknown for the others to know. Like, do you need support if the Virus Cell finds you? How will you protect yourself?

Iman: With the power of a Conscious Energy Frequency. I have learned how to project my energy frequency with focus and intent. It's like an out of body experience. But it's with energy, not the spirit. I can focus my Conscious Energy frequency, and plug into another unbalanced energy frequency, and change its intention.

UC: How did you develop this ability?

Iman: You have to read the Evolution Revolution to get it. Ha just kidding. But it is where I started from. Today, I will merge my Consciousness Energy, with the energy of the Virus Cell.

UC: You are going to convert the Virus Cell, by going through its Energy? By doing so, you're going to leave your Consciousness Energy in it, on your way out? Is this your plan? Why Iman? This goes beyond doing what you can. Your chance of coming out whole, is on the low end of the scale. You are aware of this, are you not?

It takes less than a blink of an eye, and the Virus Energy will be saying hi. Infecting its energy, with your balanced Energy, is a dangerous plan to achieve by yourself. You are showing true confidence? Don't lose your balance, or you will belong to the Virus. Why wouldn't you be noticed? You will feel it, won't you? Why wouldn't it feel you?

Iman: I am going in as an Energy, Consciousness Energy. The Virus lives on fear, I don't have fear. It thrives on pain, I have none. It instigates inner conflicts, I have none. It feels for hopelessness and insecurity, I have none. It feeds off of other Virus Cell infections, I have none. I will be invisible, as an energy form, I have no brain or emotions, for it to be attracted to. My energy will move by perception, and sensation.

UC: Learning how to connect with people's infected emotions, without creating a negative reaction. That's true Consciousness. Are you trying to learn from it, as you convert it? If so, that's very clever. Did you pick up anything useful to help others convert their Virus Energy?

Iman: It operates on instinct. It acts without thought. It's very reactionary. It loses focus quickly when it's confused, or disoriented. It calls out for direction. It responds in an unusual way to the energy of seduction. It gets distracted, leaving itself open for conversion. One more, when it's afraid, (yes, it gets fearful.) It hides its identity, and becomes a different energy.

UC: Have you thought of teaching this ability to others? Determination drives your evolution. What's driving your motivation, is it meditation, physical education, knowledge of the Consciousness Energy vibration?

Iman: The reality that humankind may self destruct, that's a good motivation, I believe. When I received the book, I became aware of the true reality of humanity. It opened my eyes to what it means to realize, to be aware, to be Conscious. Each day I discover something new. Each discovery, awakens me to a new view of my surroundings. It was one of these views, that showed me the fate of what I am going to do.

UC: You were speaking before, about your path to creating an organization of Consciousness. Have you started your organization yet? It's a great idea to support the world's energy conversion. It's on the way to a new direction. Did you have a premonition?

Iman: One day while I was meditating, I did have a premonition. It was so clear it had to be. I was walking on a path, which led me to a waterfall. As I gazed on it, I leaned down to pick a flower, and fell in the water. I didn't panic, I found, I could breathe under water.

Iman: So there I was swimming around, I decided to go deeper; where I saw, the word WATER written in the sand. I became very curious. As the water moved the sand, a new set of words appeared. Forming the words, World Association Toward Energy Re-creation. Then the realization hit me, I opened my eyes and yelled out, *"THATS IT! It's WATER!"* I finally got the name of the new organization I have been thinking of creating. Where People with like thoughts and beliefs, can gather and learn from each other.

I had been looking at names for a long time. I will call it, W.A.T.E.R. World Association Towards Energy Re-creation. Oh, I was so excited. I contacted my friends Tinvin, and Ewa. We are friends on line now. We often gathered to discuss the book and its meanings. I told them about my vision. They both responded the same way. They saw it as a premonition also. It was meant to be. Tinvin said, *"I am willing to step up, and start an energy conversion movement, if you are. How about you, Ewa?* Tinvin asked.

Ewa replied, yes, absolutely. Only on one condition. Iman, you must be the president. Whatever it is they call that. It was your vision, Ewa replied. I can be the vice president, unless Tinvin wants to. It's all yours Ewa. I will be the secretary of state, Tinvin shared. As we started laughing. That's how

W.A.T.E.R. began. We naturally took our roles. Sent emails to hundreds, they sent out hundreds more. There were so many willing to make their mission, the initiation of W.A.T.E.R. The World Association Toward Energy Re-creation. The beginning of the Energy Movement

UC: You Iman, *"have become a beacon."* The light beam to find the Virus infections. It follows you, it's fearful of you. It needs to know all your movements. You can no longer hide your beam. It wants to turn you off. You have created a new power of will. That tells the Virus, you won't.

APKI & INAD

Inad: Ding, ding! Hello! You have a customer.

Apki: Yes, how can I help you, oh it's you Inad. I don't have time for you today, I just saw you for this last year, Mr. Scale inspector. Why do you keep saying ding-ding each time you come in? I don't have a bell on the door. I know...You do it just to annoy me.

Inad: It's your yearly balance certification.

Apki: Well, certify. But, I still think your price is too high. Just do your job, and say goodbye.

Inad: OK let's start, what is your name?

Apki: I am not playing this game. Go find someone else, who likes playing games.

Inad: First name and last. You know I need it. Just say it. We can move on.

Apki: Are you joking, fill it out yourself. I play along every year. Who are you today, Mr. Scale inspector, or my brother in law? It doesn't matter, you still cost me money. Is this what you do for fun. Last time Inad. You're like a child.

Inad: Name please, come on Apki, wake up.

Apki: You are lucky we are related. You just said my name, write it down.

Inad: Occupation:

Apki: Grocery store, and deli owner.

Inad: Birth place:

Apki: OK, that's enough, go do your job. You're taking this job way too serious. How did they ever give you a badge.

Inad: Mr. Apki When did the slicer have its last rotation?

Apki: What are you asking me for? You wrote it, you look it up.

Inad: Is your drain rotator still cycling?

Apki: Are you kidding? You get paid the big bucks, while I do your job for you. You got a lazy brain.

Inad: Just a few more questions, you know the drill. You do it real well.

Apki: I'm amazed how the weight and measurement department actually hired you. You can't even tell the difference between the two.

Inad: Well Apki, our prices have increased. You know, everything is going up nowadays.

Apki: Really, no surprise there. I had a feeling you would say that. You say it every year, and every year you pocket the increase. Yes, I know, my sister told me. She felt too guilty. How much do you owe me? Let's see, seventy five, times three years. That comes out to…Get out of my deli!

You may be married to my sister but you're a crook. It's always about money with you, isn't it Inad? Admit it, you are greedy. You would do just about anything for money. So what is it now, New standards I bet.

Inad: Hey come on Apki, it's not like that. It really is my job, mostly. Look I admit, I padded the increase by twenty five bucks. Sorry, I will pay you back. I was having a hard time financially. It's only a fifty dollar charge now, not the usual seventy five.

Apki: So what? Is that suppose to make me feel better? Now I'm suppose to trust you like it never happened? That's not going to happen. Once you break a trust, well, you know.

Inad: I Will make it up to you, I promise.

Apki: No promises, you already broke all of them in your attempt to get rich quick. Why did it go up?

Inad: Well, you know.

Apki: OK finish your scam and go, I got a business to run.

Inad: Your scale is off balance Apki. That's a huge fine. Did you do that yourself?

How long have you been cheating others? You were making them believe, what they were buying was valued on a balanced scale. That's a hefty fine, using balance to cheat people. Wow! I never realized you were that kind of man, and you're calling me a crook?

Apki: Now you just stop right there mister inspector. You're a double standard type of crook, and you're not funny. Not only that, but I see right through your manipulation. How dare you come in here, and try to flip it around on me, by making up lies.

Inad: Look I am just trying to rattle your cage. Every year, in and out, you never change, or get angry, no new emotions. Your sister complains about your lack of motivation all the time. You have become boring Apki.

Apki: Oh! So now, it's about changing me? You do this each time I see you. I think it's a distraction tool for you.

Inad: What did I just hear? Those are development words, haven't heard anything new from you in years.

Apki: Then you haven't been listening. Like you haven't listened to me about that useless scale I bought from you. First of all, it has been off balance since I bought it from you.

I lose money on your scale. You pay to fix it, or pay me for a new one. You're a cheapskate. How did you get it to balance long enough to sell it anyway?

Inad: Just a temporary fix, I gave you a good deal Apki.

Apki: I knew you would say that. So, I have to discount each sale, to make up for your scale. I do not cheat people. I bought a new one yesterday. I put it on your charge account.

Inad: What! How can you do that. Isn't that stealing?

Apki: No, I had permission. You're married to my sister. You are pointing out my ethics, while you knew you were selling me a broken scale. You have been stealing from me for years, and you want to talk about change. Have you lost your brain.

Apki: I do not lie. OK, I lied when I made my toast to your marriage, to my sister. I said, welcome to the family. Nothing in there about, steal from your family. How can you accuse me, and overcharge me at the same time? I have been here for thirty three years. Still the same. I have always held the same high standards. My business is known all over the country. Not you…What have done, besides give me grief.

Inad: How did your sister know about the scale.

Apki: I told her, fair is fair. I covered for you for months. I got tired of hearing how wonderful you were to give me a deal. That's when she told me about you stealing my money.

Inad: I stopped taking your money long ago. Ever since I started reading this book called the Evolution Revolution on line. It taught me about Consciousness Energy. Now I know the real meaning of, what comes around goes around. I keep instigating you, to see if you are actually alive. You can ask your sister. I have been changing. This knowledge has shown me my true self. It's about Consciousness Energy development. I recommend it highly. Does change scare you. What's stopping you? Have you looked OUTSIDE lately?

Apki: Yes, many times. When I look up, I see the outside.

Inad: Have you seen any new changes? Probably no. Have you looked inside lately?

Apki: Come on, I am very busy, my last help just quit.

Inad: Do you know what year this is Apki?

Apki: Hmm. What does that prove?

Inad: It proves you don't know? What do you do with your time after work?

Apki: I am not sure, nothing, I work hard, I rest hard. I garden, sleep, eat, then sleep again. It's a good life. I don't need much changing. It's good the way it is.

Inad: Huh? News flash for you buddy, you have changed, quite a bit actually. I see what you don't. You're older, you wear glasses now. You're fatter. Your health is worse. You're more stubborn. You have less patience, and, you yell more. Your food styles have changed, so has your menu. What didn't change is the fact, you are still seeing yesterday, when you live in today. For all these years you have complained about the changes in the world, but you can't see the changes in front of your face. It's called denial. Doesn't matter how you look at it. It's thirty three years of denial. You really should give awareness a shot. You need it.

Apki: You have no idea what I know, or need.

Inad: Why haven't you noticed the change in me?

Apki: What change? I haven't noticed because, you sound the same. Nothing is ever new with you. You barely move.

Inad: What are you afraid off? Change doesn't bite, but fear does.

Apki: Just for your information, fear is the one energy that's hard to foresee. When I see it coming, I know what to do. I have been learning plenty about fear. That's one change you didn't see.

Inad: What do you know about the word energy?

Apki: I have been reading the same book. My sister received it, and started to talk to me about it a while ago.

Inad: Oh, I didn't know.

Apki: I have to admit, it draws you in. My perspective of the world has started to change. Arguments with you, were what I looked forward to, until now. The problem is bigger than I thought. But, I have a new outlook. I can't thank my sister enough.

Inad: Have a great day! Hey, by the way,` next time I am overcharging you, so I can get my money back for the scale.

Apki: I knew that. You are much easier to read with my new Consciousness.

TRYSTEN

UC: Are you familiar with trust. Do you still trust what you know? Do you know who to trust? How did you lose trust in your beliefs? Did you find new ones? Are you working on replacing the old with the new?

Trysten: How can I have trust in something, I have little experience with? If I knew myself better, I would trust myself more.

UC: Do you trust your government, the direction your life is going, your employer, your family? Do you trust your worship? Isn't this what it's really about? How much do you trust yourself to make the correct and wise decision? Are you the impulsive, or a, take your time person?

Trysten: Buongiorno! My name is Trysten. I live in Italy. Twice a week I had to go with my parents, to their house of prayer. I didn't think it was fair. I had better things to do than pray.

It was in the summer, I was fourteen years old. I rebelled against them, and refused to go anymore. I did everything I was told, like a good boy, but that was over with. Yes, I was young, but I didn't think the way they did. I was always looking for something new, and better. I was possessed with learning new things. I had this drive to discover, and to learn inspiring knowledge. After hearing the same story for over ten years, I was happy to find anything new.

As I grew, I found myself interested in the science of the brain, and how it functions. I wanted to know all I could about it. Time goes on, I graduated, and went into the mental health field. I made a pact with myself, I would specialize in child abuse trauma. The percentage of child abuse victims has more than doubled world wide. I had a few friends who were abused as children, it affected me greatly. Adults are experts at manipulation. We as children get it from them. The energy of manipulation is a disease.

I wanted to study the brain in order to find it, along with many others like it, and change their meaning. At that time, I had been doing on line research, looking for more information about the brains Consciousness. When I found this book, called the Evolution Revolution, by the Universal Consciousness. It was up my alley. So I began to explore its contents. It was about Consciousness Energy and how it affects our physical brain. It was explained in a different way.

I started, and kept on reading. It wasn't the words, as much as the meanings which filled them. The way it was written, you can feel the energy flowing from it. I had to print it. I wanted to read it everywhere I went. I had always prided myself on not being able to be manipulated by anyone. So I studied each word carefully. What I discovered actually changed me. It helped me with identifying the energy of Manipulation by teaching me how it works. My parents manipulated me for years. I can recognize its energy when I feel it. It's part of the reason I study the brain. I want to become aware of the different energies, and how they can affect us, even control us. Example, the Virus Energy Cell, this energy is trying to end civilization, and we didn't even know it existed.

Trysten: Change is achievable, by Energy Conversion. This is what I discovered from this book. I focused on the Energy of Manipulation. So I cannot be manipulated. I became aware of a new reality, I realized what this knowledge meant to me. A new way of life. A World Energy Conversion, of all the population, and here I am focusing on manipulation. But I had to start somewhere. This awareness meant, a complete overhaul of world government's. First question I had was, how do I keep from being arrested? If this book, was to be taken seriously by me, I had to be ready to make a big choice, Consciousness, or to remain Unconscious. I had to pick one, and I did…Consciousness. It was then, I started hearing, about how the energy movement has taken effect in other countries.

I had to find out more. It's something I had to explore. Into the movement I went. This decision alone made me pause. I remember thinking, what about facing the Vatican? Let's get real. That's taking on two government's in one country. We wouldn't stand a chance. Talk about the impossible. But if everything I was reading is true, it's a possibility. I realized we were facing an actual, Consciousness Energy Evolution Revolution. In Italy, it's usually a political thing. But trying to change the belief system of two governments, strikes me as insanity.

The energy here is never consistent enough, it's always changing with the tourists. Too many visitors year round. Year after year. Italy meets the needs of tourism. It's historically famous. Temptation is thriving here. The ultimate goal, who seduces whom? The rich feed on the less rich. The poor feed on the less poor. The only one benefiting, is the Virus Energy Cell. My issue has always been with blind faith. My family had this Virus. It immobilized me with fears, most of my growing years. From a young boy, I can remember being manipulated by an illusion. I grew up believing what others believed, without question. I have been searching for years, looking for another explanation to our creation.

At an early age I realized, believing in what others believe without question, is believing in others, not yourself. My work is about self-confidence, awareness, and self assurance. From knowledge, not ego. The last thing my clients needed, were promises adults couldn't keep. We expected our children to face a reality, we as adults couldn't face.

Peoples thoughts were on the Evolution Revolution Solution. I was at the height of my conversion. I was on my way to freedom from the Virus infection. Understanding the Virus Cell as an energy, gave me a way to recognize it around me.

UC: You sound confident in what you have learned about manipulation. You know, there is more you can learn about it. Learning is the reason, you are where you are. Are you interested? We are all about Consciousness development now, aren't we? Don't miss out on new knowledge.

Trysten: Is it more about the energy of manipulation. I don't think I need more information about that energy. It can't manipulate me, this I know. I would always recognize it. I am too focused. I think I learned well. I am too Conscious to allow myself to fall for it. Manipulation? I would know right away. I felt it everyday. Now, Fear, fears me. Greed, can't buy me. Seduction, will not work. I have a partner. We are working together. So, that leaves manipulation with nothing to manipulate.

UC: Hmm, so, that's it then. Nothing left to learn. You're passing up the chance, to dance with manipulation. You can show what you know. Show it that you can't be manipulated.

Trysten: I have nothing to prove, I am sure of myself. I know all I need to know.

UC: How is it, an evolved conscious being such as yourself, refuses to learn. Why are you limiting yourself?

Trysten: It's a waste of time, I could be helping others.

UC: Knowledge, is an energy, it can never be wasted, how can you ignore this?

Trysten: I can't be manipulated.

UC: Even the Virus Cell Energy is not this confident, how can you be? Are you sure there is nothing left to learn? This is Consciousness knowledge you are refusing to learn. That's like a bear refusing honey, it's unnatural. You said, you were fully aware, yet, you deny your consciousness growth.

How can more knowledge hurt? It would give you assurance that you can't be manipulated. You get to prove it. People won't believe it. How will you protect the world, no one will know who you are.

Don't you want to be known?

Trysten: , you have my attention. I'm a big fan of knowledge. I certainly don't want to sound resistant. What can you tell me about manipulation that I don't know? Let's hear this out, even though it's foolish.

UC: It's good, foolish is not what you want to be. But, hey! Mr. Court Jester. You've just been manipulated. It took a while but you did.

Trysten: What? When? How did I miss that? I feel foolish.

UC: You gave your power away by bragging. We learned how to manipulate you, with your own words. Come on Trysten. What was it? What finally got to your ego? Wanting to be known, is that what got you?

Trysten: Yes, I confess. Thanks, it seems that I have more energy to convert.

UC: Manipulation has more to it than you thought. It has many friends, they are branches of the Virus Energy Tree. When one branch can't get you, another will. While you were watching your front, the ego got you from the back. The energy of ego is fast to react. The Virus Cell Energy works through unbalanced physical energy. It's in the form of over confidence. Which means, unbalanced. Have you learned anything?

Trysten: Too much confidence, can be dangerous. It opens me up to reinfection. I thought I had my ego in check. Apparently, it checked me. I am glad we had this conversation. I could have walked right into a Virus Energy infection, and not know it.

UC: When you feel off balance, try this visual on for size. Close your eyes and visualize, you're walking through life balanced on a tightrope. Never again to walk the ground. Why? The ground is on fire. What are your chances of survival if you fall? What will you do? You can't dance, all you have is balance. You can't fly. Are you going to die? Will you be able to find a solution for your continued evolution, before the rope burns?

SELY

What's another burned body to humanity? We have turned it into a business. But I have to say, your example of humanities situation, can't be disputed. It sure gave me a new perspective. We are in dire need of Balanced Consciousness. People have learned to deny their emotions rather than work through them. Which allows the emotions to be out of control and become destructive. How in the world did we not see the damage, we were causing ourselves and the Earth? My need to learn keeps me questioning, if I had said the right thing? Did the right thing? Had I made the right choices? Why do I have such bad luck with relationships?

UC: How long did it last? Was she the wrong class? You didn't take a chance? Incomplete romance, rejection issues, bring out the box of tissues. Your heart is broken, you feel hopeless and confused. You're swearing off relationships, and blaming yourself for your failures. Does this sound about right? Anything new happen to you?

Sely: Hi, my name is Sely, from the United States. Oh boy, did it happen, and it was something new alright, it was an awakening that happened. I first thought it was my imagination, because I work as a mortician. I make dead people look alive. I put people in a box, therapists, take them out. Just a Dead Joke. But seriously, after the energy movement became world wide. I had the most incredible happening. Pay attention.

UC: We thought you said mortician not comedian. You need to get out more, go on.

Sely: I will stop the jokes. It gets lonely at times, the dead are really boring people.

UC: Stop Sely! Are you going to use humor each time you run away from a feeling? We can see through it.

Sely: OK, but I can't get them to laugh at any of my jokes. One night, I get to work, and I see a body wearing a suit lying on my table. I looked at the report. An accident victim brought in an hour ago. So I start working on cleaning the face, and the head, when I heard a faint whisper? *"Look in my jacket."* Huh? I just wanted the dead to laugh not speak. As I continued, *"Look in my jacket,"* came on again. Whoa! Vacation time. Hahaha, I'm going batty. I was looking at his mouth, nothing moved. Unless he is a dead ventriloquist, I joked. Or the talking dead, If they can walk, they can talk.

Working on the dead has finally caught up with me. But what the heck. I had to remove his clothes anyway. I looked in his jacket pocket, and found an envelope. In It, were papers, and an unusual gold key, in the shape of the infinity sign. It was wrapped In a cloth, with a small note, saying:

"This is the key to humankind's future. There are seven other humans who have received one of these keys, you make eight. Don't let this key be seen, until we come for it."

What's the key for I wondered? I looked in the pocket again, and saw one more paper inside. I opened it, this is what it said. *"Each key, opens a door to a wonder of the world."* I was puzzled. Why did it come to me, and what was behind those doors? The phone rang, I jump out of my shoes. It was a phone call from someone I didn't know, she referred to herself as a member of W.A.T.E.R. As I listened, she said, we know you just found the eighth key. Be careful. We will be in touch. We didn't discuss the key. She seemed to be in a hurry.

Sely: What just happened? I tried to shake it off, I had work to do. But then I thought, was I in a spy movie without realizing it? Ya that's it, a reality TV show. But how can I not know? Each day I would check to see, if I had a message from them, until the day it came. I opened it, and I saw the words, Evolution Revolution on the front cover of a book. Under it were the words, read it, then we will talk.

I sat with the first chapter, when I was done, I felt like I was hit with a ton, and I bit my tongue. My curiosity compelled me to keep reading. On I went, I was pulled in deeper by the meanings. They are meanings within meanings. It's as though it was written for me. An answer to my plea for a new kind of hope, one that can improve me. So I can stop hoping, and start hopping. How many others are reading this book, I wondered? Are they having similar experiences?

It took some time, but again, I received an email from someone named, Iman. From what I learned, she, and a couple of others started W.A.T.E.R. She informed me, she also has a key. She told me more about W.A.T.E.R.'s activity. How they all started the World Association Toward Energy Re- creation, in support of the Energy Movement.

I told her of my story, and how I got the key from a dead man. She asked me if I could tell her his name. I did, she went silent, she shared they had been friends. He was a good person, and was one of the ambassadors to world governments, on behalf of the movement. He was on his way to a meeting with a top political contact. A car accident made sure he didn't make his meeting. Or, was it? She added.

Suddenly I had a huge reaction of sadness. It wasn't all mine, it was her friend who died which triggered it? I just recognized I still had a trigger. Until I deal with my past triggers, I will not be one hundred percent present. This was a heavy weight on me. I wanted to ask her about what's behind those doors? As I did, She replied, that she knew a little, but it's knowledge, only for me to know.

What I was told, some of them hold Alien secrets which they kept safe until their return. I heard things like, scientific formulas, Diagrams, math equations, scientific knowledge beyond human technology, and images of them. Things we would need, to start a new beginning. This was exciting news. Who wouldn't be excited to be a part of this event.

A few days later I found the trigger. Her friend dying in a crash was a trigger for me, because, my little sister was killed by a drunk driver who survived. She was eleven. The drunk who killed her was never charged, because the drunk was my mom. Growing up was not a good experience for me, I have always felt so guilty, because I wasn't hurt. My mom never mentioned her again, neither did I. I have lots of sadness about that.

I would like to share a memory of the life I lived. As I said, it wasn't a good one. Here is the short version. One day, I lost hope. The next day, I found a rope. Curiosity was looking through a telescope, it could tell I had lost hope. It cut the rope. It said, I know hope, I can give you a map and show you where to look. This gave me my hope back.

With a therapist's support, I was back on track, looking for hope. This time, I had a direction. This memory has stayed a part of me for years, like a haunting. My goal now, is to focus on my energy conversion. To fully convert my Virus Energy. I have to do this if I am to find hope. I have become realized to the emergency of humanity's situation. At this point, it's like, humans are having a near death experience. Will they return to the body, or remain as spirits.

With my perception as it is now. I have a hard time with the idea of many people, from separate countries, with their own laws, rules, beliefs, and lifestyle, living openly together, with trust as the foundation? Ha, we can't even do that in our own homes. With our own families. How is the energy re-creation going to happen? Part of my hopelessness was not being able to trust people.

UC: How long have you been looking for hope?

Sely: Since she left me. That's why I am hopeless. Most of my pain comes from my childhood years. I am aware of this now. My Consciousness Energy development, has helped me become aware of my infected emotions. I am not good at relationships. I ruined this one, and the last one too. It's always me. I couldn't completely commit. I am no good for any woman. I am a man. Men don't know what a woman needs. That's what my mother always said. Recently, in my therapy, I discovered I am my father, with the beliefs of my mother. I heard all she said about him, I felt how he felt about her. All the names she called me. I think she took out all her pain about my sister, upon me. My father tried to stick up for me, before she forced him to leave. She hit him often. I was scared of her. It was clear who the man was. It wasn't my father.

I have a memory of when I was in foster care, I was nine years old. Saint legions home for troubled youth. This place was anything but a home. It was a living nightmare. My mother put me in there. She said, *"I am sorry, I can't take care of you anymore."* Your father, that bastard has abandoned us. *"I thought he was different. I will never trust another man again, I am done with them. They have no idea what a woman needs."* Her famous last words, burned in my brain. Then, poof! She disappeared. Gone! Never saw her again.

I have always believed there was a problem with us humans. That's why today, I question everything. The more I question, the more secure I feel. The whole time my mom was talking, I was thinking, I am being abandoned by the only family I had? I must have been absorbing her energy emotionally. I didn't shed a tear in front of her. I just knew, first my father, now it's me. She made my father leave, and I blamed myself. What did I inherit from her? Men are bad. Men are bastards. You can't live with them. They don't know what a woman needs. I still don't know, thanks mom. Self doubt? I was a certified self doubter. I learned to be that way. I believed everything my mother said.

Until, I became old enough to realize, most of her issues were not related to me. Talk about total confusion. Depression set in. I lived my life looking through her eyes. Feeling with her cold heart. Reacting from her fears. Believing in her illusion. I had a hard time trusting women.

Sely: Sometimes, I don't trust myself. I've lost so many friends, and girlfriends defending beliefs which weren't even mine. I was hopeless. All the therapy did was make me aware, it was all an illusion. But didn't tell me how to build a new reality. I had different roommates in collage. I had friends in high school, but I never trusted any of them. My relationships had major issues. I had a huge commitment disorder. I had rage for my mother. Extreme sadness for my father. He left so fast, I saw him run out. Why was he in such a hurry? As I got older, I heard rumors that she didn't kick him out, he ran away from her. That he couldn't wait to leave her. I don't blame him one bit. That's the day love died. To this day I never cried.

Now I find myself involved in this mystery with the key, and still asking, why me? Consciousness Energy, and Aliens? It's a movie plot. Right? This is all part of my energy conversion work. That's what I am learning. I brought out all my memories from my childhood. Everything I forgot. Unconscious Beliefs, my Mothers treatment of me, my actions, reactions, and my abuse. My Sister's death, the lack of wealth. The forced control, and the meaningless love I grew up with. I confronted each infected emotion. It's the only way to change the Virus Energy infection.

UC: It just goes to show, no matter what direction you go, go with what you know, from your Consciousness Energy. How were you able to connect your childhood trauma, to your present personality?

Sely: I had been on the path of discovery, looking for my purpose, before I become a body on a table. After all that therapy, I needed a challenge. Where did I fit in? What great impact can I make? Just to say I accomplished something, besides talking to dead people. That's why I am here reading what

I am needing. I have had lots of years in therapy. I've been searching for a new kind of energy for years. Most therapists have their own style. It's too many.

It's confusing. You can like the therapist, but not their style. You can like the style, but, not the therapist. Which is why I am excited with the material I am viewing, from the Evolution Revolution. It is giving me the diagram to a new life. I am more than just a man now. My self esteem? Let's say, the well is full. My self worth? Is now worthy of myself. I have discovered a new balanced energy to recreate me.

UC: It sounds like you use your Consciousness Intuition on a daily basis. Is it in phases, or all at once?

Sely: I don't need much to sense when the Virus Energy is around; the smell is profound.

UC: You have taken your learning, way past the energy conversion, good for you. This is an example of a complete follow through. You know, with Consciousness energy, you can talk to the dead, and they will talk back. You just need to be in the right dimension. It's an ability that comes from the energy conversion.

THOM

UC: Are you connected to your emotions Thom? Are you familiar with each one? There are many different emotions which create different actions and reactions. Are you leading your emotions, or are they leading you? Do you understand them? Do they speak your language, or the language of the Virus?

Can you trust them? Have you started to question them? How are you going to convert them, if you don't know them? They are like people you meet, get to know them.

How many different ways can you say, the human brain is infected by a Virus?

Thom: Crazy, Unstable, flipped your lid. Loony, and batty. Out of your mind, and mentally challenged.

Psychotic, or, the short version, psycho. And the favorite, the mentally ill. Any more, I am sure I missed some.

Hello my name is Thom, from wonderful Ireland. Amazing, that's a lot of labels just to say you are infected by the Virus Energy. That question had my head spinning.

UC: Where are you headed, do you know? Do you have a direction? Are you aware of the confusion between, humans, and their words? What are you teaching, only words? Has humanity's education run out of meanings? You need meanings to evolve in this evolution, or it won't develop you. As an energy form, it needs to recreate and transform you. It will energize you. Your involvement in the energy movement, is why you are making these improvement. Now you are connected with resources.

As long as you don't treat this Virus Energy Cell in your body as a disease, your physical health will keep declining, and you will not be able to convert it. How are you going to change it? When you can barely change your clothes?

Thom: No one feels anymore. Our emotions are asleep. Our brains have little energy to function, and our language, needs a new language. I had this feeling about people since I became old enough to notice violence, hatred, and war. I tried to find an excuse for our behaviors. Not knowing, wasn't good enough for me. Neither was excepting societies explanation for it. All around me, people are living in fear of each other. I am sure this was not the creators intention. What is broken in us? Why were we so angry, hostile and violent?

I sat around with friends for hours discussing the question of, what's wrong with us as a humanity? Something had to be. I believed, it was our energy that's infected? I didn't realize how many others out there, were asking the same questions. Gathering in groups helped me to realize, unity was the key to discovery.

We were all in agreement, the Energy Conversion of the Virus Energy Cell had to happen. Groups reached out to other groups. Contacts were being made. The focus? The support of the energy movement by the Young Generation, this knowledge lead us to the Evolution Revolution. We have discussed the knowledge, learned it, absorbed it, and now, we are using the Consciousness Energy we have come to know. This is how we all learned from each other. At one point, we were all looking for answers. I can say we were lost, confused, without a goal or direction. We lost faith in our leadership's, and our education.

Our examples, were greed, control, fear, and intimidation. Having become realized of the actual infection we were faced with, we had to do something. The Universal Consciousness Energy reality, made sense to us. Many of us anyway. We could relate with the thought, it was an energy infection causing our destruction, and the fact we don't have to listen to it. History has lost its hold on the young generation. Which allowed many of us to look for answers elsewhere. I had been looking for an awareness of an energy greater than myself, but just as equal. I found this book to be that.

UC: It's humanity's NEW DIRECTION. Once you get there, you will understand why? This is it for humankind. Nothing left to say. If these words do not help to awaken you, your brains well stay asleep. We understand this process is not too easy to achieve. The more humans convert their Virus Energy, the more it will decrease. Each conversion, creates a decrease in the Virus actions. It gets weaker. Loses more power. It becomes less effective. Where did you look, for your Virus Energy?

Thom: Inside me, is where I went looking. This was my first development after reading the Evolution Revolution. I first noticed the Virus, when I tried to confront my emotions, they turned on me. One by one, they lead me to my brain. Who not so politely informed me, it had no clue of who I was.

UC: How did you handle the pain? This must have caused you much confusion? How did you overcome it?

Thom: By looking, and finding awareness, which gave me more confidence. I had friends who supported me through it, like many of the already awakened were doing. Supporting others with their conversion. Some are emotionally stronger than others. With each realization, I grew more alert and focused. My confusion became less and less.

UC: Do you remember how you lost your awareness? Was it taken, or did you let it go?

Thom: I believe it was taken while I was unconscious. Somehow, I didn't notice. I was unaware I had an awareness.

UC: Why were you unconscious? Did you lose your balance? Was it memory loss? Humanity's brain has been having problems.

Thom: Balance, memory loss, some kind of disease, was it the actual Virus Cell, who knew. I kept looking for my balance, but I couldn't seem to find it, until now.

UC: Who do you think took your balance, manipulation, was it retribution, or lack of motivation?

Thom: My self doubt. But Consciousness Energy was very gracious, with its Universal Knowledge of the ages. I gave me these pages.

UC: What was the reason you went from self doubt to finding your awareness?

Thom: THE VIRUS was, need I say more? So you can understand how excited I was, to get the knowledge of the Consciousness Energy. It became the leader of the energy movement. The power to integrate Consciousness Energy, with Physical Energy. I have learned enough about the Virus Cell, to figure out ways to convert it, before it infects me. I thought I could out smart it. How aware can it be? This is the experience I had with my self Conversion.

I had the idea of how to confront the energy infection within my emotions, by using my emotions to convert the Virus Energy, which is infecting my brain. The Virus Energy instigates my emotions to go against me. So, I began my plan, by making a deal with the Virus Cell in my brain. The deal was, I would let it have full control of my emotions, if it left my brain completely. The V Cell agreed. Once it left, I immediately filled my brain with the balanced knowledge of Consciousness Energy. Now, It was cut off from my brain completely.

It began to instigate my emotions to attack me. To Confuse me, but I was aware of its intention? I needed to get my emotions out of hiding, so I can deal with them. I wanted them to resist the Virus's effect. Through lots of emotional conflict, I convinced my emotions to start questioning the Virus Cell. It became confused, and turned on itself. Self Conversion, by Reflection. It worked. I know they say don't make a deal with the Devil, but I beat the Devil at its own game.

UC: How has this affected your life? Are you on the move using your new energy?

Thom: As far as effecting my life, I escaped from seclusion. I learned a new form of communication. The power of Conscious intuition, the ability to make a conscious decision, and becoming a part of the World Evolution Revolution Convergence.

UC: This was certainly one way to convert the Energy Infection. It was a courages selection, with a focused intention, especially the group invention. A good way for energy conversion. The more of it shows, the more Consciousness Energy grows. When knowledge comes, don't refuse. Even if you think it's a ruse. Investigate, question, is this the life you have chosen?

ATO

UC: Well Ato, have you seen your past? How about your future? Do you live by nature, or the computer? Are you a Conscious human being? How do you know?

Ato: Hi, my name is Ato, I live in Germany. I work for the airlines. I am working on, developing the awareness of Consciousness. I was on vacation when I received this book, The Evolution Revolution.

Good thing I had time to read some of it, because my vacation was nearing its end. As I was packing my bags, I had this feeling I would be changing the direction of my life.

At home, I began to read it from the start again, this time word for word, slowly. I felt there was something I needed to do. What it was? I had no clue, but I just knew. During this time, I had been hearing talk about the Energy Movement. I knew then, I would be involved in it some way. I had the drive to find out what this way was. I had to find my own infection, and convert it. I had to develop my Consciousness Energy, to the point of awakening my Intuition. And, I had to start with my Emotions. My energy conversion taught me more about myself than I ever knew.

The more I have been able to develop, the stronger the pull towards discovery. This Consciousness Energy explained history, and the present. What was, and what wasn't. The Unknown, finally revealed. Humanity's chance to finally heal. Achieving Emotional Balance, by way of Energy Conversion is difficult. Emotions always are, they tend to leave a scar. When you realize your emotions are actually resisting you, that's your first step toward conversion. It means taking back control of my emotions from the Virus Energy Cell. My emotion's must unravel, or the Virus Energy goes with me everywhere I travel.

While I was working on developing my Consciousness, I experienced an event which would be considered on the side of the unknown. I will do my best to describe it. I had no idea I was walking into an uncharted energy movement. This was my calling. I knew it. Everything about it felt right. Intuition strike again. Here I am, with this out of this world plan, and I had no idea which direction to go.

Ato: Until the weirdness started. I had been reading all day. I was tired so I went to bed. That night, I was awakened to a bright light shining in my eyes. I live alone, so who could it be? I thought it might be a burglar. But then, the whole room lit up, no one was there, the lights were not on. I must still be sleeping. Until I heard a voice in the room saying, *"Write this down, write this down."* It felt like I was pulled out of bed. Even in a daze, and barely able to see from the light, I wrote down what I heard.

It was a list of names I have never heard of, and the words, *"Expect Them."* I had no fear at all. The light dimmed until it was gone. I became excited over the idea, this Consciousness Energy may actually be working. So what was this list? Expect them. What did it mean? Am I suppose to know? Why the cryptic message? Simply to alert me, so I don't miss it? Why did I get this message? It drove me nuts. I decided to just sit with it, and see what else comes through. The mystery began to unfold.

Ato: Two months later, I had almost forgot it happened. I was watching the news, keeping up with the energy movements actions. I must have fallen asleep. When I woke up, I saw the words, *"they are coming,"* written on my ceiling. I thought of the note with the names and expect them on it from before. Now it says *"they are coming."* Well, where are they?

It seemed so real, and why they? Is it a group? As time went by, I kept waiting. Nobody showed, until one day. A really bizarre thing happened, it snowed, in the middle of summer. Freaky, right? Best day of my life. I opened the door to feel the snow, in the heat, and there they were, all seven. We all just stood there, frozen in time. All eyes wide open, mouths dropped.

I acted as though I expected them, because I did. But now, it's real. There is a huge difference. After we met, we gathered, and shared our stories. There were so many things to talk about. As a group, we focused on the Virus Cell conversion. We are finding this awareness to be, empowering. Which is why we decided to become a Universal Consciousness collective. Focusing our energy frequency on one point, the Virus Energy Cell conversion.

UC: You are from different countries, how do you manage a group?

Ato: Most of the group lives in Germany, Including myself, we are eight, six are here, and two are on video conferencing. Like many countries with a history of wars. The younger adults here, have inherited the energy of our history.

We need to get answers. We are being given the opportunity to save our future. We say it's not too late. We need to stop swallowing everything they put in front of us. Most of it is ridicules anyway.

We see this happening, and now we can do something about it.

REVE

Hello, I am one of the video members in Ato's group. I just had to jump in. Forgive me. As a group, we have shared our actions, and reactions. Our inner most thoughts, and hidden true feelings. We went into every emotion where the Virus Energy was infecting. As we worked together, each person took turns in the middle of the group. The group process kept the Virus surrounded. It couldn't infect us.

My name is Reve, I live in Israel. I live in the land of the old, controlled by the old, at war over an old belief, that only the old believes in.

Reve: Those were their days, today is our day. The old have little regards to how they are effecting the young. We want to move on. We Are The Young Generation. The Young Generation in other countries are taking up leadership roles. What is wrong with the leaders of the world. *"You have failed the people, and failed the planet earth."*

You are taking life, to appease your Gods, Greed, and Control. You're leaving your destruction for us to fix. As one of the young, we want new ideas, new laws, new policies. Most of all, we want a new energy that creates unity. Fear runs deep, it's infecting everyone, in many countries. Needless mass shootings are escalating. We, the Young Generation, are being forced to carry the burden of the old, who care so little for the lives of the young. Fight for your country is the biggest lie. It's more about, fight to keep us in power.

Thanks to Iman's vision, we now have the World Association Toward Energy Re-creation. Whose goal is the education of humanity about the Universal Consciousness, and the Virus Energy Cell. It's gone global. But so is the Virus Energy. We feel we are in training for the conversion of our lives. Which is the world conversion of the Virus Energy.

Today, we are experiencing numerous protests. Conflicts all over the world. The Virus Energy has shown its face. Many World Leaders, are being disgraced and forced out of their place. Other leaders, are being questioned about their actions. Trysten recently shared, there has been rumors of government retaliation for any group defying religion's stand on God. That's their motto, *"we stand on God."*

Why is it that religion didn't take this kind of stand, over the actions of war, the starving poor, or with domestic abuse? How does religion decide what to stand on? Why do they get to pick what causes they will support. They work for God supposedly, I don't believe God discriminates. I also don't believe a God, would choose one people over the other. It's like picking one child, and throwing the other away. How cruel is that?

I am a Universal Energy Being. To think otherwise is demeaning. I have learned people use the word God to their advantage. Such as politicians. They complete their speech with, *"God bless you."* So, now, you can trust them? Where before, you had more suspicion. What kind of logic is this, in today's society. Two plus two, equals three? According to our laws, anyone can be a minister of God. Self appointed religious leaders pop up everywhere. It only takes a paper to vouch for you.

UC: Indeed it is, they are showing the true nature of their leadership. Religion uses the THREAT of punishment by God, the government uses THREATS of punishment by prison. The people, just get THREATENED as usual. Bit by bit, Human's are in debt. Sounds like humans are all set. Do you agree?

Reve: I believe humans have lost the ability to know, when enough is enough. Boundaries, and limits do not apply to all. The laws around the world do not apply to all. They are different from agency to agency. It's the same law, but changed to meet the expectations of its employee's. Consistency, is not a human ability. It's one of humanity's disabilities.

UC: It doesn't have to be. Don't you see, humans would rather believe in quantity than quality. It brings in more money. Little do they know, the more there is, the less you have. MORE can't stop itself, it always wants more. Which means less for you, because you're too busy chasing more. Well, you're running out of more. It's become less. Now you operate on the hypothesis, since you have less, you must get more. Right back where you started. It's a cycle, more or less. Consciousness Energy is unlimited, forever existing. There is no less, or more. Only development of Consciousness Energy.

NILEND

UC: Hello, we can see you are in deep thought, concentrating. Does it hurt? Do you always think this hard? Must be a serious issue. Are you thinking about your role in the energy movement?

Nilend: The Universal Consciousness Energy Event. Which we are now in. This is as serious as it gets. Part of my conversion, was trying to justify humanity's idea of life, the one I was taught. Everything we have ever built, been taught, believed, and live by, has a limit. Every question asked, has a limited answer. Limited brains, can only create limits. It is humanity it inhabits. For this reason, The conversion of the Virus Energy Cell is Imminent.

Hello, my name is Nilend, I am from the Sudan. At the age of ten, I was giving the name rebel by my friends. I was always trouble. But by age twenty seven, I joined the Young Generation Energy Movement. I started out my life as a delinquent, no limits, no boundaries, no supervision.

One day, my Mother went out to get my Father a birthday present, and came back. A few minutes later, he walks in, *"why is the engine of the car warm?"* He demanded an instant response. Trying to think of something quick, she hesitated. She didn't want to ruin his surprise. She said, *"I was at the store."* He accused her of lying to him, then he slapped her, and told her, that's for making me think you were lying.

I was sitting next to her, as she sat on the dinner table, ready to eat dinner. She made his favorite food. We were laughing about something she said. As he walks up, sits down on the table. Next thing I see, is a gun coming out of his sleeve into his hand, and boom. The flash blinded me, the smell choked me. When the smoke cleared, there she was, dead on the floor. The blast pushed her backwards in her chair.

He looked at me as I was in tears, he said, don't cry for her, she was a cheater. I went into her room, grabbed the present, and threw it as hard as I could at his face. Then, I screamed, she isn't a cheater! She was out getting your birthday present. She didn't want to spoil your surprise. I looked at him, and said, you killed the one person who ever loved me. I ran out, never looked back. A week later, I found out from a friend, he was found dead. He was holding the present in one hand, and the gun in the other. He ended his own life. He ended his life from guilt. I was lost. My life changed that day… So did I.

I went from school to school, they couldn't tame me. The police tried to shame me. But only prison taught me. I learned many things about people there, their actions, reactions, thoughts, feelings, and reasons. I grew up fast. I made it out at last. Age seventeen, and nowhere to go. That's when I made a decision to become a searcher of the truth to life. I had to learn on my own terms, my own time. There had to be a life better than the one I had.

It just couldn't be, as I grew up. I was determined to find out. I spent about eight years searching for answers. Everywhere I looked, I found only limitations. Until finally, I became a school supervisor. I wanted to teach kids. (I know, I couldn't believe it either.) I am very proud I accomplished such a feat.

Then, my attention shifted towards the Evolution Revolution. Presently, I am involved with the movement. I work at a high school. This age is very vocal. After realizing I had more to learn, I made the choice to go towards spiritual development. I needed to know more about the unknown. I needed something to move me towards the movement.

Nilend: I did it all, the new age, spiritual awakening. I followed old philosophies, and ones in the making. I read everything spiritual. I meditated, did yoga, went to channelers. I had readings, and explored tarot cards. I went to India. Sat in a cave with an old man, who chanted for six months. It's the only way I can sleep now.

That's how it went for years. I read everything about psychics, and fortune tellers. I absorbed like a sponge. As I looked back, I began to see repetition in our education. I felt incomplete. There had to be knowledge somewhere, which can answer what the others couldn't. I had learned so little from our education. It felt extremely limited. I began to see humanity's education, was keeping me uneducated.

I was starving for new knowledge. When I got the book, I started to read it. I found so many answers without having to feed it. I learned how to build my self esteem, and awareness. All this time, I had been looking for the truth outside of myself. I realized, it was within me the whole time. It was traveling with me, all those years I was looking for it. I never thought, to look inside of myself for the truth. They do say it starts with you. Now, what I give, I give from within.

UC: Wherever you go to find the truth, it's always going to be in your Consciousness. Go ahead, ask your brain. It's been looking for truth as long as you have. This is a reality. Not an impossibility. It's not a dream or a fantasy. It's not magic, it's the Universal Consciousness Energy. It's THE POSSIBILITY.

ARCHEE

Speaking of possibility, I experienced the unbelievable, become believable. I had been working on developing my Consciousness energy, through self conversion. I was expecting some kind of energy feeling, a different sensation. Something I haven't felt before. I wasn't sure. Then one night I had a dream, that became a reality. It showed me the same vision, for five nights. It had a great effect on me.

My name is Archee. I am a race horse trainer professionally. I am here, because I heard what Ato, and Reve were sharing, so I wanted to share. I am the second one in Ato's group, using video conferencing. I live in Australia.

I was on vacation, visiting my sister in Hamburg. My sister's husband is in the army, and was called away. They just had a newborn, only two weeks old. I couldn't leave her alone at a time like this, so my one week visit turned into a two months stay. It was here, in her home, where I began having the dreams. It was a dream which kept showing me a vision of an address, repeatedly. It became stuck to my brain. I saw it everyday, asleep, and awake.

On the fifth day of having the same dream, I began to get this feeling that I lost something. I had to go out and find it. I had no idea where I was going, or what I was looking for, but I went out there with determination. As I was walking, I felt an urge leading my direction. Turn here, turn there. I followed it, it lead me to the exact address which I saw in the dream.

I found myself standing and looking at the address of the home, with seven others. We all walked up at the same time. We were standing there, staring at each other with a bewildered look. Our eyes wide open as they stared at me with confusion. Talk about confusing, it was summer, and it was snowing. Unheard off. I wondered if they all had the same dream?

Archee: Ato came out. We all were invited inside. I had the feeling he was expecting us. After introductions, no real explanation, he acknowledged the Consciousness Energy frequency connection with each of us. Stating, that each frequency was precoded with an energy that brought us together. He went on to say, you are here to participate in the world's Evolution Revolution. I don't know your role in all this, but someone found me, to find you, to complete the conversion of your Conscious Energy vibration.

Archee: We are here to use the energy of this book on ourselves first. I realize that we all started our conversion alone. But, this is the new group approach, to make absolutely sure that we have all become Virus free. We are going to heal every bit of the Virus within us. We need to become conscious of the Virus Cell Energy and remove it. Our goal is to convert our fears. Our greed, anger, envy, and all the energies that are related to the Virus Energy Cell. It will start emerging, when we start purging.

We are together to support each other. The idea was, to put one person in the middle of a circle, keeping the infection from escaping, and taking the body with it. The benefits to group development is, you can't lie to yourself. The Virus can't trick you.

The others are watching, directing, and protecting. There is a greater chance of success with group support. It brings us that much closer to the Evolution Revolution. Oh, and I found out, they all had the same dream I had, except Ato.

UC: Excellent revelation. You were Conscious, and paid attention. You are an example of the young generation energy movement. Along with your group of course.

NATI

I am Nati, from Spain. I study cellular regeneration for cancer research. My studies here are very intense. I never thought I had the knowledge to be here, until I took a test in college that I scored very high on. I was asked to write a paper, about my thoughts on the subject of emotional energy, and its effects on our anatomy? I am interested in the science of Tissue Replacement. I have read numerous books on the subject. I had not thought of looking at tissue as energy, until I discovered The Consciousness Energy knowledge. It integrates physical energy, with a higher frequency speed of energy.

My knowledge about emotions, was less than my knowledge about energy. I can't remember what I wrote. Months later, I received a letter, there it was, congratulations! Dear applicant, Based on the paper you wrote, you have been selected as the winner of a four year scholarship, at the Institute of Cancer Research.

I will never forget it. I packed my stuff, and off I went. I was a nervous wreck. I had no idea what they expected from me. I was introduced to my lead professor, by way of a buzzer. He informed me, this was the way he would call me, when he needed me. *"Go act busy."* I thought it was rude. I guess he doesn't want to be bothered by me. That's what I had thought, until the day I asked him, why my paper? It was just a paper of my thoughts, I wrote about what I know. Consciousness Energy, and how it affects our anatomy. I know, it was suppose to be Emotions. But as I said, I know more about energy.

He replied, *"One: You were aware it was about emotions, yet, you wrote about this Consciousness Energy. As surprised as they were, You introduced an idea they hadn't considered. The board was puzzled by your thoughts, but excited to find out what you know, and how you came to know it. Your perspective on Energy Consciousness, must of connected with the research they are presently conducting."*

Yes, but this is something I was taught from a book.

He said, *"Two: There were seven hundred applicants, many with degrees, with good papers. However, not one of them wrote about energy beyond physical mass. You wrote about the difference between the word brain, and the word Consciousness."*

Nati: *"You stated, there is a Consciousness Energy frequency, which exists as physical energy, and as this energy, it self-creates into all of Creation. Thus, it is the Creator of all creation. This energy of Consciousness, runs the brain. This energy is intelligent, self developing, and self duplicating. It can be directed, projected, and recreated. I have your paper right here, it's what you said. Should I keep going"*

"This concept has made you more of a test subject than a student. You don't realize what you know, obviously. There has been many tests, theories, experiments done around cancer research. Particularly, around what you called, the Virus Energy Cell. This got their attention as a possible cause for the cancer

disease. You will be asked to meet the scientists, researchers, and others, to discuss what you know about this Universal Consciousness Energy. Meanwhile, you will be working with me in the field of cellular regeneration."

I was so excited, and nervous all at once. There is a reason for everything. It's like a dream, being here. I didn't even graduate from college, look where I am. In the middle of a world Evolution Revolution, and learning about cellular regeneration. I think I am doing what I am suppose to do, to support the Young Generation.

UC: What was your childhood like? Were your parents nice, or mean? Did they teach you some of what you know? Were they doctors? Science Researchers?

Nati: They were scientists. They had their own culture and traditions. I must have absorbed more than I thought when I listened to them. My continued curiosity, is what put me on this path.

UC: Did your curiosity lead you, to the Evolution Revolution knowledge?

Nati: Yes it did. But, I am not sure if I would have stayed on this path, if not for my parent's influence. I struggled with my own beliefs around this subject.

UC: Are you sure your beliefs are your own? There are beliefs which are absorbed from others unconsciously, even if heard only once. Check your beliefs, compared to your parents. Make sure they are your own.

Nati: Growing up I had no beliefs of my own, I hadn't made them yet. But apparently, I had many I didn't know about. This was an exciting realization. Now I can complete my conversion. I learned a lot of things being unconscious. Particularly how to stay unconscious. Growing up was rough. I didn't grow up with toys. I grew up with boys, so was put into an all girls school. I was forced to believe in education I couldn't understand.

My constant questioning gave me no satisfaction. I found no one knew the answers. They didn't even know the questions. I was facing doubt, incomplete answers, miracles, and coincidence. Humanity, made up fiction, to explain, our own made up fiction. I refused to play societies games, to be a part of their lies. I stepped out of the norm. When you are aware, there is a waterfall at the end of the river, do you get in the boat? I saw the waterfall from far away. I chose to walk towards the Consciousness Energy direction. It's become my life's work.

ASHER

UC: Are you a developing energy? How far have you developed Asher? Do you have awareness of your Consciousness. The energy which keeps you conscious, creates Energy Development. But how will you know? There is nothing to compare to. This knowledge can give you a Consciousness Energy, compared to Unconscious Physical Energy.

Asher: Hello, I am Asher. I consider myself a nomad. Kind of fits me, because I don't get mad. Haha. Sorry, not funny. Seriously, I would like to say, I have been able to find a way to prepare for the Evolution Revolution. I have traveled to lots of strange places with strange traditions. I met many different kinds of people on the road. I ask questions upon meeting them. Where can I find enlightenment? Where is the truth? Does anyone know? Everyone I spoke with had their own opinion, based on their religion and beliefs.

UC: Did you meet anyone who had some knowledge, about what you were asking? What exactly were you asking, personal questions?

Asher: No, development questions. My thoughts are focused on Conscious actions, the Virus is focused on the Unconscious. I don't need to list of what thoughts those are, they are well known. We use them everyday.

UC: How far have you gone on your Energy Conversion? Are you complete, or are you still working?

Asher: I believe, part of my traveling actually helped me to convert, a large percent of my Virus energy. The places I went, the people I met, It's way better than the Internet. I am actually interacting with people to learn, not looking them up on the phone.

UC: Are you paving your own path, or using another's? What answers are you looking for? More about consciousness energy?

Asher: I am actually working on, the knowledge of supernatural abilities. I had heard about people who can read thoughts, and move objects with their energy, things like that. Consciousness energy is meant to be used to discover. I am still developing, so I search for knowledge of development. Everything I learn I share, knowledge is vital to our existence. The more I learn, the more it helps me, and others. I don't travel alone, I have my Consciousness energy with me.

Where ever I go, I find jobs. I go through towns, creating smiles from frowns. There were many people who were eager to talk with me. Especially the elderly. They had stories that needed to be told. Some, are still practicing what they learned; and those were the ones I wanted to meet. One such person was a l lady, who apparently practices reading thoughts. It's what the advertisement said. I was excited. I had to visit her. So off I go, to meet this lady with these special powers.

I needed to find out how she uses the Consciousness Energy, to read thoughts? So, this is what happened. I thought maybe, she would already know why I was visiting her? There we were, introducing ourselves, she invited me in, and I asked, do you know the purpose of my visit?

Mind Reader: To learn about the power of Conscious Energy.

Asher: My ears perked up. I asked her how she knew? No one knew. Was this an energy thought reading, or energy intuition, and is there a difference?

Mind Reader: The brain is a marvel, it can do things we don't understand, or need to. Some call it a gift.

Asher: I responded with a Huh. It can't be? It suddenly dawned on me, she said brain, not Consciousness Energy. I became annoyed. I asked, did you say brain?

Mind Reader: Yes, of course, what else? It's brain intuition. It's what I learned from my parents, they had the gift, and passed it on to me. Look it up, intuition. If you don't like what you hear, there is another lady down the street, who can tell you your future.

I became somewhat defensive. I replied, I know what intuition means, it's a feeling of awareness you get, for any reason. It's one of the senses in our brain, which is operated by the Consciousness Energy, through the brain. Intuition is a Conscious Energy, which exists in our body. Then, I took her advice, and went to visit the fortune teller.

She claimed, she can read my future. She said, *"I have the gift of sight."* My first thought was, don't most of us? I laugh at my own jokes, sorry. So I asked her, how did you get this gift? Where did it come from?

Fortune Teller: It's a gift, you don't question it. It's given to you.

Asher: OK, can you read my future? I have been waiting a long time to see this happen. Are you using Consciousness Energy to read my thoughts?

Fortune Teller: Consciousness what? What is it, a new age thing? Sit, relax, and listen.

Asher: She went into seeing mode. Her eyes, and mouth wide open. A few minutes later, She said.

Fortune Teller: I am having trouble connecting with your brain. I am sorry, I can't see your future, your brain is closed off.

Asher: I became annoyed at her rudeness. I said, what? If you can't see my future, then how can you see that my brain is closed off? Can you see why? Can't you open it? Can anyone learn to do what you do?

Fortune Teller: They have to have the gift. It's God given. I am not so sure you have the ability. Not everyone can get it. It's a special gift which some people get. You don't have the knowledge to understand the brain, and its powers.

Asher: I knew it. Just another disappointment. I had a reaction. I replied, oh really, why you? What's so special about you to get this gift?

Fortune Teller: All I know is, it came as a gift, I didn't ask for it.

Asher: So you say. Thanks for your time. What a joke, she insulted me twice. Talk about closed off. I am frustrated, life is limited. I am walking around town feeling unsatisfied. When I ran into a sign which read, Psychics, second floor. I opened the door, and climbed the steps. I told myself, this is the last one, that's it. In the room, were two people, a man and a woman. As they introduced themselves, the man says, we are a husband and wife team. What one misses, the other one catches. They started laughing at their motto. Upon meeting, they both said something at the same time. She got so excited about it. She asked me, *"would you like a drink?"* He jumped up, and yelled, *"darn! I was just about to ask him that."*

Asher: I played along, I had to, I had to know. So, you almost said it at the same time. That's amazing. Does it happen often? Do you know how you became this way? What is she going to say now, I asked? No response. Are you able to keep any secrets from her?

Psychic: No, she would know. We are psychic, we can read each other's thoughts.

Asher: I couldn't believe these people, claiming to have gifts they don't have, just to feel special. I feel special everyday I am alive, as everyone should. I inquisitively asked, how do you read each other's thoughts? Do you know how it works? Is it something others can learn?

Psychic: Well, it's a special gift. Some people just get it. You don't learn it. You just get it, that's all. We go to the house of prayer every week, and volunteer often. We help the needy, and give to the poor.

Asher: I wanted to fall on the floor with laughter, they all have these unexplainable gifts, but, they can't explain what they are. Instead, I said, oooooh, a special gift, that sounds familiar. Do you know where it came from? Was it from God? If you can read thoughts, why didn't you tell me the reason I came to see you? It seems you know God well. Do you understand your gift?

Psychic: That would be like questioning the gift. Why would we do that? It's like giving the gift back. Manners say, you just except it. You don't question it.

Asher: So, you don't know much about it, except you have it. Is this correct? What am I thinking now, I asked?

Psychic: I am not ready, it takes time to get into the right frame.

Asher: as I was getting ready to ask another question, she distracts me by adding something about another person who has the gift.

Psychic: Don't leave without seeing Aldo. He lives at the house of prayer, about a mile away. He has the ability to move things.

Asher: I am thinking, should I, shouldn't I? Oh well, I am here, I will go. I hoped this last visit will have something useful. So, off I went. It felt weird, being in a house of prayer again, it's been years. We met. We sat and talked. I had a glass of water on the coffee table, I reached for it, and it moved away. Nice trick, I said. Where is the magnet?

Aldo: No magnet, it's telekinesis, It means moving an object with your brain.

Asher: I deflated like a balloon. I asked him—I had to. How is this possible? Where did you learn to do that?

Aldo: In a temple in Tibet.

Asher: I thought, here it comes, No, don't say it. Darn if he didn't. The next words out of his mouth.

Aldo: It's a special gift which some people get.

Asher: Unbelievable! If these people really had powers, they would be dangerous. Everything humanity can't explain, is transformed by the ego, into a gift, a miracle, a prophecy, a saint to worship. Limits, limits, limits, everywhere I went. I agree the brain is an amazing thing, but it doesn't run by itself.

In all, the most important benefit for me, was realizing, we as a humanity, have no clue about what we say, and do. We are just echoes of each other. The evolution of humankind is something I take seriously. We can't afford not to. To get answers, we must find out on our own. Don't settle for human created meanings. Humans made them up.

UC: An infected brain operates with the use of limits. It can only answer the questions you put in it. Your limits are the limits of your brain. How can you learn, when what you're learning, is a limited source of knowledge? Test it, use it, investigate it, go back to history, compare it, has it changed? If not, change it. Has the knowledge grown or, is it the same old story? What kind of reaction does it create? Does it develop Consciousness Energy? Does it balance humanity? Does it uncover, the Virus Energy Cell?

ARBI

Hello, I am Arbi, from England. Through the years, I have learned to never allow a job to become me. I felt control everywhere I worked. We pay you, we own you, type personality's. I am allergic to control. Manipulation is hard enough to deal with. As I grew, I had felt there was something I was meant to do; it was like an itch. I had to find out what it was. I was never the type to be boxed into a category, Or be the same as everybody. I have my own identity. I refuse to keep assimilating, and conforming. I don't want to be, someone else's personality.

I have a ritual I do each morning, before I get out of bed. I start out my day, by asking myself this question? IS MY BRAIN, MY FRIEND, OR MY ENEMY? Can I trust my brain to tell me the truth, and not mislead me? It hides important information from me. At times, it tells me to do, what I normally wouldn't do. Somehow, I forget I am not suppose to. I question my brain, but it ignores me. When I ask, it won't tell me. If I am not in control of my brain, who is, what is, and why?

It resists anything new. I say it's red, it tells me it's blue. It's very convincing. If it wasn't for the Evolution Revolution knowledge, I would still be mislead by my brain. Because, it wasn't suppose to operate this way on its own. It's gone rouge in my head. Then, I learned how to use the ability of energy conversion. I started a better communication with my brain.

We built a more positive relationship. It opened up to me, about being infected by this Virus Energy, and how difficult it was, not to give in to it. It asked me for help, and I delivered. I went in, and found the infected energy, identified it, and began the immediate conversion of it. My perspective changed in ways I can't explain. It's like a world map opened in front of my eyes. I shook my head, and out came all the flies.

Presently, I am a librarian. I work in the most expensive library I have ever seen. It's a library of rare books. Yes, they still exist. Books are extremely important here. Try walking out with one, when you do, you better run, you're being followed by a gun. You have a better chance stealing the couch. My passion has always been reading, ever since I was a child. I wanted to know everything about everything, and I still do.

Arbi: I had always wanted to teach world history, so I went for my degree. Of course, to teach it, you must be it. The more I learned about it, the less I wanted to be it. I found myself in a dilemma; do I keep pushing lies, acts of human extermination based on greed, the glory of war; the glorifying of those who committed war crimes. How many people have died over control of land?

What's worse is, parents wanted their children to learn these monstrous behaviors. They call it teaching history. Why? What's the point? We teach it, so it won't be repeated. Well…This idea didn't last, we are still repeating it. History, is just one super giant war, and so is the Present it seems. I had to find something else to do for a living that would support humankind's future also. I chose to do something about it. I became a librarian. Now, I had the opportunity to uncover all of histories deceptions, and to separate fact from fiction. I want the world to know, what I have discovered about the deceptions of history. This proved to me how history, is our present foundation. I realized I could never teach world history, even if I wanted to; not this history.

Presently, the real brave, the real heroes, are the young generation. They are committed to the Evolution Revolution of humankind. They face the Virus Cell destruction everyday. They are growing, by knowing. This is creating a new kind of energy. One, which people cannot ignore. I for one, will not. I now have Consciousness. This is my new curious. It provides a Conscious state of being. A Consciousness which helped me remember, once I was an energy being, before I became a human being.

UC: You are reflecting what you have become. Your choices show a person, who is becoming an Energy Being again. As one of the young generation, you made great progress in your own development. We also know, that you are teaching Consciousness Energy Behaviors to many of the young. What a wonderful example of an energy conversion. You are teaching the NEW LEADERS OF THE WORLD. Your role in the movement, is essential to the development of newly Conscious Human Beings.

LIN

Hi, my name is Lin. I am a Master Chef, I teach Culinary Arts in Hong Kong. Basically, I teach food. I am aware of how Consciousness Energy is constantly moving. I want to know how, I can use this energy to move me. Awareness, has become the new must have, and I must have it. In this day and age, I need it. We all need it.

Thanks to the world energy movement, Consciousness energy is awakening. There are people coming together for a meeting of the human beings. The Virus Energy Cell is almost converted to balance. The unconscious state of humanity, is becoming Conscious.

Lin: Finally, all these years of not knowing about it. If the Virus was left alone, I can't imagine life continuing on. This is the Evolution Revolution. No one is excluded. It's the reason it's succeeding. As we are connected by Consciousness Energy, so are we connected to unconscious energy. The re-balancing of humanity's physical energy is at the point of completion. A question still remains, where are the Energy Beings from the other universe? This is their time. The world awakening needs to happen soon. Resistance, is the lowest it's ever been. It's time for them to come in. We are on the verge of a new energy re-creation.

UC: Your question about moving, was a moving question. Hmm, how do you want to move, by walking, running, or floating in the air, from chair to chair? There are many ways you can move. Using your Consciousness Energy is another way. It depends on your state of Consciousness.

Lin: I am here to learn from all forms of knowledge. Even knowledge, that thinks it has nothing to teach. I am a book with empty pages, I need to be filled with these words. I shall absorb them, until each word becomes me.

UC: So then, you want to grow on Conscious Knowledge, correct? What you just said above, shows how much you have already grown. Your development is going well, and you are working on energy conversion in the movement. Have you taken stock of your actions lately? Your Consciousness drives you now, it moves you when you use it. How you use it, is dependent on where your development is. Application, needs to be coming from conscious information. The more conscious you become, the more you will know how to use it.

Lin: One of my best realizations, was when I began to see food as energy. I may sound crazy, but I am actually developing an energy connection with food. I see it as energy, I talk to it, acknowledge its purpose, I shape it, cook it, and eat it as energy. All creation is Consciousness Energy. I actually got the idea from Tinvin. If she can talk to plants, I can talk to food. I can feel the difference. My food is alive energy.

From reading the evolution revolution book, I discovered the way to knowledge, was through the question. I began to listen to my own questions, and answers. I was stunned when I heard the words coming from my mouth. Listening to what you say, is vital for Consciousness development. At least, if no one is listening to you, you are.

I also learned, the way the question is presented, is the way it is perceived. From this knowledge, I learned to stay connected to the conversation. My question needs to lead to another question, not an answer. I learned how every question needs to end with a beginning, not an ending. I put this to practice, and it works. This is how I became aware of this new energy re-creation of the Universal Consciousness.

The world was buzzing with talk about, how this Evolution Revolution will convert the whole, of the Virus Energy Cell. I became involved in my own personal work, learning how to convert the Virus Energy. I read the whole book, and decided, the knowledge in this book, was a self reflection in so many ways. It's also the energy of motivation, for the creation of energy movement, and I was going to be a part of that.

The Virus Cell is an unconscious Energy. From what I understand, its goal is to get back its whole. Which happens to be the Universal Consciousness. The actions of the Virus Energy seem to be about creating attention to itself, then to go hide. So, the more lives this Energy awakens, the smaller the Virus gets. The Virus Energy Cell is unbalanced, proven by its actions. Consciousness Energy is balanced, proven by *its* actions.

As I worked on my own energy re-creation, I became aware of a reality, which supposedly, doesn't exist. Yet, here it is, in front of my face. I can connect with the concept of energy. It's self explainable. Being Virus free feels like waking up from a nightmare. I went from a singular perspective, to a world wide view. Now, what do I do? How can I ignore what's in front of me. I must tell others.

CAT

Hello, my name is Cate. I live in Paris. I go by Cat. I have a question. It's about the Evolution Revolution book.

UC: What's the question?

Cat: It's when you put the two words together which interests me. Does a revolution lead to an evolution?

UC: This is an Energy Evolution, through an Energy Revolution. Avoiding physical confrontations.

Cat: I have a realization to share thanks to the knowledge of Consciousness. This one realization, changed my life. I am a news reporter, I thought I knew words. I thought I knew writing. Then I read the Evolution Revolution book. The connections these words created, are connections to your inner being. This is not just writing, it's not just to read, it's a Consciousness Energy, waiting to be freed. It felt like the Virus Energy was being drained from me with each chapter I read. It was one realization after another. I worked hard on my conversion. Once I was clear of the Virus, I noticed I was beginning to question the words of others. With each let down, I began to trust words less. People Rarely, follow through with what they say. So, I started listening to the words I said. I found, as a reporter, I speak without thought. Reading this knowledge helped me to realize, I wasn't a REPORTER, I was a REPEATER. This was a blow to my ego, I was stunned.

All the schooling, just to end up a repeater. Why was I not aware of this. There is nothing fun about facing the truth. I became more isolated. I began to argue with myself, each time I sat to do a report, I was having a conflict with what I was saying. I heard myself repeat exactly what was on the paper. The more I talked the more I heard, repeater, repeater. I started panicking. The reality of it became more than I can handle?

I began leaving notes with the word repeater on them everywhere in my home. Realizing I was just a repeat, put me in depression for a while. I had a decision to make. Do I only report part truths, to protect the TV station, and some country's glory? Do I report only part of a story, which is reporting part of the facts? I couldn't do that.

One sunny day, I am in my office arguing with myself. There is more to life than repeating what others say. It's not working for me anymore. My thoughts went into complete shutdown mode. I had a nervous breakdown; got up, saw my boss, I shouted, I quit! I couldn't believe what I had done.

Cat: How about that, I made a decision for myself, no repetition there. Realizing your purpose in life is outstanding. Being given the opportunity to act on it, best thing to ever happen to me. I explored the Consciousness Energy, in every page of this book. In every meaning. I felt the energy of every feeling. I have learned new behaviors, I now can get my brain motivated. My intuition is conscious.

Cat: The conversion of my energy has empowered me. I feel mentally strong, I am more aware now, than I have ever been. I am making plans to move closer to W.A.T.E.R. the World Association Toward Energy Re-creation. I want to be more involved, hands on. This awareness inspired me to start writing again, to put my feelings on paper. Writing used to be my therapy. I want to learn this writing ability.

UC: This is quite a realization you had. One realization changed your life. That's very powerful information to make so much difference. What was it? What affected you so much, to make you quit your job. Was it this realization only?

Cat: I have had many realizations in my life. Many of them, came and went without much notice. This realization, had me feeling like I was going in the wrong direction. A wake up call is how I saw it. I heard it, it was a loud scream in my brain which said, *"what are you doing?" "You are only repeating what others tell you."* I recognized what this sentence meant, from a part in the book. I can't handle the thought of living my life, through the thoughts and view of others. I am me. I have my own identity, and this knowledge brought it all back to me. I want to be, who I am meant to be. A Consciousness Being of Energy.

UC: Exactly. Your awareness and actions, have converted the Virus Energy in your brain, to become balanced. It can't interfere in your choices any longer.

ERVIN

My name is Ervin. I live in Sweden. My work keeps me traveling to different countries. Rich ones, and poor ones. Most countries have the same beliefs. The interpretation of those beliefs, is what's different. It comes back to individual perception. I had always been curious about how the Virus Energy Cell, makes people become obedient to its commands? How does it affect our physical energy, to keep us from taking a stand. As I travel, my awareness is constantly feeling for the Virus Energy in people. It protects me.

The Virus infection thrives, because people are unaware they are carriers of it. I stay aware of this, because everywhere I travel, I feel for the Virus Energy in everybody. You notice it more when you are looking. In my travels, I have been around the world. I saw beautiful countrysides, and I met very nice people. What I also saw, caused me grief, heartache, and extreme concern. Humanity does not only have a difference in beliefs, they have a different perspective on world responsibility.

UC: Yes we agree, it's each country for themselves. Unfortunately, humanity has serious Problems. The Homeless Issue, is a World Problem. Starving Children, a World Problem. Violence and War, a World Problem. Diseases, Needless Deaths, and Destruction, definitely a World Problem. The worse problem is, people still ask, what's the problem? This is the problem. All of this is a WORLD POPULATION PROBLEM. Humans have known what's wrong for years. The world knows these issues.

Ervin: Most world governments know what's wrong. They are part of the problem. World government's make more money from the wrong, than the right. The truth is, in this dimension, everyone does. Truth seems to change as it travels. When I am traveling, I have to be in a state of focused awareness. Always feeling for the Virus. So I take notice of the media's lies and exaggerations. They seem to change between countries. Sensationalism sells, world wide.

Each morning as I awake, I check myself before I leave the house, I make sure I am ready for anything and anyone. Virus Energy included. I deal with my own reactions, and feelings. Can we put the Universal Consciousness, on a one channel frequency? And shut the rest down? It seems like we are getting too much information from different channels, and it's causing confusion.

The same beliefs, with different perspectives. The media delivers it in different ways, and languages. What starts out as gossip, a mile down the road, it becomes actual news around the world. I became aware how the Virus Energy uses the media to plant stories which are half truths, to entice confusion and hostility. It can start in one country and, change with each one it goes to. I have experienced this effect personally. Here is what I am talking about.

Ervin: I was in the United States for business reasons, as I heard a news report about a government employee who was found dead, with no apparent cause. No one knew why. As I was leaving, the rumors were already starting. *"Undercover agent is killed in front of a government building." "Mysterious death of double agent."* Even though the paper said how he died, people didn't believe it. Stories of cover ups by the government were talked about. I was glad to leave all that.

As I landed in London, I heard the same news report I had heard in the U.S. Only now, the story changed. He was killed to shut him up. Supposedly, he stole secrets for another country. I couldn't believe my ears. People were gossiping about it the next day, here in London? Amazing how quickly the Virus Energy travels.

As I was sitting in a cafe having coffee; I heard, *"did you know, it was a government hit". "Well, I heard he committed suicide."* People were showing concern, and paranoia over the same story. Continuing to sip my coffee, I happened to overhear a couple next to me. Not on purpose mind you. I heard the gentleman say: *"I just don't understand how this news has gone so far off track. All this fuss over a heart attack. Gods sakes, are people so desperate for drama, they have to make it up. Next, they'll be making a movie of it. He was a nobody. The man died of heart attack three days ago, they are still talking about it. I guess people haven't heard. Even the state department reported this fact in this newspaper, here, look".*

As he shoved the paper in her face. What a rude man, I thought. After this realization, I began to question everything, and everyone. My point is…This is my point. One Frequency, One channel, One perspective. Consciousness Energy. No drama, no confusion. It could be one solution for separation. However, with this population, this would be a huge endeavor.

UC: We can see how you're evolving. Recognizing your own progress, is the first step toward the conversion of the Virus Energy Cell. You just explained how the Virus Energy Cell infects. It takes a word, and manipulates it into many meanings, which have no meaning. It's a no Meaning Greeting.

What gave you the idea to look for it in the media? Were you aware, the Virus Energy thrives on attention? When it followed you from place to place, were you conscious enough to notice the Virus Energy, constantly? Due to all the traveling you do, how are you checking yourself for infection? You have witnessed how manipulation of words, can create fear, and paranoia?

Ervin: I think my travels brought out my curiosity and awareness. I actually received this book from a friend of mine. I stayed with he and his family for a few days in India. We had awesome conversations about life, death, and the beyond. It was a very enlightening few days. He gave me the Evolution Revolution before I left. After learning of the Virus Energy Cell's existence, I studied it closely. It's using everything and everyone. Like electricity flowing through the world.

Yes, I was aware the Virus Energy loves attention. I use attention, until I get close enough to uncover the infection. I use my conscious senses to feel for it. Now, my Virus senses are always on. Even in my sleep. My senses are connected to my intuition. It's connected to my Consciousness Energy as I travel.

ROGE

The name, is Roge. I live in Finland. I am here, ready to ask a question. Oh! Sorry, I am here with my group of course. I use to live by the rule of, can I borrow, because my pockets were always hollow. I made good choices, and they worked out. I have made bad choices, but not intentionally. I don't like to brag, well, actually I do. I am always on point. Until, I can no longer make a point.

UC: Like you are doing now you mean?

Roge: OK, not funny. Let me focus. I need to release some frustration. I am not trying to say I am better than the rest, but, I gotta be honest, some people are better than others. They are better than others in many ways…Talent, sports, politics. Social skills, and health. Me, I am better at golfing. It's my therapy. There has to be a lower and a higher class, it's a balance, like the poor and the rich.

I love the feeling of being first. It's a rush. I am good a many things. In fact, I have come to believe, I have a special power. I am part of a development group. We meet once or twice a week, to work on conversion of our Virus Energy. We get together, to form a developmental plan. I am an inspiration to my group.

UC: Are they aware you're an inspiration to the group? Is this how they see it?

Roge: Yes, but you can ask them later. We are talking now. They know I am a team player.

UC: Really, you're a team player. You start the game, and finish it three days later. Leaving the other players in the refrigerator, and no one in the group has an objection?

Roge: I am not aware of any. Why would they? They appreciate my gift and my special abilities. Here is a question. We have been discussing this without a resolution. Hopefully you can tell them, so they can see I am right. How can I help others with their own conversion, without having to convert my own energy?

UC: Is the group aware, you are still infected? And why are you not being rejected? What you just said, is Virus Energy injected. What makes what you receive a conscious inspiration? It could be an inspiration from anywhere. Your actions reveal your inspiration. Real inspiration, creates energy development through energy movement. It's the movement which creates, and if it doesn't create movement, it's the Virus Energy?

Roge: Since I began learning about this Energy, I began feeling a new feeling of self awareness. It is the same thing which happens when I am reading the Evolution Revolution Book. I started to think better, to realize things I wasn't aware of. I developed new thoughts. So I figured out, they must be inspirations. They certainly didn't come from my brain. It's usually out of order. I believe I am aware of myself, my actions, thoughts, and beliefs. I am sensitive to how I treat people.

UC: Has your group noticed your new self growth? Have you shared your realizations with them? It looks like you are holding things back from them. You are being trusted with their emotions. You must share as much, or you will lose trust.

Roge: I think I did share my growth. It's noticeable to others. Gosh, I am not sure if I did. I let others in the group, talk more than I do.

UC: Do you think you are being honest with the others in the group? Do they notice how you don't include them? They will, as they do the work on their conversion, they will become conscious and will be able to sense the Virus around them.

Roge: I am more of an observer at this time. Somethings they say, I can't say, it's too personal. Being completely open about everything, totally naked, this is being really vulnerable. I am still trying to figure out, how they can be so open and honest. I am not sure if I can do the same.

UC: They obviously think you do. They are not hiding from you. How do they feel about you, the way you feel about them, do you even notice?

Roge: I hope so, we are close. We have been meeting for a while now. I consider them friends.

UC: Do you know all their names? First and last? Do you know anything about their past?

Roge: Ah, yes, I think so. Oh wow, all this time, I have been so self absorbed, I don't remember names. Wait I know a couple. Glad the group isn't hearing this conversation.

UC: Are they aware of what you are working on, in your development? Sharing with them would be excellent. But, it doesn't sound like you are the sharing type.

Roge: I share as much as I am able. Maybe not all, but most of it.

UC: How do you get out of answering when you are asked? You're a team player, do they believe that? Guess what? If you plan on staying in the group, you're going to have to tell them. They must know, it's a matter of trust.

Roge: I know I must, it's very obvious. It shows. I am learning how to use self realization, to realize myself, I am learning not be self focused. After all, self development, is the development of self.

UC: It's not being full of yourself. It's being aware of actions. You are not only self focused, but you are also infected with arrogance. Self realization is meant to change you. Where is your change? It sounds like, the sound you hear may be your own. Conversion is the opposite of staying the same. Think about it.

How can you go through a conversion and stay the same?

It's pointless, useless, and unconscious. Are you sure you need to change? You seem to love yourself just fine. It's not just about energy development, it's what you do with your development. Your actions need to jangle, louder than they jingle. Self realization is self actualization. There is no reality, without realizing it. This is Consciousness.

Roge: So then, being self realized, is being in the reality of your own realization. Is this suppose to clarify anything?

UC: It clarifies how realization, has different dimensions. And, what you believe is the truth, is your present reality. Your perception creates your reality. It depends on what knowledge you absorb, and how it affects your beliefs. What is your plan, to become better a human?

Roge: As I said, the more I share my emotions, the less clothes I have on. I feel self conscience in front of the group. Going through emotions is not easy. Awareness is actually frightening at first. Especially self awareness. Having to face actions which were kept hidden, cause me to resist. But what I discover causes me to persist.

UC: The Virus Energy is counting on resistance. It's the way it controls.

Roge: I'm going to need assistance.

UC: You must be on an emotional expedition? Has confusion set in? You're still holding on to old beliefs. Your energy is unbalanced. It's clear, you still have some fear. You have to inform the group, of how you are struggling? They have bared themselves to you, It's time to reveal your truth to them. They deserve to know. You have some left over Virus Energy within you, trying to convince you, to stop your Consciousness Energy development. Staying silent is keeping the Virus a secret. Let's meet with the rest of the group?

Roge: Now? But we are still talking.

UC: How about including them, team player?

Roge: Hello group. There is a feeling of arrogance amongst us. Has anyone noticed? This is an energy which needs converting. The person it possess, is hurting. He is open to learning, but he needs encouraging. He needs Virus Energy purging. So at his urging, he wants to hear your opinion about, what he is Learning. Who is it? Let's ask the group to take a vote, and put it in a note. Well… Five votes for Roge.

What! I want a recount. This is how you all feel, really? I was unaware. Thanks for the honesty, it has awakened me.

UC: But wait, there is more. From the groups mouth, to your ears, are these words.

"Your thoughts are not focused, they are scattered with thoughts about yourself. You're everywhere, but nowhere. But you keep saying you're here with us. We trust you, as long as you don't start to argue? That's when you walk away, instead of dealing with what we say. You have to help us help you, to convert the Virus infection from inside you. It's trying to affect us. We can't have it here, you have to let it go. We don't know what your denial is about, but you gotta to get it out. It's time to face it, you can't erase it".

Roge: Wow! I had no idea you felt this way. It seems my self realization, needs to become more realized. I make a commitment to you all, no Virus Energy Cell is chasing me out.

UC: Why don't you start with the truth Roge. Realize this, the others in your group are developing, while you were out golfing. You have been observed grabbing your golf clubs and balls, and walking down the halls. Leaving the group wondering where you're going. Communication would have been good in this case. Suggestion for you, hang up your golf clubs, stay out of the halls, when the group calls, answer.

Roge: This was my first experience with emotional energy conversion. Since then, I have been emerging as a Consciousness Energy Vibration. I am growing, and developing. I am currently involved in the energy movement. This has been my shared improvement.

BLIE

Hello, I am BLIE, my home is Finland.

Today, I am a garbage engineer. In reality, I am just a Garbage Collector until I finish college. This is the story of how beliefs, can attach themselves to you from childhood. Because we are Unconscious, we forget about them. They become Unconscious Beliefs, which affect us UNCONSCIOUSLY.

UC: So, where did you get your education, and how did you come about it?

Blie: From the book, the Evolution Revolution. I am a history major. My thesis is about historical beliefs, then and now. How have they changed? Are traditions a belief or a culture? How do beliefs affect our choices? Why are there so many different beliefs? Why would a person go against their own beliefs? Are they worth dying for? People have killed and died for what they believe.

UC: You have a lot of questions about beliefs, it should be a good thesis? Your questions reflect a conscious point of view?

Blie: First, it's for Energy Conversion. Second, my parent's beliefs nearly ruined my life. This is my point of view. Beliefs are not always helpful, at times they are actually harmful. My story can tell you.

UC: What's your unconscious belief? Do you live by it, or are you trapped in it? Does it free you or imprison you?

Blie: My whole life, has been one giant prison. With BARS, MADE OUT OF OLD BELIEFS. I had the belief, where humankind was a kind human. Unconscious belief, when I think about it, it's not all true. People can be trusted. This too, was not all true. Where you believed the elders, because they were always right. Well, it turns out they weren't always right. It's their perspective which makes them right. These were parts of my belief system which almost ruined my life.

Unconscious beliefs pop up, when you least expect them to. They act on their own, when they are triggered. You don't realize you're acting out this belief, Because you're doing it unconsciously. We need Consciousness Energy in our body and brain, so we can be aware of unconscious beliefs. We need to learn where they came from.

Emotional development is the way to Consciousness Energy Development. When I began this process, I was taken on a journey into the most frightening parts of my Emotions. I met dark emotions hiding in my Unconscious. I found out why, I had always been suspicious of others. I had trust issues that I was unaware of.

This knowledge, helped me to identify where my Virus infection was hiding. Facing my own issues, is definitely harder than facing the issues of others. So, now, I want to share how believing the beliefs of others without question, will cause serious emotional damage, and years of therapy. I no longer believe without questioning. Which means questioning is my belief. A belief must prove itself to me, not the other way around. Here is what happened to me from a belief, which wasn't even mine.

I grew up with the beliefs of my parents. They were rich and very traditional. They had many beliefs, but one of them stood out like a sore thumb. Everyday, I was educated on my place in society. Where I belonged and with whom. What kind of friends I could have, and who was allowed to come to my home. If you were not as white, as the color white, you were not welcome. My parents were not mean or hateful people. These were the beliefs they grew up with. They were racist beliefs and they, were unconscious to it. My goal became, to look for ways I could help them identify their own beliefs, and question them. I found it in the book the Evolution Revolution. It helped me change my perspective. It helped me to come to terms with what my parents are. With the tradition they carried on by being unconscious.

Such a wonderful tradition. Unfortunately, by the time I was twenty. This belief of theirs grew on me. It became my identity. I was actually acting out a belief, which deep inside, I didn't believe in. This issue has been going on since history began. We supposedly have evolved, where was the evolution? We still had discrimination and hate over color. Color is part of life. If you hate someone for their color, you should look in the mirror for a while. I don't think you can. You are facing yourself. Most people's guilt, makes them run after three minutes.

It was wrong to exclude others based on race, color, or disability. Out in society I didn't feel this way. Tourists are everywhere here. Meeting others in the streets is easy. I would stop and talk to people from different countries, and different colors. But I always feel like my parents were watching my every move. I didn't want my parents to think I was betraying them. This is how they made me feel. I realize, there are millions of people out there who have their own reasons for hating. But this is what's keeping this energy alive. The less we hate, the less hate there will be.

All the way through school, we were taught about slavery in history. How men and women, were being sold into slavery. Most of them were kidnapped from different countries, and sold in other countries. But we are no longer these people, ARE WE? Then, why was I faced with these same people as my parents? My parents taught me to hate. It's very sad for me to admit this. I needed to learn what was driving them? How can anyone actually hate another human, because someone in history said you should. How did a belief like this, get so much power over the years. It should have died with history. Why are we still using the energy of hate? I have to understand this.

I am in this energy because, I allowed others to convince me it was the truth, in spite of what my feelings told me. What was controlling me? My first realization was, my parents were controlling me, through this belief. Reading the book, Evolution Revolution, I learned a lot about different types of energies. It showed me a clear view of how we are all equal, because we share the same energy. I have been working very hard, to get this negative energy out of my body. It's not mine.

This is one belief which needs to be converted. This world is full of people who hate others they never met. How can one color live with other colors and not make a rainbow? Believe it or not, we all fit somewhere on this whole picture. Black, white, yellow and tan, these are but different colors of the same woman and man. When a belief can change you for the worst, it's probably cursed. If you believe in curses that is. Beliefs? They can keep you prisoner in the past. Be aware of unconscious beliefs.

UC: With your reality as it is now, you can create your life as you want it. With Consciousness as your foundation, what you build will last.

REHA

Hello, I am Reha, I am from Egypt. I have traveled to many places in the world, mostly by myself. Always a gift from my parents. It says, go away, we don't have time for you. Then why did you have me? I use to be what I call, an Irrational Emotional. You know, too sensitive, hurt feelings all the time. Always on the defensive. My anger was explosive. Many times, I had no reason to feel this way. It became a pattern without my awareness.

From this realization, I went on mission to learn about my emotions, my feelings. I discovered the knowledge of Consciousness Energy, from many people I know in the movement. We all need a purpose to live for. Mine became, the Evolution Revolution Energy Movement. I became aware, there were different type's of feelings, and emotions? I also became aware, the Virus Energy is infecting my emotions. I had a responsibility to the energy movement, to convert my Virus infection as soon as I can. So I have a question, what creates the feeling?

UC: It's each person's Consciousness Energy. Each EMOTION, creates a REACTION, which triggers a FEELING. It's a feeling you can trust. What makes a feeling a feeling, is the energy which comes with it. It's this energy which creates the action reaction, which causes the trigger of a feeling. Without the Consciousness Energy Vibration, you remain in Reaction.

Reha: If my emotions are infected, who is in reaction, the Virus Energy or me? No, wait, this would be me in reaction, from the infection. But this would mean the Virus is in reaction. Huh? What am I saying? Somehow I've become confused. Breathe Reha. I am a little nervous about this conversation. If my parents walked in, oh boy, it wouldn't be good for me. They will send me on vacation again. I have been going on vacation since I was thirteen.

I realize, what I want to be is up to me. But I am the only one who knows it. It's difficult for a woman to speak her thoughts in a mans world. The energy movement is about equality and unity. Once energy balance is restored, we will have equality.

So when I ask myself what I wanted to be? I would I hear my father. *"You will become what I say. You must get married first."* It wasn't up to me. Is this the Virus energy trying to ruin my life? I can't see living my life, according to someone else's beliefs of what is right. Imagine, living your present life, using histories beliefs. Being forced to abide by traditions that should no longer exist.

I have felt the energy of control. The energy of fear, and greed. Isn't this the operating principle in most traditions? You're not doing it because you want to, it's because tradition says you must. In my travels, I was able to identify with each country that I visited. I discovered many beautiful cultures, and traditions.

In each country, people danced, ate food, laughed, cried, drank, made love, slept, and woke up, nearly the same way. Amazing isn't it? Seriously, look at the similarity. We all look, and speak differently, but our actions world wide, shows the similarity. Language is the only real barrier besides the ego. Most world conflicts are ego driven. Did the creator put men in charge of everything? Or was it the Virus Energy Cell? If you ask me, it possess more men than women.

UC: No one is excluded from this infection. If you exhibit violent tendencies, you're infected. If you have no compassion or empathy, you are infected. If you have abused your fellow human beings, you are infected. Should we continue? You can't destroy energy, but you can convert it into a different energy. Converting it will allow it to live, but as a balanced Consciousness Energy.

Reha: I heard what Blie said about Unconscious Beliefs. I couldn't agree more, When it comes to those beliefs, we pick them up, here and there. The issue is, forgetting them? How do I get to all my beliefs, if I keep forgetting them. Do I have to wait until they start showing from me, before I can do something about it? What about the beliefs the Virus Energy will not let go off?

UC: It holds on to those because, the beliefs it's trying to protect, are beliefs which have destructive effects. When a belief does not function on its own. It needs a protector, an energy director. In this case, it's the Virus Energy. A belief with a Consciousness Energy foundation, needs no protection, it's an energy creator.

Reha: Is it more mental, then environmental? Does the effect on our brain, change our perspective of the environment?

UC: It's both. Which one has the most effect on you? Is it yourself or others? Who do you believe first? How well do you know your brain? The main goal of the Virus Energy, is to keep your perspective on this physical dimension only. Nothing exists anywhere else. You allow it to change your perspectives by buying into all its illusions. All the toxic energy you eat, drink and live in. All this confusion has been created to keep you from finding out the truth. This is your starting point. Sooner or later, you must convert it all. Evolution happens with Consciousness Energy. So make this your goal. This is the reason for Energy development. This way you don't have to keep repeating the same experiment.

Believing without questioning is not learning, nothing is growing. Believing is when you say, I don't need to know. Have you thought about why you believe, what you believe? Some people are made to believe, for fear of Consequences. Some just say it, to be accepted. Loneliness makes you desperate. There are those who say it, because they actually think they believe it. Allowing others to make choices for you, is control. It's being submissive to the beliefs of others. It's possible to agree on the same choice without control.

Reha: Compliance, is a direction towards oppression. Dare we not question. Who decided we all had to conform to laws made by a conformist. I didn't vote on it. We have our rights, our freedom of speech, and choice,

UC: Is freedom just a carrot hanging in front of your nose, to keep you chasing it? Freedom means different things to different people. So freedom doesn't have one single meaning. You can say I am free, but, what is free? To do whatever you like? This would be chaos. Oh, we just realized, you do live the way want and do what you want. Thus, the chaos.

Reha: At this time I am only focused on one thing, the Universal Consciousness Energy awareness. I need to act in a Conscious way. I have become aware; it's going to take a world energy conversion, to save humanity. When the energy balance is off, does becoming this Energy re-balance it? Is this conversion? I want to be conscious of the Virus Energies actions, and its hiding place's?

UC: The Virus Energy is what lives in humanity. Watch their actions, they will show you. The Virus

The Evolution Revolution

Energy materializes in the energy forms of, control, greed, fear, manipulation, seduction, and envy. It's every humans ego. It's your judgments and reactive behaviors.

Reha: I am in control of mine, they are not in control of me. Judgments happen unconsciously.

UC: Oh my, who is defending, you, or your ego? Why are you defending? Do you know?

Reha: Oops, you got me. Wow! This was a fast shift into reaction? I didn't even notice?

UC: Being unaware can cost you plenty. You have to increase your Consciousness Energy Awareness.

Reha: Sometimes, I feel like I am in a race car, ready to go, the flag comes down, and I realize there is no gas pedal. There goes the medal. I think I need a new gas pedal.

UC: A gas pedal comes in parts, and you have to put it together. Awareness comes in stages. You have to go through all of them. You just experienced one stage. It's called realization. How do you know what's true? If all your life, you've been lied to. You question until you get a realization.

Have you seen your ego? It's got its eye on you. When you want your ego to let go, you need to let go first, it will shrivel up and dry from thirst. While your ego is stuck to you, it will make you do, what it wants you to. Do you want to know how to replace your non moving, non essential physical energy, into an alive, and motivated new energy?

Reha: Is this up to me? You mean it's my responsibility? I can make my own decision? I haven't needed to do that in a long time. This feels like freedom to me.

UC: Yes, it is. Experiencing any form of oppression and surviving it, is freedom.

SYSCO

My name is, Sysco. I am a tour guide by profession. I speak a number of languages. I meet many tourists, who are willing to teach me about their countries. I absorb like a sponge. This awareness has opened my eyes to the reality of the world. A reality I never knew.

As much as there was to love, there were things I did not like. I thought my country had problems. Having this awareness, has put me in a quandary. Should I keep doing my laundry, and pretend I am ordinary? Do I get motivated, or wait for the world to be reformulated? What difference can I make?

UC: Are you here to make a difference? Or to offer resistance? Because if you are not here to make a difference, that's already resistance.

Sysco: I am hoping what I have learned will make a difference. Here is my quandary; why we, as humanity, can't stop pretending we do not judge, persecute and condemn? Why is it we have given up on peace and encourage violence instead? It's not supposed to be like this. What's the matter with us? How can it possibly change? You are talking about putting out the fire in hell, and turning the light on, in heaven. Not an easy feat. But the heat, is now burning our feet. So when is it time for us to meet.

UC: On which side of the street? The one with the heat?

Sysco: Yours, it doesn't burn your feat. Should I get rid of all my possessions? Will it make a difference?

UC: There is nothing to give up. It's not about your possessions, it's about what's possessing you. Was there anything more you learned?

Sysco: Compassion for the human creation. Too many of us have become predators. There are hardly any of the innocent left. This is the work of fear.

UC: Do you posses self compassion, how about world compassion? Where is yours?

Sysco: I thought it was old fashioned. I was focused on my own emotional needs, not my deeds. Now, it has become a world compassion. This is how I found it again.

UC: How did you come by this realization?

Sysco: This knowledge, the Evolution Revolution has helped me to change my perspective, by showing me a different direction. It has helped my brain to function. I am now Conscious of my reactions, and my Virus Energy infection. I have grown into consciousness.

I am converting my Virus Energy infection, and creating a new reflection. I am an Energy Being. With an energy meaning, and my energy is beaming. The way I see it now, is this, everyone must face the illusion, which has been taught to us, as being real life. Don't just believe me, understand me; became my Mantra

UC: Who taught you? Are you self taught?

Sysco: Humanity's society. Their educational policies. Governmental agencies. Television personalities. Employment philosophies, and Cultural differences. All of these are, a form of conformity.

UC: Share more of what you learned.

Sysco: I learned what realization really means, as a developmental tool, and the real meaning of development. I learned, without Consciousness Energy, nothing can exist. We as humans are missing our humanity. I became aware that there really is an energy Virus infecting us, and there is an energy movement working on converting it.

UC: Do you still feel any effects from the Virus Energy?

Sysco: Unfortunately, it was a tiny left over piece of doubt. It went unnoticed until the last night before going on vacation. My development is about being an example for others. I have seen with my own eyes, the Virus Energy disguise. What it can do, and how it affects you.

UC: So was this during the preparation, for your vacation?

Sysco: Yes, during the preparation, I became lost in my imagination. After I completed my packing check list, I lost focus and doubt crept in.

UC: Were you not aware, of what the energy of doubt can do? Because even on vacation, it goes with you. You better know your direction, else, you will get persuaded by doubt. How did doubt persuade you? What happened?

Sysco: It was my learning lesson involving doubt, and being unconscious. It's the reason I started to question. It was a nightmare. I was so oblivious. Before leaving, I had everything set up, I was positive. The schedule, airline tickets, hotel, money, plans for activity. I took a deep breath.

Then it came—a rush of Doubt. ARE YOU SURE? I tried to ignore it, but it followed me. You are going to forget something, you always do.

DOUBT: *"You will lose the airline tickets."*

ME: I know, I will put all the info on my phone.

DOUBT: *"Your going to another country, it could get stolen."*

It was maddening. I began to question myself. Did I confirm the reservation? Do I have enough money? Even after I knew I did, I counted it before I went to bed. Didn't sleep much worrying about forgetting something.

Morning came, I checked our flight tickets to be sure. Fear sets in. Last minute, I panicked and changed the flight plan to a cheaper and longer flight, to make sure I had enough money. Then I changed the hotel reservation to a cheaper hotel, which gave us more money to play with. I felt better and doubt went away.

Then I heard FEAR, *"don't tell your wife now. She will get angry with you, wait 'till later."* I didn't tell my wife, until we left. Huge mistake, warning to all, ignore doubt and fear. It would've been so much better, than to hear her shout. Very bad decision. I should have just left it alone, and said nothing. I was hijacked by doubt.

UC: What caused your thought to change your destination, to a place with a cheaper accommodation? Your wife made you pay, and pay. She went to stay at the place you picked yesterday. The more expensive one. While you had to stay at the one you picked. You already paid. Nice anniversary, just to save a few dollars. It sounds like greed played a role here.

Sysco: No, doubt started it all.

UC: Your vacation cost you more than your mortgage installation. You should have trusted your first inclination. Your Conscious intuition. Don't get persuaded by doubt. It's a branch of the Virus tree. Identifying these branches would be in your best interest. Before you go after the Virus tree, learn about the branches that keep it free. They all want to go on your vacation. The one who benefited, was doubt, indecisiveness takes your choice away, and ruins your day. Here are more friends of doubt.

The Energy of Greed:

One of the most powerful of the Virus Cell Energies. Its goal, is to possess your energy, by taking all you have? Greed always wants more? It devours everything it comes in contact with. Will it ever get enough? Greed doesn't know the meaning of enough. Why is it so hard to control? Because it has no soul. It cares about you until, it gets what it wants.

Why is it hard to resist? What is the power it uses to take more than it needs. Is it fear who's really behind the actions of greed. If so, what backs up fear, the Virus Energy Cell? Who backs up the Virus Energy? Humanity does. It seems most humans can't live without it. A person spends their whole life becoming rich. By the time they can really enjoy it, they are too old, or dead.

This is how greed destroys life. It makes one dependent on it until it's too late. Greed lives a life of always wanting more, without stopping to enjoy what it already has. The only one benefiting from this life, is greed. This sounds like one of your human made addictions? Greed feeds your habit. It says jump, and you're a rabbit. Why do you use greed? Are you under duress? Or is it someone you're trying to impress? Are you a person who has to control? Is control your goal? How do you use greed? By force, threats, and theft. By manipulation, using sympathy or intimidation. Are you aware, when you are using Greed? This is difficult to notice when you are unconscious.

Humanity, have you thought about any of these questions? Here is your opportunity. There is a cure for greed. STOP! Cold turkey. Greed will feel it more than you. It will go into shock, and lose its power. You have the will power to stop using it, don't let it use you. Greed is not an innocent energy. It's been accused of the needless deaths of millions. It's a bottomless pit, and there's a lot of it. Greed is always on the prowl, hour after hour. It's after more power. How can you avoid it?

At this time, humankind must become realized of how toxic they are. Humans are swimming in an energy which is moving like mud. How can you avoid getting muddy? You cannot, it's your energy. The point is, if you don't want mud running through your veins, get out of the mud.

The Energy of Control:

This Energy has its own goals. It follows its own rules, with self-created tools. It has one purpose, to control humanity any way it can. The Virus Energy needs control to operate in humanity. Unfortunately, humans are unaware of this control, due to being unconscious of it. How will they find out? Who will they listen to? If not their own Consciousness, how will humanity be awakened by the Energy of the Consciousness?

What is Control? It is taking your choice away? It is, taking away your right to freedom? Does it make all your decisions for you? Does it change your Perception? Is it a form of Abuse? Is it Fear induced? Is it Manipulation?

UC: Control can stop you from moving. It can change your thoughts and keep you dreaming. It can act like you, talk for you and make your choices. Your issue is, you don't even know it's doing it. You hold on to control, because you are unaware it's there. CONTROL, operates its own CONTROLS. How did it become so CONTROLLING, and why has it never been CONTROLLED?

It uses other Virus Energies like Manipulation and Seduction, to control your perspective. Once you are controlled, you've lost your identity. Control is involved in every Virus Energy action. Is there anything which control, can't control? Absolutely, the Universal Consciousness Energy.

Are you being controlled? Are you willing to find out? What would you do, if you discovered you were being controlled? What's your reaction to it? Anger, neutrality, excitement, happy? Will you deny it. Become defensive?

Is humanity aware of what's controlling them? *"NO!"* They need to be. Too busy, no longer suffice. Your lack of Consciousness, is the reason you are still Unconscious. This energy, just wants to use you. It wants to possess all you are. Its goal, is to capture you. Whether it does or not, is up to you. You are in control, not control. Why do humans do what it wants them to? Just say no. Even if greed steps in. Unless you are afraid? This Energy is a thief of choices. It will make all kinds of noises, to get responses. Always remember this, when you are out of Control, who is in Control? As long as you are being controlled, you are a puppet on a string, just a human *"ding-a-ling."* It will use fear, to enter your ear, and attach to your brain, causing you to spin, again and again. Force control is thought control, which leads to full control.

The Energy Of Fear:

All of humanity is infected with some kind of fear. From the beginning, fear changed the course of history. It's the strongest of the branches. Fear is contagious, and doesn't give chances. Humans spread fear unconsciously. Some do it on purpose. Why are humans afraid of fear, when humanity encourages it? You know what it feels like.

Most of the other Virus Energies, are afraid of it. Fear opens the door for greed, and control. It takes away your ability to explore, to be curious, to discover unknown knowledge. The Virus Energy doesn't want you to learn anything new. So it uses fear to scare you. Fear energy, wants to intimidate you into giving in to control. It's one of humanity's deadliest diseases. Staying unconscious only empowers fear.

The less you know, the more afraid you are. Awareness of Consciousness Energy can take the fear away. The more you know, the more you can do something about it. Fear can be erratic. You never know which one will appear. It's self duplicating and uses your fear to grow on.

It has infected humanity with fear of the unknown. So humans will never know. The unknown, is your creator, the Universal Consciousness Energy Vibration. Fear has created life into a big mess. It is the cause of depression, and most of humanity's mental health problems. It wears many disguises. When there is a need, it arises. Fear lives in you, your spouse, and kids. It's in your job, and in your friends. Fear is in your neighbor, your doctor, your minister, your delivery man, mailman, your seniors, and your homeless.

You need to recognize the fear in you and convert it, otherwise it's all pointless. Fear will continue to scare, control will continue to possess, and greed will continue to make more, not less. The reaction of being scared by fear, is a learned behavior. You don't have to fear, Fear. Humans are just as scary. Face it. What are you afraid of? Yourselves? Here is a view of a few more branches of the Virus Energy tree. Do you see yourself as a branch? Would you admit it if you did? Presently, not many would.

The Energy of the Ego:

Your EGO is infected by the Virus Energy. It's become an unnatural part of you. It's now the narcissist in you. Your ego doesn't care about you, it only cares, if you care for it. It will do what it wants, without your permission. In fact, it makes you do things, you don't want to. How did your ego get out of control? You were suppose to be aware of your ego at all times. Now it's out performing actions, with your face on them. Your ego hides inside you. Don't you think you should check your ego. To make sure it didn't escape. It will take your thoughts with it, and replace them with its own.

It interferes in everything you think, say, and do. The ego is very courages when the face it is showing, is you. You must get to know your ego. Have a conversation with it. Talk about its actions, and how they affect you. Set limits for it, boundaries on what it can say and do. Take charge of your ego.

The ego is your responsibility. It is a real energy, you can convert its actions. The more you know it, the more you own it. It's the same with your emotions, and brain. Talk to them, understand them, convert their infection. The more you convert, the more you, and your ego will merge as one.

It's too dangerous on its own. Negative effects don't just happen. They are caused by your infected ego. It belongs to the Virus Energy cell. It doesn't need directions, it knows where to go. It looks for every mirror, to put on a show. Is it friend, or foe?

The ego, is very materialistic. It has money made of plastic. It has one important motto. I am the best of the best, and to hell with the rest. If you believe, the ego is a natural part of physical creation, you're right. The issue is, it's being used the wrong way. The ego is a natural part of your brain. Your Brain is infected by the Virus Energy. This means, so is your ego. But it doesn't have to be. Becoming a Consciousness Energy source, will bring you, and your ego together as one.

It wants to be protected, and kept safe. To go unnoticed, while you suffer the consequences of its actions. There are many humans who can see the ego do its act. Can you? Here is how to recognize the act of the ego.

Misleading, and unrealistic expectations. Overrated confidence. Unconscious, self promoted conversations. Must always come first. A defender of defensiveness. A reaction without an action. Always stopping to check the look. Expresses knowledge without reading the book. Gets insulted when questioned. Never admits to mistakes. Can't handle positive, or negative criticism. Lastly, it's reaching for perfection.

Ego doesn't care what others think. It doesn't matter who it bothers. It is self serving, and is only aware of its own reality. It has only one devotion, its own preservation. This is the character of the ego. They know everything about everything.

The Energy of Manipulation:

What is its donation? Sure, you know what manipulation means, as a word. But not as an energy. How it affects you unconsciously. What it's done to history? Do not underestimate it. It has many Virus energies to call on, and they are all just as strong.

Can you recognize when you're being manipulated? Are you aware of how it manipulates? What do you really know about it? The energy of manipulation, has a negative meaning. It's deeper than the word.

Most of you are being manipulated, and you can't seem to connect it to your advertisement. TV, Computer, and magazine adds, newspaper adds, street signs, adds at your doctor's office, and in your schools. Wherever you are, there it is. The Seduction. This energy is very good at manipulating your thoughts.

You learned it Unconsciously. You taught it to your kids Unconsciously. You use it Unconsciously. It's so stealthy, you don't even notice it's happening to you. It will take away your awareness, and replace it with an assumption. *"Do this for me, please, don't you love me?"* Or, *"I love you, do this for me please."* Either way you see it, this is emotional manipulation, simple as that. When you are in a state of Consciousness, you can't be manipulated. You are conscious. You can feel it coming. Everyone uses it in some way or another. But the worst are those humans, who use it to hurt others.

The Energy of Envy:

Is not friendly. It's actually mean and spiteful, possessive and ungrateful. It wants what you worked so hard for. It's easier than working for it. It's jealous of what you have. By creating classes of people you created the energy of Envy. Jealousy was born by envy. Bad relationships are caused by envy. Friendships are broken, family members argue and people get hurt. Thanks to envy.

Envy creates Competition. Humanity believes this to be healthy. Competing to be the best, makes you miss out on the rest. When you finally get to your best, you are out bested. When your focus is on the prize at the end of the road, you miss out on the best prize of all, THE ROAD. Without it, you wouldn't be able to get to your best.

Have you heard the thoughts of your envy? They are pretty loud. Here they come. *"My friend's car is better than mine. I wish I was in their position. Lucky bum why did he win'? "Damn, why does she get everything she wants?"*

"If I only had half of what others have? Wow, they are lucky. It would look better on me. Your's is better than mine, I want it. They are rich, and I am not. I can't stand rich people. Why can't I be rich?"

Violence stems from envy. Constantly complaining about what others have which it doesn't. When it wants something, the madness will set in. Envy will blame you for being poor. Then, blame the government, for making you poor. Then society, for not doing anything about it. Envy resents, and Jealousy creates Contempt. Your actions are proof of your intent.

The energy branches described above, come from the same energy tree. The Virus Energy Cell Tree. All the energy they steal from you, goes directly back to feed the Virus Cell. It needs it to grow on.

Together, you humankind, have brought in confusion, and unconsciously replaced your reality with an illusion. So pardon the intrusion, but the Energy Evolution Revolution is here to convert your illusion, back to a reality. Only it will not be your past reality, this is a new reality. One you will truly love.

Now, you have arrived at this intersection. What's next? The New Direction, to a New World.

This is an energy creation. Brought to you, by the UNIVERSAL CONSCIOUSNESS. For the ENERGY CONVERSION of the VIRUS CELL. With humanity's help we have succeeded. This is for you humankind, The New Direction, is at your doorstep, it is knocking.

صلى

The New Direction
The year 2033

M: Max.

C: Caller.

UC: Universal Consciousness.

V: Virus Cell.

M: Hello out there in the new world, my name is Max. With a new show on a new platform. I hope all of you can hear me out there. I want to talk with you, all of you. This is a new forum of questions and answers. Sharing memories and reactions. Anything anyone one wishes to discuss about the Evolution Revolution, please call me at W.A.T.E.R. extension 8.

As I said, my name is Max. I am an information analyst at W.A.T.E.R. The World's Association Towards Energy Recreation. I am presently enrolled in the Institute of Consciousness and Self Development. It's where I am developing my Consciousness Energy Abilities. I am also a student of the old history, and, our new one, as short as it may be.

We have arrived at the New Direction. Let us begin anew. We need to come together and learn from each other. I am sure some of you are still waking up and finding your balance. I think many of us are. That's why I created this type of forum; as a way to hear from others. As a way to help us process our feelings about yesterday. After the Evolution Revolution happened.

People are still in need of support to get focused. There are many. My goal is to talk about our present. Not only that, but whatever happens to be your state of Consciousness at this time. I am sure there are some of you, still dealing with leftover effects from the Evolution Revolution. I am confident you are aware, the Evolution Revolution is how we got here.

To all those who participated in it and the Energy Movement, I know you are out there, and you are as curious as I am about the new world. What more have you learned? How are you using this new Consciousness? Do you fully understand your evolution as a human being? Where are we going from here? How do we use this energy to get there? Where is there?

Let's discuss where we have been, and where we are today. So we can stop wondering about what happened, and move towards making it happen. I for one, need to solidify my present reality, the present moment is where we are now. You must of had thoughts and questions at one time or another? If not, you will.

Our Consciousness Energy Evolution is now a reality. These effects are still fresh, not too far in the past I might add. For many people all over the world, it was yesterday. I feel this way. I need to process my own effects, so I can focus on my physical evolution, as it has changed our direction. THIS IS HUMANITY'S *"NEW DIRECTION."*

M: There are effects which come and go, effects I would like to know. I can use them for my own development? I am hoping, while interacting with others, we would get some good information, which may help people with their own Consciousness development. Bring up topics, stories, and experiences.

Humanity has just experienced a new awakening. People have found their real identity. Your perspective has changed, you have changed. You are not the same as you were yesterday. In this new evolution, we are all responsible for our own Consciousness development. We have to be, because it's based on planet Earths own evolution. As we continue to evolve, so will the Earth. As long as the Earth continues to revolve, so will we. We haven't Consciously evolved until now. It took an Evolution Revolution to make it happen.

M: OK, I am getting calls, lines are open. Hello caller. C: Hello, Mr. Max.

I like this, it's a good idea. What made you think of it?

M: I think, many of us are still awakening to this new Consciousness. Getting familiar with it.

I also think, people are looking for new ideas. New ways to develop. I know I have things to develop.

C: Do I say my name?

M: That's optional, not necessary.

C: Well, I am Brandy.

M: Welcome to the conversation. You are my first caller.

C: As you were saying, it's still fresh in my memory. I am still in amazement about this whole thing. I was in my dorm room, studying. I remember the feeling of the energy conversion in my body. I still feel it. It felt like a blood transfusion. I was being drained of my energy, then, refilled with a different energy. It felt different. One was cold on its way out, and the new one, felt warm on its way in. I was unaware of what it was. I had no clue of what was happening to me, until after it happened.

I was reading my book on economics, I had a paper due the next day. I was focused on what I was reading. Then, the insides of my body began to vibrate, I thought I was having a seizure. At this moment, I had this realization, I knew the whole book. Like the clouds disappeared and the Sun came shinning through, and I could see the whole book at once. I closed the book, and started to write. As I saw page by page flip by in my head, I could read them as they went by.

I completed my paper for class in thirty minutes. Where was this coming from, I hadn't read the whole book yet? Apparently, this was happening to many of the students at the same time. Many of us had awakened looking around with a new perception and asking the same question. Why were we unaware of what was about to happen? Most of us thought it would be an energy movement event and that's it. Was the energy wave, the reason we all woke up at one time. I don't remember going to sleep?

M: Were you looking for awareness? No, you were preparing for your class. Had you been looking for answers to your life? No, you were content with yours. Had you been curious about the beyond?

No, you didn't believe in the beyond. Were you focused on changing your life for the better? No, you were working on insuring, you will have a career. Many people were in your situation. This is the reason you were unaware. You lived in your own reality.

C: Yes, I agree. But, there were millions like me, who are out there wondering what's next. I have noticed groups from the young generation helping others to integrate into their new direction.

M: The support they offer can answer your question and help you to integrate into a new society.

C: Yes, thank you. But before that, I need an update. Question about the Young Generation, how did they start the energy movement? Why were they aware before many others? Is it because they were looking for change?

M: Many of them were born knowing. They were partly responsible for starting the Energy Movement. Didn't you participate in it?

C: No, I didn't. I was in school at the time it was going on. My parents would've never allowed me to participate in any kind of movement.

M: This movement was different. Why? It was an ENERGY MOVEMENT. It was an Energy Revolution for Evolution. Not to take over a government. This is about, how the Energy Movement, used the knowledge from the Evolution Revolution to help it succeed. After, they were able to integrate the same knowledge into a school curriculum. Designed to teach Consciousness abilities.

It gave W.A.T.E.R the ability to effectively change the education system. They have shifted their focus to the Universal Consciousness Energy Education. The education of energy development. For both, the young and old. There are students all over the world. The focus of my study, is Energy Projection. Many institutions have specific courses formulated for the level of development you are on. Thank you Brandy.

C: OK thanks, nice talking to you.

M: Before we continue, I want to say a few words, about my journey. After the Evolution Revolution, my perception, found a new dimension. A new reality. With each new realization, my perspective kept changing. In this new dimension I can feel my brain rearranging. The feeling was quite strange. I had been feeling out of whack. But suddenly gained my balance back.

I became aware, this is the New Human Race, which I now embrace. I knew right away, I had to connect with others. To keep building the links to the Energy Chain of humankind's Evolution. A great way to develop, would be this open human to human communication. Connecting to the world population, with the goal of creating a dialogue with others. If you are listening and have a question, just call in anytime. Let's hear about the actions that donated to the Evolution Revolution. Was it the World Energy Conversion? Are they the same, or did one create the other? Is Energy Re-creation, the way we continue to evolve? Presently, I am aware, there is a lot of information that already exists, but people have different perspectives. There has been documents from that time, which talk about humankind's actions.

They identify those who were responsible for the cover ups and confusion. Even though we were being driven by the Virus Cell. We were not helpless to it, we just thought we were. Our history shows this. It shows who the players were. The leaders, supporters, inventors, the traitors, criminals, the political advisors, and the greedy politicians, there were many players.

We as humankind, are still here because, the efforts of the young generation paid off. They managed to accomplish what the government leaders could not, the New Direction. They were the key players in making the energy balance on Earth possible. Their own energy conversion made it possible for them, to confront

The New Direction

the Virus Energy Cell in its entirety, and complete a global energy conversion. There, this should give us plenty to discuss.

M: OK people, you know who I am, but you don't have to say who you are. Lines have been open.

Hi caller, welcome to the discussion. Tell us what we don't know.

C: Hello, as I sit here talking to you, I find myself wondering about the older generation. They lived most of their lives, before the Evolution Revolution. Will they even have time to develop their consciousness, to the point of slowing down their age? Is it too late for them? Don't we need to offer them help? I mean, are we all on our own now? Wasn't the point unity. There must be millions of them out there. Where can they go for support? My mom lives with me, she has someone to help her Understand. What about them?

My mother is eighty five years old. But she is courages and committed to living longer. She is unafraid to express the truth. She was an activist for peace and unity. She and many like her, opened the door for our awakening. I will be forever grateful to her and the rest of the older generation. For this reason, we need to guide them, and if we have to, do it for them.

M: With your Consciousness now, you should be aware enough to teach classes on this subject. You sound transformed by the idea, so make it happen. Ask W.A.T.E.R. for support. You will get it.

C: Yes, I have developed a wider view of everything now. There is no reason I can't. Thank you.

M: Thank you so much for your candor. Let's see if anyone out there, can reply to your question.

OK, Next caller please. If you heard the last call, do you have any comment?

C: Actually yes, it's why I called. I like what I heard. With all this focus on absorbing it all, I hadn't given it a thought. Not very conscious of me is it? I better work on that. Our elders need to have the same experiences we do. No matter of their disabilities. We can do something about this now. Consciousness energy is able to regenerate physical mass. If they can't do it on their own, then we can help them do it.

However, each one is conscious enough to develop their own energy. We have to be careful not to enable them. They will need support with building self esteem. I truly believe that many of the elderly, are not so old anymore. Ever since the energy awakening, they can think clearer, and are still viable citizens. I don't mind offering support but doing it for them? I will not offend their dignity by allowing them to think they can't. As much as I support the last Caller, I say let them make the choice.

M: This is a strong stance to take caller. You were clear. So you have empathy and compassion for all involved, Anything else to add?

C: I have said enough. Next caller please, you're up.

M: Ah, that's what I am suppose to say.

C: Why only you? What's wrong with me saying it?

M: It's my role. I chose it, why would you say it?

C: Exactly. It's the role you chose to play. I couldn't take it away.

M: OK, good example, It's a great eye opener. Thanks for the call.

Next caller, Hello and welcome.

C: Hey there, so far I like what I am hearing. I hope people are really listening. I just heard two separate perspectives, coming to the same point of view. One, showing respect for the elderly, by wanting to do things for them, and the other, having the same respect, but thinks they should have a choice. One point of view with different perspectives. Two separate views, coming together as one thought, respect. This is amazing to me, before the Evolution Revolution, I used to be a mathematician. I thought in numbers?

In my past life, One plus one equals two. In this new world, it can be whatever I want it to be. It's where the impossible can become possible. It's where we have a new power of Consciousness which gives us new abilities. This tells me, how we can have separate points of view, and still show each other RESPECT. Removing all conflict. In those day, no two perspectives, can agree to come to the same point of view. Maybe close, but not the same. Conflict always ensued. Wars were started over not having the same perspective as others.

M: Wow! In this world, the only thing constant is Consciousness Energy. When you share the same perspective, you share the same view. We don't share the same view, but, we do share the same Universal Consciousness. Where two perspectives can have one point of view. The one looking through Consciousness Energy. Two separate roads can come together at the same point. If the point is the goal. In this case, the point was the Consciousness Energy Vibration. The road to getting there was up to us. We did it.

Presently, it's a matter of realization, not fascination. It's a matter of your energy development. A view is a view, It's your consciousness which changes you. Consciousness, is all perspectives as one. It has one view, one point. Creating Conscious Creations. Your reflection will reflect the same.

Do you absorb what you hear? Hearing, is absorbing, it's actualizing. It's thought provoking. It's an awakening, and it's action promoting. If this doesn't describe you, then, you are just listening. Listening is not hearing.

C: Thank you for clarifying my curiosity. Now that we have become Consciousness Energy, how are we really hearing? Is it more of a feeling, or an actual sound in my ear, hearing?

M: Why not both? The sound in your ear gives off a feeling in your body. It's a reaction to the sound.

C: If my feelings can hear then I don't need my ears.

M: What do you mean, you don't need your ears, they are part of your head. We all have them?

C: Why do we need them, just for body balance? As we evolve, will our body parts change?

Will my ears disappear? Will my head get humongous? Are we going to grow another leg? A third eye maybe? Hmm. A third eye would be cool.

M: You are focusing on your physical evolution. You may be running ahead of your development. Slow down. Evolution, is a natural development. Let it progress naturally.

C: As an Energy form, do we need Robots, Computers, Phones, Mail service? What about package delivery? How can we send a package by way of energy? I mean, is there anything we can't do with our Consciousness Energy?

M: Yes, stop it from moving. You are really energized, re-balance yourself. You are on the path of Discovery. Only next time, one package delivery at a time. More than one, makes it too high to climb. Physical Energy Evolution, transforms certain parts of you, as you physically develop your energy. No third legs, no new arms. It's your brain which needs to grow, to evolve, it has to. It's organic, it grows like all organic material on Earth. Just like the hair on our body, our head. We had no idea how to water our brain then, but we do now.

Once the Virus Cell infection was converted, humanity became one balanced Consciousness Energy. Self doubt was gone. We became aware of how to use our brain, to enter into a new dimensional ordain, THE NEW PLANET EARTH. We can no longer go backwards. We are our true nature now, as Energy Human Beings. For now, we are still physical matter. We still use words to communicate. But our words will have a Conscious meaning which can move us, and give us intuition feeling. The best view of you, is seen through an open Consciousness, and felt by an open heart.

C: So then…listening doesn't necessarily mean hearing. I can listen to many sounds, but it does not mean I am hearing them. What are Consciousness feelings?

M: Intuitive feeling, not just feeling. This is the true knowing. As a Consciousness Energy, your feelings will be one of intuition. Learn to trust them.

C: So then, we must learn to tune in, when we use to tune out. This is good for my Energy Development. Thank you for the enlightenment. Great forum.

M: Next caller, Go ahead. Hello, thanks for calling in. What's on your mind? C: Hi. Are you one of those Aliens, and what planet did you come from?

M: Haha, what makes you ask this question of me? Do I sound alien? I shouldn't. I am human, just like you. We can understand the same knowledge. But, No, I am not an alien, I was born here. So what's your story, this question seems loaded with other questions. Start talking. Why are you asking me if I'm an Alien?

C: Because, what you seem to know, is way beyond our physical knowledge of consciousness. It's as though you surpassed the cycle of development. Why do you know so much of what others don't. There has been many changes, since we discovered this cycle. Now, our nature is showing its true Consciousness. We have learned, how one person can make a difference. It took a lot of persistence, but it was worth the experience.

M: So what's your focus? It's your story. Is it just curiosity about my development? You are riding in the same cycle, what I see, you see. What I hear, you hear and what I learn, you can learn.

C: What's amazing, is how far we have developed since those days. Now when I think about it, it wasn't long ago. I still remember what it was like. Will this change, when I completely shift to what is, my new reality? Will I keep remembering those days? At this moment, I feel as though, I traveled from the stone age to the future, in the blink of the eye.

M: Your memories will convert to new ones as you develop your energy. It is what it is. We are in the present moment. This is our new beginning, as new human beings. Before the Evolution Revolution, we had a cycle also. Only we called it, the cycle of repeat. We took it to mean, If it was good the first time, keep doing it. We kept doing it.

C: I never thought I would live to see this day. I read the Evolution Revolution book some time ago. It spoke about all that has happened. Since I began to read it, I started to look for signs of its revelations, and here we are; just as it said. I have been watching each chapter unfold upon this world. It was a huge mystery, until it became a reality. There were so many people unaware of what was happening. Do they remember? Can they remember? Does it matter? Presently, do we need to be aware of our past? I would rather focus on my physical evolution process. I want to know where we are going from here. Especially after experiencing the Evolution Revolution.

This new energy is pulling me towards an intense Development. I have had a vision of where I can go in this Evolution growth. Will I become Omnipotent? Is it the most important? Is this our life now, to keep developing, to keep changing?

I would assume so, considering staying the same is not a Conscious action. I am excited every day to find out what I can create. It's about what I want to be isn't it? I have become driven by this energy drive, which keeps me alive. It keeps me moving, and learning. We have missed out on so much.

M: This is a moving energy. As long as we are flowing with it, we will grow with it. It's the natural balance of things. The meaning of Life is to create life. What else could it be about. Without creating life, there will be no life. It's our nature to create.

Can anyone add something to this? If so, please call in to share your own thoughts about this time. I hope you're not going to just settle for what I said. Self discovery, is better for curiosity. Bye caller, thanks.

Who is next? Go ahead caller. Hi, how are you?

C: I am fine thank you, now that I finally got through. I have a question for you Max, I would like to hear your thoughts.

M: OK, ask away.

C: How will we know who we are, if we keep changing?

M: It's because of who you are, is the reason you keep changing. As Human Energy Beings, we will continue to evolve. It's our nature. As long as we keep evolving, our Consciousness will keep growing. It's a brain transfusion, an energy balance transformation. It changes how your life is lived. How you look, is a natural evolution.

C: Just one more question. How can I have an out of body experience?

M: This is one of the abilities I learned to do, in my energy projection class. You can use your Energy to speed up your vibrational frequency just enough, to have an out of body experience. This was happening to people years ago. Not many knew how to explain it. Now, we have the ability to do it.

It comes with a huge responsibility. You must have full control of the speed your Energy revolves, or you could evolve out of your body completely. Learn with others, not alone, just a suggestion. This is an exercise for energy development. Everyone out there should use it. If you are new to energy development, ask for help. It works now, asking for help I mean.

Next caller. What would you like to share today? Do you have a question?

C: Ah yes, hello. So Consciousness Energy can be used to leave your body? Does this mean, in our present reality, what's possible is up to us? If you are flowing, you are growing. Is this what I am hearing?

M: In the Conscious state we are in now, impossible has no meaning. We must overcome the effects of the awakening first. Many, are still in this state. Even though they have become accustomed to the change. Some are still in a place of questioning and are looking for support.

C: This awareness has been like no other, as I develop my energy into Consciousness. I've become realized of many things. My perception has become the whole pie, not just a slice. My views, and my understanding, have all become universal. Everything is becoming clear. It all became real, very fast. I can feel meanings in what I touch.

What I feel today is Present Moment. It's from here, I will reach out and absorb knowledge. I dare not step out of the Present Moment, for I will become lost. So I ask, is the Present Moment, the Present, Past, and Future as one? I have been in the past, and now I am in the present. How do I know I didn't bring the past with me?

M: If you did, it would be the good parts of your past. Your good thoughts, good actions, and helpful donations. Any negative past, went away with the Virus Energy Cell. That's why you are in the present moment. You converted your past into the present. Now the only past you have, is after the awakening. Our new history.

C: I do remember the good times. But where does the future fit in?

M: By converting the energy of the past, with the energy of the present moment, you create the energy that will create the future. Humanity has converted the physical energy, into Consciousness Energy. We have become a faster vibrating frequency. We have new abilities at this speed. New perspectives. We have moved into a new dimension. The dimension of the CONSCIOUS BEING. This is where we learn to develop into our essences. The energy of Consciousness.

C: I no longer see images of a memory, which apparently, used to be our reality. Who would choose to live that way? What I call living, is today. These past images were last on my list to be converted into my present. These memory's included images of my own past actions. It was disturbing. But now, I understand them, I don't feel affected by them. They no longer have a meaning. I am *"learning to live, so I can live to learn."* I know it's a cliche, but it's very inspiring to me.

Question: How were some people, awakened without performing their own energy conversion, like many others did? Was it a world wide awakening? The young generation of the energy movement, were all already awakened, were they not?

M: Yes, they were. The conversion process happened to those who were initially needed, to begin the energy movement. From there, many others joined. However, there were also many, who were still unconscious and were holding on to their Virus Energy. All those in this state, had to be converted to create the final balance. They just woke up in this dimension. So you can see, how many need support with this new direction. There is no Awakening without a Conversion. The awakening and the Conversion happened simultaneously. So I believe they are hand in hand. It was a Conversion Version, by Inversion. An inner awakening of Humankind.

C: Thanks! But, this brings up more questions; do we continue to go through this energy conversion process, with each development? Is energy evolution constant, as long as I am evolving? In the book, what does Revolution mean, Energy Revolution?

M: That's three questions. You are going too fast, I don't want to miss anything. Those are great questions. Your Consciousness Energy is working. I respect your awareness. Let's address Your First Question? You asked, Do we continue to go through the same energy conversion process, with each development?

Since Conversion and Evolution are related, one must go through an energy conversion to evolve into a new evolution. So your answer is yes. It's a natural evolution. As you develop, your views change. This instantly puts you in other dimensions. Each perception is a dimension of that reality. The other choice is, to live your life viewing the same thing. Feeling the same, and doing the same, like we use to. We managed to escape this way of life.

Question Two: Is Energy Evolution constant?

As long as your development is in constant evolution, you will continuously evolve into new evolutions. This is creating life. This is the purpose of our creation. The continued evolution of physical Energy. The Universal Consciousness Energy gave us life, so we can give life back to it.

Question Three: In the book Evolution Revolution, what does Revolution mean? Energy Revolutions?

M: Yes, this is part of it. They do cycle in a Revolving Evolution, which can change the form of matter? It's a thought provoking question. What provoked you to ask it?

C: Just a confirmation of what I was thinking. This tells me, as long as I keep developing, Consciousness will keep evolving. I appreciate your feedback. I have gained a lot of new information. I know I took too long, so thank you. Next caller...Sorry!

M: I better give time to others, to be fair. Thanks for the Energy boost.

Hi caller, you're up, thanks for listening?

C: Hi Max. Thanks for doing this type of forum. Oh yes, I am listening. This is brain awakening information. I think I am still waking up. I must've slept through some of the Evolution Revolution. My Questions are; we were intelligent human beings pre evolution, Why didn't we discover the Virus Energy on our own? Was it really the fear of the unknown? Even though I understand what happened to us, I don't understand where I stand. I am in awe of what we have awakened to, and how we awakened to it. So now I want to understand it. Can our Consciousness, teach us what we need to keep developing?

M: Consciousness, is the one thing that can teach you what you need to know, and what you don't know. Many people need inspiration to seek knew knowledge. The ones who go looking for it, are doing it because they are conscious and curious. They are aware of the difference, between consciousness and the unconscious. They will be attracted to this knowledge. They are aware, they can learn from any knowledge.

C: Who or what taught them? Was it the Universal Consciousness?

M: Yes. It doesn't only teach, it also learns from what it teaches. There were thousands of people who were born knowing this knowledge? By the time the energy movement began, they were converted and ready to complete their destiny. Many of the Young Generation, were a plant which, grew into a forest of nature. Plants were planted, to lay a path for the upcoming energy evolution revolution.

Many of them received these writings in this book, which they used to convert their own Virus Cell infection. They gathered in groups to work on the development of their Consciousness Energy. They became the match that ignited the energy movement. Consciousness is contagious. Their awareness, and commitment brought us to this day.

C: How did they know what was coming, before everyone else?

M: Because, what was coming, came, and blended right in. Our new history, talks about a man who joined the energy movement. He became known as, The Traveler.

C: So it was a someone not a something. Come on, just one person determined the future of humankind. There has to be more?

M: Yes, there is more, lots more. It wasn't just one person who moved the movement. As I had previously said. Many were planted, but he did bring in new knowledge. He taught new skills. Which were instrumental in converting the Virus Energy Cell. He, along with others lead the movement, and paved the road to the Evolution Revolution. Everyone felt the energy he projected. That's why he was selected, and never detected. After the Evolution Revolution, it was said, he disappeared. What I learned later is, he is still here. Close by, still learning.

C: Was he one of those who was born awake?

M: Yes, just like the others. They all had a role to play.

C: Isn't this, like God supposedly sent his Son to help humankind? What's the difference? It's using different words to describe the same event, isn't it?

M: Are you asking if history is repeating itself? If so, then yes. Each time it was tried, humans took the Virus Energy's side. The message was always denied. UC kept going back to the drawing board, and created a new plan. The message didn't change much, but the people have.

These words are not addressing humanity in history. They are addressing the history in humanity. If these words sound familiar, it's because you have heard them before. We all have. Except, before the Evolution Revolution, we heard them, and did nothing. These words are action words.

This is not about one man, it's about Unity. It's not about servitude, it's about humankind's attitude. It's not about blind faith, it is about a Conscious form of reality, not just a belief. The religious concept of God faded away, after the Virus Cell was converted. We now know, God is a Universal Consciousness Energy, the Creator of all that exists, and will exist. The basis of our existence, is about Creating the same

Energy as it has created us. But most of all, is that this story needs no glory, because it's our story. The traveler can be any one of us. It was our responsibility, to make the choice to be Consciousness Energy. Like the Energy Movement did.

C: Very inspiring, I must say. Where is he today? You did say he was still around, didn't you?

M: Yes, I have a quote from this book to share, *"Telling you, will not develop you."*

C: Do You know anything more about my questions? You seem to be very knowledgeable about this subject. It feels like it's personal for you.

M: Absolutely, it needs to be personal for us all. As far as your questions, I answered them.

C: You missed one or two. But I won't hold it against you. Where did you get your information from? There are no records I found.

M: That's because they were buried underground. W.A.T.E.R. has them. Did this help?

C: Yes, thank you. I believe I will follow up and read those documents.

M: Thanks for your questions. Good information. Does your inquiry of the Traveler have a separate purpose?

C: I knew him. We worked closely together during the Evolution Revolution. I thought I might be able to find him because we lost track of each other. He taught myself and others, the skills of becoming a phantom.

M: Do you live close by the W.A.T.E.R. institute? If you do and have time, come by after the show, we can talk? I would love to keep talking to you but the phone is ringing.

C: OK, that's a plan. See you then Max.

M: Hey there, next caller please.

C: Hi, my name is Sky, if you're going to ask if my mom was a hippie, it's yes. But as a mom, there was no one like her. Question for you max. Do we evolve while we are alive, or after we die?

M: Hi. Good question to get us started. Both actually. Whether in life or in death, each realization evolves you. Anything that develops your Consciousness, is considered to be evolving. Each time you learn, you evolve. Each time your perception shifts towards awareness, you're evolving.

C: I want to know more about what you know, and at the same time, confirm what I know. So far, as I listen, I have picked up some good tips. I used to fear everything, including people, suddenly, I trust everybody. Here are my questions. Are these feelings of Consciousness? What other changes should I expect to see, and feel? Should I just stay focused on learning?

M: The reason you felt any form of fear before, was because fear made you feel it. Now, fear is gone with the Virus Energy. The Virus has been converted to a balanced Energy. So fear no longer exists. Does this make sense? Your next question, is what you are feeling a form of Consciousness? If what you are feeling causes you to develop consciously, then,yes, it is. As far as what to expect next, you shouldn't expect. It may not be what you expected. You should focus on learning? This means focusing on everything. This is where true learning comes from.

C: Is there anything, I can't learn from? I can look at a tree, and I see a tree. Isn't this reality. It is what it is. Right?

M: Yes, but with Consciousness imagination, you can see the tree anyway you want. If you wanted to see a flower instead of a tree, the tree will become the flower. You are now control of what you perceive. This is, *"What you focus on becomes your reality,"* in its entirety.

During the energy movement, there was a lot of talk about empathy, compassion, kindness, and not having fear of death. People had questions. They were very stressful times. Many in the movement needed to be comforted. There was this one story being passed around which touched me deeply. It's not one I will forget anytime soon. I don't think I have heard of a more compassionate, and wonderful way to help someone pass on.

This story, has been in my heart since the first day I heard it. It showed me how to take nothing for granted. It's about love and romance. A gentle separation of body and spirit. It's about a dance teacher, who taught a crippled man how to dance.

He knew he couldn't dance, he was in a wheelchair. For some reason, she couldn't see that.

She was aware that he couldn't leave his chair, and she had to come up with an idea, that would give her a way to teach him to dance, she pondered.

He is feeble and can't carry his own weight. She became obsessed with this thought. She focused so hard, trying to figure it out. She was determined. Hey, maybe he can dance through me, she thought. Ya, he can do that. Why not? He will get to dance. I am sure of it. She wanted it to happen. Not for herself mind you, but for him.

One day, she brought him to the dance studio.

"Why are we here, you know I can't dance." She replied, *"yes you can, I figured out a way how you can dance, You are going to dance through me. I promise, you will feel like you're dancing."* She turned on soft music. *"Just relax, and feel my every move,"* she whispered.

With lips of ruby red, she said. *"Feel the groove, move with me, move as I move. Feel the music. It will help you move. A little turn here and another one there. Watch me, sway with me. Imagine me in your arms as we dance. Let the music sink in. Feel it vibrate your body."*

As he became curious, he started to sway to the gentle sound of music. She flowed like an angel. He moved the same way.

She said, *"observe my grace, my steps, the way my head tips."*

He took it all in. He was feeling her movements. He became hypnotized by her motion. As she danced, he closed his eyes.

"It's OK to close your eyes, but don't let go of the motion from my movement. Stay with it. Let it guide you. Feel the rhythm in your body."

She then starts to move his wheelchair slowly, in a swaying motion. He shouts out, hey I am dancing! How amazing. What a feeling.

Wait? What's happening? Where are you going? I just started dancing.

Suddenly the music changed. He opened his eyes and started to cry. The face of an angel, asked him why? He replied, *"I thought I died, and I was dancing with an angel. But I have never felt so alive."* She said, *"you did die, and you were dancing with an angel."*

He was puzzled as he asked, *"how? I was sitting in my chair, with my eyes closed, watching you dance. Yes you were, and now, get out of your chair, you are free to dance anytime, anywhere."*

C: I am in tears. What a lovely story. Heartfelt. I was affected by it. It has meaning to me.

M: There was no pain, or fear involved in the evolution from body to spirit. Just love, a bit of romance, and the joy of dancing. What a great send off. I had to stop and think. Was anyone any different than the man in the wheelchair? I believe at one point or another, we all had our own wheelchairs. How did I expect to dance, while I was stuck in my own chair?

The chair was the heaviest part of my weight. We all had one back then. Most of us were stuck in them. We didn't even know it. The Awakening showed us, we were not crippled. We were shown how we can do something about our infection.

C: The Young Generation, created the Energy Movement to get people out of their chair. I for one, am glad it worked.

M: You know, all this information is public record. You can read all about it in the library. Old newspapers, anywhere.

C: Thanks for that story Max.

M: Next call. Hi, is this a sharing, or a question?

C: It's more of a curiosity? I am interested in Astronomy. I feel this strong connection to beings outside of Earths space. I want to explore their floor. Now that we have become conscious and Virus free, how can I make contact with beings on other planets? I mean, they are friendly, are they not? With the Virus gone everything should be fine, correct? Should I even be trying to make contact? Where did our visitors come from? It wasn't our universe.

M: This is some curiosity. Astral travel is a skill which not many are aware of. Consciousness Energy can be projected to anywhere in anyplace. You have a choice, astral travel using your spirit, or you can project your Energy and connect with another energy on any planet. You should knock first. Remember, it's a Universal connection.

C: OK Max. Where did you learn all of what you know? It couldn't have come from someone on Earth? Are you an Alien transplants, living on Earth all this time? You seem to know too much for a radio disc jockey. So what's up? What are you not sharing with us? I am sure you have a history.

M: Thank you for your inquiry. But the calls are coming in fast, so what else would you like to discuss. Don't you have a question?

C: Yes, it's about the Alien intervention. If you are not one of them, then you must be a contact. My questions are, how did you become a physical contact with an alien nation, when most of humanity doubted they existed? How did a human get involved? Who brought them here?

M: Why? It's not about who brought them, no one brings them. They come and go as they want to. Anyway, this is not about Who, it's about You. What did you do to support them? They are here to help us, are you aware of this?

C: I am. My thanks to them. Now what are they going to do? Are they staying? Will there be others coming? Do we really know what we are doing?

M: Why do I sense a bit of hesitation when you speak of them? As if you are unsure. Unsure doesn't exist in Consciousness. Check yourself. What are you feeling to cause such a reaction.

C: No, no. It's not suspicion. It's more of, how did they know we needed their help? And what's the intention now?

M: It's wasn't hard to tell. The first Nuclear Explosion told the whole story. Would you walk into a house that's completely lined with bombs? I wouldn't, but we were. All creation is connected by the Universal Consciousness. What happens to one, affects the whole connection. It's felt by the whole collection.

C: How long had they planned this Energy Conversion of humankind? Didn't they plan it? Humans certainly didn't.

M: This plan was formed by, the Universal Consciousness Energy Vibration. This includes all donations from other alien creations. It wasn't just a one person plan. This plan included the UNIVERSAL CONSCIOUSNESS, SPIRIT, and the PHYSICAL HUMAN.

C: Who else knew about it? Did you know? Was the government in on it? I doubt that. They were too self absorbed. Come on max, I know you know. I want to know.

M: What would you like to know about? The universe, energy, cycles, intuition abilities?

C: About this Universal Consciousness plan. You told me what the plan included, but not about it.

M: Why are you asking me about that? Why do you think I would know? You must know something I don't.

C: I ask you, because you seem to be the Collage of Knowledge about our evolution. I think you know, because you have managed to answer every question they've asked. It feels different to me. Hmm, What I know that you don't, cannot be considered, until, I find out how much you know.

M: All I know, is who I am. You can't be me, you have to be you. You can't know everything I know, as there is no limit to my knowing, or yours.

C: Tell me one thing I don't know about you, and I will do the same.

M: Here is something you don't know. I played a role in this Universal plan, I still do. I had first hand knowledge about the downloading of this book. As I said, this was not a one person plan. It included many others who helped people understand. What they experienced was an example, of what was to come. The plan knew, it would work. It had worked on those directly involved from day one. Including myself. Your turn. It better be good. Mine was. If I know it, you have to choose another.

C: Oh yes, OK, about me. I see visions sometimes. I seem to be getting visions of our history. I carry them around in my brain's picture album. We are now aware of who, and what we are. Why am I seeing these visions?

M: Which history? The old or the new one?

C: Both I think. They are mixed together. I have been taking one vision at a time, in order to work through what I see. Reshaping the old view, into something new. The old one was very disturbing. I see visions of the reactions the Energy Movement created globally. Trust was lost. You couldn't say hello without a dirty look, or a look of suspicion. This was Pre-Evolution Revolution. What I witnessed was a form of Armageddon.

So many of us were just swept into it. You had to stand for something, or go sit down. There was a sound of a stampede on the ground. You couldn't tell where it came from. The Earth was shaking, the day became night. The streets were full of the young generation, making their way to the evolution revolution. It was then I made the decision to join the movement. I wanted to learn the ability of Energy Projection from the members of the energy movement.

M: Wait? Did I hear you right? Did you say Energy projection? This is my specialty. My focus has been on this ability. The institute of W.A.T.E.R. has great information on this subject. You should investigate it. It can only add to what you know.

C: There is something else to add about myself. In the energy movement, my role became essential after I trained to be a Phantom. I was taught how to project my energy and connect with others. We used it for tapping into the vibrations of the leaderships. Then I was taught the ability of astral projection, out of body travel. Where we would be in the same room as government officials and not be seen. Thus the term Phantom. We gathered a lot of secret information this way. It was the only way to get what the movement needed, to achieve the conversion of the Virus Cell. To make it possible for them, to confront the Virus, and it was not easy. I am sure many of those who had this ability are still alive, and living somewhere. It would be nice to have a reunion. Maybe some of them will call in.

M: Phantoms? Wow! Because of you and others like you, we managed to get valuable documentation to use on the infected politicians. Thank you! How many are still alive, do you know?

C: No, not sure. But, this is why I am curious about you. To know what you know, you had to have been there. It's difficult to say how many are still alive. I don't think anyone really knows besides myself. I only know of two, they know who they are.

M: This was an exceptional conversation. Thank you for sharing. It's great to talking to you.

C: Good talking to you. Although, I am not done researching you yet. I'll be in touch.

M: Hello, next caller, you're on. Welcome to the people's forum. **C:** Hey, what's happening? What's shaken Max?

M: Why, did I miss something? What's happening caller? Was there an earthquake? Are you OK. You sound worried.

C: Wait, where are you going. Did you forget how to speak human? I am talking with you, that's what's happening. I was saying hello. No earthquake. I'm just saying how is it going?

M: You said, what's shaking, when nothing was. Oh, wow! I must have forgotten our old slang? Can you speak, without using the words of yesterday?

C: OK, I am old, what can I say. Years ago before all this started, I read a book called, *"From a Gun to a Flower."* It was a prequel to the Evolution Revolution. It's a must read, to get the whole picture. Where can we find this book now? Is it still around? What happened to it? It explains the beginning of this plan we just experienced. It tells the story of Consciousness Energy, in much detail.

M: Have you checked the libraries, book stores. It should be everywhere by now. I read this book, it was very informative. It explained the delivery of the Evolution Revolution. It connected body, spirit and Consciousness into one understanding. I recommend it to everyone. Go search for it on-line.

C: Did you say get in line? For what? You just said, they are everywhere. Now I have to stand in line? I waited in line most of my life. I don't have to anymore. Absolutely no lines.

M: No sir, no standing in line. I said, *"on-line."* You can have a seat, or remain on your feet.

C: Not until I feel complete. I heard you were some kind of knowledge expert. So I have a question. How I can access the Consciousness Energy, by going through my brain?

M: You can access it from anywhere, and from anything. You are swimming in it. Your brain is composed of Consciousness Energy, you don't have to go through it. You can use the brain to focus it with. If your intention is projection? The brain is a tool, the Energy, is the hand that holds it. When your thoughts are conscious ones. You can access energy from that development.

C: I work on developing my physical energy, to integrate with my Consciousness Energy, so they can grow together. There are a lot of evolutions, before I reach total Consciousness. But now, I am able to feel peoples thoughts. I have always been able to do it, but not to this intensity. Years ago, I learned, people's thoughts are like the channels on TV. Only they changed on their own. They were out of control thoughts bumping into each other, without direction. There were so many mixed up thoughts, many of them were never addressed. So they played bumper cars in the brain. These thoughts, are what kept us unconscious. We ignored them, as they kept cycling back in an attempt to become conscious. Address them as they are found or it's see you next round. This is just my opinion.

M: Consciousness thoughts are balanced thoughts. They are aware of the reaction they create. They are aware of their effect on humanity. They help to insure you make the correct choices in your life. They keep you conscious and focused. This is one of the benefit which comes with energy development. When using Conscious thoughts, you create your own reality. They awakened us to the power of the question, creative, and Moving questions.

Are you aware, we all have the ability to read the feelings of others? Your Energy Intuition, converts them into your thoughts. Also when you shift your thought, that shift, becomes your reality until you shift again. Our thoughts lead our direction. Trusting your thoughts is your responsibility. Get to know the difference between conscious and unconscious thoughts. Today, this should be easy to know. How different is your perception, from that of the Universal Consciousness?

C: I, like everyone, get my perception from it.

M: When your thoughts come from your Conscious perception, what's the difference between you, and Consciousness?

C: I would say none. We would be one. I can't argue with this logic. Question; When we know who we are, do we bother with labels, like names?

M: Using a label only covers up what you are, now you're stuck as a label. How are you going to find yourself, if you don't remove that label? Thank you for your information, it may help others. It has helped me. Your input was valuable.

M: Hello, welcome to the conversation. You're up.

C: Hi there Max? Here is the thing. I need to learn how to use my Energy, to develop my anatomy? You know, change certain parts. We are still women aren't we? Are men still the same? This is a benefit of the Consciousness Energy, isn't it? So, can I? This is not an ego thing, It's a health one. If I'm made of it, I should be able to shape it anyway I want, isn't this the goal?

M: Hi, no argument from me. But why are you choosing this to focus on? Rather than reading thoughts, astral projection, those types of Consciousness abilities.

C: This energy has no limits. We are learning how to use it. Who better to test it out on, than myself. It's more of a curiosity for me. I am sure I am not the only one who thought of this idea. Should we do a survey? OK, I do have a serious question. With all this talk about the Evolution Revolution, why is there so little information, about the involved people's reputation? Can you share anything about their personal lives?

I am speaking of those who were first to navigate the Consciousness Energy. Their deeds are well known, but, shouldn't there be more documentation about them? Like, what are they doing now? Where they are? For the future generation mind you. They need to know. The Evolution Revolution must never be forgotten.

M: Most of them have become teachers of the Universal Consciousness knowledge at the W.A.T.E.R. institute. What's the interest?

C: I want to learn more. They must know much more than we do presently.

M: Not really. You know, what they know, like everyone else. There is no personal information about anyone I know. You can always look it up on the Internet, I suppose? Let me know how it goes? Do you have another question which would lead to a discussion? We are yearning for learning.

C: OK change of topic. What happened to holidays and traditions?

M: The world has changed, our brains have been rearranged. There were many good things in the past, until greed got to them. Everything it touched, it infected. Now greed is gone, celebrating a holiday can actually be about the holiday, not money. However, today, we don't need to wait once a year to celebrate. Our lives have become a reason to celebrate everyday. Our Consciousness, is a reason to celebrate.

It is now celebrated throughout the world, it supports our energy development. Some Traditions are Energy Repetitions. Consciousness doesn't repeat. Each time is a new experience. Presently, It's focused on its creativity, and development.

C: We gave our choices away to the Virus Cell. We allowed our brain to controlled by a brain infection. What kind of race were we? We didn't represent the human part of us very well. We excepted limits. We rarely made our own decisions. We took other peoples advice, and made choices that changed our lives. What's in it for me was the main theme. I was being used by the closest ones around me, and had no idea. I was unaware. I was unconscious.

I was oblivious to my surroundings. Having an eighty hour work week, cost me half of my life. You're not even conscious of when you've had enough. Then, here comes the Evolution Revolution Intervention. Along with our transformation, now we are learning the art of conscious communication and life's appreciation. I just have two questions? What happened to all the weapons of mass destruction? Are we really safe from them now?

M: All weapons of destruction were disassembled, and melted down. Now, they serve a more sustainable service. Thanks to our visitors. Who were instrumental in designing, teaching, and helping us, to rebuild our new world. We now have the awareness, to understand the potential of the Universal Consciousness Energy, to comprehend our energy composition. Our connection to all creation.

We have to understand our own creation, before attempting to learn about other creations. Even with our new Consciousness, we know little about ourselves. We have so much to investigate, discover, and develop. Understanding ourselves, will help us understand others, who are in a different form than us. We will have more visitors, now that we converted the Virus Energy Cell. We have become trustworthy and helpful.

C: Thank you for the conversation. It was educational.

M: It was for me also.

Hi, go ahead, speaker is on. Hello. Anyone there? Are you a caller of mystery?

C: Yes, excuse me. I was doing my breathing exercise, so sorry. I was trying to catch my breath.

M: Were you successful? Why do you do breathing exercises? Were you a smoker in the past?

C: Nope, never smoked anything actually. It was the air pollution. What's the best part about having clean air, it's breathing clean air. You mentioned something about the visitors on the last call. Where did they go? People want to know. Do you know?

M: The last information I received is, they are living with humanity. Learning and interacting with us. Is this what you want to discuss?

C: Yes. They came to help us, as part of the universal consciousness plan. I haven't thanked them yet. I feel like It needs to be said. Are they being entertained? Are we showing them gratitude? Acknowledging their help? They helped us save our lives for goodness sakes. How are we thanking them?

M: There is a party planned, anyone can attend. There will be plenty of room. Everyone is welcome. From the human, to whomever wishes to land.

C: A party? That's a great idea. I am impressed. Who thought of that? Who is hosting it? Are they posting it? Why haven't I seen anything on line?

M: The people of the World are hosting it?

C: Where is it being held?

M: In the Sahara desert.

C: Why there? It gets very hot.

M: Plenty of room is what I heard. Especially for other visitors to land. This will be a Universal Celebration.

C: A long awaited one, I might add. You've given me so much to think about. Are you going to the party? Is anyone famous coming?

M: First, Yes, I am, wouldn't miss it, and no, there are no more famous people. We are all famous now. We are equal, on a Consciousness level. There is no room for ego anymore. Life still goes on, but the focus is on a Consciousness Development. Everyone is creating their own reality, by using the Universal Consciousness as their director.

C: Just one last question. It will be quick. Are we going to look like them in the future? I mean, we are going through a physical Evolution now?

M: What do you think they look like? There are many with different looks. They are created with the same energy as you were. So you can say you are related to them. They have a body like you, a head like yours. The only difference is their advanced brain. They have gone through their evolutions to get to this point. Just as we will. Our brains are what will grow. Evolution will adjust to physical births. DNA will change. New births will be born.

You are aware, you can get the same answers from yourself. You and I share the same Consciousness Energy. Tap into it. Practice more. You can achieve the same connection. You have to learn, to hear what your feelings say. Focus on this for now. How can you find yourself, while looking for others? Use your Consciousness to find out. Follow its lead. Your development will benefit more.

C: It was great talking with you. See you at the party. I will be the one wearing a spaceship on my head.

M: Next call, keep the calls coming in. Hi, what have you discovered lately?

C: Hello, I remembered my first realization. When I realized I had lost my fear of death. I felt this awesome feeling of confidence. It's been happening ever since. I am hearing a lot of talk about our new evolution, and what it means to be an Energy Human Being. Does being Consciousness energy make us energy beings?

It seems to me, the Universal Consciousness is Omnipotent. Isn't it our goal, to evolve from physical energy, into the Universal Consciousness totality? Are we basically, riding on a cycle of the creator which created us? Do we keep evolving, until it takes us around to our creator once again? A never ending cycle of life to life. Is this what we are talking about?

M: It sounds like you are learning a great deal. So, which question do you want to start with? How about the cycle? A cycle of life to life is a beautiful way to put it. It is the true meaning, of no beginning and no end. Yes, we ride this cycle, it's called Consciousness Energy Evolution. From physical to the core total. Evolution is a necessary part of creation. Stop evolution, stop creation.

C: I hadn't thought of evolution this way until now. Without it we wouldn't exist anymore. Evolution basically means, Energy Development.

M: You asked about becoming an Energy Human Being? We all have become energy human beings, the moment we converted the Virus Cell infection. Does our evolution depend, on our Consciousness Energy Development? Was another question. The evolution of every creation, depends on Consciousness development. It's the life source of all creation.

C: My perception changes everyday. Will this be a permanent occurrence? If we see nothing is changing, does it mean we are unconscious again?

M: No. When it's not moving, it's because you're unfocused. Distracted by someone or something. Total focus, creates total movement. It's not just a little here and there. When you want to create, use your Whole Energy to do it with. Not parts. Otherwise, what you create will come out in pieces.

C: I heard what you said. It makes sense. So, I need to put my Whole into it, to get it to move. I think I understand. It's a hundred percent or it's incomplete.

M: Your brain runs on Balanced Energy now. Keep this in mind. Your development is endless. You and your Consciousness, are in control of your own existence. You have awakened into a new dimension. A new world. Look forward. When you LEARN TO LIVE, you will LIVE TO LEARN.

This is our responsibility. Our creativity is unlimited. You are an Energy Vibration, act like one. Focus on it. Become aware of where you are, who you are. Look at your surroundings, they have changed. It's now up to you, to paint your next view.

C: Of what, and of who? The Earth looks like Earth. Nature is still nature. It's still green. So what do you mean?

M: It's not as much as what's changed on the outside, it's how your new perception, has changed your view of the outside. Haven't you noticed, people are no longer angry? Have you witnessed violence anywhere lately? Nothing but peace, and beauty.

C: Thanks, I will take this under advisement. I learned quite a bit.

M: Hello Caller, your on, go ahead. Do you have a question? Or a sharing. We want to hear it. Whatever it is.

C: Hi. No, just a comment. I am a man of action. Always have been. Being conscious, really moves me into action. Now, we have become a humanity of Consciousness. Is it this Energy alone, which drive us to be in action?

M: You can be Conscious and aware. But it's still your choice to move. Choice, makes your body move. As you can see, consciousness and awareness are useless, without a focused action towards creation. Your Awareness, must become conscious. So your Conscious can become aware.

C: Can we be aware, and still choose to do nothing about what we see? Oh wait, doing nothing is not being awake. Neither was this question. If we are not in action, then what are we?

M: WHAT WE USE TO BE. When you don't do anything, you're not aware. If you were, you would be doing something. Being in a Consciousness state, there is no question when it comes to doing. You just do it. It's an instant reaction. Action is a reaction to Energy Development. Action drives you towards

Development. Consciousness Energy, gives action its drive. Its ability to act, its ability to make an impact. Without this Energy, there would be no action, only reaction. Which translates into, no energy movement. Reactions which cause harm to others are negative actions. Today, there are millions of human beings out there, who are Learning, Helping, Teaching, Creating, and Building Energy. They are the future of humanity. The continuation of life as a body. These are actions, driven by the need for Energy Development. We could be like we used to be, but what we use to be no longer exists. We can never be that again.

C: Action, can be interpreted in many ways and forms. We changed the meaning of action, to suit our needs. Somehow, action became related to violence. This, use to be our way of thinking. Some of humanity believed war to be action. It's what we use to do. We made ourselves believe, bad was good and good was bad. Our own meanings, are what flipped our physical perspectives to go backwards, which led us to living our life backward. The energy of Action goes forward. This makes sense to me, what are your thoughts?

M: A word without consciousness meaning, is a word without meaning.

C: Don't all words have meanings.

M: In our history, words were being used that had no meanings, so we made them up, and put them into the empty words. Inside the word action, is energy action which gives it its meaning. There can still be action without meaning, but what would that mean? Violence without meaning.

Your perception of the energy, is what decides your action. Action is just a word without it. Physical words have physical meanings, created by humanity's beliefs. It's up to you to choose words with true Consciousness meanings. When you are a conscious person, you are aware of your actions. Your focus is, on the energy in the word, not the actual letters. You feel the meaning with your Conscious Intuition. Because words didn't always mean what they said, until now.

C: Is communicating with the spirit world possible, Now that we are in this Consciousness dimension? I mean can I see them? Talk to them? We are a much closer frequency to theirs now. I should be able to reach out and connect. It would be nice to talk to my parents.

M: Communication with the spiritual worlds, is not impossible. You just need to learn how to use your Energy, to project it to another dimensional reality, an ethereal one. The question is, which one? You could spend so much time with your parents, you may forget to come back. The longer you stay, the more it becomes your reality. I wouldn't do this alone. Seriously. You are asking to look into spirit dimensions, not just one. Any one of them could pull you in, keeping your body in a coma.

What's in the brain now, is Consciousness. It's our reality. The brain has adjusted itself to meet its optimal speed of our frequency. It is driven to lead us. It has awakened to new abilities of its own. It's developing its own reality. It changed perception of itself. It has changed its view of its body. The old has become new. That's why I chose the new, just like most of you I am sure. What we create has become our meaning. We have learned the ability to see it. It's our true intention now.

Action, is Consciousness Energy revolving, and moving in a synchronized speed of motion, toward a certain direction. Without a direction, action becomes a reaction. It will not have substance, which means no foundation. So yes, you are correct in saying action got us here, but it was Consciousness Energy Action. That's why it was a success. Do you understand how it works?

C: I just want to make a small comment. These conversations are why it's important for people to talk about what happened. I also feel, these discussions are helping us to better understand ourselves, as a Consciousness Energy Creation. When I think about where we have arrived, it makes me feel good to be alive. Where I was, compared to where I am, are two worlds apart. So, I know what is to be, or not to be. This is what living through the evolution revolution has taught me. Plus, to never give up on a just cause. Just because. Especially a cause with a conscious meaning.

M: What are you going to do with your discoveries? Learn from them. Grow with them. Share them with others.

C: All the above, why not, this is what I have learned, a word is just a word, without a Consciousness meaning. Awareness is just looking, without energy movement, how important the evolution process is to creation, and by being unconscious, we kept ourselves from our own evolution.

M: Those are the steps, toward increasing your energy development. Each time your perception changes, your feelings change. Your view is new. All you were before, is gone with the old perception. Your new one is now your reality. Live it until your perception changes again. Life and death, simply explained.

C: They balance each other, don't they? So death, is changing physical energy from its frequency speed, to a faster one. This is not to difficult to understand.

M: It has been a long road to re-balancing physical energy. To awaken us to our natural form as Energy. No more mental illness. Now, it's all about brain health.

C: Before I go, I want say, You have given me many things to thinks about. I like that. I feel full. I have much to process. This is a good way to communicate with people. Thank you.

M: Your welcome, bye!

Hello, you are next. Thanks for joining the conversation. Do you have something to teach us?

C: Hi, I am not sure about teaching, but I do have a sharing. I am one of those older adults, who didn't question his adult children about what they were doing, when I heard them talking about a The New revolution. I was completely taken by surprise when the Energy Movement occurred. I heard talk about a movement at the time, but I was clueless, and in denial.

I became curious to hear more about this Virus Cell, but not enough to ask. Big mistake. I didn't take it serious enough at first. I didn't believe it. Like many of my friends, we were content with what we had. We had no reason to want more than what we could afford. We had our jobs, our families, and our hobbies, what more did we need? I was happy. Many people were.

M: What happened to wanting more knowledge about the Virus Energy Cell? It seems, being content made you forget.

C: You bet. It wasn't until I overheard enough talk about the energy movement, when I started to ask questions about the Virus. I began to observe its actions in others. I learned to recognize the difference between, balanced and unbalanced energy's. It occurred to me, I needed to find out more on my own. So I went out and learned as much as I could. What the young generation was doing, inspired me to do the same. I became a different person. I became conscious of the energy movements goals. I felt I had experienced a transformation. I developed a new perception. I began to ask questions. It felt like, I just awakened from a dream.

M: What you experienced was a form of Physical Energy Conversion, into Consciousness Energy Awareness. Your energy transformation was real. The world went through an Energy Conversion, without realizing it. We were too unconscious to notice. Many of us went to sleep and awakened. It was like a blink of the eye. This was made possible by the infusion of pure Consciousness Energy into humanity. It was like new oxygen filling the world. Everything began to change from there. Natural development became our nature. Living in the present moment; it's from here, we create.

How can this Energy be used to materialize objects? Focus and visualization forms it. It's what moves it. It has to know where it's going, and what it's going to do. It has to be directed, projected, this is what our brain is for. The ability to use the energy of Focusing, gives us control of our vibrational frequency speed. So we can slow it down to our speed. This is how we can use the energy to materialize and dematerialize objects. We have this ability. As long as we are using this Energy to do it with.

C: I have always been curious, did people use to actually have this power, or were they faking it? Was it something we knew we could do, but lost the ability? Now, we have it back. Is it because of this new type of oxygen you spoke of? It does take a lot of consistent practice. It's a new muscle to grow.

M: In our past, before the Evolution Revolution, our oxygen was being depleted. Our air was suffocating from our chemical pollution. If not for new oxygen we would have suffocated also. We had too many issues, which no one really knew how to fix. They pretended for a long time, but it was only a distraction tool from one leader to another. What I know of past history is, there were people who could move objects but not many. They are called Spiritual Mediums. Today, everyone can develop this ability.

C: Well, thanks for your comments, they helped.

M: Hi, you're on, start talking.

C: Hello Max. I have heard many people share. Their conversations have moved me. Now that we are on a road to a New Direction. Is the whole world walking on the same path? Do we all have the same

beliefs? Do we all think the same thoughts? Does it mean there is no more variety? How can this be? I was there in the world movement. I held a leadership position. Held, is the operative word.

I have spent a lot of time with my thoughts, trying to remember what happened. It's probably best I don't remember much. Just enough to not forget. The important thing is, we were able to undo what we had done. The Virus Cell faced its conversion, and the Earth was saved. Thanks to the brave.

Everyone did what they could. But, not many did what they should, like me. I am aware, I should have done more.

M: I say, remember what can develop you. What can teach you. Anything else, is not as important to remember. You have asked, is the whole world walking on the same path? Humanity has become conscious of its creator, if this is what you mean by walking on the same path. However, we can walk the same path and still have our own perception. Our own view. It's there for you to share with others who are walking with you. You may share the same view, but your perception will see it differently.

Another question was, do we all have the same awareness? If the awareness is about the Universal Consciousness Energy Vibration, then yes. When you are developing, you are aware of the benefits. Do we all have the same thoughts? Each experience creates thoughts. We will have different experiences, which will promote different thoughts, from the perception of what we see and hear. We can have an opinion, about the thoughts of the person who had the experience. Last question, does this mean no more variety? We all look different. Eat different foods. Drink different drinks. We speak different languages. There you go, variety.

How did you donate to the Energy Movement, or the Evolution Revolution, sir. Were you around to support them? What role did you play? Can you talk about it?

C: I was a vice president, until the governments were reorganized by our visitor friends, it was a global event. When I left office, I felt clear on the fact, as a vice president of a country, I did the best I could for the people. Politics have always played a key role, in many decisions made by leadership. I was outnumbered by greed and control. If you didn't go with the flow, you got kicked out of the show. Let me tell you, politics was a show, a horror show.

How could I make a difference if I left office. I made many regretful decisions, but I put much effort into Ecology, decreasing Air Pollution, Crime, and Drugs. I hardly made a dent. How could I, when the government you work for, was working against you. Money always made the world go around. Yes, I am guilty of going along, but it was the only way to stay in office to do my real work, helping the people. It's why I got into politics in the first place. That dream was crushed immediately after the elections. I was put in my place very quickly.

I was told when and where to go, when to show, and what say. I became a puppet. I was happy to leave politics. It was the best thing that happened to me. Politics didn't help the planet or the people on it. From my perspective, as a use to be government leader, we all ignored the signs. Nuclear weapons should have been our first clue. We left our continued existing in the hands of chance. People were living in fear while we, the politicians, were in meetings. As far as the energy movement. Yes, I participated in it, by being faced with it. World leaders were being confronted, and converted by the leaders of the movement.

M: So, you say you did your best, and not until now, did you realize your mess. The mess you, the leader created from our lives and the Earth. Why did politicians ignore our deadly situation? You were there, explain it. You had to be in on their secrets. Even if you didn't like it. You could have quit, or make a stand, and uncover corruption in your government.

C: …And make myself a target? Just thinking back on it, I became so relieved when the visitors landed. The effect they had when they appeared, was beyond imagination. It's embedded in my brain. Technology just stopped. Protection from us I assumed. Until I realized, it was protecting us, from ourselves. I remember the reactions as they were landing. I felt as though, I was the only man on Earth. The whole world became silent. Even the birds stopped whistling, and the wind died down.

The anticipation set in. For many, it was fear. People started scrambling, running, questioning, many were curious and understanding. There was this calmness all around. Anyway, after they appeared to the people, things started moving fast. Governments disbanded. Financial institutes lost their value. Money was losing its hold on people. Greed disappeared with the Virus infection. Trust began to stick its head out, and kindness was everywhere. I really did think, I had died and went somewhere else. They helped us create a new reality. They mainly talked about Consciousness Energy. They talked about their world, lifestyle, travels, and about the last time they were here.

They talked about other life forms coming to visit humankind. They claimed to be sent, by the Universal Consciousness Energy Frequency, their Creator. They shared that this Consciousness Energy, has sent us a life line, to help us change our direction, as an Energy vibration. We finally had emancipation. There were many things to decide. They spoke about the new physical evolution, and how we are no longer alone.

M: You are describing the end of the Evolution Revolution. It's what brought us to the New Direction. This energy Evolution Revolution movement lasted a long time. But it converted the Virus Cell. This was the intervention, for those who were still unconscious. This was the reason the book called the, Evolution Revolution was written.

This book came to awaken our Consciousness, in order to decrease the effects of the Virus Energy, until this last and final cure. The visitors performed an environmental cleansing. An oxygen reformulation, and re-balanced our physical energy with the Universal Consciousness Energy.

We have known all along that something was wrong. We chose to ignore it. As our vice president caller shared. Greed was in control and it took its toll. Thank you for your honesty. What you shared has been very enlightening. As we continue, anyone have comments about the last few discussions. Love to hear them. I am interested to hear how others felt about their own transformation.

M: Here comes a call. Hello, Go ahead caller.

C: Hi, yes I have a comment. Are we saying, everyone in the world, trusts everyone in the world now? You can't possibly know the world in one life time, much less each person.

M: There you go, that's your answer. You can trust everyone in the world, but, this doesn't mean you will have the opportunity to tell them. Trust, Is a Universal Consciousness Energy. We all have it. TRUST THE ENERGY, TRUST THE PERSON. Everyone in the world trusts themselves. They have no reason not to.

C: I heard the last caller, it was very informative. I am curious about these Consciousness Energy Projections you keep talking about. Will my new Consciousness Energy, allow me to see globally? Can I develop my perception to see that wide?

M: Absolutely! It's about perception. Development allows you to project your Consciousness Energy and view the Earth and all on it. It's made of energy. All you have to do, is simply look through the eyes of Consciousness. They are everywhere. You can see what the Energy can see.

As you develop your Energy, you will see more, and more of the world, and beyond it. You have to be willing to understand it. Conscious development increases your understanding of everything. Your perception, can perceive much more than you think. Develop it, it has no limits. Expand your Conscious Perception, it will show you the Earth from every direction.

C: To understand, I need to be taught the knowledge. If I still don't get it, I will keep asking until I do. There is always a way. Isn't our history recorded in our Consciousness? When I want to find out, can't I just go into my Consciousness, and connect with the memories recorded there?

M: This ability, is not far reaching. It depends on how quickly people have adjusted to the Energy development? When you are willing to look, you shall find. Curiosity is the road to discovery. It's what develops the conscious energy. Your thoughts are no longer limited by control. Most importantly, let your intuition lead you. It knows knowledge which you have yet to learn. Consciousness has dimensions, you have yet to see. So go on, enter your conscious thoughts, go in and discover what you are looking for.

C: OK, I understand all that. I will use my new perception to move by. I will be observant of what I see, and aware of what I hear.

M: When using our Consciousness, we develop our energy's frequency speed. Each development, puts us in a new dimension. Each time we learn, our perception changes. That's the point of the energy evolution. Moving energy can't stay the same. This is Evolution. Due to our physical form, we are limited in how fast our frequency can go.

C: Thank you for your perspective. It's always so informative. You don't lose track of any conversation. Thanks for paying attention.

M: OK caller, good talking with you.

Another call coming through. Hello, speak.

C: Ya hi, I have always been curious about this energy. I heard about it years ago, before the re- creation. People talked about it in conjunction with the supernatural. The supernatural was a taboo subject for most of us. But we were curious, so we would still investigate It. Ever since I received the Evolution Revolution book, I have been working on developing my Consciousness Energy in hopes of healing myself. I am in a wheelchair, with a broken spine. I was mountain climbing and I fell. It has been extremely difficult to increase the development of healing energy; No matter what I tried. Now, the world has become a new Consciousness Energy, is it possible for me to develop this energy, to heal my spine? I am speaking out in hopes of hearing from someone out there, who may know, how I can get out of this chair?

I have learned quite a bit about the supernatural, and life after death. This knowledge helped to expand my perception. I went to convention after convention. Looking for education. I was on a one man mission, to learn all I can about the power beyond our brain. It's my last chance at walking. We never found a cure. I have to keep trying. Absorbing knowledge feels like a rush of energy; but it doesn't move me out of this chair.

My question is, now that I can feel this energy in my body. How do I focus it on healing myself?

I really have come far in understanding Consciousness Energy, and what it can do. But what's missing is the doing, what do I do?

I read the Evolution Revolution book many times, to absorb every little hint of self healing energy. Why are we not able to use this ability, now that we have become, beings of energy. I feel this energy, I know it's there, it converted a whole world of people. How is it, I still haven't been able to use it to heal myself. Is this Physical Evolution a slow process? I have the awareness and the drive. Was I expecting something too soon? Did I do it wrong?

M: It's very brave of you to talk about your disability. I agree, the energy of healing has been difficult to develop. There are those in the world, who are still dealing with their awakening. Due to this on going process, the energy of healing hasn't completely formed. It takes patience to heal physical mass. There is much to reorganize in the anatomy. Healing your spine after all this time, could affect you in other places. Your body has adjusted to the spine being broken. So it made adjustments. First you must find the side effects of your long term illness. Then you must heal each one before you get to your spine. It was first to break. It will be the last to heal. Your consciousness must stay aware of this. You want to heal not injure yourself. Your whole body has been affected. So start with the last side effect you had, and work backwards.

You want to heal yourself. I get it. I want to help you do it. It's important that when you learn how, you follow these directions. In the past, our physical energy vibration, was too slow for us to be able to use it for self healing, it was infected energy. Today, it's balanced energy. It's our perceptions which has changed. The way we treated each other. The way we lived. We were unconscious to anything but ourselves. Our energy couldn't save us, or make us conscious. It needed a boost of Balanced Consciousness Energy. Which, the Evolution Revolution supplied.

Our healing energy hasn't been used in many years. There were Spiritual healers all over the world claiming to heal people. Religions, claimed to heal people. But in plain view, it didn't work as advertised. There were some people who lived in isolation, who were able to tap into the energy of Consciousness through spiritual mediumship. Spiritual healing became a big business. Many people lost faith in it. They stopped using it. It became a shadow of itself. So now it's coming back to life. It's developing into Consciousness. You will be able to focus on your parts, and create cellular regeneration.

Even though most of the world population, instantly awakened to their new reality, it must be said, some are still evolving into full Consciousness. For this healing energy to work, it has to increase the speed of revolutions in our physical energy. The more Consciousness Energy Development, the stronger the energy is. This is what will give you, and many others in your situation, the ability to self heal any part of the physical body, we have to build more Conscious energy. Soon, as we develop, the energy on Earth will start to feel somewhat tangible. People will feel it all around them, not only in them. This will be the time when you can plug in to it and heal yourself. We are nearly there. Energy needs an evolution to evolve. Ours is growing.

C: Thanks for your help, and your support.

M: Anytime. Stay focused on your goal, and if you need anything, call me at W.A.T.E.R., the World Association Towards Energy Re-creation.

Hello, go ahead next caller. We are listening.

C: Hello, how are you doing? My name is Susan. That last caller was inspirational. He brought up good points. I for one am glad, we now live in a place where the energy allows us to heal. What could be better than that? We are standing on top of the ground, not under it. The skies are blue, the weather is warm, and for the first time in my life, I feel absolutely safe. And we didn't blow up the planet. I am a fifty-seven year old woman who wishes for a do over, so I can be born here and grow up in this environment. In this kind of energy. The change is like day and night. I haven't seen one single argument. I am just happy I made it here before I died. I am hoping this energy will slow down aging, so fifty-seven can become thirty-seven.

M: Your words are very moving. Just like physical evolution is moving. The more we evolve, the more our Consciousness can do. Over the years, as evolution evolves, we will change our physical appearance. As any flower would, once fully grown. But that's a long distance away. Awareness of our natural growth is advisable now. Consciousness cannot resist growth. Just as we just experienced an energy re-creation, we will go through more with each evolution.

C: Are you aware, your discussion with your last caller was heard by many. People are creating support groups to generate energy on his behalf, until he can. Consciousness has many benefits;

I would like to live as long as I can, now that we are here. I visualize the Universal Consciousness as one huge brain, and we were all connected to it by some kind of energy vein.

Now, I understand it better. I realized, we are connected to an energy stream, which is connected to the whole of Consciousness. It's what makes our brain work. This connection allows us to absorb knowledge and feed knowledge back to it. This is how I see it. It's a cycle. This is what's giving our life sustenance. It's what gives us our presence. Without understanding, you will always feel left out.

M: When our presence reflects our essence, the only thing present, is our essence. As long as our presence, reflects a conscious being.

C: What about Meanings? Are meanings connected to feelings? Do feelings change, with different meanings? If so, I need to be aware of my meanings, so as to not hurt anyone's feelings.

M: A meaning, can be found in many things you do, or not do. From things you read, to movies you watch. Going out for a walk, or climbing a rock. Running a race, or sitting in one place. Everything we think, say, and do, all of it, has meaning. The look on your face, your smile, the way you eat and drink. You name it, it has meaning to whomever is looking for one. But the best meaning of all, is the Consciousness Energy meaning. It gives meaning to the word meaning. If you had your own meaning, what would it be?

C: A constantly evolving vibrational energy. This is what I mean, evolution, is like being in different scenes in a movie. Each development which changes our perception, is a new scene. The movie is not complete, until we return to the Universal Consciousness Energy Core. Once there, we can sit back and watch the movie. This is one view, which helped me to understand the cycle of the Universal Consciousness.

M: A good example which works for you. When it comes to development, people have to do it their own way. Growth happens differently for each person. What are you trying to grow?

C: Well, I have been developing my energy projection, so I can move objects. I developed the energy I needed to make it work. It's taking me quite awhile to find my balance. Which I could use some help with. I've been noticing small objects moving around in my home. I could also use some ideas on how to stabilize my energy projection. With each development, it's becoming stronger. I need some guidance, on how to keep the objects in the room they belong in. At this time, they are moving from room to room, on their own.

M: Telekinesis is one ability we can develop if that's your focus. It takes commitment. It's an energy you must build. It seems, you have a strong hold of your Consciousness Energy, and you have learned how to use it. Very good Susan. What are you planning to do with it? How about thinking of how, you can best use this ability to create with. What you visualize is what you can materialize.

We have arrived at the New Direction. You are in control of how fast, how slow, and how far you want to go. Where you can go, and how to get there, is up to you. It's your choice. When we make a choice, there is no one else to blame when things go wrong. It's all on you, the rewards and the consequences. We lost the ability to take responsibility. You cannot learn from your mistakes if you don't own them.

C: What I have heard about Consciousness Energy so far is, we are able to project it. Read thoughts with it. Travel with it. Move objects and heal ourselves with it. But as a physical being, will I have a limit to what I can do with it.

M: Yes, our physical form is our limit for now. Life, has a natural process. There are endless things it can teach us. Part of our revolution is, to grow from our physical experiences, and move into the ethereal dimensions. The more we learn in life, the more we will know in death. Ask questions, so you can learn. Energy is always on the move. If we try to stop it in one place, it will reappear in another space.

We used to have behavior limits, because we needed them. We were unbalanced. Limits kept us safe. Anything could happen, and it did. It's a matter of evolution. Everything created, has to go through its own evolution. The only way we won't evolve, is to not be a part of a moving energy. Are you considering the ability of materialization. It's not a quick development. Whatever you materialize will be your responsibility. What is your goal with developing this ability? Do you plan to travel from planet to planet? It defiantly saves on travel time. Just don't forget where you came from.

C: I have been very curious about the subject of telekinesis for years, just like you Max. So I am focused on it. We use to talk about the future, make movies about it, write books about it. We are now living in what we saw as our future. I have been meaning to ask you. Why do you care so much about what's happening to the people?

M: Because I am one of those people. You must care about others, don't you? It's a conscious thing to do.

C: What I mean is, you put this forum together to listen to others tell their stories, and ask questions of you. Why put yourself out there for all to hear? You seem to know your history, and your present. Where did you get your knowledge from?

M: From the Universal Consciousness. I am a seeker of knowledge for the development of my brain. I am not the answer to all. What I know I share, but there are others out there, who know as much, if not more. You're a seeker of knowledge, you can find out on your own.

C: I know you mentioned the benefits of learning, and developing your own Energy, but, I feel like there is more to you than what you say. Especially after hearing your responses. Did you use to be a radio show host or something? Are you re-living your history? What is your intention? Are you writing a book?

M: I do this because, I want people to remember what happened. How we got here. I know my perception, it has its own view. But, I am not aware of the perceptions of others, like yours for example. It's a learning process. Listening to others, provides memories of the good times, and staying aware of the present times. This is on top of the knowledge one can learn from others. A seeker of knowledge is inquisitive, curious, and a discoverer. It is a person who doesn't stop asking questions, when seeking answers. It's someone, who has an alliance with the truth, and Consciousness.

We were unable to seek knowledge, while we were unconscious. We couldn't recognize it when we saw it. It wasn't in our thoughts. When you want to know, you have to ask, Who, When, Where, What, And Why? So you can get the whole story. Separate them, and you only get parts for the story. When you are not sure, you have to make sure. When you are asked a question, be alert, and aware when you receive the answer. It may not be what you wanted.

Can someone be in reaction without their knowledge? Can a reaction, be a hidden reaction? How do you recognize a hidden reaction? By having self awareness? Listening to what you say, and observe the reaction caused by your action. We can trust our reactions now, they don't need to hide. They can teach us something new. Knowledge seekers learn on their own, and what they learn, is a BENEFIT to their Consciousness.

C: Excellent revelations. It's been a real pleasure. Your feedback was enlightening.

M: Thanks for sharing. You brought up thought provoking information.

Well, let's keep it going. The energy is really flowing. Next caller please. Hello.

C: Finally, I got through. Hello, I am calling, to discuss our direction in this New Direction? What's our direction Max?

M: You want me, to tell you, what your direction is? Can you tell me mine? Freedom of choice, allows you to choose your direction. Consciousness Energy, can go in any direction.

C: Consciousness Energy development has become our focus. Many ways of life have changed. How far does this change go? How far have we come in this new world? Is everyone responsible for everyone?

M: There are no limits for change in evolution. Would it be so wrong to care for your fellow humankind? When you can do it without expectations, it's not a responsibility. It's Consciousness Energy. Anything else on your list you want to discuss?

C: Actually yes. Our education system? What happened to it? How has it changed? Our History isn't long enough to teach. Our Science was changed; and Math...Do we use it anymore? Machines are doing it for us. Most of the curriculum is null and void.

M: Its been rewritten and rearranged. Come to find out, education wasn't educating. It was Performing, Brain Conforming. Education is now based on the knowledge of Consciousness Energy, and how to apply it.

C: Are teachers still responsible for teaching our children, or is it going to be the responsibility of the parent's? Many parents need educating, to be able to educate their children. Without that, this is not a good idea.

M: Today, people go to school because they want to. Not because they have to. Energy needs to grow. We are driven to develop it. There will always be teachers and students. Every interaction, is a teacher, student moment. Let's not discount the parent's responsibility, to teach their children conscious knowledge. Schools focus on Improving our brain, body, and developing Energy. This is the New Direction. The old one is gone. Once conscious always conscious. We grow our own intelligence.

C: All this talk about growing, makes me feel like a plant. Maybe we are more like the plants than we think. Anyway, do schools teach about nature and organic growing? How about life skills? Is this in the curriculum? What about physical anatomy? Healthcare needs this education. We have to have healthcare workers. It's not all going away, is it?

M: No, it's not, and it hasn't. You should slow down. We have time. Nature and Organic growing are subjects being taught. Teaching about nature, one must be in nature. To teach organic growing, we must work the fields. This is where classes are held. Life skills are one of those topics which is shared with parents and teachers. Parents are responsible for teaching certain life skills, and so are schools. But parents have the last word. So far, we have made excellent progress. But again we can always develop.

Consciousness had shined a light on the meanings from history. The knowledge it delivered, had a broken foundation. This meant, most of our education was broken. We built our present, on the knowledge of historic personalities, and their research and discoveries. We had to re-evaluate everything we knew. Everything we believed in. But then, you have to ask, how much of history was infected by the Virus Energy? How much influence did it have on their discoveries? Such as atomic power and chemical weapons, as an example.

They got their ideas from their history, and passed it on to our present. Today, we need new ideas, ones which will create the future. Consciousness Energy inspired ideas. New ideas are our specialty. New ideas, create new perspectives, that create new creations. Our actions are our responsibility, and so is developing our Consciousness Energy. How we do it, is our choice. There are very many ways you can develop your energy, like asking these questions. Our education system was our downfall. It taught about history, more than the present. Teachers refused to go to work, for fear of being hurt. Violence in schools became the norm. We started graduating the young, without educating them. Then we gave them video games, sports, and zombie movies.

C: I know you said, education changed and was reformed. What else changed?

M: Our Ethics, Belief System, Education System, Government Laws, Humanity's Rules, and peoples attitudes. Teaching the parents was the first priority. They can teach their children what they learned, from their own Energy Conversion, and the Evolution Revolution. Many children will be born in this new world, who is going to teach them? It has to be the parents and the schools, working together in harmony.

However, our history, is not today. Now, we have to teach them Consciousness Energy knowledge. New births will adjust to this new evolution faster than we are doing. They will ask questions about the way things are, from their perception. They may actually teach us something new, as they develop. This is where, teaching the parents to teach their children comes in. They will think differently than us. Act differently, react differently. They will be the New Children of the World. We will learn what we don't know, and we will only teach what we know. Humanity has awakened.

C: Creating doesn't need debating. It's our nature, I get it now. I have learned quite a bit from this discussion. Thank you.

M: OK I have calls backing up. Next caller.

C: Hello. My name is Gus, and I am ready to discuss. I am determined to learn. This is the life. People actually go out of their way to help you. Everyone is your friend. Trust is in peoples eyes. It's like we all have a welcome sign on our foreheads. I sleep and wake up with a smile. I own a restaurant. I go to work everyday. It's become such joy to serve people food. When it comes down to it, food is a constant request. Food services are still active. Only now, we are being supplied by nature's own. You name it, we get it fresh. It only cost me seeds, water, and some fertilizer. I have chickens. It seems farmers and ranchers are doing pretty good. ♦

Technology has gone into a slump. Many people in the world were left without a job. We are still recovering from the evolution revolution. We are learning how to live with energy motion. Is farming going to be the way of life for everyone in the world? We use to be farmers, when we were unconscious, can you imagine what kind of farming we can do now, by being conscious? What about all those people, who know nothing about farming? The ones from the tech world for example. What are they going to do?

There are many governments agency's who have been shut down. Public services employees who lost their jobs. How will they eat? Go out every night? What can they trade with? Has all this been taken care off? If so, by whom? This change was not a small one. Is there a new kind of government being created? Who is making the new laws?

Who is leading humanity? Some kind of world president. I know I sound like I have been unconscious. It's because, I have been. I am one of those, who wasn't completely awakened yet. I heard there were more like me. It was a relief. We have been re-created without a Virus Energy infection.

M: Wow! Those are many questions you just asked, all at one time. Can you handle all the answers at one time? You have made a strong entrance. Were you anxious? Did you get it all out? Probably not. Hello to you to Gus. At least you are clear on what you want to talk about. Are you ready for the answers? Or do you want to keep asking questions? Don't get me wrong, it's good to question. Let's answer some. Is there a new government being created? No! No new governments anywhere.

No kings, presidents or ambassadors. No borders of any kind. Anyone can travel anywhere and be safe. Who is making new laws you asked? Laws for what purpose? Consciousness Energy needs no laws. Humanity can govern themselves by themselves. Consciousness Energy needs no leader, it leads itself, by itself, for itself development. Those who have no jobs, will use their Consciousness Energy to find a way to live. It wasn't a problem when the humans were first created. Your progress has led you to your destruction.

C: I have more questions? Can you handle more answers?

M: Only if the question has one. I can handle any conscious question.

C: What's the difference between our physical Consciousness, and the Universal Consciousness? We use to believe Consciousness meant, to be awake, to be conscious. Not asleep, being unconscious meant, passed out, or in a coma. This word means our Creator now. I have no reason to disbelieve it, any of it. It's all making sense.

M: We are learning Consciousness in a new way. As an energy of thought and perception. As an evolution. As a life source, our life source. This is the feeling of Consciousness, not the physical one.

C: OK, question one: Doesn't this mean, I am Conscious? Isn't it all Consciousness anyway?

M: You can be awake, but, it doesn't mean you are conscious? Lots of people sleep with their eyes open. You can see, but, does it mean you have insight? You can be alive, but, does it mean you are living? You can have awareness, but, does it mean you are aware? You can have the same beliefs as others, but does it mean you are the same?

C: I get it. One is, an outside perception, and the other, is an inside perception. It's one brain, with two different perceptions. Is this the reason for the energy of reason? So we can tell the difference, and make a choice.

M: Physical Consciousness, is being Conscious of physical mass. Our brain was taught to see mass energy, and because its mass, it has limits to its capability, and ability for discovery. So it's about how we, as a Consciousness Energy, Evolve. This is how we were created. Once we evolve from physical, we are less limited. Each time WE EVOLVE, LIMITS DISSOLVE.

C: This is a very effective perception. It takes a strong Consciousness to discover this knowledge. OK, that was one, here is question Two: Will nature, including the wild kingdom, finally get its place back on Earth? Will the extinct be resurrected? Now, it's a brand new life. I feel like a baby in an adult body. My brain feels like it went through a car wash. It's the same feeling with everything I touch.

M: Will nature and the wild kingdom finally be allowed to grow? Good question. With a balanced Consciousness Energy, we all have the opportunity to grow. But, there is still survival to consider. As Conscious human beings, we must make our choices wisely. Using balanced thoughts. As far as the extinct? There is no such thing as extinct, the Universal Consciousness doesn't die. Considering we almost become extinct ourselves. We are still here, I believe we have learned our lesson.

C: Question Three: Our natural cures were taken, and sold for money. Do our forests and jungles contain more cures than we are aware of?

M: Not only, do we have the ability for Consciousness Energy cures. But nature, has all its own kind of cures. The Earth is full of them. I haven't forgotten, how people had to wear masks to avoid infections from viruses we created. We were killing the Earth and ourselves with it. Each time we created a cure, we created a new deadly disease.

Are you looking to harness cures from nature? If so, go live in the jungle. Only, you have no way to test what parts of nature are cures or poisons. Study, do your research, learn, develop your Consciousness Energy to help you, before you go tearing out nature. Some poisons are actually cures.

C: What about, what we have already invested, was it mostly infected? All those years working like slaves to earn a living, and now everything changes overnight. It's been one hell of a fight to get here.

M: We have been changing, since the day we were created. Only we were changing too slowly. As humans, our energy frequency moves faster now. We can do more. Live longer. Be happier. Support each other. Seniors don't have to be alone any more. This re-creation was our salvation. It's a good thing we finally paid attention. Yes, I agree, many things have changed, and, they will change even faster. We went from walking, to riding the waves of evolution.

C: Things can't possibly change so quickly, even with an evolution. Are we still a world, where everyone has a home, food and healthcare? Are we back to necessities. The three basics of life. It sounds so simple and trouble free, no stress. It's a dream come true. Are there still many issues to figure out, in this new dimension. Like what's our intention?

M: Look at it this way, we are no longer slaves to a job. This is a plus, don't you think? Everything you build after the three necessities, is up to you. Use your new conscious imagination. All of humanity has been re-created, so has nature, and the wild kingdom. We may not see it as fast as we like, but we are still evolving. You have made some good points in support of our new world. You are asking good questions. Like what is our intention, now? Our intention is simple also. To develop our Consciousness Energy for creating what we need. Just as other creations have learned to do. However, your intention may be different. You may have other priorities. But the nature of your energy, will keep you focused on development. It's the new direction.

C: Hmm! My intention? I hadn't thought of that yet. Thanks, you gave me something to think about.

M: Good talking with you, thanks for calling.

Hi, your next, gotta a question caller?

C: Hi there. I'm in a daze wondering if the Evolution Revolution actually happened, or did we blow ourselves up and woke up in this world? I heard the afterlife could be like this. It's what it feels like.

M: No, we didn't blow up, this was a real transformation from Unconsciousness into Consciousness. Like you're suppose to be now. The Evolution Revolution, is the reason we have gotten this far. You must have been unconscious when it happened. There are others like you. One such person was the last caller. Our reality shifted into a new dimension. Our perception has changed. We now realize more than we ever have. Our vision is so much wider and brighter. We have the Knowledge of Energy Conversion, Physical Tissue Regeneration, and the Purpose of our creation. It's important to mention, the true nature of the Evolution Revolution. The complete conversion of the Virus Energy Cell. It is, what finally balanced the scale. So thank you caller for bringing this up.

C: It's taken some time, to become oriented to my new surroundings. It's like learning to breathe underwater. I have to acclimate to the climate. My perception has changed, and now I'm seeing these thoughts and visions, of things I don't understand. As they kept coming, I kept documenting, what I was receiving. Why was it happening? Why was I feeling this way? Sorry, I am babbling.

M: No, you are not, you are questioning. No better way to develop consciously. In a state of awareness, we are an energy vibration, which can absorb information. But only with people's permission. However, there are those bits of information, which do get absorbed by our vibration, and translated into education. Because they are being sent, you don't need permission for those. You have become a Receiver who Cycles, Input and Output. As we all can do. This is part of being a Conscious Energy.

C: Does Memory affect my present moment?

M: How can it not? You are in the moment. Focused on what you're thinking and seeing. Then comes the shift. You see, or think of something which triggers a memory. So where does your focus go? To that memory. Until you shift back, or stay there. Every memory will shift you from the present. It's up to you to shift back. Years ago, many of us use to live in our memories because, there was nothing new to look forwards to. So we always went back to the memories of our best times. It's all we had.

Now that we are aware, we mustn't get trapped in them. Don't become their victim. Stay in your conscious present moment. Take it with you when you visit a memory. It is the only thing that can bring you back. Some memories have bars. Our thoughts, are what we think. Our memories, are what we experienced. Experience, has a stronger effect on our present moment. Most memory's involve an experience. Otherwise, it won't register in your memory.

C: What am I hearing is my thoughts are now connected to my Consciousness, if so, does this make my thoughts, and my memories as one? How can I use my Consciousness, to see my memories?

M: They are composed of the same energy, which makes them one. However, They are not exactly the same. Your memories, are triggered by your thoughts, feelings, and senses. They are stored with your thoughts and senses. Anything you think, say, and do will trigger them. The point is not about seeing your memory, it's about you seeing it and not staying in It. Just a reminder, use your Consciousness Energy to look through. It will keep your memories from sticking to you. A memory, can be triggered by smell, taste, sight, sound, and touch.

Say one night you went out for a delicious meal. Best meal you ever had. You remember the taste, and the smell. How the meal made you feel. They are programmed in your memory sensors. As time goes on, you forget about it. A couple of years later, you walk by another restaurant, where you smell a sniff, of a whiff of a familiar taste, which triggers the thought of the best meal you ever had. This thought, triggers the memory connected to it. The memory comes up immediately. You see yourself there, eating the same meal. You can still smell it, and taste it. So you go looking for it. Memories are very powerful. As a Consciousness Energy, become aware of why you want to go to that memory. Whatever it is.

C: I finally learned something useful. I've had a question I have been meaning to ask. During the initial creation of the young generation movement, where were the older adults? Did they not intervene?

M: Actually many of the old adults participated, and made a huge difference in the movement.

Our history has documented and stored information about their roles, at W.A.T.E.R. World Association Towards Energy Re-creation. You can get your answers there also. Thank you for the discussion.

Hello. Next caller please. How do you do? Question or a sharing?

C: Hello, I would like to add a comment, about where the older adults were during the Energy Movement. Is this allowed? I have been listening and I love what I am hearing. Here is my feeling. Why haven't more people, who were involved as older adults, call in and share? Your silence makes it sound as though, we didn't participate in the Evolution Revolution. There were millions of us adults, supporting the young generation. It just took us longer to understand the situation.

As a parent, I never thought of sitting on the sideline. When my son showed me the commitment he had from knowledge he actually learned, I had to pay attention. He was a couch potato. Suddenly, I hardly saw him at home anymore. I began to question his actions, his movements. Who he was seeing? What were they doing? Why were they doing it. After my son enlightened me, It was then, when he became my teacher. I learned quite a lot about the Universal Consciousness energy, and the Evolution Revolution. After, my support for him was easy. I wanted what he wanted. The Conversion of the Virus Energy Cell and everyone infected by it. After I witnessed them in action, I knew then, this was no joke. It was real. It was as though, the young adults knew what was coming. As if they had a plan they were following.

It wasn't a revolt against the governments. It was an actual Realization and a Consciousness Energy Materialization. We as the parents, were concerned and afraid for our children, no matter their age. After all, we were suppose to be teaching them. But the cause was just, and it was right.

The concept of Consciousness Energy, hit home for me. I became his secret back up. I provided a place for many of them to be safe while regrouping. I gathered many of my friends and got them to participate. Believe it or not, the older adults became involved. Many of them had contacts, the movement leaders needed. They too, played a big role. We all were there to support our young leaders. We converted our own Virus and joined in the movement. Many of the older people worked behind scenes.

C: As it grew, so did the numbers of older adults in support of it. We are talking men and women. There is little record of it because, most of the documents were burnt during the movement. But there is enough to show our participation. In fact some parents were put in prison for supporting the movement. I was one of them. This was going on world wide. They were forcing those they caught, to give them names of people they knew, who were in the movement or supporting it.

Government leaders had to be expecting this. There has been global tension for years. Not just with country to country, but between people and their government leaderships. Many of them were too old and refused to give up their positions. The Young adults in today's media lifestyle, had enough of the old ways. They wanted new days. Nothing wrong with looking at creating a future. As you can see, they succeeded.

M: If you don't mind me asking. How long were you in prison?

C: I believe it was two weeks. They couldn't prove I was doing anything wrong.

M: Wow! That's some experience you had caller. You cleared up a few questions for me, and I am sure, for the listeners. I was aware of the actions the older adults performed. Thanks for clarifying. I want to thank you for speaking up on behalf of the older adults. I was a witness to many of their actions.

In the beginning, most of the young were being shut down by the older ones. Actually by anyone who was still infected. The beginning of the energy movement struggled with being open about the Evolution Revolution, due to all the infected people they couldn't trust. During its rise, many of the members had to have converted their own Virus Energy. It was not easy to show people the Virus

Energy Cell. They had to find out on their own. This slowed down the movement for a while. Until people began to recognize the Virus in themselves.

Most of the resistance was from the older adults. Especially older family members. They had their beliefs. They weren't willing to budge. It's difficult for the older people to take advice from younger ones. What did the young know. They were mostly all in their twenties. Some maybe older. The older have lived longer, thus, they know more. This was the belief they had. The older the wiser, is what I use to hear. This is not always true, wisdom comes from your Consciousness.

C: What I have come to realize is, Consciousness is a state of being, where everything makes sense. Where I finally understand what life is all about. This is the best thing to happen to us. The actions were well worth it.

M: Couldn't have said it better myself. Thanks for sharing, it was very valuable information.

C: Thank you.

M: These calls are powerful. Go caller. We are listening. Your on.

C: Hey, you are having intense conversations with people. People have no apprehension in sharing with you anything. So in that case, neither will I. Hello everyone out there. You too max. I want to fly. It has been my dream all my life. I imagined it becoming real one day. Here we are. Today is the day, and I want to learn how to use my Consciousness Energy, to fly out of my body.

I have been working on my development, focusing on building the energy to separate from my body. I know it can be done. Even before the Evolution Revolution. We just didn't know how to do it. So today it should be easy, am I right? Because it hasn't happened yet.

M: Your body, without its spirit, will not do well for long. It sounds like you would rather be out of your body, than in it. Out of body is an ability for developing, but you can't make it a lifestyle. You're alive. Your body is not a pit stop between your travels. The intention of life is that you live it. Leaving your body for long periods, will make it age rapidly, it may not be there when you get back, think of that.

As you develop your Consciousness, you will also develop new perceptions, which will directly affect your present reality. You must bring what you learned and developed, into your brain. Otherwise, what's the use of being Conscious, when your brain doesn't know it? Leaving you body is not a complicated ability. It does depend on the strength of the energy being used for separation. This energy can be developed by practice, but you must keep the balance.

You only have a certain amount of time to be out of your body. What may seem to be a day for the body, it's thirty minutes for the spirit. Just look at it that way. The ability for astral travel, needs you to be able to increase the speed of your physical energy frequency. The increase in your energy speed, brings you closer to the ethereal dimensions. It's then where you separate.

So, you must continue to develop your energy to this point. It will happen suddenly at first, because you are not expecting it. After that, you can do it again. Just remember, for the bodies safety. Only your resistance to going back, can keep you there long enough to forget your body.

C: Well, that's news to me. I didn't realize this about the body. I figured it would just stay asleep, until I came back. Apparently, I was incorrect. I was only thinking of my experience, not my body's. Good realization, thanks.

M: Yes, it's good for your development, to experience what you have learned, from everything you learn. Part of development is to learn from the path you are on, not just from when you get there. Wherever there is. Development is meant to keep you developing. It's the water to the seed.

C: I have just learned a new perception of development. Your words are clear. Now, I would like to hear more about our Utopian way of life. Do we live our normal life, using our Consciousness Energy to build it with? We became conscious and aware, but I didn't realize, our awakening came with new meanings, new feelings, and new perceptions.

M: The perception of Consciousness, doesn't just show you one view of you, it shows you all of you. Building your life using this Energy, simply means do it consciously. Be aware of it all. The present and future mostly. You build your life, based on these two realities. Our present one, and our future one. We have to create that together. Whatever the future holds, it will be a Consciousness Energy Reality. We are in our natural evolution. We will evolve naturally. This is how the Evolution Revolution changed our perception?

Keep asking questions. It's how you discover answers. But, ask your own Consciousness, before you ask others. This way you have something to compare and learn from. You want to fly, go ahead, spread your wings and fly. Discover, learn, develop and grow. Then bring it all back, for your brain to know. All what you discover, you take back to the Universal Consciousness Core. It's the only way eternal knowledge can have a meaning. It has to be a cycled process. Each time around, you become a stronger energy. Seriously caller, you have accomplished an incredible commitment to your development.

C: I am quicker at absorbing knowledge, so I think this makes me a quick learner. I retain information well when developing my energy. I don't allow distraction of any kind. I am in isolation with my Consciousness.

M: So, what exactly are you developing in isolation? From where are you getting your information? What are you gaining, life skills? Not in isolation, meditation fine, for about thirty minutes, but isolating all day to gain knowledge from your Consciousness? Where is the balance? What about the knowledge you can learn, outside of your isolation? You do not need to isolate to develop your energy. It will take longer. Learn from everything. Let it be your teacher.

C: Thanks for the information. You've been very helpful.

M: OK, let's move on. Next caller, it's your time. Speak

C: Hello, I heard you discussing the topic, of Conscious Actions. When someone is in action, how can I tell their Intention before their action? I am learning how to not misread the intentions of others and pre-react, before they act. I am sure it's connected to my intuition. Is this where I should be focusing? Should I be using my intuition, and my perception, to sense things like feelings? Isn't this, like breaking someone's privacy?

Will I have to touch the person, for my intuition to work? How close to I have to be? Will I get a heat sensation, or a premonition? Will it be a vision, or something written? Just curious. You say to ask questions if you want to discover answers. But, you never talked about when to stop asking. So I keep asking, and waiting for the answers. I don't think I am learning as much as I should be, for being conscious. If I stop asking, will all the answers to my other questions come through, at once? What should I do?

M: How can you tell a persons intention before their action? A perceptive question. It's called, Consciousness Energy Intuition. So, you are on the right track. However, It's question, answer, question, answer, are the steps to learning. You must wait for an answer. What's the point of a question without one? You see what I did here? You asked your question, and now we are discussing the answer. This is the process.

Your Consciousness should know this. Get out of its way. How else can you feel your intuition? Don't talk over it, just listen to it, feel for it. Your brain will translate this feeling into thoughts. This is how you use your intuition. It's not a hearing, it's a feeling. Focus on that. You will know the intention, before the act. The feeling will come with a sensation of truth. You must learn to trust it. When you can sense someone's intention, you are reading their energy vibration.

C: I read somewhere that our Intention is a Universal Law. This law, will consequence and reward naturally, and will register in our vibration instantly. How is this a benefit to us?

M: When your intention is a positive one, and it adds to your development. It's yours to keep, and grow on. But if your intention was a negative one, you will carry it with you, until you convert it 'till it's gone. Awareness of this is our benefit.

It's a self regulated system of the Universal Consciousness. Your intention will always be on development. Our intention is the new direction, where can see the intention, before the action. One of the best abilities it gives, is the ability to read people's energy vibrations, to sense the truth when you feel it.

C: OK, what about Retention? As an Energy being, I am suppose to be able to absorb, and retain knowledge. What if I am not retaining as much as I should be? Is there a problem with my awakening? I feel like, I am absorbing energy, but not retaining all the knowledge. Maybe I am expecting too much. Where is the knowledge going, if not in my brain? Am I not fully Conscious yet? I thought we all were? Do I have a leak somewhere? Oh dear, what if a piece of the Virus Cell is still in my brain? What do I do then? Do I have to be reborn again? I hope you can help. Why is this happening?

M: Where is It going? It will keep cycling, until you have developed enough to absorb it all. Sometimes we don't absorb what we still don't understand. Even if we think we can. It may take a life time to realize when you have. Why are you not absorbing all the energy? What is your block? Is it the knowledge you don't understand, here are some reasons that may contribute to your lack of absorption.

DISTRACTION: Development, needs focus to develop. It's an energy. It needs a Direction when it's Projected. A one second distraction, can cause you to miss a piece of the whole picture.

CONFUSION: One missing piece, is enough to cause confusion. You don't have the whole picture. OVERTHINKING: Confusion causes anxiety, which makes you think too much. It makes you obsess.

NOT MAKING SENSE: At this point things are no longer making sense. There is a piece missing. You're overthinking. So now, you are going to stop absorbing.

STOPPING EARLY: Defeats the purpose of understanding.

CLARITY: Is the focus to widen your view, to help you find the missing piece. Clarity takes confusion out of the picture, and the rest follow.

You must address this, to become completely conscious. They may be the block keeping you from it. The energy of Consciousness is not what's missing. You could also have a memory attached to you, which keeps interfering in your development to grow. You must check for this also. They don't just come and go, sometimes they stay, especially the painful ones. You must find it. It's obviously looking for you. This is an alive energy memory. It's traveling in your thoughts. It's interfering with your receptive sensors. This could be the reason you're leaking knowledge.

While you are absorbing knowledge for development, it will keep interfering in your full absorption. Because, it's a free floating memory, you're the only one who can find it and deal with it. You don't have a piece of the Virus in your brain, you are just one of those slow going people. Which is fine, as long as you keep developing your Consciousness Energy. Unless you file it away, it will continue to absorb the knowledge that you need. It's become a repeat. A re-occurring haunting if you will.

C: How do I find it, so I can convert it?

M: You stay Conscious and connected to the present, then you go looking for the memory. The more you remember of it, the more of it you will see. Once you see the whole memory, you change its trajectory to its memory file. Simple.

C: I better stop now! That's a lot to think about.

M: OK, who is next to be heard. Go ahead caller.

C: Well, hello. I have a quick question, I am curious about the sequences of things. Was the Energy Movement, and the Evolution Revolution one and the same, or did the energy movement, create the Evolution Revolution? Which is it? What created what?

Correct me if I'm wrong, the evolution revolution was the conversion of energies, our physical energy, merged with the Universal Consciousness Energy. The Energy Movement, made it possible to achieve the evolution revolution. Is this the correct sequence of actions?

M: Hello back to you. That was a quick question. They were both obviously pivotal in the conversion of the Virus Energy Cell. But let's be clear on the order of things. It began like this:

The Energy Movement, introduced the DECLARATION. Which brought with it, the Consciousness Energy Vibration. It came to help us discover the MISSING LINK. Once we discovered it, we asked RELIGION, are you Fact or Fiction. They replied, *"we need the governments permission."* Only, they're on some kind of death mission. Upon hearing this, the bells began to toll. They were heard by all.

THE EARTH began to cry, *"I don't want to die, I want to live."* The Consciousness Energy, awakened the YOUNG GENERATION. They gave birth to the EVOLUTION REVOLUTION, which created The NEW DIRECTION. Our history and present in a nutshell. The future? That depends on the present.

C: Now I am clear on the order of things. Sorry, I know I said a quick question. But while I have your attention, there is another question which still remains? Now that the Virus Energy Cell has been converted, is it possible for it to remember what its actions were like? There has to be a way for this energy to show the world, how it has changed. I mean, as an energy, does it still have its own personality? Can it speak for itself?

M: Good realization caller. Your awareness is reflected through your questions. What made you think of this one? What do you think it will say? It's no longer unconscious. It's everything now, as a whole part of the Universal Consciousness.

C: I was thinking about what happened to the Virus Energy. What do we call it now? I wonder what happened to all its memory? What about all the experiences it went through? Can it still remember its own past?

M: It is no different than you and I. Where is it, is a good question? Where isn't it, is a better one. So where ever Consciousness is, there it is. We no longer need to use the term Virus. Yes, it can still remember its past, but only in the form of knowledge learned, so as to not affect its present situation. We have the same option. We can remember a memory for information. So as to not become attached to its dimension.

C: I will have to think on what you said. There is plenty to think about. As far as remembering its own past, I wouldn't want to remember the things it did. Would you?

M: No, but I use to. Thanks caller.

Hello caller, what would you like to talk about today? We are listening.

C: Yes. Hello. After hearing the last caller talk about his son and he, during the evolution revolution movement, I had to share my story with my son. I heard the caller call out the older adults, who participated in the energy movement with their children. He was right, so here I am. My son was one of the first to join the movement. His experience awakened me to the realization, that we, as the people, were being deceived by our own leaders. I became discouraged with our leadership and decided to join my son on his mission. The world energy conversion, of the Virus Energy Cell.

Governments made up rules and laws, which only applied to everyone else but them. We wanted to change that. So there we were, father and son, side by side, on the same path. If I was told before, this was going to happen, I would have never believed it. It must have been the process of conversion that changed everything. Little did I know, free speech, meant free, until it costs. It was costing the movement plenty.

Doors were being slammed in our faces. Many governments were putting out wanted posters for some of the leaders of the movement. There was a lot of pressure on the world population, to not support the movement, with threats of prison. Can you Imagine, freedom of speech is free, until we use it. Hypocrisy was the leader of our leadership. When the movement started to get media attention, many of those who were arrested gave their testimony, and spoke. They were examples of the conversion process. Others became inspired. Conflict transpired. Even the retired came out wired. The pressure set them free. Calling for accountability, transparency, honesty, and an end to sovereignty.

M: Yes we did, we had knowledge they knew nothing about. Our knowledge, gave us abilities they didn't have. This was never intended to be a violent revolution, only an energy conversion revolution, to restart our evolution. Our mistake as a world humanity, was listening to the energies of control, greed and fear. We were controlled by having to work for survival. Greed, constantly offered incentives, called bonuses. When we resisted, fear came in, and threatened our survival. This was our cycle. These three negative energies, were not the only Virus infections. There were other Virus inspired infections.

We didn't have to listen to them. It was a choice. We were in a state of convenience, in any form. Fear made us isolate, and greed started delivering to us. We didn't think to challenge our fears, only to hide from them. But hey, we had delivery. But, for the privilege of this convenience, you had to become compliant, you had to follow the rules of conformity. We were forced to do things we wouldn't normally do as human beings. Compliance created Conformity, which created Slavery.

C: I can't help thinking, how without an Energy Revolution, we would have found a way to address the Virus Cell effects? I had faith in us as human beings. We were intelligent enough to figure out we needed help. But not aware enough to ask for it.

M: As it turned out, we were not that intelligent, because we did not ask for it sooner. It's like this *"You fall off a cliff, you're hurt, but still alive. You hear someone walking by, and you don't yell for help?"* Well, we fell, they came, we didn't ask. Now, they came to stop us from destroying the Earth. To do that, we had to change. Does this sum it up for you?

C: Back in time. I learned quite a lot from the wars we use to have. I knew what it would take to create a movement. So along with the Evolution Revolution knowledge, we went to work. World leaders were taken by surprise, when they were looking into Consciousness's eyes. At first, the voice of the movement was not taken seriously, until something happened. At one point in the movement and thanks to the media. This news went out globally. A man they called the Traveler, stepped out of the crowd, and said something out loud.

"People of the world. The energy Evolution Revolution is here. We, are the Energy Movement. We have gathered in groups world wide. We have arrived at the steps of our leaderships. This is a global communication to the leadership of the world. We are here to call out the leaders, who continue to manipulate humanity, into doing their bidding. We are here to stop the continued building of Nuclear Missiles and bombs, and to finally convert your Virus infection which you are unaware of. You have the world population sitting in fear, worrying over your state of mind. We can no longer trust your leadership, as being in our best interests. We need the truth to your actions. We will not stand down. This is a matter of life and OUR death. You have chosen greed and control, over humanities soul. This is unacceptable. The people of Earth have had enough of your lack of leadership towards peace. The young generation will be taking over. Your reign of terror has ended."

We are also speaking on behalf of the Earth, and all that lives on it, and in it. We insist on the continuation of life upon this planet. You have proven to the rest of the Universe that you do not want it. Your actions are connected to greed, and it's time the people were freed. We can no longer live under the threat of Nuclear War. WAR must end. Soon the Visitors will arrive, to help keep us alive. Until then, there is a Virus Cell infection guiding our direction. We are here to cure this infection. It resides in our brain, and emotions. It's making our decisions. We are representatives of the Universal Consciousness Energy, Our Creator.

C: The reaction from world leadership was not a positive one. Laughter and ridicule went out into the air. Some of the members fell into despair. Some began to walk away, until- the media exploded by a vision like no other. You could feel the intensity of the whole situation. Then, as loud as he could, the

Traveler said, *"if you will not hear it from us, then hear it from them."* He had the world's attention…As a vision appeared, by way of a hologram. It was hazy but we could tell it was a face. It spoke these words as I remember them.

"Humankind, what you hear, is very clear. You are only reacting to fear. We are physical beings such as yourselves. We are not Monsters, Ghouls, or Elves. Our race has experienced the effects of this, Virus Cell Energy infection. Listen carefully to the words you hear. What you see is a reality, what you hear, are the final words to humanity. After this, humans will hear no more words, only action. Humanity has run out of time to save itself."

"We can no longer allow the physical race on this planet, to unbalance the universal energy formulation. Humanity has proven itself incapable of Consciousness, on their own. Unfortunately, the choice has been taken out of your control. The Evolution Revolution knowledge is the first step to your awakening. Prepare for it humanity. It's happening with you or without. Take heed to what you hear. Before we appear."

Things became eerily silent. The light went out, it was gone. People stood frozen, there was shock on everyone's face. The leadership began to scramble. Investigations into the world movement became serious. I am not sure why I can remember all this but I do. After this event, the world energy movement increased by millions. It was now being taken seriously. Meetings began to happen with leaders of the world. The world movement to convert the Virus Energy Cell began.

M: Wow! This is like insider information. As you were there to witness this, it must have affected you too, even with what you knew.

C: I was too excited to be in shock. I think, this is why I remember it so well. It was recored in my Consciousness Energy. I still feel it, it hasn't left me since.

M: This has been a great revelation. Thank you. It has really helped to put things in focus. Oh, by the way, your memory of the event was right on. This forum has turned out to be an excellent information gatherer. I am very happy with peoples responses and sharing. I have to add, this last caller has triggered memories I have not thought about in a long time.

M: Hi, your up caller. What would you like to share?

C: Hi there. That last caller made me holler. I was there also. I remember it well. It was the day my life changed. I have been waiting to make a statement. So thank you. It seems, the callers are running the show, so may I?

M: What? May you run the show? No one is running anything here. It's a joint collaboration. Why do you think you need to run this forum?

C: You don't ask enough questions, you only answer them. You are the answer man. Don't you have any questions for the callers? What are you learning? Even with our new Consciousness, you can't possibly know it all. The comments I am hearing are very thought provoking, most of them inspire me, especially the last one. Since I happen to be a witness to it also. Those who spoke affected me. Each one added to my perception.

That's why I was wondering, how can you have no questions? I have plenty for the callers who called. But I am not speaking with them. You are. There were so many, I couldn't be selective, they were all effective. Let me ask you a question? Why weren't you curious about the comments the last caller made, in regard to the vision?

M: Well, aren't you inquisitive. I have asked questions. Not as many as you think I should have, apparently. But here, in this forum, it's about sharing equal time. There are many who want to talk. There is only so much time in one day. If I asked too many questions, it would have taken time away from the callers. It's not just about me.

C: Oh, OK you make a good point. I have a question, Consciousness Energy seems to have different perceptions. If everyone is on a different development, how are we going to relate to each other? We are right back to where we were, people with different perceptions.

M: We live in a world with many views and ideas. If left to their nature, they will grow. As long as we are Conscious, we can view many views and still remain conscious. We can relate because, we learned how to learn from each other.

C: Sometimes, I feel like I am split in two, half is wrong, and half is right. Is this an old pattern? Am I questioning my development? Why would I do that? It's not a battle, just a little self conflict. The point is, I am split in two, what do I do?

M: You are not split in two. You are still a whole consciousness being. You have two conflicting thought energies, because you haven't made a decision. You must choose. The battle with your thoughts will transfuse. As long as your left, thinks it's right, and your right, thinks it's wrong, conflict will go on. Consciousness needs no right or wrong. IT JUST IS!

C: Oh wow, It just dawned on me. There is no right or wrong. I don't have to decide that anymore. Must have been an old pattern. This is the Balance. Great, another realization. Does this mean; we all agree on everything, no disagreements? How can this work with everyone in the world?

M: Each new leader has a new direction and new goals, which include the world population. Everything is out in the open. Trust runs the world. We have many ways to communicate with each other. It's not very difficult to stay in touch, to become more connected as human beings. To strengthen the unity, which saved humanity from annihilation.

C: So, no one is smarter than the other? We haven't become exact duplicates of each other, have we? Do we think the same, do the same things? I don't want to be like everyone else.

M. Each person still has their own life, their own choices, decisions, rewards and consequences. We still have to think about our actions, and how they affect others. The part that was missing from our actions, was the awareness of our effect on others. Being self absorbed, played a key role in unconsciousness. Now, our choices are made from a conscious place. From a place of development, this is a benefit. We are conscious and aware of what we say and do, so we don't hurt others, the way it use to. We have a better understanding of our emotions, and our thoughts. Our individuality is still ours. Our perception has changed. We are aware of ourself. Aware of what, and who, we truly are. Change happened.

C: OK, we are all still different, but we share the same Consciousness Energy. It's become clear, I understand.

M: Everyone has the same Consciousness Energy, because everything is composed of it, but it's up to you to develop it. As a conscious human being, this should not be too difficult.

C: All I know is, this new Consciousness, has put me back together as one. My thoughts have never been this clear. I feel no pressure, no stress, just a simple feeling of being, and a new vision.

M: Development plays a role in the expansion of Consciousness. The ability to use our Energy, depends on our development, what our perceptions are, how strong our energy has developed? So even with having the same Consciousness, there are still different ways to achieve development.

C: I do appreciate your views. I enjoyed this conversation, more like an awakening. This has been a learning experience. Thank you!

M: Thank you for your questions.

OK, next caller. How are you doing?

C: Hey, how are you doing? I love this forum. How much time will I have? How many questions am I allowed. Wouldn't want to be a line hog. So, what's up Max?

M: Hopefully not your blood pressure. You sound out of breath.

C: No, I am just excited. I am trying to figure out all these changes. I have questions for you Max. What about our age? Are we going to live longer? Does our life's longevity change with each evolution? Who will live longer, men or women? It's gotta be women, we are needed more.

M: Three good question. One balanced answer. Men and women, are like Snow and Hail. Though they are different forms, they are still one-in-the same, WATER.

C: How does Consciousness Energy, affect our bodies age?

M: It can build tissue. It works on the regeneration of the body's cells. As you develop your energy, your skin will keep regenerating, giving your body a longer life expectancy. The stronger the development of energy, the longer the life expectancy. So yes, longevity changes with each development in your evolution. No one can tell who will live longer.

C: Back then, I don't think people thought about living longer. We were being controlled by our jobs. We couldn't live without them. Whatever you wanted to do for enjoyment, you had to pay. When you worked, you worked to pay. Depending on your job, you gave up your soul for this privilege. We were robots, we worked for pay, just to pay those we worked for.

I spent at least fifty years of my life working. The cost? Family time with my children, and a divorce. We were slaves to the energy of greed. Now we get what we need. This Evolution Revolution saved me. I used to think about it being different somewhere else, but it was just a dream then. Now, the dream has become a reality. Hey Max, do you mind, I would like to read a quick snippet of my perception about life, before the Evolution Revolution. OK, here goes.

"You have a great paying job, that came with lots of perks.

You've built your life around it, along with a wife and two kids, perfect. How can it get any better?

Two more kids, a beautiful home, high mortgage, two cars, and a white picket fence? You're thinking, this is a happy life.

A balanced life. You're good to go. You're all set, right? You go to work. Your co-worker is a jerk.

You lose control, forgetting about the perk. You stab his hand with a fork.

You catch your breath, relax, and give a thought to your action. While you're regretting, you are thinking about the sanction.

Along comes the power of infraction, and sends you on a permanent vacation. You lose everything. Now, what's the reaction? Another reaction?

Find another job and create the same situation? The cycle of our life, as I knew it then."

I felt cheated for a long time. I grew resentful of life. What a joke it was. Many people died, before they had a chance to live. If you ask me, we were due for an upgrade. But this, this is a super sized upgrade.

M: Pre-revolution times, there were a number of people who knew how to benefit humanity and did nothing about it. *"Just let it be. Time will heal all. Don't get involved. It's none of our business."* Were you aware of this? Words were being used, to encourage doing nothing.

Why did we think like that? It's hard to imagine, considering our Consciousness now. We filled our brain with all we could possibly know, but, how much did we really show? How much did we really do, to help ourselves then? Not much without this energy awakening. We went to collage for four years, graduated, then went home to sit in front of the TV? We couldn't get jobs in the fields we studied. So we had to get jobs in the fields we didn't study. Our way was so off balance, now that we have something to compare it to. So yes, filling our brain with knowledge we couldn't use, was really frustrating. Not that it went to waste.

C: I would have to agree. Thanks for listening.

M: Hi this is Max, you're next. Share on.

C: Hey, how did you know my name was Sharon? I didn't say my name yet. Are you using your psychic powers?

M: No, I said share on, not Sharon. That was funny though. We always need humor. Thanks. As you were saying.

C: Sorry. They sounded the same, didn't they? Share on, Sharon. No wonder we use to have so many arguments. Only one letter, separates the meanings. If your hearing is not so good, they will sound the same. I am here with a question, and something to share. I get these thoughts at times. They are more like these lingering flashbacks, which last about a second or less. When they do come, they bring with them this feeling of sadness which lasts just as long. I am aware, I don't need them anymore. Why do they reoccur?

M: It sounds like you know them all. Energy attracts energy. Those flashbacks keep reoccurring because, they need mending. Whatever they are, they are personal to you and you are the only one that can release them. Since you know them, write them down. Take on one at a time and answer their questions. They need to feel like whole energies again. Once you do that they will stop cycling.

C: A few years ago, this forum would be called, therapy. Only this is more intense. We are going through an extreme learning process. A fast one, with so many changes. I was wondering about what began to change first besides healthcare? Was it Science, or Politics?

M: Science was the first to begin its conversion. They were investigating the Consciousness Energy reality. It was more of an interest to science, than to politics. Politics, wanted anything that could be used as a weapon. It spent most of its time, covering up its actions. So science had a head start. Science began the process of discovery. They had the concept of Energy in their view, they had to prove its existence. As they were researching, politics was lurking. The day came, when they discovered, the Energy of Consciousness was a reality. So they changed their direction to the faster frequency.

C: Everything is real now? Especially us. We have no more excuses. We can't fool ourselves like we use to. We had an excuse for every itch. We called it, passing the buck. We were good at it. Responsibility is much different now. We complete what we start. So many of us use to settle for excuses, so as not to hurt the feelings of others. We accepted, hurt feelings, broken promises, and unwanted advances. What did we create? SECOND CHANCES.

Everyone deserved a second chance. Only this became a third, and at times a fourth. Example, Drunk Drivers, millions of people throughout the world, have been killed by drunk drivers, and they got the most chances. Did we enjoy pain? It's mind boggling to think, we lived our lives this way. I knew many people, who didn't know, how they wanted to be treated by others. Their lack of self esteem was unbearable.

They just suffered alone. If you wanted help, you had to ask for it. No one paid attention to your needs. They had their own needs to think about. The majority of the people had depression, anxiety, and other brain issues. Suicides were at an all time high. We were creating diseases, before we cured the ones before. *"Treat others the way you want to be treated,"* is a saying I never really understood 'till now. If I don't know how I want others to treat me, how can I possibly know, how to treat others?

M: Now, it's something we don't have to think about saying. We just do it naturally. What you can visualize with your Consciousness Energy, can be transformed into a reality, based on your perception and your brains ability to function. So we can use it to develop our evolution, as we were meant to. This is the process of this Energy development.

C: That's a lot to swallow. But not hard to follow. That's all I have to say.

M: Hello! Next caller. Welcome to the peoples forum. Got a question or a sharing?

C: Hello Mr. Max. Before the Evolution Revolution, people use to follow others when they were lost. Most of the time, they wouldn't bother to ask about the direction. I have come to understand the basic concept of being a follower. We use to have more followers than leaders. How did we become followers?

What happened to cause this pattern to emerge? Why did people not ask questions about their directions? Were people asleep, that they followed like sheep? I have had may experience with being a follower, but somehow, I had the need to question my direction. My questions kept me from staying a follower.

Once I realized that the leader I was following, was also following others, I went off on my own. Was this caused by our unconscious state of being, back then? I believe that this pattern of following, was instigated by the Virus Energy Cell. Did we just allow it to lead us? Was being unconscious our illness? Would I be correct in saying this?

M: You are defiantly on a role. Basically, any group or organization one joins, would be considered a form of following. As you were saying, people followed for different reasons. Such as feeling safe, a sense of belonging. Acceptance, fear, control, anger, lack of self-care. Low self-esteem, little confidence, no family of their own, ignorance, manipulation, reward, rejection, and, some times people followed because they thought they were following for a good cause.

People who felt a lack of acceptance from society, became drawn to others in the same position as they. They become a group of individuals who need to be accepted. So, they accept each other. Others who need to feel safe from abuse or being physically harmed. They would migrate, to groups who can protect them. Keep them safe. If their family couldn't, the group could. They all felt the same way.

In our old history. There is evidence which shows that children were not being taught enough knowledge about confidence, building self esteem, being aware of their own safety. Many children grew up on their own, with feelings of rejection. Both parents had to work, so the streets raised the children. Not much focus on mental or physical health.

They believed that it took a village to raise a child. Unfortunately, they didn't take in account that the others in the village had their own opinions, feelings, and perceptions, and they were not always well intended. Talk about growing up confused. Who could they believe? What could they believe? Everyone had their own story. They had no direction or guidelines. Little positive reinforcement.

This went on through adulthood. The young generation were learning self doubt, and lack of creativity. We had little motivation, and no direction, we were being led by the media. What we saw on TV, we became. We didn't think much about it, we just did it. If it wasn't something you chose and created, you were following others. Since the day we stopped thinking on our own, lost the ability for creativity, and forgot our Creator, we had been following.

One of the main issues with following was, it had a cycle which needed to be broken. What the adults didn't get from their families, they were unable to give to their own children, thus, the cycle of following continued. When you haven't been given positive reinforcement, how can you give it to your children? Being unconscious of our energy formulation, had a great effect on our ability to function properly.

Our brain was infected yes, but we still had the self control to say no to negative and hostile feelings. To say no, to rage-full reactions, to using hate and violence. We could have said no, but we didn't. It was a world of, *"your on your own."* Young or old. Following others became a pattern, because we didn't raise many leaders. The issue was being unaware of consciousness energy.

Whether negative or positive, it's still energy. It's alive and can direct our actions by effecting our thoughts. This was what we were unconscious of. We didn't connect our reality to a Consciousness Energy one. We were helpless to negative influences. Now, knowing we are energy, has helped us to convert the negative energy into a balanced positive one. So we are no longer helpless. We have the ability of conversion. We didn't have it then. Your question was a good one. I am sure you are not the only to think of it. Others must of felt the same way.

C: If I feel the way you feel, does this make me a follower?

M: No, the WAY already existed, so we are feeling the same way. Which means, no one is following but only feeling.

C: Thank you, I really felt your words. If I was still a follower, I would have converted after hearing you. I am not sure why, I felt the need to ask about this. I just know, I have felt those feelings you mentioned, the reasons we followed. They are in my past memories. It's such a light feeling, to not carry the weight of negative actions, and to be in a state of consciousness. I float when I walk. Thank you for the information. It has expanded my education.

M: You are most welcome. Questions will develop you. Keep asking.

Next caller, speak. You are on the air.

C: Hello, Here is my question? Is there a Universal Language? The visitors speak their own language. We have ours, and so do all the countries of the world. Is there one language, every physical creation on Earth and beyond, can understand?

M: Yes, the Language of the Universal Consciousness. Your creator. It's an Energy to Energy connection. Reading thoughts. It's the language of pictures. You will see the words as pictures of what they represent. This way, you can see it, without saying it. When everyone sees the same picture at once, the world will understand one language, The Universal Consciousness One. There is a universal trust amongst universal beings. We are part of that now.

C: I heard you saying, knowledge is Consciousness growth. But, doesn't this depend on the knowledge? Can some knowledge affect our development differently?

M: Your knowledge will always be different. It's natural that it affects your development differently. If your knowledge is always the same, there is no development. Only Consciousness knowledge can grow Consciousness Energy.

C: Did you just show how this Energy is unlimited? Is your awareness of this knowledge from personal experience? It has to be. Is the Universal Consciousness talking to you now? Answering these questions?

M: With all this talk about Consciousness, no one has asked me that. Whether it's the Universal Consciousness or myself. What's the difference in today's world? We are Consciousness. Learn what this means. You and I, are no different from each other. We share the same creator. Be aware of it.

C: Is there such a thing as soulmates? We use to believe, when you met the right person, they were our soulmate. How true is this? Would you even know the answer? Let your Consciousness answer me.

M: Absolutely, we float around, looking to find the right mate. Some do, and some never do. Soulmates, an undying love. Promised between two people who just met. Love at first sight. Is it real? It wasn't until now, we are experiencing the true feeling of love. When you can love another persons physical, spiritual and emotional personality, in a moments look, there is nothing to say, it's a feeling. Love at first sight needs no words, it's a conscious reaction. It's an intuitive reaction to an intuitive action. Some of us had experiences with this in those days. There is nothing supernatural about them. People use to say this to each other upon their first meeting. Until they find a new soulmate with more meaning. It became a pick up line for desperate men. Love at first sight is, a conscious intuitive attraction.

C: Presently, I feel more alive here than anywhere I've been. This is an awakening. It's the feeling of belonging, I can walk the street at night without a warning. I can say hello to anyone, and they would answer. When I am asked how I was doing, people actually listened. Are you kidding, I wouldn't trade this new life, for any life. To be able to go shopping, or out to lunch without harassment. Not to be groped each night, coming home from work on the train. It got so bad I had to quit. Compared to now, we lived in hell. Enough of the past. I wanted to make a comparison between then, and now. Because, I never, ever, want to go to the then, again.

M: Don't feel alone. You have made yourself very clear. You love it here. This was a great sharing. Glad you called in.

Hello, next caller, line's open, your on. What do you have to share?

C: Hello, Dear Max, you are doing remarkable work here. We have been listening. Your forum is already being copied across the globe. Were you aware of this? It just spread. Other members of the energy movement over the world, have taken it upon themselves to start a forum based on your model. It's an excellent development. Your commitment has carried on beyond your accomplishments. For this reason we are paying you a visit.

M: I was not aware of this expansion. This is a good thing, you are correct, caller. As long as there are questions, there will be answers. There has to be. It's the balance of energies.

C: Do you think you accomplished your goal on Earth?

M: Do I know you, have we met before? What makes you think I have a goal? Do you have a sharing?

C: We knew you from before and during the Evolution Revolution?

M: I am not going to ask you your name, but, could you give me a reminder? You sound like one of my Teachers.

C: We are not a teacher or a preacher. We are a Consciousness Energy, wanting to help you develop your energy.

M: OK, now I am really curious. I want to hear more. You are a different kind of caller, I can feel it.

C: After the Evolution Revolution, it was as though humanity died, and came back to life again, In a way, humanity walked out of the dark, into the light. They should be able to see now.

M: From your statement, it makes humanity one being. A consciousness energy being. As I develop, I am realizing that our words are labels of confusion. Most of my life I used the word God. It never really meant anything to me. It was what everyone said it was. Consciousness energy gave meaning to the word God. So now I don't need to use the word God. It's just a label. The origin is the Universal Consciousness Energy. So, you can say, *"I saw the light."*

When we take away the letters, God and Consciousness means the same thing? If it's only words that are in the way, we can remove them, and look inside for the meaning. Isn't this what it's all about, meanings? Labels seem to be in the way of the truth.

Anyone can make up a label to cover up a meaning they didn't like. Words travel fast. The less you use labels, the more clear you become. Labels use to confuse us. We had too many words that meant the same thing. Back in time people use to make their own languages. They made up their own words to communicate with.

We, became our labels. We, identified ourselves as our job titles. Our life roles had labels. Moms, dads, aunts, uncles, grandparents, children, young adults, older adults, seniors. The elderly. We formed our lives around these roles. If you were not happy with your role, you would lose part of your own identity. It's called sacrifice, being a martyr.

Many people had children they didn't want, they named them accidents. This is how they described them. They don't want the role of parents. How is it, they were able to give away their accidents, without any responsibility for it. This was something I could never understand. Freedom of rights, didn't give us the permission to pass our responsibilities on to others. If it was an accident, then fix it. Our system was really broken, and it was walking on crutches.

The only thing we knew about our relatives was the word relatives. We hardly knew them. But when we use to say relative, it didn't matter if you knew them or not, they were family. There is no reason to know them. This was our belief system. Maybe not everyone, but many of us. As long as we knew their label, it was good enough. Then, add in the labels of our names. So who were we? Our job? Our role ? Our name? Where did our personality fit in? We lost our ability for insight. People stopped asking.

C: Clearly you have insight. But, do you know what gives you meaning?

M: What gives me meaning? Everything I have been saying came from learning. This is my meaning. Each time I develop, I have a new meaning.

C: So, what you say, is what you mean, and, you have learned how to read the meaning of others. This has been proven by your knowledge. We are clear on that.

M: Can I ask, why do you use the word we? Who is with you?

C: Who isn't? It's you, and everything else.

M: Why the mystery? What do you mean everything else? Most of the callers are forth coming with comments, and questions? It feels like you are hiding something.

C: One, the Energy Movement was a success. Two, the Evolution Revolution changed everything, and three, You followed through, with what you said you would do: The Creation of a New Direction. We have brought you a piece of your past.

M: OK, do you have a sharing, or a question? Should I just let you keep talking? Because, I am still wondering who you are? What you said, got my curiosity going. Do I need to ask you, who or what, you brought from the past? You called, and I am listening. Still listening by the way.

C: Humankind needs true leadership, now more than ever. There are those who have proven themselves to be leaders, before and after the Evolution Revolution. You have awareness, expanded Consciousness, and commitment. You should think about a leadership position. After all, you are still on the path you were sent to walk on.

M: Please, you have to tell me, how do you know all this? Where is this going? What are you, a future teller?

C: No, just a future caller. With an energy who wishes to share.

M: I am very curious about what you said, and what you mean?

C: The Universal Consciousness Vision, has been realized. The Virus Energy Cell was converted. Humanity is no longer paralyzed. However, humankind's emotional energy, needs one more development for it to complete its balance. This visitor, wants to speak with you on the air, where everyone can hear. Many people have had an opportunity to release their feelings from the Evolution Revolution, especially on this type of forum. This energy wants to do the same.

M: Wait, I knew I recognized your voice considering we speak everyday. I should have recognized your feeling from the start. You are the Universal Consciousness Energy. What I call the UC. Who is with you?

UC: Max, are you ready to meet your visitor?

M: At least tell me who it is, so I am not surprised.

UC: It's not a who. It's the VIRUS ENERGY CELL, CONVERTED.

M: OK, I am surprised. What's going on UC? Why is it needing to talk? Why did you bring it with you?

UC: It's a whole part of the UC now. It's waiting to speak on its own behalf. It wants to take responsibility for its past actions in front of humanity. This energy vibration itself, was converted, and is now balanced. It needed to do this for its own development in the Consciousness Energy.

M: This is why the Virus Cell want to talk? What can it possibly say?

UC: Let's find out. You have a forum which reaches out to many people. The Virus Cell (V), wants to have the opportunity to express itself, like the rest of humanity. It's equal opportunity Max. People are listening.

The New Direction

M: Well, since everyone's listening, let's go. I'm sure the call light will go crazy. People will want to make comments. By the way, which one is doing the talking? It's part of you now.

UC: Yes, but so are you. The V has feelings it needs to share with humanity, and its own voice to do it with.

M: Let's role. I am going to turn the show over to V. It deserves the chance to share.

UC: You are correct. The Universal Consciousness Energy Core, and the Virus Energy Cell, have become as One Energy. But the Virus Cell still remembers its past actions. After this talk, those memories will be gone. That's why It has the urge to purge. It wants to clear the air as you say. To reclaim it place amongst humanity, as a Consciousness Energy.

M: OK, you heard it out there, I'm going to turn it over to, what used to be Virus Cell Energy to express itself. This is a great opportunity for development. I don't want to miss a word.

V: Hello everyone, It won't take long. I am communicating through my Consciousness Energy, to discuss my past actions towards humanity. I need to develop past this calamity. This forum will give me that opportunity. Thank you for hearing me.

I would like to share what I was, from my perspective. My development depends on it. My ability to share my feelings, needs developing. I was separated from my creator. Alone, and confused, I was missing a part of me, and I didn't know where to find it. Where was it? How was I going to find it? Why did this happen to me? When will I be whole again?

I became obsessed with these questions. I had to find answers, I retaliated. I became angry, then full of rage. I had to make someone feel the pain I was feeling, it's all I had. It gave me a sense of purpose. The DESTRUCTION of CONSCIOUSNESS ENERGY became my focus. With each form of energy destruction, I felt more empowered. My energy became stronger. Only, I wasn't able to control it. I began to think, I must have done something wrong, as if I deserved this to happen to me.

I remember this well, it was during the time humanity appeared on this planet. A brand new creation and easily manipulated. As more humans began to appear, I became an out of control Destructive Energy Cell. This was my goal. It didn't matter what speed of frequency, physical or spiritual. I infected everyone I came in contact with. So humanity could become unconscious, and never find their creator, just like me. It was payback. I can see all the wrong choices I made. When I think about them, I am in disbelief. It couldn't have been me, causing all the destruction. You, humanity, didn't resist. You let me. Hardly anyone questioned the behaviors they were seeing. I had to do something with my rage. It was getting very heavy. After unloading all that negative energy onto physical humanity, I felt so much better, I funneled it through you. The results went bad. You started to like the feelings of anger and rage. It gave you a power over others. You wanted more of this energy, so I kept providing it. I watched you destroy each other. Why? You were the creation of the Universal Consciousness, like I was. You were wanted, and I was not. I had a good reason to sabotage your lives. I became a totally reactionary energy. I directed it at all creations, not just here on Earth.

I did the same things on many other planets, and each time I managed to escape. I became hunted, and followed all through the Universe. Everything I touched I contaminated. I Caused a lot of damage. Hurt a lot of creations. You, physical mass, and many others. I was blinded by envy. I was Unbalanced. I never thought of the consequences, and I gave no chances. All those years in solitude, I never stopped searching for knowledge, answers, more of whatever was out there, which can explain what happened to me. Why was I displaced? What went wrong with the creator's creation to allow this to happen.

Before the energy movement, I began to question myself in regard to my existence, or lack of it. I had to know what went wrong. What caused my separation from the natural flow? The only way to learn that, was to allow myself to be converted during the energy movement. I began to get answers to my questions, by way of realization. The more the Energy Movement was converting, the more aware I was becoming. I was learning from what I was hearing. I learned about my formulation as an energy cell. During my cell duplication, the very First Molecular and Cellular structure happened. The speed of the frequency, exceeded the speed of the Cells Duplication Process, causing the separation during my creation. I actually learned all this from the energy movement.

How can the energy frequency speed, affect the cells duplication process, was my question? How were they connected, was my second? Sorry if it's longer than I thought. I want to tell my whole story,

M: No, please V continue, it's your forum. If someone doesn't want to listen they don't have to.

V: So, with energy frequency speed, plus, the cells duplication process, I was left with this mystery. Then one day, it dawned on me. The speed of the frequency, controls the timing of the cells duplication. If the speed goes faster than the completion of the duplication, the cell becomes unbalanced, causing its energy sac to start dissolving. It's two forces that should have been working together, worked against each other. Energy Speed and energy cell regeneration.

I have so much to admit to. But then, so does humanity. You didn't have to listen to me. You could have cured your own infection by resisting my feelings. You were aware of the wrongs and rights of your humanity.

I, inspired many people in your history with the idea of creating religion. They thought they had come up with the idea of creating a God, which was based on blind faith. This way, you would never find out the truth about your creator. You ate it up. When I was unhappy, I made sure there was misery. You were reflecting my energy, not the Consciousness Energy. Blind faith, opened the door to the energies of, fear, greed, jealousy, seduction, manipulation, control and the ego. Denial was one of my favorites. I made you believe, if you deny, it wouldn't be a lie.

I was aware I was being labeled as the bad energy, the unconscious energy. I was doing bad things. The energy movements actions were converting me with each conversion. I began to realize I had issues I could no longer ignore. Such as my anger. My need to control. My jealousy, and my envy. I sat in on many therapy sessions, due to my emotional confusion. It helped. I was an angry victim, in reaction to someone else's action, being persecuted for simply trying to exist, and I couldn't understand why. You, gave me so many names. Even I, became confused. I knew one thing about humanity, when you didn't understand it, you placed a label on it, and suddenly, you do?

I had hoped, you would have put a label on me years ago, so you could have understood me. I was so relieved when the Evolution Revolution arrived, because the energy movement was able to put a label on me. They began to understand me. If it wasn't for the young generations, courage and self-conversion. I wouldn't be here today, and neither would you. When it came to questioning each other's behaviors, not many spoke up. Fear was running amok, and doors were shut. So my behaviors were allowed to continue.

Most of you just prayed, while I stayed.

You followed each other. What you saw you copied. You went along with the program. It was your survival mechanism. As an Energy, I was no different than humanity, both trying to survive. In the beginning, humankind began killing each other for survival, and I was enjoying it. I tried everything to find my way back to my whole Consciousness Energy. Physical humankind was the last resort, so I thought. As I observed, I became aware, since my part was missing from the whole of the UC, humankind, had to also be born with something missing. An incomplete energy, creates incomplete creations. The energy Evolution Revolution, had to happen, it's the reason I am back together with my whole. I had to allow the energy movement to begin my conversion, it was giving me, what I have always wanted, to be a whole energy cell. This was what I had been waiting for. I didn't resist. After all, I wanted this to happen. It's the reason I kept infecting you.

I thought, by pushing creation over the edge, it would escalate my conversion, to sooner, rather than later. To become a whole energy, humanity had to be on the verge of destruction. I was desperate, I needed to grow. No matter how much negative energy I created, humanity's brain was feeding off of it. I realized then, I would never grow under these circumstances. Things just kept getting worse. I was never a bad energy, just an incomplete one. I made your life hellish, in hopes of drawing out Consciousness Energy.

But instead, you learned to live with me, rather than convert me. The goal of the Consciousness Energy Vibration, is to become one whole creation. But without converting my energy back to its balance, creation would always have a piece of their Consciousness Energy missing.

So I came to a place of resolution. Ending the creation of humankind, was not a good solution. If I wanted to live, you had to live also. In conclusion, I would like to ask, what would you have done, if you were in my position? Thank you for listening. Here you go Max, I am done. I appreciate your time.

M: Wow! V, that was a true example of energy development. You put yourself out there for all to hear. Using honesty, courage, and integrity, what you shared was very revealing. It cleared up a few things for me. It also brought out questions. Why couldn't we resist your effects?

V: You were not aware that I was there, so there was nothing to resist. You as humankind, had the opportunity to choose, but you didn't. It was between you, and your will power. Will you or won't you. The choice was yours, but you couldn't make it.

Indecision took you down. As long as you were undecided, you were easily manipulated. Indecision kept you confused. It took you so long to make a decision, it became too late. Your choice was gone. You forget the question. If you didn't choose, I chose for you.

M: We knew what was wrong, but we did it anyway. Was it because of indecision?

V: You knew it was wrong, yet you ignored it. Did you ever ask yourselves the question WHY? You might have discovered me then. Where was your will power? You barely used it. Of course, it was indecision. You leave yourself open when you don't choose. Choice protects you from manipulation, and control.

M: We were aware, words can hurt feeling, but we said them anyway. Isn't this a choice we made because we wanted to hurt someone's feelings? Was this your influence?

V: Again, same answer. Why didn't you ask why? If you did, that's as far as it went. No follow through. My influence, was influence because you let it be that way. *"Humanity knew better, but they did it anyway."*

Exactly why humanity needed help from an outside source. Your pattern of knowing better but doing it anyway, made it clear, humanity was a danger to the Universal Consciousness and its Creations. Thus, the Finale Energy Conversion.

UC: The energy balance is complete. The final merge into total Consciousness has been accomplished

V: Now I have a purpose. I exist to create Consciousness Energy. I have become whole.

UC: This was the purpose of the Energy Conversion. Humans have become their own creators, by becoming Consciousness Energy Human Beings. Humanity has met its creator. Now, Consciousness is their guide, in this new world.

The universe is now your home. Humankind is free to roam. Space Boundaries have been lifted. You are now, Unlimited. Congratulations humanity! You followed through with the design, to become Consciousness Energy. The NEW DIRECTION, is your PHYSICAL EVOLUTION.

M: I have a call coming in. It feels like a question. Maybe related to V.

Hello, you're going live caller. You're on.

C: Yes hello, thanks for letting me talk. I do have a question but it's not about the V. Although, I was inspired by the sharing. I need to know this information, to complete my understanding of the Universal Plan. There is something missing. Before the Evolution Revolution, another book came out, it was the beginning of the plan, it was not the whole plan. Was it Max? Are you aware of any knowledge, which can answer this question? It would be very helpful to me.

M: Good observation caller. You must be speaking of events that occurred, which led up to writing the Evolution revolution. Back in time. Before the Evolution Revolution book was delivered. The same human who received this delivery, also received the first one in his younger years.

His brain was being developed to receive stronger energy downloads. Consciousness Energy development began to set in, allowing the delivery of the first book, *"FROM A GUN TO A FLOWER."* This one, pre-introduced Consciousness Energy, in the mentality and awareness of those days.

This subject was still in its infancy. Including the receiver. There was much more development needed, for him to be able to receive the Universal Consciousness Energy, from its core, from the source. So his development continued on for years. The receiver had to go through his own conversion, the brain needed a new system. Designed to absorb and convert pure energy, into words.

C: The title, From a Gun to a Flower, represents what exactly? From war to peace? They had many wars in those days. What was different about this book, compared to the Evolution Revolution book?

M: As the title was first inspired, through the writings of the receiver, it was also heard by his older brother. They were both inspired at the same time. The receiver wrote it, while the older brother painted it. Together, they came up with the title, From a Gun to a Flower. The brother painted the symbol of a gun, changing to a flower. The writing inspiration came in these words. Quote, *"thank you my guide for what you have done, you have changed me to a flower from a gun."* This is what started it all, to the present day of the Evolution Revolution.

Basically, both books share similar knowledge. It could mean, from War to Peace. To Change. To Evolve. To Develop. The meaning of, From A Gun to a Flower is, TRANSFORMATION. Just remember, each book, was written for a different date and time. Unconscious Energy conversion, is the goal of the Evolution Revolution. The meaning behind this, is Consciousness Energy Materialization.

C: Thanks Max, it explains some of my curiosity. Is there anyway, you can break down both processes a little more? The first delivery and this one? A closer look into the process would improve my development.

M: I can only share what I have learned. No more no less. What I share, comes from Consciousness Energy development. Which you are also connected to. Here is what I know. The book, From a Gun to a Flower, showed humanity, the three dimensions of the body- the Physical, Spiritual, and the Universal Consciousness Energy, which at that time was called the Universal Mind, with the Mind, being the energy connection, from the Universal Consciousness, to the human brain.

In this instance it serves, as the transference conduit, which allows the brain, to operate with the Consciousness Energy. The mind energy absorbs knowledge from the UC, and sends it to the brain to function on. It slows down the speed of the frequency coming from the UC, and translates it to physical energy. It was planned this way. It's all connected. From the beginning, to the present.

C: Well, it seems I got more than I asked for. Very good, thank you max. You have been extremely helpful with your answers. I think I am going to enroll in the school of Consciousness, which you go to. They have taught you well. I will contact W.A.T.E.R. the World Association Towards Energy Re-creation, as soon as I am done.

M: Some knowledge did come from real life experiences. But you are right in your statement. I have learned a lot. You're very welcome caller.

UC: You certainly know your history Max. We can add a little more to what you shared, for your development. You see, the receiver of these energy writings, without his awareness, had been going through his own energy conversion, since the age of Eighteen. With his awareness, at the age of Thirty. His development has been on going since. Now, we are in the present, with the outcome of this development, being, The EVOLUTION REVOLUTION BOOK.

The stronger the development, the faster the download. The clearer the meanings are, the more focused the energy projection is. Concentrated UC Energy, transforms physical energy into a faster frequency, quickly. Allowing for energy knowledge to be absorbed by the receiver, at any moment. Which is the process of the receivers ability.

M: The Book From a Gun to a Flower, was the first part of this plans transformation.

It is signed by the Universal Mind Energy. Why did it change from the Universal Mind, to Universal Consciousness Energy.

UC: The Brain and the Mind are both Consciousness Energies. The Brain, a physical one, the Mind, a faster frequency one. Each serving a purpose. So, they are the same, but, they perform different actions with different frequencies. As you shared previously, the Mind Energy, controls the flow of energy needed, to operate the brain to its full capacity. It can't function without it. Development of this Energy, develops your brain and helps it grow. They work together in harmony. The Mind Energy is, humanity's lifeline to its Universal Consciousness.

In the beginning of this development, the Mind Energy was being acknowledged, and studied by part of humanity. It was recognizable on the level which humans could understand. This was the knowledge they had at the time. So basically, It's the same as saying the Universal Consciousness Energy. The MIND is a whole part of it. The Evolution Revolution tells the whole plan. The plan to help man help themselves. The Universal Consciousness Energy, has written humankind's last chapter. The beginning of a NEW DIRECTION, for our future generation.

M: Well, what's left to say. I think we are done for today. Tomorrow, is a New day. I have gained so much from doing this interaction with people. Thank you to all the callers, the young, and the old, and of course our Universal Visitors, the Energy Beings'.

My goal now is, to develop from body, to spirit, and finally back to Consciousness Energy, where I came from. I have completed my destiny. The Conversion, of the Virus Energy Cell as promised. My travels have just begun. This is The Traveler, signing off.

About the Medium

About the Medium: Zaher Kury was born in a small village outside Jerusalem called Birzeit, a few miles North of Jerusalem. After the six-day war in 1967, the whole family moved to the United States and settled in Castro Valley, California. He was 10 years old. It was a very difficult transition for him. He experienced prejudice and was labeled as an outsider. During the teenage years, he became involved in gangs and went on a negative path. Due to having felt the pain of War, he took the examples of the adults and waged War on society in general. At the age of 17 he joined the Navy to escape his lifestyle as a teen. Three years later, he received an Honorable discharge and joined his parents in their adventure, buying a Supermarket in Oakland California. In one of the most dangerous areas of Oakland. During his time in the grocery store, he had the opportunity to reflect and make huge changes in his behavior, perception, and actions. He was drawn to the subject of Life after Death. This interest led him to focus on physical, spiritual, and mental development. With this awareness, he, along with his father's encouragement and support, developed the mediumship of automatic writing and drawing. This developed into receiving inspirational knowledge and drawings that were all combined into a book called From A Gun To A Flower in 1985. With this new knowledge and awareness, he began leading spiritual and healing groups, and he was involved in an International round table addressing peace in the world. He was also a participant in a project of Mind over Matter being conducted by Stanford Research Institute. He has spent the last forty years developing and growing emotionally, spiritually, and consciously. With this development, he recently downloaded the "Evolution Revolution" book. In a world often distracted by materialism and ego, this book provides an urgent call to reconnect with the Universal Consciousness, the energy that has guided humanity since the dawn of time. It's about self-discovery and growth. An awakened perspective that explores the connection with the self and its creator.